JAPAN AND MALAYSIAN DEVELOPMENT

In the shadow of the rising sun

Edited by Jomo K.S.

London and New York

First published 1994
by Routledge
11 New Fetter Lane, London EC4P 4EE

Reprinted 1998, 2001, 2002

Transferred to Digital Printing 2002

Routledge is an imprint of the Taylor & Francis Group

Simultaneously published in the USA and Canada
by Routledge
29 West 35th Street, New York, NY 10001

© 1994 Jomo K.S.

Typeset in Garamond by
J&L Composition Ltd, Filey, North Yorkshire

Printed and bound in Great Britain by
Intype London Ltd

British Library Cataloguing in Publication Data
A catalogue record for this book is available from the British Library.

Library of Congress Cataloguing in Publication Data
has been applied for.

ISBN 0–415–11583–3

CONTENTS

Part II

FIGURES

TABLES

LIST OF TABLES

CONTRIBUTORS

Anatory Marappan *Royal Customs and Excise Department, Government of Malaysia, Kuala Lumpur, Malaysia*

Makoto Anazawa *Associate Professor, Otaru University of Commerce, 3–5–21 Midori Otaru, 047 Hokkaido, Japan*

Anuwar Ali *Professor and Dean, Faculty of Economics, National University of Malaysia, Bangi, Selangor, Malaysia*

Mohamed Aslam *Lecturer, Faculty of Economics and Administration, University of Malaya, 59100 Kuala Lumpur, Malaysia*

Chee Peng Lim *Development Planning Division, ESCAP, UN Building, Rajadamnerm Avenue, Bangkok, Thailand*

Mehmet Sami Denker *Deputy Dean, Faculty of Economics and Administrative Science, Selcuk University, Alaeddin Keykubat Kampusu, Konya, Turkey*

Ghazali Atan *SJ Securities Sdn Bhd, 9 Jalan SS 12/1 47500 Subang Jaya, Selangor, Malaysia*

E.T. Gomez *Lecturer, Institute of Advanced Studies, University of Malaya, Kuala Lumpur, Malaysia*

Mohd Haflah Piei *Associate Professor, Faculty of Economics, National University of Malaysia, Bangi, Selangor, Malaysia*

Jomo K.S. *Professor, Faculty of Economics and Administration, University of Malaya, 59100 Kuala Lumpur, Malaysia*

Kit G. Machado *International Division, Waseda University, 1-6-1 Nishiwaseda, Shinjuku-ku, Tokyo 169, Japan*

Wendy A. Smith *Lecturer, Industrial Relations, University of Melbourne, Melbourne, Australia*

Peter Wad *Institute of Social Anthropology, Copenhagen, Denmark*

INTRODUCTION

Economic relations between Japan and Malaysia have grown since the Meiji Restoration in Japan from 1868, which is generally credited with bringing about the modernization and industrialization of the archipelagic Land of the Rising Sun under the aegis of a modernizing elite operating under the umbrella of a strengthened Emperor. By the late nineteenth century, Japanese influence had extended well beyond its shores, and even beyond its immediate hinterland in Northeast Asia. Relatively poor in terms of natural resources and still at a nascent stage of industrialization, Japan did not have much to offer then by way of exports. Petty traders offered goods and services, including prostitution, with Japanese women sacrificed for sex to earn precious foreign exchange for the resource-poor nation struggling to industrialize – a cruel situation ironically reversed at the end of this century, with thousands of Southeast Asian women now forced to provide similar services in Japan and to Japanese tourists visiting their lands.

Colonial Malaya's exports of tin, rubber and other raw materials sold to the industrializing world, including Japan, transformed the peninsula into the most precious jewel in the crown of the British Empire by the early twentieth century. Malaya's pre-war iron mining was almost exclusively for export to Japan, ironically providing the raw material for the military industrial complex with which the Japanese imperial armed forces overran the peninsula and the British armed forces three times their number in barely three months from 8 December 1941. In Chapter 2 of this volume, Denker sums up the economic implications of Japanese interests in the peninsula before the Japanese Occupation (also see Yuen, 1983).

To date, there has not been any economic assessment of the Japanese Occupation of Malaya (for a survey of major socio-political consequences, see Cheah, 1983), although there is little dispute over the hearsay accounts of massive disruption and deprivation under a brutally exploitative colonialism betraying all the pre-war sweet talk and promises of an anti-Western Greater East Asian Co-Prosperity Sphere. The ethnically divisive mode of colonial rule developed by the British became even more pronounced under the Japanese Occupation as the Chinese were especially

1

persecuted for supporting the pre-Occupation anti-Japanese movement in China and providing much of the mass support for the communist-led anti-Japanese resistance in Malaya during the Occupation. In contrast, both Malays and Indians were initially wooed as fellow Asians opposed to European, in this case British, colonialism, though the pretence was not maintained for very long, and the ravages of wartime military Occupation and the forced labour demanded by the Japanese (e.g. for the notorious 'Death Railway' linking Siam to Burma) killed any remaining illusions previously sympathetic Malays and Indians may have had by the end of the Occupation.

With the military defeat of Japan in 1945 and the post-war American Occupation of Japan until the early 1950s, Japanese business was in no position to reconstruct or build new economic interests abroad beyond securing the raw materials required for reconstruction and rebuilding industry. Even after the end of the US Occupation, foreign exchange scarcities required the Japanese government to restrict foreign investments by Japanese firms. Proceeds from the sale of Japanese properties were treated as war reparations. However, reparations demanded were considerably limited by the desire for Japanese support in the Cold War, and were primarily paid to British investors in Malaya, rather than to Malayans who had suffered most under the Japanese Occupation (see Hara, 1993). Some would later argue that Japanese economic 'aid' subsequently provided in this connection eventually turned out to be beach-heads for a 'second (economic) invasion' from the 1960s.

With the recovery of Japanese manufacturing in the 1950s, economic expansion was inevitable. After the newly independent Malayan government implemented import substitution policies from the late 1950s, Japanese firms soon sought to secure market shares through joint ventures (see Chee and Lee, 1983), mainly with ethnic Chinese businessmen. In the 1970s, Japanese firms – seeking to reduce production costs, secure raw material supplies, evade strict environmental legislation and obtain export platforms for penetrating other (mainly US) markets with country import quotas – increasingly began to move to Southeast Asia. Economic recovery meant the end of restrictions on capital outflows as the Japanese Ministry of International Trade and Industry (MITI) adopted pro-active policies encouraging such investments abroad. In the early 1980s, new global considerations resulted in declining Japanese manufacturing investments in Southeast Asia, with increasing investments in North America and Europe. In Malaysia, however, the government's heavy industrialization policy involved state enterprises forming joint ventures with Japanese firms encouraged by official development assistance (ODA).

Japanese private direct investment in Malaysia in recent decades has been motivated by several considerations, including securing raw material supplies, capturing and expanding market shares, the availability of relatively cheap, semi-skilled labour, generous and attractive tax infra-structure and other investment incentives, easier access to other markets (e.g. under the Multi-Fibre Arrangement (MFA) and the Generalised System of Preferences (GSP)) and less stringent environmental and labour security regulations. The larger picture of Japanese investment trends in Malaysia up to the mid-1980s is surveyed in this volume by Denker (Chapter 2) (also see Golley, 1983; Steven, 1990). With the yen appreciation (*endaka*) from late 1985, Japanese firms – this time including more small and medium Japanese companies – were once again encouraged to relocate abroad, mainly in Southeast Asia and China, to cut production costs. This new phase of Japanese manufacturing investments, encouraged by Japan's MITI, has contributed to the economic boom since 1987 – discussed by Anazawa in Chapter 3, this volume – which, in any case, has been largely due to this new wave of foreign manufacturing investments, primarily from East Asia. Meanwhile, in Chapter 1, Aslam and Haflah review trade and other economic relations between Malaysia and Japan (also see Lin, 1983, 1985). As an example of Japanese interest in Malaysian natural resources, Jomo (Chapter 7) examines the Japanese role in Malaysian deforestation. Smith's case study (Chapter 6) of a Japanese factory in Malaysia reveals how ethnicity has been used to maximize firm profitability, an innovative Japanese variant of old ethnic 'divide and rule' tactics; her study also reminds us how cynically Japanese-style industrial relations have been adapted in the Malaysian context.

MAHATHIR'S 'LOOK EAST' POLICY

In some respects, this book is a sequel to an earlier volume, *The Sun Also Sets* – which was inspired by two distinct images. The rising sun is, of course, identified with the East, especially with Japan. On the other hand, one of the boasts of the British Empire at its zenith was that the sun never set on its far-flung imperial realm. The title hence evoked the image that as surely as the sun must set, so too empires must surely fall, that domination and hegemony are intrinsically unstable systems. This is important to remember in an age of consolidating Japanese economic strength and a concomitant infatuation with things Japanese.

While Japan's economic strength is undoubtedly impressive, notwith-standing its problems in the early 1990s with the bursting of the 'bubble economy', the current Western fascination with the Japanese ironically stems partly from a somewhat racist naivete about non-European or non-White civilizations, societies and cultures. Hence, the Japanese 'economic miracle' acquires a more exotic hue when viewed from a Euro-centric, or North Atlantic-centred perspective, compared with, say, the equally impressive phoenix-like recovery of the West German economy after the Second World War. Confronted by a deep crisis associated with the end of

3

the post-war boom, sometimes referred to as the Keynesian 'Golden Age', the industrial West has turned to the East, specifically to Japan, in desperate efforts to seek solutions to their own problems. In geographical terms too, the very idea of 'Looking East' is necessarily defined from a Western perspective. In this sense then, 'Looking East' during this historical conjuncture has ironically become quite fashionably Western.

There are other reasons, of course, for the Southeast Asian 'delay' in 'Looking East' (actually North) to Japan. Half a century later, the bitter experience of the Japanese Occupation is still part of living national memories. Perhaps more important, the stubborn refusal of successive Japanese governments to come to terms with this bitter heritage – e.g. in official school textbook treatments of the war or official denial of forced military prostitution, euphemistically referred to as involving 'comfort women' – and instead to use its economic muscle to try to 'buy' its way out every time such issues are raised, can hardly inspire much confidence in Japanese motives and attitudes. The consequences of more recent (mainly economic) intrusions also have not won too many friends, as manifested in the 'hot welcome' students and their allies gave to Japanese Premier Tanaka Kakuei during his 1974 Southeast Asian tour.

It is a mark of Japanese diplomatic achievement from the mid-1970s that half a decade later, from the early 1980s, several Southeast Asian governments were publicly invoking Japan as a model for emulation despite the bitter heritage of the wartime Japanese Occupation. Singapore's campaign to 'learn from Japan', for instance, was well under way by late 1980, with the appointment of the former Singapore Ambassador to Japan as head of the government's Singapore Broadcasting Corporation (SBC). However, domestic resistance – not unrelated to memories of the Japanese Occupation – and other considerations necessitated a switch of emphasis to the Confucian values supposedly common to the cultures of Japan and the East Asian newly industrializing economies. (For a recent quasi-feminist critique of authoritarian Confucianism in Singapore, see Heng and Janadas, 1992.)

Reacting to criticism of the Malaysian 'Look East' policy's emphasis on supposedly Japanese work ethics, and understandably reluctant to claim a common cultural heritage once this had been claimed to be Confucian, the Mahathir administration has instead been obliged to emphasize that the work ethics being promoted were not contradictory to, but rather consistent with, Islam. But as with the earlier argument that the Weberian 'Protestant ethic' is already to be found in Islam (Alatas, 1968), this begs the question of why bother to have a 'Look East' policy at all, especially since the Malaysian government inaugurated an 'assimilation of Islamic values' policy from the early 1980s. Since the mid-1980s, the Malaysian government has actively promoted a modernist Islamic ideology emphasizing diligence at the workplace as a central element. In mid-1992, the Government provided a generous endowment of at least RM30 million (RM: Malaysian ringgit) for the establishment of the Institute for Islamic Understanding (IKIM, or Institut Kefahaman Islam) to legitimize, articulate and propagate this message more effectively.

The most cynical – and slightly irreverent – Muslim response to the 'Look East' policy has been that 'the Prophet only said China' in reference to a *hadith* (a quotation attributed to the Prophet) enjoining Muslims to 'seek knowledge even unto China'. This attitude does not, of course, seriously claim to insist on a literal, rather than a metaphorical interpretation of the Prophet's injunction, but is probably symptomatic of public cynicism at the use of religion to legitimize various campaigns and changes considered conducive to the advancement of the regime's interests and priorities, in this case of those coinciding with the requirements of modern industrial capitalism.

With the 'Look East' policy of almost the same vintage as Mahathir's premiership since mid-1981, its impact on Malaysian society has not been inconsiderable, though it is sometimes still unclear where and when the policy begins and ends. One is often tempted to conclude that the policy embraces only those policy aspects publicly deemed to have been successful or broadly acceptable, avoiding what is popularly perceived to have failed or to be unacceptable. In other words, after over a decade and numerous public clarifications of what the policy constitutes, there remains a considerable grey area of ambiguity.

Some proponents of the policy and supporters of Mahathir have even suggested that since the 'Look East' policy is implicitly anti-Western, it is hence 'anti-imperialist'. This, of course, cannot be further from the truth since – as the experience of the Japanese Occupation has shown – modern imperialism is hardly a Western monopoly. Nor is there clear evidence that deteriorating relations with the West in general – other than with Britain in the early 1980s – were responsible for Malaysia 'Looking East'.

Of course, the Mahathir administration has been more consistently vocal (some would argue that actual practice has not matched the rhetoric) in supporting demands associated with the South, e.g. for higher and more stable commodity prices, better aid terms, greater technology transfer and reduced market restrictions in the 'North' on manufactured exports from the 'South'. Since the second half of the 1980s, Mahathir has taken a higher profile internationally as a champion – albeit somewhat nebulously and occasionally inconsistently – of the South, though this is not inconsistent with the emerging new, more complex international division of labour in which Malaysia has made significant gains and aspires for more.

During late 1981 and through most of 1982, Malaysian–British relations were undoubtedly strained by several developments. These apparently included the 1981 increase in British university fees for foreign students (of whom the largest number – around 50,000 then – was from Malaysia), the change in corporate takeover regulations in London (apparently in response to Malaysia's Permodalan Nasional Berhad, or PNB's takeover of the British agency house, Guthrie, at premium prices), huge losses on the London Metal Exchange (LME) after the LME's rules were suddenly changed to subvert an attempt by the Malaysian government proxy 'mystery buyer' of tin to 'corner' the tin market (see Jomo, 1990b), the indiscretions of the then new British High Commissioner to Malaysia and the Malaysian Prime Minister's ire at the supposed indiscipline of British labour as well as at foreign, including non-governmental British, intervention in Malaysian labour and human rights issues. In Mahathir's words (in *Asiaweek*, 22 March 1987): 'Whatever you used to do before with the West, I think you should also do with the East. That is the "Look East" policy. And if you have learnt all the bad work ethics of the West before, it's about time you learnt some of the good work ethics of the East'. As Bartu (1992: 54) puts it, Mahathir's view reflected the Japanese perception of 'the "British disease", whose symptoms include a low esteem for work, a high unionisation, and outdated management and marketing methods'.

This culminated in an official 'buy British last' directive and other similar measures, undoubtedly reflecting a new low in British–Malaysian relations. Mahathir even threatened to take Malaysia out of the Commonwealth, and refused to attend the first Commonwealth Heads of Government Meeting (CHOGM) held after he became prime minister – an interesting irony in light of his subsequent enthusiasm for what he once unflatteringly described as a 'creature of the past'. This 'change of mind' culminated in Malaysia hosting CHOGM in 1989 and the prominent role he has since sought in the 'new Commonwealth'.

Also, British–Malaysian relations now appear to have been considerably mended after the inefficacy of the Malaysian countermeasures became apparent and some 'face-saving' concessions by Britain to the Malaysian government were made. By the mid-1980s, however, relations had improved considerably after a visit by Prime Minister Margaret Thatcher, several generous (tied) aid packages to Malaysia (despite its 'middle income' status) and the signing of a 'Memorandum of Understanding' between the two prime ministers in late 1988 for Malaysia to purchase 1.5 billion pounds sterling worth of British armaments.

After the considerable early confusion about it, the 'Look East' policy was defined as a campaign to boost productivity by inducing hard work and promoting greater output as well as quality, and more effective modes of labour organization and discipline ostensibly associated with the Japanese. According to Mahathir (in Jomo, 1983), 'Japan's disciplined determination lifted her up from the abyss and made her the economic power she is today. . . . What (the "Look East" policy) means is that we must learn the reason and the factors for Japanese success in modernisation: a good work ethic, social consciousness, honesty and discipline, a strong sense of social purpose and community orientation, good management techniques and aggressive salesmanship.' Such official clarifications were necessitated by initial confusion over a fairly wide-ranging and apparently unintegrated series of policy initiatives in the early 1980s to accelerate modernization and industrialization by trying to emulate the Japanese and South Korean 'economic miracles'.

To be sure, Mahathir's personal commitment to the 'Look East' policy was never in doubt. Unlike Singapore premier Lee Kuan Yew – who initiated a short-lived policy to learn from Japan, but has subsequently maintained a critical distance from the Japanese – Mahathir seems to have remained more consistently enamoured with the Japanese. According to a former cabinet colleague (quoted by Bartu, 1992), 'he practically gave the Japanese *carte blanche*. . . . He even sent his children and his family to Japan for training and studies'. When Japanese Prime Minister Nakasone visited Kuala Lumpur in 1983, the two leaders praised each other so much that the Dow Jones controlled *Asian Wall Street Journal* (10 May 1983) suggested that 'Mahathir and Nakasone appear to have formed a two-member mutual admiration society'.

Hence, it was not at all surprising that when Japanese and South Korean construction firms won many turn-key and other building contracts in the early 1980s, with significant official assistance in the form of cheap finance from Tokyo and Seoul, this was widely associated with the 'Look East' policy, even after it was denied by Mahathir himself. While the foreign construction firms were generally willing to outbid Malaysian firms in order to secure contracts after having lost much business in West Asia, in at least one well known case involving construction of the Dayabumi complex, the contract was awarded to two Japanese firms whose bid of RM314 million was RM71 million more than a lower Malaysian bid. The indigenous (*Bumiputera*) engineering firm which the two Japanese firms were required to work with subsequently complained publicly that its Japanese partners were merely using it to maintain good relations with the government, and that no technology transfer was actually taking place. In any case, the Japanese firms apparently used a construction technique unnecessary for Malaysian conditions and materials mainly imported from Japan, bypassing Malaysian suppliers in the process (Jomo, 1992). By transfer pricing, Japanese firms in the region have generally shown minimal profits, or even operating losses, to evade taxes (see Bartu, 1992: 60–1).

With the 'Look East' policy, it has been widely suggested that the other intended models for Malaysian emulation are the other newly industrializing economies or countries, or 'little dragons', of the so-called 'gang of four' of the 'East Asian edge', namely Singapore, Hong Kong and Taiwan besides South Korea. These, it has been further suggested, cannot be explicitly cited by Malay politicians as models for emulation because of their Chinese character. While this is probable in view of ethnic and cultural sensitivities in Malaysia, it should also be recognized that Singapore and Hongkong are fundamentally different kinds of metropolitan economies. Also, both the Taiwanese and South Korean economies – not unlike Japan's economy earlier – have benefited greatly from heavy United States aid because of their political significance during the Cold War as alternatives to China and North Korea respectively (see Jomo, 1993a).

It is generally acknowledged that Mahathir's 'Look East' policy has been primarily directed at the Malays in Malaysia, who have been blamed by Mahathir (1970) for being primarily responsible for their own economic backwardness due to a combination of genetic and cultural factors rooted in rural peasant culture. Bartu (1992: 54) quotes a young (presumably Malay) technician approvingly: 'Malaysians work for family and religion. Japanese work for money and country'. It should also be emphasized that the 'Look East' programme on labour involves more than exhortations to work harder, as is sometimes believed. The 'work ethic', for instance, should not be considered in the abstract. If so, even if Chinese Malaysians have to be bypassed as models for emulation by ethnic Malays, the reputed diligence of the Kelantanese or Javanese, or the known entrepreneurial abilities of Kelantanese or Minangkabaus would be less controversial and better known, especially to Malays. But these are, of course, abilities developed within peasant cultures quite irrelevant to the official desire to induce greater productivity by wage labour in an industrial capitalist context. The real thrust of the campaign appears to be the promotion of labour discipline through reorganizing industrial relations to promote company loyalty (e.g. propaganda campaigns, company welfarism, in-house unions), increase productivity (e.g. work ethics, wage flexibility with a higher proportion of income in the form of output-based 'incentive payments') and reduce losses (e.g. quality control circles, 'zero defect' groups).

Since 1982, over two thousand students and skilled workers have been sent to Japan as part of an official effort – coordinated by the Prime Minister's Department – to inculcate Japanese work ethics, discipline, diligence and management techniques. Most of these trainees stay in Japan for less than three months, and the efficacy of the programme is suspect. Apparently (according to Bartu, 1992: 65), only ten per cent of the returnees have even bothered to respond to an official questionnaire attempting to assess the value of their visits.

A host of other policy initiatives of the Mahathir administration have been linked to 'Looking East', including the early 1980s' emphasis on heavy industries and preference for 'turn-key' projects, the Proton or 'Malaysian car' project, the award of major construction contracts to Japanese or South Korean companies, the encouragement of more cooperative and complementary government–private sector relations under the auspices of the 'Malaysia Incorporated' campaign and the 'privatization' or 'denationalization' of potentially profitable economic activities by the government. Some consequences of these policies have been subject to scathing private criticism (e.g. the award of the Dayabumi construction contract to a Japanese consortium at a price of RM314 million, rather than to a local firm whose bid cost RM71 million less), but the limited avenues for public dissent and the feared consequences of public criticism have kept these to a minimum.

Also, it has been suggested that some such policy initiatives have had less to do with 'Looking East' than other influences on policy-making. For instance, while the Japanese state has – since Meiji times – developed viable economic enterprises only to pass them over to the private sector, the more immediate inspiration for 'privatization' in Malaysia appears to be the dismantling of the public sector consistent with 'Reaganomics' and 'Thatcherism' in the West, and the new opportunities for 'rent appropriation' derived therefrom (see Jomo, 1993b).

Reflecting executive dominance of Malaysian society, especially under Mahathir, the rest of the state quickly fell into line: 'The media lapped it up, the bureaucrats scrambled to uncover and discover all manner of ways to implement it, while the Malaysian public at large were bombarded with an unending barrage of propaganda about the "Japanese miracle"' (Saravanamuttu, 1983). Dissenting voices were ridiculed: 'Only anglophiles are likely to be flabbergasted. But even they should know that the days of colonial straightjacket [*sic*] are over. Their bias has been inherited from another era under *Pax Britannica*', according to the *New Straits Times* (quoted in Jomo, 1983a).

However, in his 1984 speech, 'The Second Opening of Japan' (Mahathir, 1985) – apparently written by a speechwriter, and delivered by his cabinet colleague and rival, Tengku Razaleigh Hamzah – a different, critical and almost threatening tone emerged, which Mahathir subsequently distanced himself from. Bartu (1992: 63) claims that this 1984 speech marked the end of Mahathir's infatuation with Japan after the Japanese government refused to give a Malaysia Airlines (MAS)–Northwest Airlines joint flight service traffic rights through Tokyo's Narita Airport.

With mounting public criticism of his policies in the mid-1980s, Mahathir became more muted about his 'Look East' policy. However, right after the August 1986 general election, in which the policy hardly figured as a campaign issue on all sides, Mahathir claimed that his electoral success was a popular mandate for the 'Look East' policy. The resurgence of private Japanese investments in Malaysia – as in much else of Southeast Asia – after the *endaka* (yen appreciation), especially in the late 1980s, mollified Mahathir, and to some, is perceived as a vindication of his 'Look East' policy.

The remaining articles in this volume have been included to contribute to developing a critical understanding of the implications of Mahathir's 'Look

East' policy. Wad and Jomo in Chapter 8, this volume, critically review the changes in official trade union and industrial relations policy under the Mahathir administration, particularly its emphasis on the promotion of in-house or enterprise unions. Chee Peng Lim and Edmund Terence Gomez in Chapter 9, examine the sad fate of the half dozen Malaysian *sogoshoshas* set up in response to the Prime Minister's request to set up such companies, apparently at considerable cost to the participating investors. Chee Peng Lim, in Chapter 10, also critically reviews Malaysia's mixed experience with heavy industrialization from the early 1980s, paying particular attention to questions of timing, sequence, choice and priorities. All the new heavy industries set up in the early 1980s were established as joint ventures between Malaysian public enterprises – mainly HICOM, the Heavy Industries Corporation of Malaysia – in collaboration with East Asian, mainly Japanese firms. These included Mitsubishi's involvement with the Malaysian car or Proton project, Nippon Steel's involvement with Perwaja to produce steel using a prototype system (which eventually turned out to be a failure), Nichirin's contract to set up the Kedah cement plant on Langkawi and the South Korean firm's involvement with the Perak–Hanjoong Daewoo cement plant. Jomo then reviews Malaysia's experience with the 'national car' (Chapter 11), while Kit Machado (Chapter 12) elaborates on the implications of the project in terms of Japanese transnational firm strategies in the Southeast Asian regional context. Finally, in Chapter 14, Wendy Smith explores some broader cultural ramifications of the 'Look East' policy.

EAST ASIAN ECONOMIC REGIONALISM?

After the collapse of multilateral ministerial-level negotiations to conclude the Uruguay Round of the General Agreement on Tariffs and Trade (GATT) in Brussels in mid-December 1990, Mahathir quickly announced his proposal for a regional response through the formation of an East Asian Economic Grouping (EAEG). Visiting dignitaries from the region, including Singapore Prime Minister Goh Chok Tong, were obliged to publicly endorse the proposal. This was accomplished after intense negotiations to scale down the nature and implications of the original proposal, especially sought by Singaporean officials, who subsequently indiscreetly claimed credit for saving the Malaysian government from acute embarrassment.

But even in its watered-down form, the proposal has only received lukewarm endorsement within the region, with Japan continuing to distance itself from it. While probably pleased by the unexpected multilateral official endorsement of its regional economic hegemony, the Japanese government was clearly reluctant to offend the Bush administration, which was unequivocal in its opposition to the Malaysian initiative. The Miyazawa government may also have been mindful of the potentially heavy costs and other obligations as well as other implications of an increased commitment to the region while trying to protect and advance its interests elsewhere, in the face of consolidating European as well as North American regional economic integration.

It has been noted that Japan prefers to treat the region in terms of sub-regional groupings (Bartu, 1992). In some versions of this, Northeast Asia has been subdivided into three areas – around North Japan, South Japan and South China (including Taiwan and Hong Kong) – while Southeast Asia is sometimes divided into a Thai-centred 'Indochina' or 'baht bloc' (including Myanmar) and the rest of insular or Malay ASEAN (Association of Southeast Asian Nations). Somewhat surprisingly, this reluctance has not been associated with the EAEG proposal's obvious reminder of the wartime Japanese government-mooted Greater East Asian Co-Prosperity Sphere and the associated image of becoming a Japan-dominated 'yen trading bloc' – an image greatly feared, among others, by former Singapore Prime Minister Lee Kuan Yew (see Bartu, 1992). Rather, US objections to the EAEG proposal appear to have been decisive in deciding the official Japanese stance. In 1989, Australia successfully initiated and promoted the reputedly Nakasone-mooted Asian Pacific Economic Cooperation (APEC) forum, with delayed, but crucial endorsement from and the (soon dominant) participation of the US – to which Japan appears quite willing to play 'second fiddle', perhaps for fear of further exacerbating bilateral ties. The deterioration of bilateral Australian ties with Malaysia in the early 1990s probably also muted the Australian government's public disagreement with the EAEG initiative.

Virtually forced to obtain sub-regional endorsement from ASEAN before being able to take the EAEG idea any further, the Malaysian Government was obliged to further dilute its proposal under a new name, the East Asian Economic Caucus (EAEC). In 1991, at the APEC Forum meeting in Seoul, the United States government – led by then Secretary of State James Baker – launched a direct and apparently successful attack against the Malaysian initiative. Two months later, despite earlier tacit approval for the EAEC proposal among ASEAN foreign ministers, at the ASEAN Heads of Governments Summit in Singapore in January 1992, Indonesian President Suharto publicly insisted that the existing APEC arrangements were adequate for regional cooperation beyond the Southeast Asian level, thus implicitly rejecting even the much watered-down EAEC proposal. Suharto's stance was probably due to a combination of factors, including Indonesia's continued heavy dependence on Western aid, its general reluctance to antagonize the West, particularly the US, related concerns after the much-publicized Dili massacre in East Timor of November 1991, its disapproval of the lack of Malaysian consultation before unilaterally announcing the EAEG initiative in December 1990 and its view of itself as the first among equals in the ASEAN club.

INTRODUCTION

There is widespread recognition within East Asia of some potential gains from greater regional economic cooperation, especially in the face of apparently protectionist regional integration in Europe and North America. However, continued US political hegemony – enhanced by the end of the Cold War and the disintegration of the Soviet Union despite US economic decline relative to both Japan and Europe – has discouraged most other governments in the region from taking more independent positions. Furthermore, the US continues to be very significant economically for the region – as the main export market for the region and also as an important source of foreign investment and, for several regimes, foreign aid and military protection. Hence, unlike the other two major regional economic blocs, East Asian economic cooperation and coordination must necessarily be of the 'open regionalism' variety as a 'closed' or 'protectionist' regionalism would be contrary to the interests of and hence unacceptable to most, if not all governments of the region.

For other East Asian governments, generally less enamoured with the Japanese than Mahathir, the prospects of further Japanese ascendance in the region as a consequence of such regional cooperation is hardly attractive. Distinguished by its relatively poorer record on trade liberalization, tied aid, technology transfer as well as entrusting and promoting non-Japanese managerial personnel (compared with most North American and European firms), most East Asian political leaders do not quite share his enthusiasm for the Japanese. Mindful of its militaristic and expansionist past, concerned about the future course of its resurgent hegemony, resentful of its apparent cultural arrogance, economic vulgarity as well as political opportunism, and concerned by its apparent lack of public moral and democratic commitments, most East Asian populations are not looking particularly kindly to Japan for regional leadership.

Given Mahathir's close personal identification with the proposal and his well-known persistence, it is quite likely that the Malaysian Government will continue to pursue the proposal for some time more unless it finds a 'face-saving' way to drop it or, as is more likely, until a new prime minister succeeds Mahathir. In the face of the Clinton administration's effort to elevate the status of APEC by hosting the Seattle Heads of Governments meeting in November 1993, it is still possible for the EAEC to be further reconceived as a sub-regional caucus in the larger APEC arrangements still favoured by the new US and Japanese administrations in 1993. However, Mahathir's refusal to participate at the Seattle summit – where he could have continued 'lobbying' for such an interpretation of the EAEC – may unwittingly have defined the EAEC as inimical to APEC, and thus foreclosed any such compromise. Unfortunately, the likely demise of the EAEG proposal will occur without a full, serious and informed consideration of regional cooperation alternatives, mindful of historical precedents and likely global trends, especially on both sides of the North Atlantic.

BIBLIOGRAPHY

Alatas, Syed Hussein (1968) 'The Weber Thesis and Southeast Asia', in *Modernisation and Social Change*, Angus and Robertson, London.

Amante, Maragtas, Marie Aganon and Rene Ofreneo (1992) *Japanese Industrial Relations Interface in the Philippines*, School of Labor and Industrial Relations, University of the Philippines, Diliman, Metromanila.

Anon, 'Exporting QCCs: Japanese-type Industrial Relations Abroad' in Jomo (1983).

Aoki Takeshi (1992) 'Japanese FDI and the Forming of Networks in the Asia–Pacific Region: Experience in Malaysia and Its Implications' in Tokunaga (1992).

Bartu, Friedemann (1992) *The Ugly Japanese: Nippon's Economic Empire in Asia*, Longman, Singapore.

Bix, Herbert P. (1973) 'Regional Integration: Japan and South Korea in America's Asian Policy', *Bulletin of Concerned Asian Scholars*, 5, 3 (November).

Buchanan, Keith (1971) 'Japan and the Pacific Rim Strategy', *Indochina* 15 (June).

Chan Chee Khoon and Chee Heng Leng (eds) (1984), *Designer Genes: IQ, Ideology and Biology*, INSAN, Kuala Lumpur.

Chang Yii Tan (1985) 'Tilting East: The Construction Problem' in Jomo (1985).

Chandra Muzaffar (1983a) 'Hard Work – The Cure All?' in Jomo (1983a).

Chandra Muzaffar (1983b) 'Overkill?: In-House Unions for Malaysia' in Jomo (1983a).

Cheah Boon Kheng (1983) 'Malaya Under Japanese Occupation: Socio-political Consequences' in Jomo (1983a).

Chee Peng Lim (1983a) 'Malaysian Sogoshoshas – No Go So Far' in Jomo (1983a).

Chee Peng Lim (1983b) 'The Malaysian Car Dream: A Need for Reconsideration' in Jomo (1983a).

Chee Peng Lim (1985) 'The Proton Saga – No Reverse Gear! The Economic Burden of Malaysia's Car Project' in Jomo (1985).

Chee Peng Lim (1992) 'Managing Structural Change and Industrialization: the Malaysian Experience', ISIS-HIID conference on the Malaysian economy, 1–3 June, Kuala Lumpur.

Chee Peng Lim and Lee Poh Ping (1979) *The Role of Japanese Direct Investment in Malaysia*, Occasional Paper no. 60, Institute of Southeast Asian Studies, Singapore.

Chee Peng Lim and Lee Poh Ping (1983) 'Japanese Joint Ventures in Malaysia' in Jomo (1983a).

David, Abe and Ted Wheelwright (1989) *The Third Wave: Australia and Asian Capitalism*, Left Book Club, Sydney.

Dore, Ronald (1973) *British Factory – Japanese Factory*, George Allen and Unwin, London.

Emmott, Bill (1989) *The Sun Also Sets: Why Japan Will Not Be Number One*, Simon & Schuster, New York.

Fong Chan-Onn (1992) 'Foreign Direct Investment in Malaysia: Technology Transfer and Linkages by Japan and Asian NIEs' in Tokunaga (1992).

Golley, Linda (1983) 'Investment Paradise: Japanese Capital in Malaysia' in Jomo (1983a).

Haflah Piei, Mohd (1989) 'Malaysia–Japan Economic Relations' (mimeo).

Halliday, Jon (1983a) 'The Meiji State and Economic Policy' in Jomo (1983a).

Halliday, Jon (1983b) 'Japan's Southeast Asian War' in Jomo (1983a).

Halliday, Jon (1983c) 'Education, Examinations and Employment in Japan' in Jomo (1983a).

Halliday, Jon and Gavan McCormack (1973) *Japanese Imperialism Today*, Monthly Review Press, New York.

Hara, Fujio (ed.) (1993) *Formation and Restructuring of Business Groups in Malaysia*, Institute of Developing Economies, Tokyo.

Heng, Geraldine and Janadas Devan (1992) 'State Fatherhood: The Politics of Nationalism, Sexuality and Race in Singapore', in Parker, Russ, Sommer and Yaeger (eds) *Nationalism and Sexualities*, Routledge, London.

Higuchi Tokuzo (1983) 'Japanese Labour Divided: Unions and Unorganized Workers' in Jomo (1983).

Holland, Stuart (1991) 'Europe, the United States and Japan: Multinationals and Triadic Competition', paper presented at the Waseda international symposium on 'Japanese Firms in a Changing Tri-polar World', 11–13 June, Tokyo.

Hosmer, Ellen (1988) 'Aid, Incorporated: the Real Beneficiaries of Japanese Foreign Assistance', *Multinational Monitor*, November.

Ishihara Shintaro (1989) *The Japan That Can Say No: Why Japan Will Be First Among Equals*, Simon & Schuster, New York.

Jamil bin Mohd Jan (1990) 'Heavy Industries in Malaysia – Lessons from the 1980s and Challenges for the 1990s (HICOM's Experience and Views)', INTAN economic lecture series, 21 February, Kuala Lumpur.

Jensen, Nini (1980) 'Nakane Chie and Japanese Society', *Bulletin of Concerned Asian Scholars*, 12, 3 (July–September).

Johnson, Chalmers (1977) 'MITI and Japanese International Economic Policy', in Robert A. Scalapino (ed.), *The Foreign Policy of Modern Japan*, University of California Press, Berkeley.

Johnson, Chalmers (1982) *MITI and the Japanese Miracle: The Growth of Industrial Policy, 1925–1975*, Stanford University Press, Stanford.

Jomo K.S. (ed.) (1983a) *The Sun Also Sets: Lessons in 'Looking East'*, INSAN, Kuala Lumpur.

Jomo K.S. (1983b) 'Project Proton: Malaysian car, Mitsubishi profits' in Jomo (ed.) (1983a).

Jomo K.S. (ed.) (1985) *The Sun Also Sets: Lessons in 'Looking East'*, second edition, INSAN, Kuala Lumpur.

Jomo K.S. (ed.) (1989) *Mahathir's Economic Policies*, second edition, INSAN, Kuala Lumpur.

Jomo K.S. (1990a) *Growth and Structural Change in the Malaysian Economy*, Macmillan, London.

Jomo K.S. (ed.) (1990b) *Undermining Tin: The Decline of Malaysian Pre-eminence*, Transnational Corporations Research Project, University of Sydney, Sydney.

Jomo K. S. (ed.) (1992) *Suria Terbenam Jua: Ajaran 'Pandang ke Timur'*, INSAN, Kuala Lumpur.

Jomo K.S. (1993a) 'Prospects for Malaysian Industrialization in Light of East Asian NIC Experiences', in Jomo K.S. (ed.) *Industrialising Malaysia: Policy, Performance, Prospects*, Routledge, London.

Jomo K.S. (1993b) 'Privatization in Malaysia: For what and for whom?' in Thomas Clarke and Christos Pitelis (eds) *The Political Economy of Privatization*, Routledge, London.

Kaneko Fumio (1988) 'Japanese ODA: Politics of Strategic Assistance', *AMPO Japan–Asia Quarterly Review*, 20, 1, 2.

Kaneko Fumio (1991) 'Japanese Capitalism: Spreading Its Tentacles' *AMPO: Japan–Asia Quarterly Review*, 22, 2–3.

Kimbara Tatsuo (1991) 'Localization and Performance of Japanese Operations in Malaysia and Singapore' in Yamashita (1991).

Kitamura Hiroshi, (1972) 'Japan's Economic Policy Towards Southeast Asia', *Asian Affairs*, 59, 1 (February).

Kitazawa Yoko (1987) 'Setting Up Shop, Shutting Up Shop', *AMPO: Japan–Asia Quarterly Review*, 19, 1.

Kua Kia Soong (1983) 'Why Look East?' in Jomo (1983).

Lee Poh Ping (1985) '"Japan Incorporated" and Its Relevance to Malaysia' in Jomo (1985).

Lee Poh Ping (1988) 'The Japanese model and Southeast Asia with particular reference to Malaysia', *Kajian Malaysia*, 6, 1.

Lim, Linda (1985) 'Singapore As Number One' in Jomo (1985).

Lin See Yan (1983) 'Malaysia's Trade with Japan' in Jomo (1983a).

Lin See Yan (1985) 'Malaysia's Trade with Japan' (revised) in Jomo (1985).

Lin See Yan (1988) *Japan–Malaysia Relations: External Debt, with Special Emphasis on Official Assistance*, Institute of Strategic and International Studies (ISIS) Malaysia, Kuala Lumpur.

Livingston, Jon, Joe Moore and Felicia Oldfather (eds) (1973a) *Imperial Japan 1800–1945*, Pantheon, New York.

Livingston, Jon, Joe Moore and Felicia Oldfather (eds) (1973b) *Postwar Japan 1945 to the Present*, Pantheon, New York.

Machado, Kit (1987) 'Malaysian Cultural Relations with Japan and South Korea in the 1980's: Looking East', *Asian Survey*, 27: 638–60.

Machado, Kit (1989–90) 'Japanese Transnational Corporations in Malaysia's State-sponsored Heavy Industrialization Drive: The HICOM Automobile and Steel Projects', *Pacific Affairs*, 62: 504–31.

Mahathir Mohamad (1970) *The Malay Dilemma*, Donald Moore, Singapore.

Mahathir Mohamad (1983) 'New Government Policies' in Jomo (1983a).

Mahathir Mohamad (1985) 'The Second Opening of Japan' in Jomo (1985).

McCoy, Alfred (ed.) (1980) *Southeast Asia under Japanese Occupation*, Yale University, Southeast Asia Studies, New Haven.

Morris-Suzuki, Tessa (ed.) (1989) *Japanese Capitalism Since 1945*, London.

Motoyama Yoshihiko (1988) 'Securitization and New Trend of the Acquisition of the Third World's Assets', *AMPO: Japan–Asia Quarterly Review*, 20, 1, 2.

Murakami Hyoe and Johannes Hirschmeier (eds) (1979) *Politics and Economics in Contemporary Japan*, Japan Culture Institute, Tokyo.

Muto Ichiyo (1983a) 'Japan at a Crossroads: US–Japan Relations, Politics and Labour' in Jomo (1983a).

Muto Ichiyo (1983b) 'Japanese Labour in the "Company World"' in Jomo (1983a).

Muto Ichiyo (1989) 'Possibilities of New Internationalism: A View from Japan', *Communique*, 5, July.

Nakase Toshikazu (1983a) 'Sogo Sosha, the Japanese Conglomerate' in Jomo (1983a).

Nakase Toshikazu (1983b) 'Japanese Multinationals Today: Some Characteristics' in Jomo (1983a).

New Times (1985) 'The Myth of Homogeneity: Japanese Treatment of Minorities' in Jomo (1985).

Newsweek, 5 August 1991 (cover story: 'The Yen Bloc').

Nishikawa Atsushi (1983) 'Japanese Transnationals and Asian Trainees' in Jomo (1983a).

15

Nishikawa Jun (1981) 'Japanese Overseas Investment and Developing Countries', *Waseda Economic Papers.*

Nishikawa Jun (1991) 'Japanese Private Direct Investment in the Asia-Pacific Region', paper presented at the Waseda University international symposium on 'Japanese Firms in a Changing Tri-polar World', 11–13 June, Tokyo.

Norman, E.H. (1983) 'The Establishment of a Modern State in Japan' in Jomo (1983a).

OECF (1989) *Japanese Contribution to Economic Development of Malaysia Through OECF Loans*, Overseas Economic Cooperation Fund, Tokyo.

OECF (1991) *Outline of OECF's Economic Cooperation in Malaysia*, Overseas Economic Cooperation Fund, Kuala Lumpur.

Pura, Raphael (1985) 'Doubts Over Heavy Industrialization Strategy' in Jomo (1985).

Puthucheary, Mavis (1985) 'Privatization – Proceed, but with Caution' in Jomo (1985).

Raghavan, Chakravarthi (1993) 'Japanese Study on State's Role Refutes Free-market Myths', *Third World Economics*, 16–31 May.

Robertson, Eric (1979) *The Japanese File: Pre-war Japanese Penetration in Southeast Asia*, Heinemann Asia, Hongkong.

Rodo Joho (1983) 'Recent Trends in Japanese Labour' in Jomo (1983a).

Ryder, James W. (1985) 'QCCs: Management's New Velvet Glove' in Jomo (1985).

Ryusuke Kijuiri (1973) 'Shosha: Organizers of the World Economy', *The Japan Interpreter*, 8, 3 (Autumn).

Saravanamuttu, Johan (1983) 'The 'Look East' Policy and Japanese Economic Penetration in Malaysia' in Jomo (1983a).

Saravanamuttu, Johan (1988) 'Japanese Economic Penetration in ASEAN in the Context of the International Division of Labour', *Journal of Contemporary Asia*, 18: 139–64.

Sekiguchi S. (ed.) (1983) *ASEAN–Japan Relations: Investment*, Institute of Southeast Asian Studies, Singapore.

Shahari Ahmad Jabar, Mohd (1985) 'Government Support for Private Enterprise' in Jomo (1985).

Shiode Hirokazu (1989) *Japanese Investment in Southeast Asia*, Centre for the Progress of Peoples, Hongkong.

Sim Ah Bah (1977) 'Decentralized Management of Subsidiaries and Their Performance: A Comparative Study of American, British and Japanese Subsidiaries in Malaysia', *Management International Review*, 17, 2: 45–51.

Steven, Rob (1979) 'The Japanese Bourgeoisie', *Bulletin of Concerned Asian Scholars*, 11, 2 (April–June).

Steven, Rob (1980) 'The Japanese Working Class', *Bulletin of Concerned Asian Scholars*, 12, 3 (July–September).

Steven, Rob (1983) *Classes in Contemporary Japan*, Cambridge University Press, Cambridge.

Steven, Rob (1990) *Japan's New Imperialism*, Macmillan, London.

Sono Haruo (1983) 'Japanese Car Business: Anatomy of a Success Story' in Jomo (1983a).

Sudo S. (1988a) 'Japan–ASEAN Relations: New Dimensions in Japanese Foreign Policy', *Asian Survey*, 28: 509–25.

Sudo S. (1988b) 'From Fukuda to Taskeshita: a decade of Japan-ASEAN relations', *Contemporary Southeast Asia*, 10: 119–43.

Sunoo, Harold Hukwon (1978) 'Economic Development and Foreign Control in South Korea', *Journal of Contemporary Asia*, 8, 3.

Taira Koji (1970) *Economic Development and the Labour Market in Japan*, Columbia University Press, New York.

Tan Boon Kean (1991) 'Changing Patterns and Issues in Japanese Investment in Malaysia', in Waseda University international symposium on 'Japanese Firms in a Changing Tri-polar World: Their Production Network in the Asia-Pacific Region', 11–13 June, Tokyo.

Thong, Gregory (1991) 'Foundations of Human Resources Management Practice in Japanese Companies in Malaysia' in Yamashita (1991).

Thong, Gregory and H.C. Jain (1988) 'Human Resource Management Practices of Japanese and Malaysian Companies: A Comparative Study', *Malaysian Management Review*, 23, 2.

Tokunaga Shojiro (ed.) (1992) *Japan's Foreign Investment and Asian Economic Interdependence: Production, Trade and Financial Systems*, University of Tokyo Press, Tokyo.

Tse, Christina (1983) *Reflections on Japanese Management Lessons to a Woman Worker*, Centre for the Progress of Peoples, Hongkong.

Tsokhas, Kosmas (1981) 'Social Capital, Interdependence and Japanese Multi-Nationals', *Journal of Contemporary Asia*, 11, 4.

Tsuda Mamoru (1983) 'Big Corporations and Business Groups in Contemporary Japan' in Jomo (1983a).

Tsurouka, Doug (1993) 'Ticket to Ride: Daihatsu Gets Its Way on Malaysia Car Plan', *Far Eastern Economic Review*, 18 February.

van Wolferen, Karel (1989) *The Enigma of Japanese Power*, Macmillan, London.

Watanabe Ben (1988, 1989) 'The Japanese Labor Movement: Towards Total Dissolution?', *AMPO: Japan–Asia Quarterly Review*, 20, 4; 21, 1.

Woronoff, Jon (1979) *Japan: The Coming Economic Crisis*, Lotus Press, Tokyo.

Woronoff, Jon (1980) *Japan: The Coming Social Crisis*, Lotus Press, Tokyo.

Woronoff, Jon (1981) *Japan's Wasted Workers*, Lotus Press, Tokyo.

Woronoff, Jon (1982) *Japan Inc.*, Lotus Press, Tokyo.

Yamashita Shoichi (ed.) (1991) *Transfer of Japanese Technology and Management to the ASEAN Countries*, University of Tokyo Press, Tokyo.

Yuen Choy Leng (1983) 'Japan's Penetration of Pre-War Malaya' in Jomo (1983a).

Part I

1

MALAYSIA–JAPAN: UNEQUAL TRADE PARTNERS

Mohamed Aslam and Mohd Haflah Piei

At least since the 1980s, Malaysia has relied heavily on Japan, not only for trade, but also for investment, aid, technology transfer, services and even education. Japan replaced Europe as Malaysia's principal trade partner in the mid-1970s. Malaysia has become more import and export dependent on Japan after trying to reduce its dependence on Britain and the European Economic Community (EEC) since the early 1980s (Nester, 1991: 90).

However, even as Japan has become a more important trade partner, its trade surplus with Malaysia has grown, especially since 1988. Since the *endaka* (yen appreciation), Japanese corporations have shifted more production plants to Southeast Asian countries to cut production costs and improve access to markets and raw materials (Japanese External Trade Organization (JETRO), 1988: 38). Since the yen appreciation – from September 1985 and in early 1993 – has reduced Japanese price competitiveness in the world market, internationalization of Japanese capital accelerated during the 1980s to preserve Japan's market share in world trade. Internationalization is not a new phenomenon, but more Japanese manufacturers have come to recognize the importance of low labour costs and stable markets, spurring a rapid increase in foreign direct investment (JETRO, 1988). More than 60 per cent (by value) of Japan's machinery imports from the Asian newly industrializing economies (NIEs) and Association of Southeast Asian Nations (ASEAN) are produced by Japanese machinery industry affiliates based in these regions (JETRO, 1992: 142).

MALAYSIA'S TRADE PARTNERS

Despite the efforts by the government to diversify Malaysia's export markets, Japan, the US, the EEC and ASEAN remain Malaysia's major trading partners, accounting for 75.9 per cent of Malaysia's total trade in 1991 compared with 73.9 per cent in 1975 and 74.5 per cent in 1980, respectively. Table 1.1 shows the growth of Malaysian trade with these trading partners since 1970. Total trade with these countries has increased

Table 1.1 Malaysia: trade and trade balance with major trade partners (RM million)

	Japan		USA		EEC		ASEAN		Singapore	
	Total trade	Trade balance	Total trade	Trade balance	Total trade	Trade balance	Total trade	Trade balance	Total trade	Trade balance
1971	1,798.4	26.4	931.0	342.4	2,019.0	−188.2	1,965.3	705.3	1,459.8	788.4
1972	1,886.6	−220.8	1,082.1	250.9	2,078.4	−1.4	2,002.5	562.1	1,490.2	770.6
1973	2,790.6	−118.6	1,315.5	283.3	2,902.6	330.8	2,722.4	933.8	2,164.2	1,250.0
1974	3,933.9	−496.7	2,470.5	390.3	4,260.2	66.6	3,886.6	992.0	3,028.2	1,387.8
1975	3,131.6	−456.8	2,447.4	530.8	3,868.0	406.8	3,522.7	944.7	2,595.7	1,152.1
1976	4,900.0	775.8	3,330.9	857.7	4,491.2	1,135.2	4,280.2	1,497.2	3,297.5	1,612.2
1977	5,661.1	436.3	4,092.5	1,342.7	4,898.9	1,009.5	4,458.8	1,201.0	3,319.8	1,451.4
1978	6,872.0	534.0	5,085.4	1,280.4	5,613.5	652.9	5,127.9	1,216.3	3,928.2	1,595.0
1979	9,508.5	1,827.9	6,747.8	1,617.2	7,283.2	1,289.2	7,374.9	2,348.5	5,806.3	2,645.5
1980	11,794.6	1,064.0	8,137.0	1,080.6	8,394.6	1,153.4	10,155.2	2,440.2	8,138.0	2,632.2
1981	12,243.6	−788.4	7,414.2	336.0	7,831.1	427.7	11,968.4	2,417.4	9,663.7	2,691.3
1982	12,979.4	−1,526.8	8,302.8	−1,854.8	7,750.1	683.1	14,015.5	2,695.3	11,185.8	2,856.4
1983	14,248.2	−1,315.6	9,276.1	−607.7	9,103.3	462.9	15,047.7	3,441.1	11,669.8	3,102.8
1984	17,279.0	−13.2	10,599.4	−122.8	9,290.8	461.4	16,685.2	3,932.2	12,181.6	3,618.0
1985	16,278.0	2,266.0	9,518.3	263.7	9,686.2	1,036.6	16,628.3	2,982.5	12,184.6	2,529.0
1986	13,775.1	2,331.1	11,191.8	685.8	9,316.6	1,142.2	13,884.0	1,872.6	10,289.0	1,892.6
1987	15,753.0	1,902.0	13,468.2	1,501.0	10,725.5	2,169.3	17,579.1	4,273.7	12,937.6	3,502.0
1988	19,500.9	−805.9	17,259.9	1,961.7	13,776.6	2,191.4	21,607.9	5,353.9	16,397.6	4,981.0
1989	25,620.9	−3,823.9	22,967.9	2,388.7	18,942.7	1,952.1	28,778.2	5,803.6	21,678.4	5,115.8
1990	31,562.7	−6,384.9	26,719.5	254.5	23,418.2	307.6	38,010.4	8,086.0	29,852.1	6,252.1
1991	41,365.6	−11,347.8	31,461.8	507.6	27,736.2	210.8	47,707.5	7,652.3	37,740.1	6,375.3

Source: Bank Negara Malaysia, Quarterly Economic Bulletin, various issues.

rapidly over the years. The leading partners are ASEAN (led by Singapore) and Japan. Of all these major trading partners, only trade with Japan has involved major trade deficits, especially since 1988 (Table 1.1).

Trade with Japan during 1971–91 averaged 19 per cent of exports and 23 per cent of imports. Malaysia's trade with other ASEAN members averaged 25.6 per cent of total exports and 18.7 per cent of all imports during the same period (Table 1.2). Singapore was the second most important trading partner for Malaysia after Japan, with exports averaging 20.4 per cent, while imports averaged 13.1 per cent during 1971–91. Exports and imports with the United States averaged about 16 per cent. Overall trade with EEC nations also grew considerably, with most trade involving the United Kingdom and the Federal Republic of Germany.

MALAYSIA–JAPAN BILATERAL TRADE RELATIONS

As is quite evident from Tables 1.1 and 1.2, Japan has been a very important trade partner for Malaysia. Over the period 1971–91, total trade between the two countries increased from RM1.8 billion to RM41.4 billion (RM: Malaysian ringgit). In 1991, Japan accounted for 15.9 per cent of exports and 26.1 per cent of imports. From Japan's perspective, Malaysia's trade with Japan accounted for only 2.6 per cent of total trade in 1991, compared with 1.5 per cent in 1986 and 1.8 per cent in 1982 (JETRO, 1983, 1988). Obviously, Malaysia is more trade-dependent on Japan than Japan is on Malaysia. Japan still remains the most important single country export market for Malaysia, absorbing 16–24 per cent of Malaysia's exports during the period 1970–91 (Table 1.3). Japan's imports of Malaysian goods averaged 2.6 per cent of total imports during 1990–91 compared with 2.1 per cent during 1982–86 (JETRO, 1983, 1988, 1992). Malaysia's imports from Japan averaged about 20 per cent of total imports during 1990–91. Japan's exports to Malaysia averaged 2.2 per cent during 1990–91 compared with 1.3 per cent during 1982–86.

Exports to Japan involved many raw materials. Exports of crude materials, inedible and mineral fuels to Japan have increased greatly (Table 1.4). Items such as rubber, sawn timber and saw logs (SITC section 2), liquefied natural gas (LNG) and crude petroleum were major export items to Japan; nearly 100 per cent of Malaysian LNG exports go to Japan. Other primary commodities important to Malaysia–Japan trade are tin, palm oil, palm stearin and palm kernel oil. Exports of manufactures to Japan have not been impressive, even though Japanese manufacturing investments in Malaysia have grown rapidly. However, exports to Japan of machinery and transport equipment as well as manufactured goods (SITC 6) and chemical products have increased significantly after 1988, reflecting the huge Japanese investments in these industries in Malaysia after the *endaka*.

Malaysia's total exports of manufactured products (SITC 6, 7, 8) to Japan

Table 1.2 Malaysia: direction of trade, 1970–91 (percentages)

	1970	1975	1980	1984	1985	1986	1987	1988	1989	1990	1991
Total exports (RM millions)	5,162.4	9,231.1	28,171.6	38,646.9	38,016.7	35,720.9	45,138.4	55,260.0	67,824.5	79,646.4	94,496.6
Japan	939.0	1,337.4	6,429.3	8,632.9	9,272.0	8,053.1	8,827.5	9,347.5	10,898.5	12,588.9	15,008.9
Shares (%)											
Japan	18.2	14.5	22.8	22.3	24.4	22.5	19.6	16.9	16.1	15.8	15.9
USA	13.0	16.1	16.4	13.6	12.9	16.6	16.6	17.4	18.9	16.9	16.9
EEC	20.0	23.2	16.9	12.6	14.1	14.6	14.3	14.4	15.4	14.9	14.8
UK	6.6	6.0	2.8	2.6	2.6	3.5	3.2	3.5	3.8	3.9	4.4
FRG	3.1	4.3	3.6	3.1	2.6	3.6	3.4	3.4	3.6	3.9	3.6
ASEAN	23.0	24.2	22.4	26.7	25.8	22.1	24.2	24.4	25.5	28.9	29.3
Singapore	21.5	20.3	19.1	20.4	19.4	17.1	18.2	19.3	19.8	22.7	23.3
Total imports (RM millions)	4,340.1	8,638.4	23,451.0	32,925.9	30,437.8	27,921.3	31,933.9	43,293.4	60,858.1	79,118.6	100,831.1
Japan	767.8	1,794.2	5,365.3	8,646.1	7,006.0	5,722.0	6,925.5	10,153.4	14,722.4	18,973.8	26,354.7
Shares (%)											
Japan	17.1	20.8	22.9	26.3	23.0	20.5	21.7	23.5	24.2	24.0	26.1
USA	8.5	11.1	15.0	16.3	15.2	18.8	18.7	17.7	16.9	16.7	15.3
EEC	24.6	20.0	15.4	13.4	14.2	14.6	13.4	13.4	14.0	14.6	13.6
UK	13.4	9.9	5.4	3.6	4.0	4.5	4.3	4.9	5.4	5.5	4.6
FRG	4.8	5.0	5.4	4.1	4.5	4.5	4.2	3.9	3.8	4.3	4.3
ASEAN	15.4	14.9	16.4	19.4	22.4	21.5	20.8	18.8	18.9	18.9	19.9
Singapore	7.2	8.3	11.7	13.0	15.9	15.0	14.8	13.2	13.6	14.9	15.6
Trade balance (overall)	822.3	592.7	4,720.6	5,721.0	7,578.9	7,799.3	13,204.5	11,966.6	6,966.4	527.8	-6,334.5
Japan	171.2	-456.8	1,064.0	-13.2	2,266.0	2,331.1	1,902.0	-805.9	-3,823.9	-6,384.9	-11,347.8

Source: Bank Negara Malaysia, *Quarterly Economic Bulletin*, various issues.

Table 1.3 Malaysia: trade with Japan, 1970–91 (RM million)

Year	Exports	% Total exports	Imports	% Total imports	Trade balance
1970	939	18.2	768	19.7	171
1971	912	18.2	886	20.1	26
1972	833	17.2	1,054	23.2	−221
1973	1,336	18.1	1,449	24.4	−113
1974	1,719	16.9	2,215	22.4	−497
1975	1,337	14.5	1,707	20.0	−369
1976	2,838	21.1	2,062	21.2	776
1977	3,049	20.4	2,612	23.4	436
1978	3,693	21.6	3,145	23.0	548
1979	5,668	23.4	3,832	22.3	1,836
1980	6,429	22.8	5,365	22.9	1,064
1981	5,728	21.1	6,516	24.5	−788
1982	5,726	20.4	7,253	25.0	−1,527
1983	6,466	19.7	7,782	25.3	−1,316
1984	8,633	22.3	8,646	26.3	−13
1985	9,272	24.4	7,006	23.0	2,266
1986	8,053	22.5	5,722	20.5	2,331
1987	8,828	19.6	6,926	21.7	1,902
1988	9,348	16.9	10,153	23.5	−806
1989	10,899	16.1	14,722	24.2	−3,824
1990	12,589	15.8	18,974	24.0	−6,385
1991	15,009	15.9	26,355	26.1	−6,335

Source: Bank Negara Malaysia, *Quarterly Economic Bulletin,* various issues.

in 1987 reached RM954.3 million. By 1991, there was an increase by over 330 per cent to RM5139 million. Nevertheless, this is still modest as it represents barely 2.6 per cent of Malaysia's total exports and 8.4 per cent of Malaysia's total exports of manufactures. Malaysia has yet to make significant inroads into Japan's market for manufactures. Much of the limited growth of manufactured exports from Malaysia to Japan has been due to Japanese investments in Malaysia rather than to exports by Malaysian manufacturers.

As for Malaysia's imports from Japan, intermediate (SITC 5, 6) and capital (SITC 7) goods continue to account for a large proportion of Malaysia's total imports from Japan. Imports of machinery and transport equipment (SITC 7) have grown rapidly, mainly since 1987 (Table 1.5). Such imports include various manufactured products such as general machinery, electrical machinery, metalworking machinery, constructing and mining machinery, transport equipment (including motor vehicles and parts) and electronic products. Besides that, imports of manufactured goods (SITC 6) and chemicals (SITC 5) also increased considerably despite increased exports of similar manufactured goods.

In 1991, the imports of intermediate and capital goods from Japan

Table 1.4 Malaysia: exports to Japan by commodity section (RM million)

SITC	0	1	2	3	4	5	6	7	8	9	Total
	Food and live animals	Beverages and tobacco	Crude materials inedible	Mineral fuels	Animal and vegetable oils and fats	Chemicals	Manuf. goods	Machinery, transport equipment	Misc. manuf. articles	Other imports	
1970	24.7	—	629.0	4.5	3.0	0.5	266.2	0.2	0.1	4.0	952.2
1971	58.3	—	486.2	93.8	4.6	0.5	265.3	0.8	0.1	4.3	913.0
1972	58.8	—	445.6	38.5	10.4	0.6	273.7	1.4	0.3	3.2	832.5
1973	84.1	—	843.3	42.2	18.7	1.7	337.9	1.0	3.3	4.2	1,336.4
1974	60.2	—	915.3	233.2	78.1	3.2	394.6	22.1	7.1	4.8	1,718.6
1975	72.2	—	560.3	350.0	64.0	4.0	211.5	51.4	18.7	5.6	1,337.7
1976	127.2	—	1,303.8	824.0	87.2	5.7	389.8	50.4	39.4	7.7	2,835.2
1977	106.2	—	1,359.9	946.8	115.4	1.9	408.6	45.2	38.8	5.9	3,048.7
1978	127.0	—	1,516.1	1,192.7	177.1	10.5	538.9	79.3	38.6	12.6	3,692.8
1979	207.5	—	2,532.6	1,877.8	196.3	7.8	653.6	131.2	47.7	13.7	5,668.2
1980	117.2	—	2,275.5	2,868.7	182.1	11.2	752.1	150.6	57.8	14.1	6,429.3
1981	145.4	—	1,915.2	2,601.4	187.2	10.4	647.6	172.8	36.8	11.4	5,727.6
1982	144.6	—	2,504.5	2,131.4	167.9	12.5	488.4	214.2	46.0	16.8	5,726.3
1983	176.7	—	2,306.9	2,717.0	198.2	24.5	611.9	324.3	46.5	23.2	6,429.2
1984	149.2	—	2,344.7	4,627.5	306.3	33.5	669.7	422.0	49.0	31.0	8,632.9
1985	138.5	—	2,340.5	5,486.4	267.0	52.4	424.5	476.2	53.6	32.9	9,272.0
1986	195.5	—	2,388.2	4,093.8	181.2	85.2	342.4	667.0	62.7	36.9	8,053.1
1987	207.4	—	3,443.0	3,616.2	228.7	108.1	511.9	586.3	93.1	29.3	8,824.5
1988	236.2	3.2	3,489.0	3,465.3	325.0	217.6	531.5	914.6	138.3	26.9	9,347.5
1989	195.4	4.6	3,873.3	3,941.6	341.9	162.1	594.4	1,561.1	204.2	25.2	10,904.3
1990	215.6	4.0	3,467.2	5,092.4	277.7	212.7	608.6	2,275.0	388.7	48.7	12,590.5
1991	272.3	6.7	3,358.6	5,372.4	361.6	287.6	763.4	3,659.2	716.4	41.4	14,839.6

Source: Department of Statistics, *External Trade Statistics*, various issues.

Table 1.5 Malaysia: imports from Japan by SITC commodity section (RM million)

SITC	0	1	2	3	4	5	6	7	8	9	Total
	Food and live animals	Beverages and tobacco	Crude materials inedible	Mineral fuels	Animal and vegetable oils and fats	Chemicals	Manuf. goods	Machinery, transport equipment	Misc. manuf. articles	Other imports	
1970	23.9	0.1	6.4	0.5	0.4	47.7	218.9	234.7	36.3	1.3	570.2
1971	21.6	0.1	7.7	6.6	2.0	70.9	321.3	388.1	40.5	2.6	861.4
1972	22.4	0.1	12.1	2.2	2.2	83.0	342.3	424.0	42.5	1.9	932.7
1973	26.0	0.1	15.3	6.5	2.4	111.4	516.6	612.6	54.1	2.5	1,347.5
1974	28.0	0.1	20.3	9.9	1.5	197.7	826.7	1,034.1	81.6	4.2	2,204.1
1975	41.5	1.6	15.2	5.6	1.8	172.0	601.6	784.1	77.0	6.2	1,706.6
1976	40.7	0.1	28.8	7.3	2.3	247.5	674.0	972.6	84.6	4.5	2,062.4
1977	44.9	0.1	30.3	9.7	3.1	259.4	764.0	1,369.3	125.1	6.5	2,612.4
1978	52.0	0.3	32.4	8.0	3.0	264.6	857.8	1,792.9	126.7	7.6	3,145.3
1979	66.8	0.8	40.4	11.3	3.0	316.6	1,039.7	2,202.8	142.6	7.8	3,831.8
1980	88.2	0.9	53.2	15.8	2.2	357.9	1,447.1	3,198.2	190.9	10.9	5,365.3
1981	95.5	1.2	83.1	19.2	1.7	384.7	1,740.4	3,926.9	253.9	9.4	6,516.0
1982	91.7	1.0	56.3	14.1	2.0	403.1	2,102.5	4,225.0	346.4	11.0	7,253.1
1983	86.0	1.8	64.4	13.4	3.3	428.3	1,905.7	4,877.3	378.6	9.9	7,768.7
1984	105.3	1.6	67.8	16.0	4.5	419.1	1,802.1	5,713.3	503.3	12.9	8,646.1
1985	95.9	1.4	63.7	13.8	4.8	411.9	1,541.6	4,371.8	489.0	12.1	7,006.0
1986	80.5	1.6	71.2	16.5	3.8	464.6	1,245.5	3,392.3	432.6	13.4	5,722.0
1987	67.3	1.3	70.9	19.6	2.8	575.4	1,374.3	4,290.6	501.6	14.3	6,918.1
1988	69.0	2.2	89.5	19.4	2.7	893.2	1,978.1	6,406.1	676.8	16.5	10,153.4
1989	73.3	3.5	113.6	25.1	3.0	1,070.4	2,706.1	9,782.5	920.8	23.5	14,721.9
1990	68.9	2.9	122.3	25.6	2.4	1,365.4	3,299.7	12,831.5	1,299.5	53.1	19,071.3
1991	81.8	5.5	174.0	35.0	3.3	1,661.2	4,670.1	17,852.3	1,782.3	23.0	26,289.2

Source: Department of Statistics, External Trade Statistics, various issues.

Table 1.6 Malaysia: manufactured imports and direct investments from Japan

Year	Intermediate goods (SITC 5, 6) (%)[a]	Capital goods (SITC 7) (%)[a]	Total (SITC 5, 6, 7) (%)[a]	Direct investment (RM million)
1970	266.6 (46.8)	234.7 (41.2)	501.3 (88.0)	43.1
1971	392.2 (45.5)	388.1 (45.1)	780.3 (90.6)	34.7
1972	425.3 (45.6)	424.0 (45.4)	849.3 (91.1)	36.7
1973	628.0 (46.6)	612.6 (45.5)	1,240.6 (92.1)	308.7
1974	1,024.4 (46.5)	1,034.1 (46.9)	2,058.5 (93.4)	110.9
1975	773.6 (45.3)	784.1 (45.9)	1,557.7 (91.2)	134.7
1976	921.5 (44.7)	972.6 (47.2)	1,894.1 (91.9)	132.1
1977	1,023.4 (39.2)	1,369.3 (52.4)	2,392.7 (91.6)	162.8
1978	1,122.4 (35.7)	1,792.9 (57.0)	2,915.3 (92.7)	106.1
1979	1,355.9 (35.4)	2,202.8 (57.5)	3,558.7 (92.9)	152.7
1980	1,805.0 (33.6)	3,198.2 (59.6)	5,003.2 (93.2)	32.6
1981	2,125.1 (32.6)	3,926.9 (60.3)	6,052.0 (92.9)	69.1
1982	2,505.6 (34.5)	4,225.0 (58.3)	6,730.6 (92.8)	136.9
1983	2,334.0 (30.0)	4,877.3 (62.8)	7,211.3 (92.8)	37.8
1984	2,221.2 (25.7)	5,713.3 (66.1)	7,934.5 (91.8)	67.3
1985	1,953.5 (27.9)	4,371.8 (62.4)	6,325.3 (90.3)	264.4
1986	1,710.1 (29.9)	3,392.2 (59.3)	5,102.3 (89.2)	116.3
1987	1,949.7 (28.2)	4,290.6 (62.0)	6,240.3 (90.2)	715.1
1988	2,871.3 (28.3)	6,406.1 (63.1)	9,277.4 (91.4)	1,222.0
1989	3,776.5 (25.7)	9,782.5 (66.4)	13,559.0 (92.1)	2,690.4
1990	4,665.1 (24.5)	12,831.5 (67.3)	17,496.6 (91.8)	4,212.6
1991	6,331.3 (24.1)	17,852.3 (67.9)	24,183.6 (92.0)	3,157.7

Source: Dong-Sung Cho, 'Globalization of Japanese and Korean Firms: Implications For Other Asian Countries', paper presented at the MIER National Outlook conference, Kuala Lumpur, 8–9 December 1992. Ministry of Finance, *Economic Report*, various issues. Trade figures as in Table 1.5

[a] Percentage of total imports from Japan

accounted for more than 90 per cent of Malaysia's total imports from Japan. As shown in Table 1.6, the proportion of capital goods in the total imports from Japan was more than 60 per cent during 1987–91, while imports of intermediate goods proportionately declined from 46.8 per cent to 24.1 per cent between 1970 and 1991. Hence, while the Japanese mainly import primary commodities for their industrial needs, they export manufactures – especially capital goods – to Malaysia, reflecting the changing international division of labour involving Japan and Malaysia. This pattern of imports from Japan is likely to continue in view of Malaysia's 'Look East' policy, heavy industrialization and renewed export-oriented industrialization with foreign investments, dominated by East Asian investors.

Malaysia depends on Japan for supplies of intermediate and capital goods, technology and direct foreign investment (DFI). Table 1.6 shows that Japanese DFI has increased greatly since 1988, and this DFI has presumably involved huge amounts of imported capital goods from Japan, reflecting Japanese investments in assembly-type production and high technology industries.

Most Japanese investment in Malaysia, as in the other ASEAN nations and in the East Asian NIEs, involve assembly-type manufacturing of machinery, electronic and electrical appliances. Investment in these types of industries has increased substantially since the yen appreciation (the *endaka*) resulted in higher costs of production in Japan. Protectionist measures against Japanese exports have also induced large multinationals as well as small and medium sized firms in export-oriented Japanese industries to move their production facilities and production to other Asian countries. As a result, Japan's direct investment in the East Asian nations more than doubled over the five-year period from 1983 to 1988. Much of this investment has been in manufacturing, particularly in the machinery sector. Through such investments, Japanese firms have been spearheading the internationalization of manufacturing in Asia. The recent strength of the yen has thus encouraged this new international division of labour in East Asia (Petri, 1991) with a changing pattern of international trade.

Japan's increased exports to ASEAN since 1986 have been led by intermediate goods and manufacturing equipment (e.g. general machinery, electronic parts, machine tools). This corresponds to the period when many Japanese corporations have moved production to the Asian NIEs and ASEAN, with imported machinery from Japan accounting for more than 40 per cent of total machinery imports (JETRO, 1992: 128). Imports of processed materials (e.g of metal products and chemicals, used as industrial supplies) also increased during this period. Thus, Japan has been a key supplier of capital goods and intermediate products to the East Asian NIEs and ASEAN as they expanded their manufactured exports (JETRO, 1992: 128). This is particularly the case for the machinery sector, where the dependence of ASEAN nations on machinery imports from Japan gradually increased in the latter half of the 1980s to about 40 per cent of their total machinery imports in 1990 (JETRO, 1992: 129).

Malaysia's trade deficits in the late 1980s were basically due to the sharp increase in imports of intermediate and capital goods. The deficits were exacerbated by the yen appreciation, since the value of imports increased with the yen. Between 1980 and 1990, the yen appreciated by 95.8 per cent in nominal terms, by 70.3 per cent in real terms, and by 51.9 per cent in terms of the real trade weighted exchange rate (indicated by e[ppp] (purchasing power parity) trade weighted in Figure 1.1). By early 1993, the yen was more than twice its value in 1970–73, when the yen first emerged as a major international currency. The rapid appreciation of the yen since the Louvre Accord in 1985 has increased Malaysia's trade deficits with Japan. As pointed out (Corker, 1989), the yen appreciation 'corrected' Japanese surpluses by approximately two per cent of the gross national product

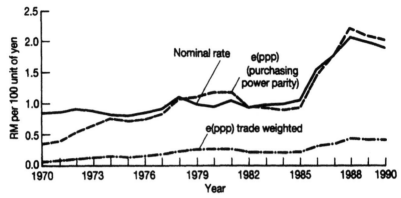

Figure 1.1 Malaysia–Japan nominal exchange rate and purchasing power parity.

Table 1.7 Japan trade indices

Year	Volume of exports	Volume of imports	Unit value of exports	Unit value of imports
1970	27.9	56.5	59.4	37.3
1971	33.0	56.3	60.6	38.0
1972	35.1	64.1	59.8	34.9
1973	37.5	83.7	63.5	38.5
1974	45.2	83.1	85.2	67.4
1975	45.1	73.0	87.2	72.8
1976	54.6	79.5	86.7	74.6
1977	59.3	81.5	86.9	72.3
1978	59.7	86.9	82.1	59.3
1979	59.8	96.8	89.6	77.2
1980	70.0	91.9	99.8	107.3
1981	77.5	89.9	102.8	107.8
1982	75.7	89.4	108.2	112.5
1983	82.3	90.5	100.9	102.1
1984	95.3	100.0	100.8	99.5
1985	100.0	100.0	100.0	100.0
1986	99.4	110.5	84.6	60.3
1987	99.8	120.5	79.5	55.7
1988	104.2	140.5	77.5	52.7
1989	109.4	152.1	82.2	58.6
1990	115.5	160.9	86.1	64.7
1991	117.5	165.2	85.7	59.4

Source: International Monetary Fund, *International Financial Statistics Yearbook 1992.* Base year: 1985

(GNP). This is evident from Table 1.7, showing Japanese import–export values and trade volume index trends. While export volume growth has been below import volume growth, export value growth has exceeded import value growth, with the yen appreciation strengthening Japan's trade surplus.

Table 1.8 Malaysia–Japan intra-industry trade index (percentages)

SITC	0 Food and live animals	1 Beverages and tobacco	2 Crude materials inedible	3 Mineral fuels	4 Animal and vegetable oils and fats	5 Chemicals	6 Manuf. goods	7 Machinery transport equipment	8 Misc. manuf. articles	9 Other imports	Total
1970	93.8	—	2.0	20.0	23.5	197.9	90.3	199.8	199.5	49.1	75.9
1971	54.1	—	3.1	13.2	60.6	198.6	109.5	199.6	199.5	75.4	97.1
1972	55.2	—	5.3	10.8	34.9	198.6	111.1	199.3	198.6	74.5	105.7
1973	47.2	—	3.6	26.7	22.8	197.0	120.9	199.7	188.5	74.6	100.4
1974	63.5	—	4.3	8.1	3.8	196.8	135.4	195.8	184.0	93.3	112.4
1975	73.0	—	5.3	3.2	5.5	195.5	148.0	187.7	160.9	105.1	112.1
1976	48.5	—	4.3	1.8	5.1	195.5	126.7	190.1	136.5	73.8	84.2
1977	59.4	—	4.4	2.0	5.2	198.5	130.3	193.6	152.7	104.8	92.3
1978	58.1	—	4.2	1.3	3.3	192.4	122.8	191.5	153.3	75.2	92.0
1979	48.7	—	3.1	1.2	3.0	195.2	122.8	188.8	149.9	72.6	80.7
1980	85.9	—	4.6	1.1	2.4	193.9	131.6	191.0	153.5	87.2	91.0
1981	79.3	—	8.3	1.5	1.8	194.7	145.8	191.6	175.0	90.4	106.4
1982	77.6	—	4.4	1.3	2.4	194.0	162.3	190.3	176.6	79.1	111.8
1983	65.5	—	5.4	1.0	3.3	189.2	151.4	187.5	178.1	59.8	109.4
1984	82.8	—	5.6	0.7	2.9	185.2	145.8	186.2	182.3	58.8	100.0
1985	81.8	—	5.3	0.5	3.5	177.4	156.8	180.4	180.2	53.8	86.1
1986	58.3	—	5.8	0.8	4.1	169.0	156.9	167.1	174.7	53.3	83.1
1987	49.0	—	4.0	1.1	2.4	168.4	145.7	176.0	168.7	65.6	87.9
1988	45.2	81.5	5.0	1.1	1.7	160.8	157.6	175.0	166.1	76.0	104.1
1989	54.6	104.5	5.7	1.3	1.7	173.7	164.0	172.5	163.7	96.5	114.9
1990	48.4	84.1	6.8	1.0	1.7	173.0	168.9	169.9	154.0	104.3	120.3
1991	46.2	90.2	9.9	1.3	1.8	170.5	171.9	166.6	142.7	71.4	127.8

Grubel–Lloyd intra-industry index calculated as defined:

$$IIT_i = [1 - \frac{|X_i - M_i|}{(X_i + M_i)}] \cdot 100$$

where X_i and M_i are exports and imports of a product category i.

Table 1.8 shows a number of significant changes in Malaysia–Japan intra-industry trade. It seems Malaysia has a comparative advantage in producing raw materials rather than manufactures. Such an argument thus seems to legitimize a particular international division of labour and resulting pattern of international trade. With this logic then, Malaysia is said to be more competitive in SITC section 2 (which comprises natural rubber, cork and wood, both saw logs and sawn timber), section 3 (i.e. mineral fuels including crude petroleum and LNG), and section 4, mainly of palm oil. As one would then expect, Japan is supposed to have a comparative advantage in chemicals, manufactured goods, machinery, transport equipment and other manufactured products. This suggests that Malaysia–Japan trade relations are typical of those between developing and developed economies with Malaysia enjoying a comparative advantage in producing primary commodities and Japan with manufactured goods.

SERVICES ACCOUNT

Discussion of Malaysia–Japan trade relations would be incomplete if nothing is mentioned about Malaysia's trade in services. In contrast to the merchandise account, the services account has always been a focus of concern because the size of its deficit has been on the increase since the 1960s with no sign of abatement. Over the years, gross payments for services rendered by non-residents has increased significantly. During the period 1961–68, the deficit was less than RM407 million, but by 1973 it exceeded the RM1 billion level. Thereafter, it expanded progressively to reach nearly RM5 billion in 1979 and peaked at RM10 billion in 1984. In 1986 and 1987, reduced gross payments led to a slight narrowing of the services deficits to RM8.8 billion and RM9.1 billion respectively. Nevertheless, the services deficit remained at about 12.5 per cent of GNP.

Malaysia's net services balance with Japan has always been in deficit, and at least up to 1985, these deficits were increasing from RM0.7 billion in 1981 to RM1.7 billion in 1984, before declining to RM1.2 billion in 1985 and 1986 during the recession (Table 1.9). At its peak in 1984, this deficit with Japan accounted for about 16.1 per cent of Malaysia's net global services deficit. While the deficit with Japan has been less than those experienced with other major trading partners, particularly the US and UK, they have been a major cause for concern to Malaysia since the Malaysian merchandise balance with Japan has also been in deficit. This puts extra pressure on the Malaysian current account balance.

Breakdown of the bilateral services account is unavailable except for an old estimate of the Malaysia–Japan invisible trade balance by Bank Negara. According to the estimate, a major proportion of the services deficits with Japan has been due to increasing net payments for freight and insurance, increasing from RM0.7 billion in 1981 to RM1.2 billion in 1984. Net

Table 1.9 Malaysia: net services account with major trading partners, 1984–86 (RM million)

	1984	1985	1986
USA	−2,583.8	−2,526.4	−2,681.4
	(24.5%)	(23.7%)	(28.4%)
UK	−2,225.8	843.9	2,177.9
	(21.1%)	(26.7%)	(23.0%)
Japan	−1,701.8	−1,144.9	−1,193.0
	(16.1%)	(10.8%)	(12.6%)

Source: Haflah (1988)
Figures in parentheses represent percentages of Malaysia's total services deficit.

payments of investment incomes accounted for the remainder of the services deficits. It is expected that with the yen appreciation, the post-*endaka* increase in Japan DFI and more liberal foreign investment conditions, deficits in the services balance are likely to increase further.

It is evident that Malaysia and Japan have become increasingly interdependent in terms of trade, investment and technology. While these relations have been relatively harmonious in the past, the future may not continue to be so unless some of the present imbalances and various critical issues in existing bilateral economic relations are addressed quickly and resolved amicably. This is even more urgent in view of the accelerating global economic restructuring process taking place, in which Japan can offer major economic contributions in terms of market access, investments and technology. In addition, the future of Malaysia's export-oriented industrialization policy, which is vigorously being pursued now, critically depends on its success in penetrating major markets for manufactures, including Japan. In the process, it is inevitable that present problems will intensify and new issues will crop up between Malaysia and Japan. What follows is a discussion of some critical issues in bilateral economic relations between the two economies that need to be addressed, given the importance of the relationship, at least from Malaysia's standpoint.

TRADE ISSUES

One major focus of trade issues between Malaysia and its ASEAN neighbours on the one hand and Japan on the other has been the former's concerns with *market access*. Trade barriers have dampened the drive to export to Japan and have caused potential exporters to shy away from the Japanese market and seek outlets elsewhere (Sanchez, 1987). While the Japanese government has repeatedly promised to liberalize trade barriers, they continue to restrict competitive foreigners, especially if they have a technological edge (Balassa and Noland, 1988: 215).

Since the establishment of the ASEAN–Japan Forum in 1977, the ASEAN countries, including Malaysia, have presented a number of memoranda on trade, requesting Japan to provide better market access for imports from ASEAN through improvement of Japanese general system of preferences (GSP) schemes and liberalization of quota restrictions, tariff and non-tariff barriers. Similar requests have been made at a number of dialogues, conferences and negotiations held at various levels between the two trading partners. Despite a few significant concessions made by Japan, most critical issues and problems raised by Malaysia have remained unresolved or are not even addressed by Japan.

In terms of tariff barriers to imports, like other developed countries, Japan significantly reduced its tariff rates during the 1960s, 1970s and early 1980s. In 1985, import duties were eliminated on about 1800 narrowly defined product categories (tariff lines), for which tariffs were generally below 5 per cent, while duties were reduced by a fifth on selected products with tariffs above 5 per cent (Balassa and Noland, 1988: 49).

On the whole, tariff rates on non-agricultural products in Japan approximate those of the European Community and the United States. Before the latest reductions, Japanese tariffs averaged 0.5 per cent on raw materials, 4.6 per cent on semi-manufactures, and 6.0 per cent on finished manufactures, compared with 0.2, 3.0 and 5.7 per cent respectively in the United States, and 0.2, 4.2 and 6.9 per cent in the European Community (Balassa and Noland, 1988: 50). At the same time, however, Japanese tariffs tend to be higher than the average for raw and processed agricultural commodities (including fishery and forestry products). This is particularly the case for fresh and preserved fruits, alcoholic beverages and wood products. Also, other labour-intensive products subjected to considerable protection – such as textiles and clothing, footwear, and wood products – are significant manufactured exports for Malaysia. In addition, some tariff lines discriminate between imports from developed and developing countries, such as between softwoods and hardwoods, and between some temperate and tropical fruits and commodities. For instance, until 1987, softwood sawn timber was imported duty free, while tropical sawn timber was subjected to a most favoured nation (MFN) rate of 10 per cent, and a GSP duty of 5 per cent up to a quota ceiling of 74.2 million metric tons, after which 10 per cent duty was applied. Similarly, tariff disparity was maintained for imports of tropical wood and softwood plywood at 20 per cent and 15 per cent respectively.

Related to the tariff issue is the problem of *tariff escalation*. A study of the Japanese tariff system shows that tariffs increase as one moves from primary to more processed stages of production in the processing chain (Haflah, 1988: 43). Such tariff escalation involves higher effective rates of protection for more highly processed items. This, in turn, restricts the market for manufactured products exported by developing countries, and hence stifles their efforts to industrialize through further processing of their primary commodities. For Malaysia, these products include preserved seafood and fruits, processed vegetables, cocoa products, paper and paper board, textiles and clothing, leather products and vegetable oils, whose effective rates of protection are substantially higher than their nominal rates would indicate (Haflah, 1988: 43).

Malaysia has every reason to ensure that such barriers to trade of processed and semi-processed goods be liberalized as the scope for expanding export earnings from processed items is considerably greater than for unprocessed goods. This is so since the import elasticities of demand are significantly higher for finished items than for semi-processed products, and are greater for semi-processed products than for crude materials (Haflah, 1988: 44). Hence, the demand-stimulating effect of a reduction in protection on finished products would be far bigger than those on unprocessed commodities.

In addition to tariffs, imports are also restricted through the use of quantitative restrictions. Japan maintains 22 quotas on imports of agricultural, including fishery products (Christelow, 1986). The use of such restrictions for manufactures is more limited: there are also quotas applied to leather products, coal briquettes, raw silk and twisted silk yarn, and a number of foodstuffs of interest to developing countries. These restrictions have caused complaints by industrial and developing countries against Japan for imposing them. The full extent of such quantitative restrictions is not generally known; according to official submissions to the General Agreement on Tariff and Trade (GATT), such information has not been made available by the Japanese government (Balassa and Noland, 1988: 50).

Malaysia has mainly been concerned with import quotas imposed on canned pineapples, which resulted in considerable loss of export opportunities for Malaysia. The quota was originally set at 1.4 million cases in 1974, and gradually decreased in subsequent years to 800,000 cases in 1981 and 738,000 in 1985. Later, more items of export interest to Malaysia were subjected to more restrictive Japanese import quotas, including wood and wood products (particularly veneer sheets, plywood sheets, particle board, laminated wood); some textile and clothing items (batik, woven fabrics, garments); leather and leather goods (footwear), iron and steel products (iron bars and rods; iron tubes and pipes) and toys.

While Japan's quantitative restrictions apply to a limited range of Japan's manufactured imports, the scope of less tangible trade barriers is broader. Intangible barriers, also known as informal barriers, take a variety of forms, including administrative guidance; customs procedures; standards, testing and certification requirements; public procurement practices; the defence of depressed industries, the promotion of high technology industries;

Table 1.10 The foreign trade barriers of Japan

	Heads	1989	1990	1991
Import policies	*Tariffs*			
	Cigarettes and tobacco products	x	–	–
	Leather and leather footwear	x	x	x
	Wood and paper products	x	x	x
	Aluminum	x	x	x
	Quantitative restrictions			
	Agriculture products	x	x	x
	Feed grain	x	x	x
	Rice	x	x	x
	Fish products	x	x	x
Standards, testing, labelling and certification	Telecommunications terminals, radio equipment	x	x	x
	Pharmaceutical/medical devices	x	x	x
	Food additives	x	x	x
	Fresh agriculture products	–	x	x
Bidding on government contracts	Supercomputers	x	x	x
	Satellites	x	x	x
	Government procurement code implementation	x	x	x
	Computers	–	–	x
Subsidies	Shipbuilding	–	x	x
Lack of intellectual property protection	Patents	x	x	x
	Trademarks	x	x .	x
	Copyrights	x	x	x
Service barriers	Construction, architectural, and engineering services	x	x	x
	Legal services	x	x	x
	Insurance	x	x	x
	High cube containers	x	x	–
	Obligatory harbour fund contributions	–	–	x
Investment barriers	Direct investment	x	x	x
Other barriers	Semiconductors	x	x	x
	TRON (The real-time operating system nucleus)	x	x	–
	Amorphous metals	–	x	–
	Optical fibres	x	x	–
	Aerospace	x	x	x
	Auto parts	x	x	x
	Soda ash	x	x	x
	Distribution system	x	x	x
	Law on retail stores	x	x	–
	Marketing practice restrictions	x	x	–
	JFTC ecurities of international contracts	–	–	x
Additional articles	Automobile markets	x	x	x
	Financial services	x	–	–

Source: JETRO (1992: 219).

regulations on intellectual property; and on distribution channels (see Table 1.10).

In addition, a number of products of export interest to Malaysia – such as the electrical and electronics products, toys, processed foodstuffs, and textiles – are subjected to several laws, each of which sets particular requirements. Thus, electrical and electronic products come under the Electrical Appliance and Material Control, the Consumer's Product Safety Law and the Industrial Standardization Law; toys come under the Food Sanitation Law, the Explosive Control Law, the Electrical Appliance and Material Control Laws as well as the Safety Toys Safety Good Standards; food products under the Food Sanitation Law and the Law Concerning Standardization and Proper Labelling of Agricultural and Forestry Products; and textiles under the Industrial Standardization Law.

Japan's industrial and agricultural standards are yet another set of qualitative restrictions which have made it extremely difficult for some Malaysian products to be sold to Japanese consumers because of the stringent standards and certification rules enforced by approved testing organizations for foreign imports to qualify for the Japan Industrial Standards (JIS) mark (Haflah, 1988: 46). There have been instances where Malaysian products, complying with international standards, have been rejected due to alleged non-compliance with Japanese standards.

Another formidable obstacle faced by Malaysian goods seeking to penetrate the Japanese market is the complex *distribution and marketing* channels in Japan, characterized by a large number of wholesale and retail firms. Traditional Japanese commercial practices are perceived as restrictive to both domestic and foreign firms seeking access to the Japanese market (Haflah, 1988: 46). This was particularly true when import channels were more limited than they are at present, and shorter distribution routes, such as direct imports by retailers, had not yet been established. It is hardly surprising that foreign firms in particular feel that the Japanese market has been difficult to enter. It is standard practice for imported products to pass through some complicated and cumbersome system involving large trading companies and a long chain of 'middlemen' before reaching final display shelves. By then, these products would probably have lost some of their price competitive edge *vis-à-vis* local substitutes. It will go a long way towards promoting Malaysian and other imports if Japan's current distribution and marketing channels are simplified.

The earliest efforts to promote Malaysia's exports to Japan emerged with the inception of Japan's GSP scheme in 1971. Since then, the GSP has contributed quite significantly to increasing Malaysia's exports to Japan, contributing about US$256 million, or 5.6 per cent of Malaysia's total exports to Japan (Haflah, 1988: 47). This amounted to 2.6 per cent of Japan's total GSP imports, making Malaysia a significant beneficiary of the Japanese GSP. Nevertheless, despite several reviews and revamps, the

Japanese GSP – like others – still suffers from several shortcomings and is therefore not very effective in promoting exports to Japan. Some major concerns for Malaysia include:

1 early exhaustion of quota ceilings;
2 exclusion of products of export interest to Malaysia;
3 stringent provisions on cumulative rules of origin;
4 insignificant and eroding margins of preference.

Malaysia and other ASEAN countries welcomed the improvement of Japan's GSP scheme from April 1989. However, Malaysia has expressed dissatisfaction because some products of vital interest to Malaysia were not included, despite requests, while quotas for some Malaysian products are still limited and the stringent criteria to qualify for GSP treatment under the ASEAN Cumulative Rules of Origin are still in force.

For a product to qualify for the GSP under the ASEAN rules of origin, Japan still requires the product to be manufactured entirely from ASEAN inputs or from both ASEAN and Japanese inputs. A product will not qualify for the GSP if it contains inputs from non-ASEAN third country sources. This contraint has resulted in marginal use of the scheme by Malaysian manufacturers. It is not always practical or cost effective for raw materials or components to come exclusively from ASEAN and Japan. In addition, Malaysia has repeatedly expressed concern over the exclusion of 17 intermediate inputs of Japanese origin used to manufacture certain products – due to the Donor Country Content rules – and hence, the ineligibility of the resulting exports for GSP treatment.

In terms of coverage, Japanese GSP still excludes crude petroleum, LNG, crude and refined palm-kernel oil, some processed pineapples, bananas, some varieties of plywood, textiles, clothing, woven fabrics and footwear, to name a few products of export interest to Malaysia. Of the 33 items that ASEAN requested for ceiling quota liberalization under Japan's GSP scheme from 1987, only three were accepted, but none of the items requested by ASEAN for tariff reduction were accepted by Japan (Haflah, 1988: 49).

JAPANESE OFFICIAL DEVELOPMENT ASSISTANCE TO MALAYSIA

Another issue in Malaysia–Japan relations besides trade and investment is Japan's Official Development Assistance (ODA) to Malaysia. Japan aid grants to Malaysia have increased significantly mainly since the early 1980s. This increase occurred when Malaysia was grappling with some critical structural problems, particularly with the growing budget deficit as well as deficit in the current account of its balance of payments which hit peaks of 17.9 and 14.1 per cent of GNP respectively in 1982 (Haflah, 1988: 34).

Since 1976, Japan has been the second largest source of external finance to Malaysia after the United States (Appendix, Table A1.1). Total Malaysian debt to Japan increased tremendously from 1968 to 1987, before declining marginally thereafter. Japan's external loans to Malaysia are mostly from Japanese government financial institutions or agencies such as the Overseas Economic Cooperation Fund (OECF) and the Export–Import (EXIM) Bank of Japan. Japanese bilateral grant assistance has been more significant than market loan financing government and non-financial public enterprise projects, even after the mid-1980s *endaka* (Appendix, Tables A1.2, A1.3). Japan's project loans have mainly been disbursed through OECF and the EXIM Bank of Japan, which have much lower rates of interest and longer maturity periods.

The Japanese began to use aid as a tool to reduce trade frictions with Malaysia, while forging political and strategic links between the two countries. Also, since Japan extracts a large 'surplus' from its trade with Malaysia, it is expected that Japan will 'share' some of this surplus with Malaysia in the form of aid. But Japan extends the aid to Malaysia primarily to promote its own commercial and industrial interests. Aid is extended mainly to enrich the Japanese economy at the expense of Malaysia. This can clearly be seen in Appendix, Table A1.4, which shows Japan financing infrastructural development such as utilities and transportation projects. Improving infrastructure and telecommunications in Malaysia eventually facilitates Japanese investments in Malaysia and brings more returns to Japanese firms.

Japan also increasingly extends technical cooperation aid to Malaysia (Appendix, Table A1.5). In fact Malaysia is not entitled to aid, because the per capita income of Malaysians is more than the per capita level suggested by the World Bank.

CONCLUDING REMARKS

Malaysia–Japan bilateral trade relations have grown in significance more than with other Malaysian trade partners. However, the pattern or composition of trade with Japan reflects the traditional pattern between developed and developing countries, favouring Japan. Furthermore, the internationalization of Japanese capital since the *endaka* has raised Malaysian imports of Japanese capital and intermediate goods, eventually exacerbating Malaysia's trade deficit since the late 1980s. A parallel situation is reflected in the services account. One major reason for this unequal trade has been Japanese trade restrictions, resulting in Malaysian goods, especially manufactures having difficulty of access to Japanese markets, thus further aggravating trade relations. To alleviate this situation, Japan should be more 'sincere' in collaborating to reduce trade frictions.

APPENDIX

Appendix A1.1 Malaysia: external debts (RM million)

Year	USA	UK	Japan	IBRD	ADB	FRG	West Asia	Others	Total
1964	45.1	340.0	–	–	–	1.4	–	–	386.5
1965	121.7	338.4	–	–	–	3.8	–	–	463.9
1966	113.5	382.5	–	–	–	6.4	–	–	502.4
1967	104.2	373.7	–	18.9	–	18.1	–	–	529.6
1968	96.2	374.3	2.9	46.1	–	43.7	–	–	592.2
1969	145.7	382.1	22.4	77.2	–	81.5	–	–	746.9
1970	107.2	365.7	26.7	120.5	1.6	82.5	–	–	745.2
1971	277.8	469.4	55.2	143.5	11.8	81.2	–	–	1,089.5
1972	402.8	434.2	88.6	209.6	26.8	148.0	–	–	1,395.5
1973	397.0	354.0	121.0	203.0	39.0	155.0	–	46.0	1,360.0
1974	454.0	338.0	202.0	246.0	50.0	115.0	–	94.0	1,499.0
1975	1,108.0	355.0	341.0	330.0	91.0	104.0	–	96.0	2,425.0
1976	1,287.0	278.0	428.0	416.0	116.0	93.0	3.0	235.0	2,856.0
1977	1,362.0	212.0	492.0	477.0	383.0	248.0	5.0	170.0	3,349.0
1978	1,358.0	253.0	571.0	541.0	427.0	279.0	9.0	421.0	3,859.0
1979	1,566.0	246.0	703.0	641.0	477.0	274.0	20.0	611.0	4,538.0
1980	1,619.0	282.0	845.0	703.0	512.0	260.0	34.0	605.0	4,860.0
1981	4,107.0	281.0	953.0	900.0	620.0	251.0	50.0	607.0	7,769.0
1982	8,177.0	165.0	1,517.0	1,088.0	741.0	226.0	96.0	367.0	12,377.0
1983	10,370.0	165.0	2,302.0	1,230.0	855.0	292.0	141.0	791.0	16,146.0
1984	12,053.0	163.0	3,365.0	1,316.0	925.0	274.0	166.0	1,063.0	19,325.0
1985	11,283.0	123.0	4,724.0	1,375.0	982.0	1,418.0	214.0	1,863.0	21,982.0
1986	12,913.0	114.0	6,863.0	1,446.0	1,103.0	1,980.0	131.0	2,748.0	27,298.0
1987	9,992.0	116.0	7,794.0	1,427.0	1,112.0	2,642.0	255.0	3,293.0	26,632.0
1988	8,930.0	105.0	7,757.0	1,565.0	1,234.0	2,621.0	261.0	2,717.0	25,190.0
1989	8,604.0	85.0	6,340.0	1,604.0	1,227.0	2,956.0	242.0	2,570.0	23,628.0
1990	8,903.0	87.0	5,922.0	1,773.0	1,274.0	3,461.0	233.0	2,654.0	24,307.0
1991	9,505.0	74.0	6,331.0	1,929.0	1,345.0	3,405.0	115.0	2,457.0	25,161.0
1992	8,082.0	61.0	5,721.0	1,917.0	1,316.0	3,290.0	100.0	2,106.0	22,593.0

Source: Ministry of Finance, *Economic Report*, various issues.

Appendix A1.2 Malaysia: external market loans (RM million)

Year	USA	UK	Japan	FRG	Others	Total
1973	335.0	250.0	n.a.	116.0	46.0	747.0
1974	336.0	250.0	n.a.	78.0	46.0	710.0
1975	982.0	250.0	n.a.	70.0	46.0	1348.0
1976	1,205.0	155.0	n.a.	62.0	46.0	1,468.0
1977	1,281.0	109.0	n.a.	159.0	79.0	1,628.0
1978	1,225.0	109.0	n.a.	150.0	294.0	1,778.0
1979	1,409.0	109.0	n.a.	141.0	544.0	2,203.0
1980	1,409.0	109.0	n.a.	131.0	541.0	2,190.0
1981	4,023.0	109.0	n.a.	123.0	541.0	4,796.0
1982	8,126.0	n.a.	473.0	115.0	286.0	9,000.0
1983	10,332.0	n.a.	1,065.0	201.0	673.0	12,271.0
1984	12,008.0	n.a.	1,627.0	200.0	817.0	14,652.0
1985	11,234.0	n.a.	2,276.0	1,376.0	1,413.0	16,299.0
1986	12,729.0	n.a.	3,545.0	1,875.0	2,161.0	20,310.0
1987	9,970.0	n.a.	3,747.0	2,437.0	2,786.0	18,940.0
1988	8,917.0	n.a.	3,761.0	2,358.0	2,229.0	17,265.0
1989	8,596.0	n.a.	3,318.0	2,487.0	1,974.0	16,375.0
1990	8,899.0	n.a.	2,415.0	2,804.0	2,064.0	16,182.0
1991	9,505.0	n.a.	2,554.0	2,787.0	1,847.0	16,693.0
1992	8,082.0	n.a.	2,285.0	2,752.0	1,576.0	14,695.0

Source: Ministry of Finance, *Economic Report*, various issues.
n.a. not available

Appendix A1.3 Malaysia: external project loans (RM million)

Year	USA	UK	Japan	IBRD	ADB	FRG	West Asia	Others	Total
1973	62.0	104.0	121.0	203.0	39.0	39.0	–	–	613.0
1974	118.0	88.0	202.0	246.0	50.0	37.0	–	48.0	789.0
1975	126.0	105.0	341.0	330.0	91.0	34.0	–	50.0	1,077.0
1976	82.0	123.0	428.0	416.0	116.0	31.0	3.0	189.0	1,388.0
1977	81.0	103.0	492.0	477.0	383.0	89.0	5.0	91.0	1,721.0
1978	133.0	144.0	571.0	541.0	427.0	129.0	9.0	127.0	2,081.0
1979	157.0	137.0	703.0	641.0	477.0	133.0	20.0	67.0	2,335.0
1980	210.0	173.0	845.0	703.0	512.0	129.0	34.0	64.0	2,670.0
1981	84.0	172.0	953.0	900.0	620.0	128.0	50.0	66.0	2,973.0
1982	51.0	165.0	1,044.0	1,088.0	741.0	111.0	96.0	81.0	3,377.0
1983	38.0	165.0	1,237.0	1,230.0	855.0	91.0	141.0	118.0	3,875.0
1984	45.0	163.0	1,738.0	1,316.0	925.0	74.0	166.0	246.0	4,673.0
1985	49.0	123.0	2,448.0	1,375.0	982.0	42.0	214.0	450.0	5,683.0
1986	184.0	114.0	3,318.0	1,446.0	1,103.0	105.0	131.0	587.0	6,988.0
1987	22.0	116.0	4,047.0	1,427.0	1,112.0	206.0	255.0	507.0	7,692.0
1988	13.0	105.0	3,996.0	1,565.0	1,234.0	263.0	261.0	488.0	7,925.0
1989	8.0	85.0	3,022.0	1,604.0	1,227.0	469.0	242.0	596.0	7,253.0
1990	4.0	87.0	3,507.0	1,773.0	1,274.0	657.0	233.0	590.0	8,125.0
1991	–	74.0	3,777.0	1,929.0	1,345.0	618.0	115.0	610.0	8,468.0
1992	–	61.0	3,436.0	1,917.0	1,316.0	538.0	100.0	530.0	7,898.0

Source: Ministry of Finance, *Economic Report*, various issues.

Appendix A1.4 OECF financed projects by sector as of 31 March 1991

Sector	No. of loans	Loan amount	
		(Million yen)	(RM million)
Electric power and gas	25	231,680	2,528
Transportation	15	57,955	741
Telecommunication	2	6,158	62
Agriculture	1	2,997	26
Mining and manufacturing (industry)	2	38,397	369
Financial intermediary loans	4	36,787	736
Social services	2	41,816	789
Total	51	415,790	5,251

Source: Overseas Economic Cooperation Fund (OECF), *OECF Economic Corporation in Malaysia*, Kuala Lumpur.

Appendix A1.5 Japan's ODA disbursements to Malaysia (US$ million)

Year	Grants			Loan aid		Total
	Grant aid	Technical cooperation	Total	Gross	Net	
1984	11.03	26.81	33.83	n.a.	209.31	245.14
1985	0.55	23.06	23.61	131.28	101.98	125.59
1986	7.06	36.43	43.49	42.46	−5.73	37.77
1987	7.85	40.82	48.67	300.58	227.72	276.39
1988	2.89	54.74	57.64	71.20	−32.80	24.83
1989	1.76	56.96	58.71	117.29	20.92	79.63
1990	1.77	58.54	60.31	410.84	312.31	372.62
Total	52.45	399.07	451.51	1,920.64	1,349.35	1,800.86

Source: Japan, Ministry of Foreign Affairs, *Japan's ODA 1991*, Tokyo, 1991.
Lee Poh Ping, 'Japanese Official Assistance To Malaysia', *Development and ODA*, UN University, Tokyo, 1991.

REFERENCES

Balassa, Bela and Marcus Noland (1988) *Japan in the World Economy*, Institute for International Economics, Washington DC.
Christelow, Dorothy (1986) 'Japan's Intangible Barriers to Trade in Manufactures', *Federal Reserve Bank of New York* (Winter): 11–18.

Corker, Robert (1989) 'External Adjustment and The Strong Yen: Recent Japanese Experience', *International Monetary Fund Staff Papers*, 36, No. 2: 464–93.

Haflah Mohd Piei (1988) *Malaysia–Japan Economic Relations*, Universiti Kebangsaan Malaysia, Bangi (mimeo)

JETRO (1983) *White Paper on International Trade Japan 1983*, Japanese External Trade Organization, Tokyo.

JETRO (1988) *White Paper on International Trade Japan 1988*, Japanese External Trade Organization, Tokyo.

JETRO (1992) *White Paper on International Trade Japan 1992*, Japanese External Trade Organization, Tokyo.

Nester, William R. (1991) *Japan's Growing Power Over East Asia and The World Economy: Ends and Means*, Macmillan, London.

Park Yung Chul and Park Won Am (1991) 'Changing Japanese Trade Patterns and The East Asian NICs, in Paul Krugman (ed.), *Trade With Japan: Has The Door Opened Wider?*, University of Chicago Press, Chicago: 85–120.

Petri, Peter A. (1991) 'Market Structure, Comparative Advantage and Japanese Trade Under Strong Yen', in Paul Krugman (ed.) *Trade With Japan: Has The Door Opened Wider?*, University of Chicago Press, Chicago: 51–84.

Sanchez, Aurora (1987) 'Non-Tariff Barriers in ASEAN–Japan and Intra–ASEAN Trade', *ASEAN Economic Bulletin*, 4, No. 1, July: 1–8.

2

THE EVOLUTION OF JAPANESE INVESTMENT IN MALAYSIA

Mehmet Sami Denker

This chapter will study the general investment trends, patterns and motives of Japanese companies investing in Malaysia over three successive periods: 1957–69, 1970–80 and 1981–86 respectively, i.e. before the full impact of the post-1985 East Asian-led industrial boom was felt in Malaysia. The first period coincides with the leadership of Tunku Abdul Rahman, the nation's first prime minister after Independence in 1957. It is often said to have been characterized by generally *laissez-faire* policies except for efforts to encourage import-substituting industrialization. The second period is usually associated with an unusual mix of increased state intervention, public sector growth and a foreign-led export-oriented industrialization under premiers Tun Abdul Razak and Tun Hussein Onn. The final period considered coincides with current Prime Minister Mahathir Mohamad's early policies, including 'Looking East' and heavy industrialization, before his more recent economic liberalization precipitated by the Malaysian economic crisis of 1985–86.

This periodization enables us to analyse the kinds of industries that Japanese capital invested in as official Malaysian policy priorities changed over time. The motivations for investment in Malaysia by Japanese companies will also be discussed. This paper also studies the types of Japanese investments in Malaysia, the incentives the Japanese companies enjoy, their location, financial sources and market conditions.

1957–69

By the end of 1968, there were 48 Japanese companies in Malaysia, 40 of which were joint ventures, with four holding pioneer status. By the end of 1969, total Japanese investments in Malaysia with pioneer status amounted to $32.2 million. Japan was listed fifth in 1969 among foreign countries investing in Malaysia. Table 2.1 sums up Japanese investments in Malaysia between 1957 and 1986. Of the 54 Japanese companies established during 1957–69, 33 were in the manufacturing sector. Of these, there were 7

Table 2.1 Japanese investment in Malaysia, 1957–93

	Number	%	Cumulative %
Manufacturing			
Pre-1957	11	1.8	1.8
1957–69	33	5.5	7.3
1970–80	104	17.2	24.5
1981–86	37	6.1	30.6
1987–93	420	69.4	100.0
Total	605	100.0	100.0
Non-manufacturing			
Pre-1957	32	8.9	8.9
1957–69	21	5.9	14.8
1970–80	70	19.6	34.4
1981–86	111	31.1	65.5
1987–93	123	34.5	100.0
Total	357	100.0	100.0

Source: Unpublished JETRO data.

companies in petroleum and chemicals, 10 companies in steel and other metals, 3 in wood products, 2 in food, 1 in textiles, 3 in electricals and electronics and 3 in transport machinery (see Table 2.2). The concentration of Japanese investments in steel and other metals, petroleum, chemistry, and wood products suggests that they were mainly interested in processing natural resources to supply inputs for Japanese industry at home. The large Japanese investments in Daishowa Pulp Company and Felda Oil Products Sdn. Bhd. are examples of such exploitation of natural resources by Japanese investments. Japanese investment in this period seemed to be quite *ad hoc*, being determined primarily by the immediate needs of the Japanese economy.[1] The fact that 15, or 71 per cent, of the 21 companies outside manufacturing were only dealing in foreign trade suggests that their basic interest was in supplying raw materials like timber, iron-ore, copper, etc., required by the Japanese economy.

Japanese investment grew more slowly in this period (1957–69) than subsequently.[2] The *Far Eastern Economic Review* has suggested that this slow growth was due to a 'wait and see' policy: 'Investors in both Britain and Japan have shown a great deal of interest in Malaysia's industrialization although both tend to shelve or sit on their plans, waiting for the tendency towards economic separation to be reversed'.[3] Nonetheless, the Japanese economic presence was consolidating itself, as the Malaysian Prime Minister then admitted: '. . . with Merdeka, the trade policy had veered more strongly towards Japan. Japanese industries which manufactured electronic and other goods grew in large numbers. Assembly plants were set up to assemble cars and motorcycles for local use and export'.[4] There is

Table 2.2 Japanese direct investment in Malaysian manufacturing industries, 1957–93

Year	Food and beverages	Textiles and products	Wood pulp	Petro-chemicals	Steel and metals	Electrical products	Transport machinery	Other manuf.	Manuf. for sales	Total
Pre-1957										
Number	0	1	2	2	1	1	0	1	3	11
% of row	–	9.1	18.2	18.2	9.1	9.1	–	9.1	27.3	–
% of column	–	7.1	15.4	7.7	4.0	4.3	–	4.3	8.8	1.8
1957–69										
Number	2	1	3	7	10	3	4	1	2	33
% of row	6.1	3.0	9.1	21.2	30.3	9.1	12.1	3.0	6.1	–
% of column	33.3	7.1	23.1	26.9	40.0	13.0	15.8	4.3	5.9	5.5
1970–80										
Number	3	11	8	14	10	18	9	14	17	104
% of row	2.9	10.6	7.8	13.5	9.6	17.3	8.7	13.5	16.3	–
% of column	50.0	78.6	61.5	53.8	40.0	78.3	47.4	60.9	50.0	17.2
1981–86										
Number	1	1	0	3	4	1	7	7	13	37
% of row	2.7	2.7	–	8.1	10.8	2.7	18.9	18.9	35.1	–
% of column	16.7	7.1	–	11.5	16.0	4.3	36.8	30.4	35.3	6.1
1987–93										
Number	6	3	11	33	34	199	20	78	38	420
% of row	1.4	0.7	2.6	7.8	8.1	47.2	4.7	18.5	9.0	–
% of column	50.0	17.6	45.8	55.9	57.6	89.6	51.3	77.2	52.8	69.4
Total	12	17	24	59	59	222	39[a]	101	72	605
% of row	2.0	2.8	4.0	9.8	9.8	36.7	6.3	16.7	11.9	100.0

Source: Calculated from unpublished data, JETRO.
[a] Including machinery.

little doubt that these investments were in response to Malaysia's import-substitution policy.

1970–80

Japanese investment was welcomed after Merdeka, and ironically, even more conspicuously during the administrations of Tun Abdul Razak and Tun Hussein Onn, which adopted the pragmatic view that 'the more money you have, the faster you can carry out development'.[5] By the 1970s, there were plenty of criticisms of Japanese–Malaysian joint ventures, encouraged by attractive incentives and other infrastructural facilities provided by the Malaysian government.[6]

Starting from the early 1970s, Malaysia adopted a policy to woo Japanese investors to Malaysia, e.g. through participation in the week-long exhibition sponsored by the Southeast Asian Promotion Centre for Trade, Investment and Tourism, with facilities provided by the Japanese External Trade Organization (JETRO). This exhibition was the first for Malaysia and the third organized by the Centre for individual Southeast Asian countries. The then Deputy Trade and Industry Minister, Musa Hitam, said that he hoped to discuss the possible joint industrial ventures between Malaysian and Japanese entrepreneurs. He was confident that the 'Sell Malaysia' campaign would make Japanese investors aware of the attractive investment climate in the country.[7] On 11 July 1972, a Malaysian investment seminar was held in Osaka to woo more Japanese investors to Malaysia; a Malaysian Investment Centre in Tokyo was opened by Federal Industrial Development Authority (FIDA), again in Musa Hitam's enthusiastic presence.[8]

This strong bid to woo Japanese investment to Malaysia was explained as follows: 'Considering the international competition we are facing from other developing countries in attracting the investment dollar from developed nations, we must step up our efforts in this direction'.[9] The actions taken by the Malaysian government to attract Japanese investment soon brought results, with Japanese investigating teams arriving one after another. In late 1974, a sixteen-member Japanese industrial delegation arrived in Malaysia; its deputy leader, Takutaro Nishijma, expressed their aim: 'All of us want to invest here as quickly as possible, but it is rather difficult at the moment to say when. However, we want this to materialise in some form in a year or two.'[10] The team's aim was essentially to investigate the climate for Japanese investment in Malaysia. It is noteworthy that its leader felt obliged to urge that anti-Japanese sentiments (a legacy of the war) should not be a decisive factor in determining investment. The real aim of this delegation was to find out whether the government was stable, and whether there was relatively cheap, skilled labour available to enable the Japanese to reduce their costs. As Isamu Sakamoto, the leader of the delegation and Vice-Chairman of the Osaka Foundation of Science and

Technology, put it: 'Your political stability, infrastructure and human resources are better than in other countries. ... Many Japanese industrialists are keen to invest in your country. This is because wages have gone up tremendously in many countries. In Japan, wages exceed those in Italy, France and the United Kingdom'.[11] He also pointed out that 'cheap labour is an available resource that could be used in labour-intensive industries, which in turn might be used to support other more advanced industries',[12] and that 'textile industries and electronic equipment assembly plants can be transplanted to this country'.[13]

Malaysia's new policy of encouraging Japanese investment saw the establishment of 124 Japanese firms between 1970 and 1974. In 1973 alone, a total of 40 Japanese firms were set up, either on a joint venture basis, or totally Japanese-owned. As of 1975, there were over 200 Japanese companies, with a total investment of RM625 million (RM: Malaysian ringgit). Of these, 143 were joint ventures, and 20 wholly Japanese-owned.[14]

However, between 1973 and 1974, there was a sharp drop in Japanese investments. The Japanese invested RM315 million in 1973, dropping to RM120 million in 1974.[15] This was explained by the First Secretary of the Japanese Embassy, S. Wakaboyashi, who claimed that Japanese investors were generally reluctant to get involved in fresh overseas commitments. He also pointed out that investment regulations in Malaysia were getting stricter, prompting some investments to be diverted to other, more attractive countries in the Association of Southeast Asian Nations (ASEAN). Japanese complaints about Malaysia's investment regulations can be attributed to Malaysia's increased economic nationalism in the mid-1970s as well.

However, K. Senoo, the chief representative of Mitsui United Bank, said that Japanese investors were expected to flock to Malaysia as soon as the economic situation in Japan improved. The world recession after the oil shock, coupled with tight finance, were reasons given for the temporary dwindling of overseas investments by Japanese firms. The sharp drop in Japanese investments in Malaysia in the mid-1970s was mainly because the oil crisis was felt so strongly in Japan at that time.

The post-1975 diversification of Japanese investments overseas provided a new opportunity for Malaysian business, according to Goh Cheng Teik, then parliamentary secretary in the Prime Minister's Department, who saw it as a chance 'to tap Japanese capital resources in order to finance the Third Malaysia Plan and to push the Malaysian economy into the take-off stage'.[16] He advised that 'government statutory bodies and private sector should not lose sight of this end and make use of the situation to grab as much investment as we can'.[17] The new situation resulted in a number of trade missions to Japan, one of these under the then Deputy Prime Minister, Dato' Seri Dr Mahathir Mohamad. He expressed the opinion that since

Table 2.3 Japanese direct investment in Malaysian non-manufacturing industries, 1957–93

Year	Agriculture and forestry	Fishing and marine	Mining	Construction and engineering	Foreign trade	Finance and insurance	Services	Transport and warehsg.	Real estate	Other non-manuf.	Total
Pre-1957											
Number	0	1	0	2	23	3	2	1	–	0	32
% of row	–	3.1	–	6.3	71.9	9.9	6.3	3.1	–	–	–
% of column	–	100.0	–	2.9	28.4	9.4	11.1	5.9	–	–	8.9
1957–69											
Number	1	0	2	0	15	1	0	1	–	1	21
% of row	4.8	–	9.5	–	71.4	4.8	–	4.8	–	4.8	–
% of column	50.0	–	100.0	–	18.5	3.1	–	5.9	–	8.3	5.9
1970–80											
Number	0	0	0	21	19	14	3	7	–	6	70
% of row	–	–	–	30.0	27.1	20.0	4.3	10.0	–	–	–
% of column	–	–	–	30.4	23.5	43.8	16.1	41.2	–	50.0	19.6
1981–86											
Number	1	0	0	46	24	14	13	8	–	5	111
% of row	0.9	–	–	41.4	21.6	12.6	11.7	7.2	–	4.5	–
% of column	50.0	–	–	66.7	29.6	43.8	72.2	47.1	–	11.7	31.1
1987–93											
Number	2	0	0	28	12	13	36	15	3	14	123
% of row	1.6	–	–	22.8	9.8	10.6	29.3	12.2	2.4	11.4	–
% of column	50.0	–	–	28.9	12.9	28.9	66.7	46.9	100.0	53.8	34.5
Total no.	4	1	2	97	93	45	54	32	3	26	357
% of row	1.1	0.3	0.6	27.2	26.1	12.6	15.1	8.9	0.8	7.3	100.0

Source: Calculated from unpublished JETRO data.

imports from Japan would become more expensive as a result of the yen appreciation, the setting up of more supportive industries should be encouraged.[18]

Thus, it appears that the Malaysian policy of attracting Japanese investment yielded positive results in the 1970s. In fact, 104 new Japanese investments in manufacturing industry, along with 70 others outside manufacturing, clearly testified to this success (see Tables 2.2 and 2.3). There were remarkable increases in Japanese investments, especially in textiles, electrical and electronic sectors, i.e. industries seeking cheap labour. These included 18 electronic and electrical firms, 11 in textiles, 14 in petrochemicals, 9 in transport machinery, and 10 in steel and other metal industries. Investments aimed at resource exploitation and processing also gained momentum in this period. In general, this period saw more new Japanese investments than the earlier period.

Of the 70 Japanese firms outside manufacturing, 30 per cent were in construction, 27 per cent in trading, and 20 per cent in finance and insurance. Japanese finance capital, i.e. banking capital, increased in importance in this period. The growth in construction had much to do with the importance given, in both the Second and Third Malaysia Plans, to projects such as highways, airports, ports, new townships, etc., i.e. infrastructural developments, partly to create an attractive climate for FDI.

1981–86

The Malaysian government's attitude towards Japanese investment became even more indulgent with the 'Look East' policy initiated under the prime ministership of Dr Mahathir Mohamad from mid-1981. In the 1980–86 period, an interesting new situation developed. As we can see in Tables 2.2 and 2.3, 37 new firms were established in the manufacturing sector, with 7 in transport machinery, 4 in steel and other metal products, 3 in petrochemicals, 7 in other miscellaneous manufacturing branches, and 13 in product marketing. A significant decrease was observed in this period compared with the earlier periods, with the number of new non-manufacturing firms going up by 111 firms, or 75 per cent of all firms established. 46 new firms were established in construction, 24 in foreign trade, 14 in banking and insurance, 13 in services, 8 in transport, 5 in other non-manufacturing and one in agriculture and forestry. Trading, services finance and insurance accounted for much of these new investments.

The basic reason for this was the decrease of investment enthusiasm, especially in manufacturing, related to subdued economic conditions in Malaysia and internationally. The rapid growth of profits from the construction and real property sectors in Malaysia also contributed to the relatively lower attractiveness of other sectors. The Malaysian construction sector grew fourfold between 1970 and 1984, with its share of national output increasing from 3.9 to 5.4 per cent. In this period, its annual growth rate was 9.3 per cent in real terms, i.e. higher than the gross domestic product (GDP) growth of 7.9 per cent. During 1976–80, construction grew even faster, at 13.1 per cent per annum; and in 1981–84, this sector's growth reached 13.3 per cent per annum.

The overall pattern of Japanese investments can thus be ranked as follows: steel and other metals, electricals and electronics, petro-chemicals, textiles and textile products in the manufacturing sector, and foreign trade, construction, finance and insurance, and services outside manufacturing. Comparing the three periods mentioned above, we see Japanese investments in the first period being generally oriented to raw material acquisition and trade. In the second period, labour-intensive industries employing inexpensive workers as well as raw material processing and trade-related investments became more evident. This reflected economic conditions in Japan after 1970, with Japanese investors seeking opportunities to increase market shares and export competitiveness on the basis of the inexpensive labour and favourable investment conditions offered by Malaysia. The subsequent general decline of Japanese manufacturing investments in Southeast Asia was partly compensated for by Malaysian government-sponsored heavy industries, largely financed by official Japanese credit, as well as Japanese firms' inroads into construction.

MOTIVATION FOR JAPANESE INVESTMENTS

Japanese companies in electronics and electricals, textiles and other manufacturing activities have different motives for investing in Malaysia (Table 2.4). The fear that tariff protection could exclude them from the local market was given as the main reason by companies in the Malaysian consumer-oriented Japanese electronic and electrical industry. The proven success of their other overseas operations was cited as the main reason why textile companies invested in Malaysia. Lastly, the enhancement of resource extraction – either through setting up of local offices to export raw materials such as timber, iron ore, copper, tin, or of resourced-based industries that make use of such raw materials – was also cited as a motive for investing in Malaysia. Other than the specific motives stated above, the political and economic stability of the country was apparently also considered very attractive.[19]

According to Katano,[20] 32 per cent of the Japanese companies in Malaysia in 1978 were motivated by 'resource security', 37 per cent by 'labour utilization' and 61 per cent by 'market security' (the categories were not considered mutually exclusive). In the manufacturing sector, the companies not dealing in food, textiles, chemicals, metals and machinery (54 per cent) were motivated by 'labour utilization', whereas the companies in research and development were motivated by 'resource security'. 'Labour

51

Table 2.4 Motivation of Japanese private direct investment in Malaysia, May 1978 (%)

| | Total | Manufacturing | | | | | | | Development | Commerce | Others |
		Subtotal	Food	Textile	Chemicals	Metals	Machinery	Others			
Resource security	32.0	21.0	–	–	–	8.3	–	53.3	100.0	–	–
Labour utilization	37.3	46.9	100.0	100.0	23.5	33.3	52.2	33.3	8.7	25.0	21.9
Market security	60.6	70.8	50.0	100.0	23.5	66.7	69.6	63.3	17.4	75.0	45.5

Source: Hikoji Katano, Japanese Enterprises in ASEAN Countries: Statistical Outlook, Kobe: Kobe University, 1981.

utilization' was the main motivation for food (100 per cent) and textile (100 per cent) companies to invest in Malaysia. This motivation, however, was only cited by 24 per cent of chemical companies. All the textile companies were motivated by 'labour utilization' and by 'market security' considerations.

In the manufacturing sector as a whole, 71 per cent claimed that market security was the main motivation for investment in Malaysia. If we break this figure down, food (50 per cent), textiles (100 per cent), chemicals (24 per cent), metals (67 per cent), machinery (70 per cent) and others (63 per cent) cited 'market security' as a reason for investment in Malaysia. It thus seems that by 1978, the main motivation for Japanese companies investing in Malaysia was 'market security', followed by 'labour utilization', and thirdly, to secure resources. A more recent study claims that Japanese as well as other foreign companies have invested in Malaysia primarily for cheap labour:

> Foreign capital interests have been able, as import substitution, to take immediate advantage of Malaysia's Export Orientation policy, simply by exploiting Malaysia's so-called 'comparative advantage' (in the form of cheap labour) in producing labour-intensive industrial items such as electronic products.
>
> The nature of such offshore production is to import 100 per cent of their inputs from the parent company and to export 100 per cent of the output assembled or manufactured in Malaysia back to the parent company for further fabrication and re-export. The domestic value added (economic contribution) and backward linkages (internal economic integration) are minimal.[21]

There have been other factors related to the broader needs of the Japanese and Malaysian economies which also explain the drive to invest. In the 1970–80 period, the .Japanese government was in fact directly responsible for much Japanese investment in countries like Malaysia: 'In 1972, Japanese investment was relocated according to the Tanaka plan. This plan encouraged rejected categories of industries to invest abroad and they were basically land, labour, pollution-intensive industries and those industries with low skills, like textiles. While they were encouraged to go overseas, Japan encouraged the growth of the high-technology industries at home'.[22] Another study found that 'in the early 1970s, Japan's most prestigious business council recommended a strategic restructuring of the Japanese economy through the decade. This called for exporting low value-added and high-pollution manufacturing processes while developing "clean" and "high-technology" industries in Japan'.[23] Furthermore, it can be said that: 'the oil crisis of 1973–74 accelerated Japanese investment and the business circle of Japan's dependency on the rest of the world, for its industrial inputs and agricultural commodities'.[24]

Malaysia's political stability seems to have been the most important factor for Japanese companies to invest, followed by other factors such as investment-promotion measures by the government and inexpensive labour.[25] While economic stability is often seen as an assurance of profits, political stability is considered absolutely crucial for protecting foreign companies' assets, providing guarantees against confiscation and nationalization, as well as labour and other unrest. In Malaysia, the government's statutory limitations on trade union activities, official efforts to depress wage levels, and the existence of laws giving the government rights to directly intervene in disagreements between employers and employees have rated highly in the decisions of Japanese companies to locate in the country.

WAGES

With the internationalization of Japanese capital, a principal reason for expanding into developing countries such as Malaysia has been low wages compared with wages for similar jobs in more developed countries. Throughout the last two decades, this wage disparity has increased, resulting in a shift of labour-intensive industries away from the developed world to developing countries. Differences in wage levels among developing countries have also become increasingly important. For instance, in Singapore, the relatively rapid rise in wages in the 1970s and 1980s, especially during 1979–81, reduced its previous advantage of offering cheap labour, and some of its industries have had to relocate to countries offering cheaper labour. Fong's research on the differences between Japanese firms investing in Malaysia and their mother companies – covering Hitachi, Matsushita, Kao Denko and Toshiba – found: 'On the basis of wages alone, one dollar spent on labour by an average Malaysian electronic firm gives it a value-added (or worth) about double that of an average Japanese electronics firm'.[26] This comparison is interesting for it demonstrates that, notwithstanding the higher labour productivity of Japanese electronic firm employees, after adjusting for the different wage rates, Malaysian workers' contributions are about double that of their Japanese counterparts.

JOINT VENTURES, INCENTIVES AND LOCATION

Joint ventures

Japanese investments in Malaysia are mostly in the form of joint ventures as elsewhere in ASEAN. According to Yoshihara, many Japanese investors who locate overseas do not have adequate funds and their most practical strategy is therefore to set up affiliated companies as joint ventures. A local partner can be useful for the initial establishment of the company and even after operations begin, because at the beginning, government approval must be obtained, workers must be hired, products must be marketed, and a local partner can supply all these facilities. The experience of Japanese overseas investors has also encouraged joint ventures.[27] Furthermore:

> Japanese businessmen and officials in export promotion agencies of the government are more sensitive to the undercurrent of nationalism embodied in the new investment laws of developing countries. Joint-venture agreements were considered necessary not only to conform to these laws, but also to provide a hedge against political roles. Sharing ownership with nationals offers an opportunity for national identification, and reduces the appearance of foreigners, and hence the risk of expropriations.[28]

Chee and Lee found that 'the reason for selecting joint ventures varies with the dominant partners involved. The most important reasons for setting up a joint venture generally had to do with the Malaysian government's requirements in those JJV (Japanese Joint Ventures) where the Japanese are the dominant partners'.[29] Whether a decision to set up a joint venture was encouraged by the Malaysian government, or was required by the Japanese government, or was for a company's own reasons, it generally proved beneficial for both partners. The Japanese company could use local funds to finance its operations and it could secure or improve its market share in the country. Furthermore, it could use the import quotas given to Malaysian exports, e.g to the USA. This is especially true of textiles under the Multi Fibre Arrangement (MFA). Japan's textile investors have taken advantage of Malaysia's quotas to export indirectly to the EEC and the USA via joint ventures in Malaysia.

An examination of the distribution of Japanese and local paid-up capital showed that the proportion of local capital was higher during the Tunku Abdul Rahman period (1957–69) than in the Tun Razak and Tun Hussein Onn periods (1970–80). The companies' total paid-up capital amounted to US$544.305 million in the period 1970–80. The amount of paid-up capital by Japanese partners amounted to US$165.602 million, whereas the share of local partners amounted to US$378.703 million. In other words, local capital put out $2.286 for every dollar of the Japanese partner. The ratio during the Tunku Abdul Rahman period was $4.132 for every dollar of the Japanese partner.[30]

During the period 1970–80, 88 companies were established in manufacturing, 16 companies in agriculture, fishery and forestry, 11 in banking, 4 in commerce, 7 in construction, 2 in mining, 2 in warehousing and one company each in real estate, services and transportation. An interesting aspect of these investments is that total paid-up capital in warehousing came second after manufacturing, with only two companies

Table 2.5 Japanese manufacturing firms in Malaysia: distribution of incentives by industry, 1987

Industry	PC	PS	ITC	Incentive LUR	WTI	SU	Total
Food							
No. of firms	3	2	2	–	5	–	12
% with incentive	3.4	11.1	9.5	–	9.4	–	6.5
% in industry	25.0	16.7	16.7	–	41.7	–	100.0
Textiles							
No. of firms	12	2	1	–	3	1	19
% with incentive	13.8	11.1	4.8	–	5.7	25.0	10.3
% in industry	63.2	10.5	5.3	–	15.8	5.3	100.0
Wood pulp							
No. of firms	4	1	1	1	7	–	14
% with incentive	4.6	5.6	4.8	100.0	13.2	–	7.6
% in industry	28.6	7.1	7.1	7.1	50.0	–	100.0
Paper							
No. of firms	–	–	–	–	3	–	3
% with incentive	–	–	–	–	5.7	–	1.6
% in industry	–	–	–	–	100.0	–	100.0
Chemical							
No. of firms	9	1	1	–	6	–	17
% with incentive	10.3	5.6	4.8	–	11.3	–	9.2
% in industry	52.9	5.9	5.9	–	35.3	–	100.0
Petroleum							
No. of firms	–	–	–	–	1	1	2
% with incentive	–	–	–	–	1.9	25.0	1.1
% in industry	–	–	–	–	50.0	50.0	100.0
Rubber							
No. of firms	4	–	1	–	–	1	6
% with incentive	4.6	–	4.8	–	–	25.0	3.3
% in industry	66.7	–	16.7	–	-	16.7	100.0
Plastics							
No. of firms	4	2	–	–	3	–	9
% with incentive	4.6	11.1	–	–	5.7	–	4.9
% in industry	44.4	22.2	–	–	33.3	–	100.0
Non-metal							
No. of firms	6	2	3	–	3	–	14
% with incentive	6.9	11.1	14.3	–	5.7	–	7.6
% in industry	42.9	14.3	21.4	–	21.4	–	100.0
Basic metal							
No. of firms	6	1	2	–	2	–	11
% with incentive	6.9	5.6	9.5	–	3.9	–	6.0
% in industry	54.5	9.1	18.2	–	18.2	–	100.0

Continued

Table 2.5 (continued)

Industry	PC	PS	ITC	Incentive LUR	WTI	SU	Total
Fabric metal							
No. of firms	4	1	2	–	4	1	12
% with incentive	4.6	5.6	9.5	–	7.5	25.0	6.5
% in industry	33.3	8.3	16.7	–	33.3	8.3	100.0
Machinery							
No. of firms	2	1	3	–	4	–	10
% with incentive	2.3	5.6	14.3	–	7.5	–	5.4
% in industry	20.0	10.0	30.0	–	40.0	–	100.0
Electrical and electronic							
No. of firms	27	–	1	–	5	–	33
% with incentive	31.0	–	4.8	–	9.4	–	7.9
% in industry	81.8	–	3.0	–	15.2	–	100.0
Transport							
No. of firms	1	3	3	–	6	–	13
% with incentive	1.1	16.7	14.3	–	11.3	–	7.1
% in industry	7.7	23.1	23.1	–	46.2	–	100.0
SC Measure							
No. of firms	1	–	–	–	–	–	1
% with incentive	1.1	–	–	–	–	–	0.5
% in industry	100.0	–	–	–	–	–	100.0
Miscellaneous							
No. of firms	3	1	1	–	1	–	6
% with incentive	3.4	5.6	4.8	–	1.9	–	3.3
% in industry	50.0	16.7	16.7	–	16.7	–	100.0
Hotel							
No. of firms	1	1	–	–	–	–	2
% with incentive	1.1	5.6	–	–	–	–	1.1
% in industry	50.0	50.0	–	–	–	–	100.0
No. of firms	87	18	21	1	53	4	184
% of firms	47.3	9.8	11.4	0.5	28.8	2.2	100.0

Source: Analysis by author from raw data obtained from Statistics Department, Manufacturing Section, 1987.
PC: pioneer certificate; PS: pioneer status; ITC: investment tax credit; LUR: labour utilization relief; WTI: without tax incentive; SU: status unknown.

having a total paid-up capital of US$301.757 million, compared with total paid-up capital in manufacturing of US$988.851 million. Most important, most of the capital in these two industries was provided by the Malaysian partners. In manufacturing, the paid-up capital by Japanese partners amounted to US$138.072 million, whereas paid-up capital by Malaysian

Table 2.6 Japanese manufacturing firms in Malaysia: distribution of incentives by state, 1987

State	PC	PS	ITC	Incentive LUR	WTI	SU	Total
Kuala Lumpur							
No. of firms	2	–	–	1	3	–	6
% in state	33.3	–	–	16.7	50.0	–	100.0
% with incentive	2.3	–	–	100.0	5.7	–	3.3
Selangor							
No. of firms	32	4	5	–	21	–	62
% in state	51.6	6.5	8.1	–	33.9	–	100.0
% with incentive	36.8	22.2	23.8	–	39.6	–	33.7
Penang							
No. of firms	23	4	1	–	12	1	41
% in state	56.1	9.8	2.4	–	29.3	2.4	100.0
% with incentive	26.4	22.2	4.8	–	22.6	25.0	22.3
Sabah							
No. of firms	1	1	–	–	1	–	3
% in state	33.3	33.3	–	–	33.3	–	100.0
% with incentive	1.1	5.6	–	–	1.9	–	1.6
Johor							
No. of firms	11	3	7	–	7	–	28
% in state	39.3	10.7	25.0	–	25.0	–	100.0
% with incentive	12.6	16.7	33.3	–	13.2	–	15.2
Sarawak							
No. of firms	–	1	1	–	3	1	6
% in state	–	16.7	16.7	–	50.0	16.7	100.0
% with incentive	–	5.6	4.8	–	5.7	25.0	3.3
Perak							
No. of firms	10	1	3	–	2	1	17
% in state	58.8	5.9	17.6	–	11.8	5.9	100.0
% with incentive	11.5	5.6	14.3	–	3.8	25.0	9.2
Trengganu							
No. of firms	–	–	–	–	1	–	1
% in state	–	–	–	–	100.0	–	100.0
% with incentive	–	–	–	–	1.9	–	0.5
Kedah							
No. of firms	4	–	3	–	–	1	8
% in state	50.0	–	37.5	–	–	12.5	100.0
% with incentive	4.6	–	14.3	–	–	25.0	4.3
Negri Sembilan							
No. of firms	2	1	–	–	1	–	4
% in state	50.0	25.0	–	–	25.0	–	100.0
% with incentive	2.3	5.6	–	–	1.9	–	2.2

Continued

Table 2.6 (continued)

State	PC	PS	ITC	Incentive LUR	WTI	SU	Total
Melaka							
No. of firms	2	2	1	–	–	–	5
% in state	40.0	40.0	20.0	–	–	–	100.0
% with incentive	2.3	11.1	4.8	–	–	–	2.7
Pahang							
No. of firms	–	–	–	–	1	–	1
% in state	–	–	–	–	100.0	–	100.0
% with incentive	–	–	–	–	1.9	–	0.5
Perlis							
No. of firms	–	1	–	–	1	–	2
% in state	–	50.0	–	–	50.0	–	100.0
% with incentive	–	5.6	–	–	1.9	–	1.1
No. of firms	87	18	21	1	53	4	184
% of state	47.3	9.8	11.4	0.5	28.8	2.2	100.0

Source: Analysis by author from raw data obtained from Statistics Department, Manufacturing Section, 1987.
PC: pioneer certificate; PS: pioneer status; ITC: investment tax credit; LUR: labour utilization relief; WTI: without tax incentive; SU: status unknown.

partners amounted to US$850.779 million. In warehousing, the paid-up capital by Malaysian partners amounted to US$300.851 million.

These comparisons of paid-up capital by Japanese and local partners in joint ventures reveal that most of the capital invested was concentrated in manufacturing, and most of the capital was provided by local partners, rather than by the Japanese partners. The Japanese share was concentrated, in order of importance, in textiles and textile products, followed by wood and wooden products, electrical machinery and transport equipment. Malaysian paid-up capital was concentrated in chemicals, followed by wood and wooden products, transport equipment, textiles and textile products, and metal and metallic products.[31]

Incentives

Tables 2.5 and 2.6 show the incentives granted to Japanese firms investing in Malaysia. Of the 184 firms established in the manufacturing sector, 87 firms had pioneer certificates, 18 firms had pioneer status, 21 firms had investment tax credit, one firm had labour utilization relief, 53 firms had no incentives, while the incentive status of the remaining four firms was unknown.

Table 2.7 Japanese manufacturing firms in Malaysia: state location by paid-up capital, 1987

State	Paid-up capital (thousand ringgit)							
	<250	250–499	500–999	1,000–2,999	3,000–4,999	5,000–9,999	>10,000	Total
Kuala Lumpur								
No. of firms	130	13	7	13	1	10	6	180
% in state	72.2	7.2	3.9	7.2	0.6	5.6	3.3	100.0
% by capital-size	12.7	31.6	32.0	26.4	50.0	27.8	37.5	43.2
Selangor								
No. of firms	28	6	8	14	12	10	15	93
% in state	30.1	6.5	8.6	15.1	12.9	10.8	16.1	100.0
% by capital-size	12.7	31.6	32.0	26.4	50.0	27.8	37.5	22.3
Penang								
No. of firms	4	–	6	7	6	6	7	36
% in state	11.1	–	16.7	19.4	16.7	16.7	19.4	100.0
% by capital-size	1.8	–	24.0	13.2	25.0	16.7	17.5	8.6
Sabah								
No. of firms	27	–	1	1	–	1	1	31
% in state	87.1	–	3.2	3.2	–	3.2	3.2	100.0
% by capital-size	12.3	–	4.0	1.9	–	2.8	2.5	7.4
Johor								
No. of firms	2	–	3	3	1	4	5	18
% in state	11.1	–	16.7	16.7	5.6	22.2	27.8	100.0
% by capital-size	0.9	–	12.0	5.7	4.2	11.1	12.5	4.3
Sarawak								
No. of firms	21	–	–	3	–	–	–	24
% in state	87.5	–	–	12.5	–	–	–	100.0
% by capital-size	9.5	–	–	5.7	–	–	–	5.8
Perak								
No. of firms	3	–	–	4	1	3	2	13
% in state	23.1	–	–	30.8	7.7	23.1	15.4	100.0
% by capital-size	1.4	–	–	7.5	4.2	8.3	5.0	3.1
Trengganu								
No. of firms	1	–	–	–	–	–	1	2
% in state	50.0	–	–	–	–	–	50.0	100.0
% by capital-size	0.5	–	–	–	–	–	2.5	0.5
Kedah								
No. of firms	1	–	–	4	3	1	1	10
% in state	10.0	–	–	40.0	30.0	10.0	10.0	100.0
% by capital-size	0.5	–	–	7.5	12.5	2.8	2.5	2.4
Negri Sembilan								
No. of firms	–	–	–	2	–	1	–	3
% in state	–	–	–	66.7	–	33.3	–	100.0
% by capital-size	–	–	–	3.8	–	2.8	–	0.7

Continued

Table 2.7 (continued)

State	Paid-up capital (thousand ringgit)							
	<250	250–499	500–999	1,000–2,999	3,000–4,999	5,000–9,999	>10,000	Total
Melaka								
No. of firms	2	–	–	1	–	–	1	4
% in state	50.0	–	–	25.0	–	–	25.0	100.0
% by capital-size	0.9	–	–	1.9	–	–	2.5	1.0
Pahang								
No. of firms	–	–	–	1	–	–	–	1
% in state	–	–	–	100.0	–	–	–	100.0
% by capital-size	–	–	–	1.9	–	–	–	0.2
Perlis								
No. of firms	–	–	–	–	–	–	1	1
% in state	–	–	–	–	–	–	100.0	100.0
% by capital-size	–	–	–	–	–	–	2.5	0.2
No. of firms	219	19	25	53	24	36	40	416
% of firms	52.6	4.6	6.0	12.7	5.8	8.7	9.6	100.0

Source: Analysis by author from raw data obtained from Statistics Department, Manufacturing Section, 1987.

When we look at the industrial breakdown of the incentives granted, we see that textiles and textile products, chemical industry, non-metallic mineral and basic metal industries have benefited most from these incentives: 63 per cent of firms in the textile industry, 53 per cent of firms in the chemical industry, as well as 43 per cent and 55 per cent of firms established in non-metallic mineral products and basic metal industries respectively, have benefited from pioneer status and pioneer certificates.

Location and size of firms

From the early 1970s until the mid-1980s, Malaysia's development policy was also aimed at promoting more balanced regional development. However, the value of such economic development programmes and projects for rural and less developed areas depends critically on the spatial implications of investments. Data on per capita GDP in the different states in Malaysia provide some measure of regional inequalities and poverty.[32] In 1970, Selangor, including the Federal Territory, had a per capita GDP almost 63.0 per cent higher than the average for Malaysia. The per capita GDP in Negri Sembilan, Penang, Pahang and Perak were about average, with those of Sabah, Sarawak and Melaka lower by some 10 to 20 per cent. The poorest states of Kedah, Perlis, Trengganu and Kelantan had per capita

Table 2.8 Japanese firms in Malaysia: state location by labour employed, 1987

State	<25	25– 49	50– 74	75– 99	100– 249	250– 499	500– 999	>1,000	Total
					No. of employees				
Kuala Lumpur									
No. of firms	128	12	19	6	10	3	1	1	180
% in state	71.1	6.7	10.6	3.3	5.6	1.7	0.6	0.6	100.0
% of firm-size	55.2	44.4	59.4	31.6	20.0	13.6	4.5	7.7	43.2
Selangor									
No. of firms	35	7	3	8	16	11	8	5	93
% in state	37.6	7.5	3.2	8.6	17.2	11.8	8.6	5.4	100.0
% of firm-size	15.1	25.9	9.4	42.1	32.0	50.0	36.4	38.5	22.3
Penang									
No. of firms	13	2	2	1	7	2	4	5	36
% in state	36.1	5.6	5.6	2.8	19.4	5.6	11.1	13.9	100.0
% of firm-size	5.6	7.4	6.3	5.3	14.0	9.1	18.2	38.5	8.6
Sabah									
No. of firms	23	2	1	1	1	–	3	–	31
% in state	74.2	6.5	3.2	3.2	3.2	–	9.7	–	100.0
% of firm-size	9.9	7.4	3.1	5.3	2.0	–	13.6	–	7.4
Johor									
No. of firms	3	1	1	1	7	1	3	1	18
% in state	16.7	5.6	5.6	5.6	38.9	5.6	16.7	5.6	100.0
% of firm-size	1.3	3.7	3.1	5.3	14.0	4.5	13.6	7.7	4.3
Sarawak									
No. of firms	20	2	1	–	1	–	–	–	24
% in state	83.3	8.3	4.2	–	4.0	–	–	–	5.8
% of firm-size	8.6	7.4	3.1	–	2.0	–	–	–	–
Perak									
No. of firms	4	–	3	–	4	–	1	1	13
% in state	30.8	–	23.1	–	30.8	–	7.7	7.7	3.1
% of firm-size	1.7	–	9.4	–	8.0	–	4.5	7.7	–
Trengganu									
No. of firms	1	–	–	–	–	–	1	–	2
% in state	50.0	–	–	–	–	–	50.0	–	100.0
% of firm-size	0.4	–	–	–	–	–	4.5	–	0.5
Kedah									
No. of firms	2	1	2	–	2	2	1	–	10
% in state	20.0	10.0	20.0	–	20.0	20.0	10.0	–	100.0
% of firm-size	0.9	3.7	6.3	–	4.0	9.1	4.5	–	2.4
Negri Sembilan									
No. of firms	–	–	–	1	1	1	–	–	3
% in state	–	–	–	33.3	33.3	33.3	–	–	100.0
% of firm-size	–	–	–	5.3	2.0	4.5	–	–	0.7

Continued

Table 2.8 (continued)

State	No. of employees								Total
	<25	25–49	50–74	75–99	100–249	250–499	500–999	>1,000	
Melaka									
No. of firms	1	–	–	–	1	2	–	–	4
% in state	25.0	–	–	–	25.0	50.0	–	–	100.0
% of firm-size	0.4	–	–	–	2.0	9.1	–	–	1.0
Pahang									
No. of firms	–	–	–	1	–	–	–	–	1
% in state	–	–	–	100.0	–	–	–	–	100.0
% of firm-size	–	–	–	5.3	–	–	–	–	0.2
Perlis									
No. of firms	1	–	–	–	–	–	–	–	1
% in state	100.0	–	–	–	–	–	–	–	100.0
% of firm-size	0.4	–	–	–	–	–	–	–	0.2
No. of firms	231	27	32	19	50	22	22	13	416
% of firms	55.6	6.5	7.7	4.6	12.0	5.3	5.3	3.1	100.0

Source: Analysis by author from raw data obtained from Statistics Department, Manufacturing Section, 1987.

GDPs of between half to two-thirds the Malaysian average. Therefore, in order to reduce regional differences and other income differences, the Malaysian government granted various incentives to encourage foreign investments in these regions.

The total number of firms in these four more developed states thus comprised 78 per cent of the total number of Japanese companies located in Malaysia. In contrast, the four underdeveloped states in Peninsular Malaysia only had 14 Japanese companies. As can be seen in Table 2.8, 232 Japanese firms (or 54 per cent of the total) employed less than 25 persons each, and 128 firms (or 55 per cent of the total) were in Kuala Lumpur, 35 in Selangor, 23 in Sabah, 20 in Sarawak and 13 in Penang. Firms employing more than 1,000 workers each were concentrated in Penang and Selangor, with five such firms in each state.

The number of firms employing 100–249 workers was 50 (i.e. 12 per cent of the total), while 32 firms employed 50–74 workers each. Twenty-seven firms employed 25–49 workers, and 19 employed 75–99 workers each. Very large firms (employing more than 1,000 workers) constituted 3 per cent of all firms, medium-large firms (100–249 workers each) made up 12 per cent of the total, small-medium firms with 50–74 workers and 75–99 workers each made up 7 per cent and 5 per cent respectively, while small firms (25–49 workers each) made up 7 per cent.

These statistics suggest that the Japanese firms located in Malaysia were, generally, of medium and small size, and have preferred to be situated in developed regions such as Kuala Lumpur, Selangor, Penang and Johor. By thus concentrating job-creation in already developed regions to the relative neglect of less-developed ones, these firms have not fulfilled one of the major social and economic expectations of DFI in Malaysia.

As shown in Table 2.7, for 220 of the Japanese firms, or 53 per cent of the total, paid-up capital was less than RM250,000 each. A further 19 companies had paid-up capital of between RM250,000 and RM500,000 each, 25 had between RM500,000 and RM1 million, 53 companies had RM2 to 3 million, 24 companies had RM3 to 5 million, and 36 companies had RM5 to 10 million. These data complement the data in Table 2.8 to confirm that in terms of both capital and labour, Japanese companies tend to be of small and medium size, while capital-intensive investments were mainly found in the developed regions, i.e. Kuala Lumpur, Selangor and Penang.

As Table 2.9 suggests, there seems to be a direct relationship between capital intensity and the number of workers employed, with the larger the paid-up capital of a company, the larger the workforce. A total of 185 Japanese firms had paid-up capitals of RM250,000 or less and employed less than 25 workers, while these same companies constituted 80 per cent of the firms with workforces of less than 25 workers. They also constituted 84 per cent of the companies with paid-up capitals of up to RM250,000, all of which suggests that Japanese companies in Malaysia tend to be of medium and small size.

As Table 2.10 shows, of the 416 Japanese firms investing in Malaysia, 106 were established in free trade zones (FTZs) and industrial estates, while 311 firms or 75 per cent were located outside them. The number of firms with less than 25 workers was 232, and 92 per cent of them were outside the FTZs. In short, Japanese firms tended to concentrate in developed regions and where well-developed infrastructure already existed; by so doing, they did not serve to reduce regional differences and locational poverty. Thus, the overall contribution of Japanese companies to Malaysia's own socio-economic goals may be questioned, as suggested by Chee and Lee[1] and Saravanamuttu.[21]

Transfer pricing

Transfer pricing is an accounting method used by multinational companies to maximize their post-tax retained profits. Internationalization and intra-firm trading among the branches of a multinational company e.g. between the head office and its subsidiaries, often involve selling, importing or exporting goods at prices different from their arms-length international prices, thus transferring profits or proceeds to or from the countries concerned. In a sense, the lucrative possibilities from transfer pricing have been an important motivational factor for transnationalization.

Table 2.9 Japanese firms in Malaysia: paid-up capital by labour employed

No. of employees	Paid-up capital (thousand ringgit)							
	<250	250–499	500–999	1,000–2,999	3,000–4,999	5,000–9,999	>10,000	Total
≤25								
No. of firms	185	11	12	16	3	2	3	232
% by firm-size	79.7	4.7	5.2	6.9	1.3	0.9	1.3	100.0
% by capital-size	84.1	57.9	48.0	30.2	12.5	5.6	7.3	55.5
25–49								
No. of firms	11	2	5	4	2	2	1	27
% by firm-size	40.7	4.7	18.5	14.8	7.4	7.4	3.7	100.0
% by capital-size	5.0	10.5	20.0	7.5	8.3	5.6	2.4	6.5
50–74								
No. of firms	9	3	3	9	3	4	1	32
% by firm-size	28.1	9.1	9.4	28.1	9.4	12.5	3.1	100.0
% by capital-size	4.1	15.8	12.0	17.0	12.5	11.1	2.4	7.7
75–99								
No. of firms	6	1	2	6	–	3	1	19
% by firm-size	31.6	5.3	10.5	31.6	–	15.8	5.3	100.0
% by capital-size	2.7	5.3	8.0	11.3	–	8.3	2.4	4.5
100–249								
No. of firms	5	2	2	12	7	13	9	50
% by firm-size	10.0	4.0	4.0	24.0	14.0	26.0	18.0	100.0
% by capital-size	2.3	10.5	8.0	22.6	29.2	36.1	22.0	12.0
250–499								
No. of firms	2	–	1	5	5	3	6	22
% by firm-size	9.1	–	4.5	22.7	22.7	13.6	27.3	100.0
% by capital-size	0.9	–	4.0	9.4	20.8	8.3	14.6	5.3
500–999								
No. of firms	2	–	–	1	3	6	10	22
% by firm-size	9.1	–	–	4.5	13.6	27.3	45.5	100.0
% by capital-size	0.9	–	–	1.9	12.5	16.7	24.4	5.3
>1,000								
No. of firms	–	–	–	–	1	3	10	14
% by firm-size	–	–	–	–	7.1	21.4	71.4	100.0
% by capital-size	–	–	–	–	4.2	8.3	24.4	3.3
No. of firms	220	19	25	53	24	36	41	418
% of firms	52.6	4.5	6.0	12.7	5.7	8.6	9.8	100.0

Source: Analysis by author from raw data obtained from Statistics Department, Manufacturing Section, 1987.

Many Japanese transnational corporations overprice sales to their subsidiaries situated in tax havens and underprice purchases from them to reduce tax liability. This transfer of prices, and hence profits, occurs within the same transnational corporation. Such internal transfers of

Table 2.10 Japanese firms in Malaysia: labour employed by location

Firm location	<25	25-49	50-74	75-99	No. of employees 100-249	250-499	500-000	>1,000	Total
Outside FTZs/IEs									
No. of firms	213	21	25	11	25	6	7	3	311
% of all firms	68.5	6.8	8.0	3.5	8.0	1.9	2.3	1.0	100.0
% of employees in column	91.8	77.8	78.1	57.9	50.0	27.3	31.8	23.1	74.6
Free trade zones (FTZs)									
No. of firms	2	–	–	1	2	6	7	6	24
% of all firms	8.3	–	–	4.2	8.3	25.0	29.2	25.0	100.0
% of employees in column	0.9	–	–	5.3	4.0	27.3	31.8	46.2	5.8
Industrial estates (IEs)									
No. of firms	17	6	7	7	23	10	8	4	82
% of all firms	20.7	7.3	8.5	8.5	28.0	12.2	9.8	4.9	100.0
% of employees in column	7.3	22.2	21.9	36.8	46.0	45.5	36.4	30.8	19.7
Total no. of firms	232	27	32	19	50	22	22	13	417
% of all firms	55.6	6.5	7.7	4.6	12.0	5.3	5.3	3.1	100.0

Source: Analysis by author from raw data obtained from Statistics Department, Manufacturing Section, 1987.

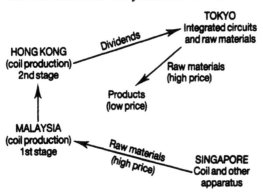

Figure 2.1 Trade and transfer pricing between branches of Toko Corporation.
Source: Khor Kok Peng (1983) *The Malaysian Economy: Structures and Dependence,*
Maricans, Kuala Lumpur.

profits often emerge as 'losses' in some headquarters' or subsidiaries' official accounts, which can be offset against tax liabilities, with the subsidiaries in tax havens showing huge profits as a result. The fact that many tax havens permit the repatriation of any amount of capital without restriction, including exemptions from all forms of customs duties and taxes, means that Japanese and other transnational corporations can extract profits without giving much in government taxes. The importance of transfer pricing cannot be over-emphasized: 'it was argued that the possibilities for international profit transfer through intra corporate pricing manipulation to the Asian low tax zones was as important as the cheap labour factor in the choice of location by Texas Instruments'.[33] Here is a possible scenario for Japanese transnationals involving Toko Corporation, an electronics company with its head office in Tokyo and subsidiaries in Korea, Taiwan, Hong Kong, Singapore, Malaysia, Europe and Latin America (see Figure 2.1). The Malaysian branch imports raw materials from the main Toko plant in Japan, the Toko branch in Singapore and another (non-Toko) Japanese company located in a Taiwanese free trade zone. After assembling, Toko Malaysia exports semi-finished coils that have been through the first stage of processing to a Toko factory in Hong Kong, where they are finally processed and then sold on the world market. In this example, the profits of the Malaysian branch are artificially depressed and those of the Hong Kong branch artificially inflated by overcharging for imported inputs into Malaysia and underpricing the exported coils from Malaysia to Hong Kong. The tax-free profits are then sent to Japan. The director of the Toko branch in Malaysia offers this candid admission:

In this area, Malaysia and Hong Kong factories are one group. Therefore, when we export semi-finished products from our Malaysian factory to the Hong Kong factory, there is no need to add up the profits here. We are successful as long as a large profit is left in Hong Kong when the finished products are exported to the world market because these profits are sent straight to the Toko head office in Tokyo as dividends. When exporting semi-finished products from Malaysia to Hong Kong, they are cheaper than the market price, although we cannot engage in those too extensively, as it is unwise to do it openly.

SOURCES OF FINANCE FOR JAPANESE AFFILIATES IN MALAYSIA

The response to the question 'How do Japanese companies investing in Malaysia finance their activities and expansion?' is important for several reasons. The answer to this question might help answer the questions: 'Why are these companies investing in Malaysia?' and 'What are their contributions to Malaysia's capital stock?' Table 2.11 shows that Japanese local and parent companies as well as financial institutions play an important role in financing the activities and expansion of Japanese companies in Malaysia. However, the main source is not capital transferred from the headquarters in Japan, but sources created in Malaysia by these companies. In other words, after some initial support, there is a self-supporting process dependent upon local sources. From my survey, 59 per cent of the Japanese companies covered had relations of at least 10 years with financing institutions in Malaysia.

The four basic sources for financing Japanese companies' activities and expansion can be identified as: (1) undistributed profits; (2) revolving funds; (3) Japanese banks and foreign finance houses; (4) parent company sources. Undistributed profits and revolving funds constitute a company's internal sources, while the others are external sources. As can be seen from Table 2.11, external sources, especially parent company sources, are as important as local sources in providing finance. Nevertheless, when we look closer, the importance of Japanese and local banks becomes clearer.

Local bank mediation in obtaining loan-finance – especially from Japanese banks and finance houses – by issuing guarantees, points to the important role of local banks in such relations. Since the funds provided by

Table 2.11 Japanese manufacturing firms in Malaysia: sources of finance

Proportion of finance	1–24%	25–49%	50–74%	75–100%
Local financial institutions	8	3	7	14
Japanese financial institutions	11	7	4	10
Parent company	14	1	3	14

Source: Questionnaire survey.

foreign loans are obtained with local bank guarantees, in effect, these funds are provided from local sources and reduce the actual transfer of capital from Japan. Thus, the basic source of finance is not funds transferred from headquarters, but provided from local sources. Indeed, the contribution of Japanese companies' own finance to capital stocks in Malaysia is not especially large compared with local finance. Thus, 81 per cent of the Japanese firms in the electronics industry depended upon local banks, while the remaining 19 per cent utilized parent company sources. In the textile industry, 27 per cent of the Japanese firms utilized foreign sources, whereas 73 per cent utilized local banks.

Funds held within a company, mainly from undistributed profits and depreciation allowances, constituted the most important internal source of funds. Both field research and interviews lead us to the conclusion that these two types of funds form a very large portion of most companies' financial resources and constitute the basic sources financing the company's activities. To illustrate this, it can be noted that the undistributed profits of the semi-conductor producer, Hitachi Semi-Conductor Sdn. Bhd. – active in the Malaysian electronics industry since 1971 – amounted to RM73.162 million as of 1987. Undistributed profits of the Japanese textile giants, Pen Fabric Sdn. Bhd., Pen Fibre Sdn. Bhd. and Woodard Textile Mill Sdn. Bhd., were RM10.0 million, RM56.1 million and RM3.3 million respectively. Furthermore, funds held by these firms from depreciation allowances amounted to RM5.4 million for Pen Fabric, RM72.9 million for Pen Fibre and RM4.5 million for Woodard. The total undistributed profits and depreciation allowances for these four companies amounted to RM377.253 million, representing nearly 17 per cent of total Japanese investments in Malaysia!

FACTORS AFFECTING FINANCIAL POLICIES OF JAPANESE COMPANIES

The main financial sources for Japanese firms in Malaysia are their profits, funds provided from parent firms or headquarters as capital or loans, funds obtained from local and foreign banks and, less important, funds from the sale of stock in Japan and Malaysia. How much these firms utilize these sources for their activities and expansion depends on several factors. Our findings from field research and interviews show that these companies tend to hold a substantial portion of their incomes within the company in the form of undistributed profits and depreciation allowances, and utilize these funds to finance the company's activities and expansion.

Dividends from Japanese–Malaysian companies to shareholders are generally very low. One reason appears to be the rapid growth rates of and, consequently, the larger investment funds needed by these companies. Another is the desire to avoid tax payment by re-orienting profits for investment, instead of distributing them to shareholders. This works because minimal tax is payable on profits held for re-investment, whereas profits transferred to the parent country or distributed to shareholders are subject to several corporate and other taxes. One tactic used by Japanese companies in Malaysia is to accumulate undistributed profits as depreciation allowances, which are non-taxable. Their declared and taxable profits thus appear as less than their actual profits.

An important source of loans for these firms is the local credit market. As can be seen from Table 2.11, 75–100 per cent of the funds of 14 firms and 50–74 per cent of the funds of seven firms are provided by funds from the credit market in Malaysia. Japanese firms choose to borrow substantially from local sources, not only to secure investment funds, but also to keep their capital commitments and debts in the same currency as a precaution against possible devaluation of the local currency, which would reduce the yen value of their assets. They can also thus take advantage of fluctuations in exchange rates. The Malaysian ringgit's depreciation against the Japanese yen by more than 50 per cent in the period 1983–87 thus means that these companies probably obtained substantial additional earnings from foreign exchange developments. Similarly, high inflation in the Malaysian economy would encourage such companies to secure local loans. Another factor is the fact that interest payments on local loans are tax-deductible.

A substantial portion of the funds used by Japanese firms to finance international expansion and activities is made up of intra-firm loans granted by the parent company to subsidiary or affiliated companies. The importance of such funds provided by the parent company can be seen in Table 2.11. Intra-firm loans have several different functions in the operations of transnational companies. Affiliated companies may easily transfer surplus funds to their parent companies in the guise of debt and/ or interest payments. The transfer of a company's earnings to its headquarters in this guise, rather than as a transfer of declared profits, enables it to evade taxes. The practice has the further advantage of enabling the company to claim loan repayment status for such funds, which can then be offset against tax liabilities.

Other considerations which enter into the financial policies of Japanese (and other international) companies in Malaysia include company size, technological level, ownership and profitability of the Malaysian investment. In general, large companies transfer more funds than small companies to their headquarters. Firms established entirely with Japanese capital utilize more funds and intra-firm loans from headquarters than joint ventures. Capital-intensive firms borrow more locally than labour-intensive ones, while small companies tend to borrow from local banks, whereas large ones tend to obtain loans from both domestic and international capital markets.

MARKETS

Two oft-cited motives for Japanese companies to invest in Malaysia to manufacture goods are 'to expand the market' and 'to benefit from the advantages offered by the host countries' (inexpensive and abundant labour, raw materials and investment incentives). If a company's motivation for locating abroad is simply to expand its market, or secure a market share, then it is likely to emphasize local sales, and exports to (third) countries and regions are likely to be of only secondary importance. In short, the basic motivation of these companies seems to be to 'sell where you produce'.

However, the general trend of Japanese electronics and textile firms in Malaysia suggests that this is not their main motive. Of the textile firms surveyed, Pentley exported 95 per cent of its production, Woodard 99 per cent, Pen Fabric 88 per cent and Pen Fibre 38 per cent. For companies expanding abroad to reduce their manufacturing costs by taking advantage of inexpensive labour, raw material and energy as well as investment incentives for export to Japan and other markets, their basic aim is to produce where costs are lower and to sell to the world from there. As may be deduced from Table 2.12, some of the Japanese companies studied sell primarily within the Malaysian market, while others use Malaysia as a springboard for export to foreign markets, especially to Japan, the USA and EEC.

The situation of the electronics industry is similar to that of the textile sector, with production aimed almost completely at foreign markets. For example, Hitachi's production is exclusively for export, with Japan taking 87 per cent of its total output, Singapore 3 per cent, Hong Kong 8 per cent and the USA 2 per cent. Although the entire output of the Naito electronic firm is for export and its manufactured products qualify as finished products, it serves NEC as a subcontracting manufacturer, with 97 per cent of its production going to NEC Malaysia and other countries. While the

Table 2.12 Japanese textile firms in Malaysia: exports to foreign markets (%)

| | Pentley | Woodard | | Pen Fabric | Pen Fibre |
		Fabric	Yarn		
Singapore	10.0	–	1.5	7.7	0.6
Hong Kong	15.0	–	10.0	12.5	17.0
Taiwan	20.0	–	–	3.7	–
EEC	29.0	26.0	75.0	13.3	–
Japan	0	0	0	0	0
USA	20.0	59.0	2.9	9.3	0.4
Other countries	10.0	15.0	5.2	35.3	49.0

Source: Questionnaire survey.

Asahi electronic firm exports all of its production to Singapore, the Matsushita room air-conditioner manufacturer exports 93 per cent of its production, with 40 per cent going to the USA, 20 per cent to Hong Kong, 1 per cent to Singapore, 37 per cent to other countries and 7 per cent to the Malaysian market.

Local sales for firms producing foodstuffs, rubber and chemicals are higher than those of firms involved in textiles and electronics. NGK Spark Plugs (M) Sdn. Bhd. sells 90 per cent of its production to the Malaysian market, while Tokai Cigar Litein sells 85 per cent, Yung Kong Galvanising Ind. Bhd. 100 per cent and Dipsol Chemical (M) Sdn. Bhd. 20 per cent. It can be seen that Japanese manufacturing investments display a dualist character, with electronic and textile firms exporting to international markets, while other industries produce mainly for the domestic market.

APPENDIX

Table A2.1 Number of Japanese subsidiaries by industry in Malaysia

Industry	Malaysia	Up to 1980	1981– 85	1986– 90	1991	1992
Total	592	146	95	257	58	33
Agriculture, forestry and fisheries	3	2	–	1	–	–
Mining	3	–	–	2	–	1
Construction	52	9	28	10	4	1
Manufacturing	371	89	39	186	39	18
Food	8	3	1	3	1	–
Textiles	11	8	–	2	–	1
Wood furniture	14	2	1	9	–	2
Pulp and paper	3	–	–	1	1	1
Printing	1	1	–	–	–	–
Chemicals	48	15	5	23	4	1
Petroleum and coal	11	1	–	8	2	–
Rubber and leather	11	3	1	7	–	–
Pottery and ceramics	15	6	–	5	4	–
Iron and steel	13	6	1	4	2	–
Non-ferous metal	27	3	4	16	3	1
Metal products	24	3	5	12	3	1
Machinery	12	1	6	4	–	1
Electrical and electronics	121	24	4	73	16	4
Transport equipment	9	2	2	4	–	1
Automotive and parts	18	3	7	5	–	3
Precision tools	11	4	–	5	2	–
Other manufacturing	14	4	2	5	1	2

Continued

Table A2.1 (continued)

Industry	Malaysia	Up to 1980	1981–85	1986–90	1991	1992
Commerce	94	28	12	36	8	9
Wholesale	85	28	11	29	7	9
Agriculture, forestry and fisheries	–	–	–	–	–	–
Textiles	–	–	–	–	–	–
Wood furniture, paper and pulp	3	1	–	1	–	1
Chemicals	8	4	1	1	1	1
Petroleum and coal	–	–	–	–	–	–
Rubber and leather	–	–	–	–	–	–
Pottery and ceramics	–	–	–	–	–	–
Iron and steel	3	–	1	1	–	1
Non-ferous metal	2	–	–	1	1	–
Metal products	–	–	–	–	–	–
Machinery	11	6	1	4	–	–
Electrical and electronics	19	7	2	4	2	4
Transport equipment	2	2	–	–	–	–
Automotive and parts	3	1	–	2	–	–
Precision tools	4	–	1	2	1	–
Foreign trade and others	30	7	5	13	2	2
Retail	9	–	1	7	1	–
Restaurants	–	–	–	–	–	–
Finance and insurance	15	9	3	3	–	–
Securities and investments	2	2	–	–	–	–
Real estate	4	–	1	2	1	–
Transport	18	2	3	9	2	1
Services	24	4	9	6	3	2
Equity holdings and others	6	1	–	2	1	1

Source: Toyo Keizai, Kaigai Shinshutsu Kigyo Soran, 1993.
Local corporations in which the share capital held by Japanese companies is less than 10 per cent are not included.
Withdrawn or dormant corporations are excluded. As the total figures include the number of corporations whose inaugurated year is not available, it is not consistent with the accumulated figures of the columns below.

NOTES

1 Chee Peng Lim and Lee Poh Ping, The Role of Japanese Direct Investment in Malaysia, Occasional Paper no. 60, Institute of Southeast Asian Studies, Singapore, 1979, p. 10.
2 Jacinta Chin, 'Japanese Investment and Foreign Aid to Malaysia', Graduation Exercise, Faculty of Economics and Administration, University of Malaya, 1974, p. 24.
3 Far Eastern Economic Review, 3 February 1966, p. 188.
4 Tunku Abdul Rahman, Contemporary Issues in Malaysian Politics, Pelanduk Publications, Malaysia, 1984, p. 42.

5 Statement by Tun Abdul Razak, *Straits Echo*, 21 January 1984.
6 *Straits Times*, 12 September 1972.
7 *The Star*, 14 March 1973.
8 *New Straits Times*, 12 July 1973.
9 Ibid.
10 *New Straits Times*, 21 October 1974.
11 *Straits Echo*, 23 October 1974.
12 *New Straits Times*, 23 October 1974.
13 Ibid.
14 *Straits Echo*, 20 October 1975.
15 Ibid.
16 *New Straits Times*, 29 December 1975.
17 Ibid.
18 *New Straits Times*, 26 August 1978.
19 Chee and Lee, op. cit., pp. 9–11.
20 Hikoji Katono, *Japanese Enterprises in ASEAN Countries: Statistical Outlook*, Kobe: Kobe University, 1981, p. 47.
21 J. Saravanamuttu, 'The Role and Impact of Japanese Direct Investment in Malaysia', paper presented at seminar on *Japanese Experience: Lessons for Malaysia*, Penang, Malaysia, 1983.
22 Chua Wee Meng, 'The Future of the Japanese Industrial Structure and Its Bearing on Japanese Trade and Investment in Southeast Asia' in *The Future Pattern of Japanese Economic and Political Relations with Southeast Asia*, Institute of Southeast Asian Studies, Current Issues, Seminar Series No. 5, Singapore, September 1975, p. 45.
23 Linda Goley, 'Investment Paradise: Japanese Capital in Malaysia', in Jomo K.S. (ed.), (1983) *The Sun Also Sets: Lessons in 'Looking East'*, INSAN, Kuala Lumpur, p. 235.
24. Ibid., p. 236.
25 M.S. Denker, 'Internationalization of the Malaysian Economy: Role of Japan', PhD thesis, University of Malaya, 1990, Chs 12, 13.
26 Fong Chan Onn, *Technological Leap: Malaysian Industry in Transition*, Singapore: Oxford University Press, 1986, p. 57.
27 K. Yoshihara, *Japanese Investment in Southeast Asia*, Honolulu: University Press of Hawaii, 1978, p. 82.
28 G. Gregory, 'Japanese Joint-Ventures Abroad: Source of Tension', in Jomo K.S. (ed.), (1983) *The Sun Also Sets: Lessons in 'Looking East'*, INSAN, Kuala Lumpur, p. 242.
29 Ibid., p. 246.
30 See my previous research, 'External and Domestic Sources of Malaysia's Foreign Policy Towards Japan', M.Soc.Sc. thesis, Universiti Sains Malaysia, 1985, pp. 134–36.
31 Ibid.
32 See Chee and Lee, op. cit., p. 11.
33 E. Sciberras, *Multinational Electronic Companies and National Economic Policies*, Greenwich, Connecticut: JAI Press, 1977.

3

JAPANESE MANUFACTURING INVESTMENT IN MALAYSIA

Makoto Anazawa

This chapter will discuss direct investment by Japanese companies (JDI) in the manufacturing sector and the performance of Japanese companies in Malaysia. In examining recent JDI, the yen appreciation has been an important turning point, especially for the global management strategies of Japanese companies. It seems that before 1986, fewer Japanese multi-national corporations (MNCs) had clear global strategies. However, after 1986, they were forced to reconsider their strategies to adjust to the drastically changing global economic environments. More significantly, this saw the international appearance of the new investors, mainly small and medium scale companies (SMCs),[1] which had seldom invested abroad previously.

JAPANESE MANUFACTURING COMPANIES IN MALAYSIA

Features of Japanese companies

Japanese direct investment in the Malaysian manufacturing sector can be traced back to the period immediately after independence in 1957. Through joint ventures with Malaysian partners, some Japanese companies invested in the food, textiles and pottery industries in the late 1950s. Since then, JDI has grown, albeit with fluctuations. The enormous inflow of JDI after the appreciation of the yen, dubbed the 'Third Wave',[2] has been quite impressive, replacing those of other major investors such as the UK, Singapore and the USA, making Japan the largest investing country in Malaysia.[3]

Table 3.1 breaks down Japanese companies in operation in Malaysia in 1991. Though the table only considers 235 manufacturing companies, while the Japan External Trade Organization (JETRO) recognized 431 Japanese manufacturing companies in Malaysia by the end of 1991. According to the table, the manufacturing sector accounted for 69.5 per cent of the companies, 91.2 per cent of the paid-up capital, 75.0 per cent of sales, and 82.8 per cent of current profit, respectively. Within the manufacturing

Table 3.1 Japanese companies in Malaysia, 1991

Manufacturing industry	No.	Paid-up capital (mil. ¥)	Sales (mil. ¥)	Current profit (mil. ¥)
Food	5	1,118	9,500	−10
Textiles	11	9,497	57,672	6,156
Wood	6	1,742	1,717	297
Chemicals	30	39,291	26,960	785
Iron/steel	9	9,426	35,872	2,699
Non-ferrous	10	7,726	13,564	−63
Machinery	8	2,701	7,701	361
Electrical	89	116,873	409,062	16,804
Transport	18	18,924	195,230	18,686
Precision	8	6,333	24,653	−125
Petroleum	1	183	137	−24
Others	40	17,545	43,957	3,100
Sub-Total	235	231,359	826,025	48,666
Agriculture	2	60	2,356	260
Mining	0	0	0	0
Construction	28	1,214	40,255	322
Commerce	49	4,365	218,732	8,262
Service	12	11,239	10,304	1,272
Others	12	5,413	3,968	−17
Total	338	253,650	1,101,640	58,765

Source: Ministry of International Trade and Industry (Japan), *Dai 21 Kai Wagakuni Kigyou no Kaigai Jigyou Katsudou* (The 21st Overseas Business Activities (The 21st Survey of the Overseas Business Activities by Japanese Companies)), Government Publication, Tokyo, 1992.
One Malaysian ringgit (RM) was equivalent to 52.32 yen (¥).

sector, the electrical/electronics industry took the lion's share, accounting for 37.9 per cent of companies, 50.5 per cent of paid-up capital, 49.5 per cent of sales, and 34.5 per cent of current profit, respectively. Despite their small share of the number of companies (7.7 per cent) and paid-up capital (8.2 per cent), the transport equipment industry accounted for 23.6 per cent of sales and 38.4 per cent of current profit, respectively. Among the other industries, chemicals were important in terms of number and paid-up capital, while textiles contributed significantly to sales and current profits, despite its limited number and paid-up capital. Outside the manufacturing sector, commerce has the largest number of companies, sales, and current profits, respectively, while services had the largest share of paid-up capital.

Motivations and favourable environment

A company survey published by JETRO in 1992 revealed the motivations of Japanese companies investing in Malaysia.[4] It recognized 431 Japanese

Table 3.2 Japanese manufacturing companies by industry and year of establishment

Industry Year	A	B	C	D	E	F	G	H	I	J	K	L	M	Total
1950s–1960s	1	1	1	2		1	2			2				10
1970–1974		6	1	4		1	1	3		9		2	6	33
1975–1979	1									1	1		5	8
1980–1984			2	1			1	4		5	5		5	18
1985	1							1		1			1	4
1986						1			1	1				3
1987			2	1		1	1	1		10			5	21
1988		3	1	4		3	2	3		13		3	7	39
1989			2	2	1	1	4	6	1	19		1	7	44
1990				1			1	3		7		1	1	14
1991				1							1			2
Total	3	10	9	16	1	8	12	21	2	68	7	7	38	202

Source: JETRO KL Center, *NIES, ASEAN ni okeru Nikkei Seizougyou Kigyou no Katudou Joukyou-Malaysia* (The Activities of Japanese Manufacturing Companies in NIES, ASEAN–Malaysia), JETRO, Kuala Lumpur, 1992.

A: Food, agriculture, and marine products processing;
B: Textile and textile products;
C: Wood, pulp, and paper;
D: Chemical and pharmaceutical products;
E: Petroleum products;
F: Ceramics;
G: Iron, steel, and non-ferrous metals;
H: Metal products;
I: General machinery;
J: Electronic and electrical equipment;
K: Transport equipment;
L: Precision equipment;
M: Other manufacturing sectors.

manufacturing companies in operation at the end of 1991, of which 202 companies responded to JETRO's questionnaires. Table 3.2 shows the breakdown of the companies by industry and year of establishment. The electrical/electronics industry was predominant with 68 companies (33.7 per cent), followed by metal with 21 companies (10.4 per cent), chemicals with 16 companies (7.9 per cent), iron/non-ferrous metal with 12 companies (5.9 per cent). It also revealed the concentration of these establishments in the period 1987–90.

Of the 202 respondents, 67 companies (33.2 per cent) stated that local market share was the major motivation, followed by the supply requirements of Japanese assemblers for 47 companies (23.3 per cent), exports to third countries involving 41 companies (20.3 per cent) and availability of appropriate labour for 38 companies (18.8 per cent) (see Table 3.3).

The local market includes supply to Japanese manufactures as well as to

Table 3.3 Motivations for Japanese manufacturing companies to invest in Malaysia

Industry	A	B	C	D	E	F	G	H	I	J	K	L	M	Total
Motivations														
Keeping local market share	1	1	1	10		4	5	9		23	3		10	67
Requirement by Japanese assemblers			1	4			6	7		13	1	1	14	47
Export to third countries		5		2		1	1	6		20		2	4	41
Acquisition of labour force		3	4		1	2	1	3		16		2	6	38
Secure materials	2	1	7	2		1		1		3		1	5	23
Counter-measures to the strong yen						2		2	2	11	1		4	22
Avoid import restrictions		2								4	2		2	10
Secure technology and information	1									1			1	3

Source: Same as Table 3.2.
Some companies cited several motivations.
Industries are the same as for Table 3.2.

Malaysian manufacturers and wholesalers, with supply to the former being more important. The local market consideration does not necessarily mean supplying the domestic market as import-substituting companies, which was generally the case in the 1960s and 1970s. Twenty-three electrical/electronics companies, ten chemical companies and nine metal companies cited this as their motivation.

Supply requests by Japanese assemblers is a relatively new phenomenon since the yen appreciation, even though limited cases have been observed in the past. Relocation of production facilities by assemblers, mostly MNCs, has encouraged their subcontractors also to invest in Malaysia. Assemblers thus increased their local content besides reducing costs instead of using more expensive materials imported from Japan. For subcontractors, this has made up for decreasing domestic and export demand in Japan. Thirteen electrical/electronics companies, seven metal companies and six iron/non-ferrous metal companies cited this.

Exports to third countries have been the predominant consideration for typically export-oriented industries such as electrical/electronics (20 companies) and textiles (five companies). However, companies in the metal industry, which have generally been recognized in the past as import-substituting, have switched to being export-oriented.

The availability of an appropriate labour supply was most important for the electrical/electronics industry, reflecting the labour-intensive nature of the industry, with sixteen of them citing this as their reason for investing in Malaysia.

Different motivations by industry reflect the industry-specific features of JDI. Under the strong yen, the electrical/electronics industry has witnessed the relocation of companies to establish export platforms, with their subcontractors also relocating to Malaysia. In other industries, such as iron and metal, one notes a similar trend with the relocation of principals, as well as their subcontractors or affiliated companies to Malaysia.

Other attractive factors offered by Malaysia to Japanese investors have been political and social stability for 146 companies (72.3 per cent), attractive investment incentives for 130 companies (64.4 per cent), low labour costs involving 106 companies (52.5 per cent), decent infrastructure for 100 companies (49.5 per cent) and the quality of the labour force involving 83 companies (41.1 per cent). One cannot find any industry-specific pattern to the conditions deemed necessary for Japanese companies to invest in Malaysia.

Japanese direct investment in historical perspective

Based on data from Japan's Ministry of Finance, the total number of JDI projects in Malaysia was 1,645, involving US$4,111.2 million at the end of 1991. Of these investments, the manufacturing sector accounted for 999 projects (60.7 per cent) and US$3,015.5 million (73.3 per cent), respectively. As mentioned before, JDI in Malaysia has been concentrated in the manufacturing sector since the 1960s. Table 3.4 shows us the changing patterns of JDI in the manufacturing sector. The historical changes in JDI should, however, be understood in the context of Malaysian industrial development policies and Japanese company strategies.

The 1960s

From the late 1950s into the 1960s, Malaysia's import-substituting industrialization strategy saw Japanese companies primarily interested in expanding and protecting their market shares. Thus, they established subsidiaries supplying the domestic market, protected by tariffs. This was true of the electrical/electronics industry then, with the establishment of subsidiaries for Matsushita, Sanyo, and Sharp. The other important industry in the 1960s was resource-based wood manufacturing. For Japanese companies, then subject to strict foreign exchange controls by the Ministry of Finance, JDI was generally discouraged until the end of the 1960s.

79

Table 3.4 Japanese direct investment in Malaysia's manufacturing sector
(US$ thousands)

Year Industry	1972 No.	Amount	1976 No.	Amount	1979 No.	Amount	1980 No.	Amount
Food	7	4,663	17	12,000	21	16,708	2	764
Textiles	6	1,928	34	70,000	36	98,151	2	6,707
Wood	24	15,222	51	34,000	57	43,123	5	1,815
Chemicals	15	2,350	31	12,000	36	58,114	5	109,366
Iron/metal	5	8,661	23	24,000	25	27,674	6	2,035
Machinery	2	246	7	3,000	9	8,799	1	60
Electrical	16	10,612	41	31,000	51	43,571	4	8,279
Transport	3	682	7	4,000	8	7,010	1	596
Others	17	6,407	36	15,000	53	20,525	10	2,560
Total	95	50,771	247	205,000	296	323,690	36	132,188

1981 No.	Amount	1982 No.	Amount	1983 No.	Amount	1984 No.	Amount	1985 No.	Amount
1	1,830	1	218	7	2,630			4	678
3	2,272	6	13,199		16,362			2	555
2	503	4	488	1	1,279	2	4,383		
3	799	1	8,456	1	1,646		1,296	4	3,420
7	2,757	7	26,824	3	6,422	4	72,163	2	9,514
3	442	1	87	5	689	1	699	2	1,822
8	6,072	4	8,049	7	8,253	17	19,949	7	2,259
	1,803	1	765	9	73,381	4	5,499	4	3,587
5	1,623	6	1,188	4	628	6	10,082	7	10,943
32	18,101	31	59,276	37	111,293	34	114,071	32	32,790

1986 No.	Amount	1987 No.	Amount	1988 No.	Amount	1989 No.	Amount	1990 No.	Amount
7	10,098	3	3,418	2	1,471			2	2,663
	89			4	5,785	3	1,335	1	3,401
1	51	4	1,071	7	7,331	7	7,562	15	22,899
4	5,432	3	5,190	8	20,504	10	49,468	6	96,057
3	6,401	4	10,755	13	22,990	17	45,389	14	51,651
3	2,259	1	179	7	36,949	10	25,935	7	80,784
18	30,332	13	26,217	29	229,089	40	272,672	39	261,039
5	2,618	3	84,577	2	4,037	3	2,865	5	10,683
5	7,284	11	16,385	19	18,042	21	65,357	30	53,076
46	64,568	42	147,796	91	346,202	111	470,586	119	582,257

Continued

Table 3.4 (continued)

1991		Total	
No.	Amount	No.	Amount
1	7,240	51	47,723
2	7,770	59	155,631
8	15,579	113	106,092
8	41,323	89	401,078
11	94,126	116	378,708
4	26,061	54	184,772
27	283,806	264	1,199,603
1	26,876	46	224,304
30	109,936	207	317,634
92	612,720	999	3,015,549

Sources: Ministry of Finance (Japan), *Okura-shou Kokusai Kin-yu Kyoku Nempou* (Annual Report of Department of International Finance), Kin-yu Zaisei Jijou Kenkyu-kai (Committee for Monetary and Public Finance), Tokyo, various issues.
Ministry of Finance (Japan), *Zaisei Kin-yu Toukei Geppou* (Monthly Statistical Report on Public Finance), Ministry of Finance, Tokyo, various issues.
The figures for 1976 were expressed in million US$.

The 1970s

With the changing industrialization strategy at the end of the 1960s, export-oriented companies began to invest from the early 1970s to establish export platforms to take advantage of relatively cheap labour. The introduction of Free Trade Zones (FTZs) coupled with the special incentive for the electronics industry which was later extended to other labour-intensive industries created favourable conditions for export-oriented companies. On the other hand, owing to rising wage levels in Japan, some labour-intensive industries began to lose their comparative advantage and relocated their factories. In the first half of the 1970s, export-oriented electrical/ electronics companies established themselves in the FTZs, mainly in Selangor.[5] In the mid-1970s, investment in the textiles industry ballooned, with the establishment of the Pen (Toray) group and Kanebo in the Prai Free Trade Zone in Penang, as well as Toyobo in Perak and Kedah. However, the wood industry was still the largest in terms of the projects and the second largest in terms of the amount of investment after the textiles industry. The electrical/electronics industry showed steady growth in terms of both number of projects and amount of investments. At the end of the 1970s, the textiles industry still led in terms of the amount of investment, followed by electrical/electronics and wood. In terms of number of projects, the wood industry had the most, followed by electrical/electronics, textiles and chemicals. Thus, JDI in the 1970s had a

81

mixture of investment in both import-substituting and export-oriented companies, reflecting the dualistic industrialization strategies of the decade.

The early 1980s

The 1980s started with huge investments in the chemical industry (urea fertilizer plant under the ASEAN cooperative project) in 1980, which made it the largest in investment terms in the first half of the decade. With the national car project (JV with HICOM (Heavy Industries Corporation of Malaysia), Mitsubishi Motors Corporation, and Mitsubishi Corporation) in 1983, investment in the transport equipment industry soared. Japanese direct investment in the iron/metal industry jumped with the participation of Nippon Steel in the Perwaja steel mill in Trengganu in 1984. Hence, while other manufacturing investments declined in Malaysia, as in the rest of Southeast Asia in the early 1980s, JDI concentrated in some specific heavy industries involving joint ventures between Malaysian public corporations and Japanese large MNCs.

Post-endaka

The yen appreciation from late 1985 caused tremendous growth and drastic changes in JDI, with new JDI concentrated in the electrical/electronics industry, contributing to rapid growth of JDI in Malaysia's manufacturing sector until the early 1990s. As shown in Table 3.4, from 1986 to 1991, US$ 2,224.1 million was invested in 501 projects, accounting for 73.8 per cent of total JDI in Malaysia and 50.2 per cent of total number of JDI projects in the manufacturing sector. In the electrical/electronics industry JDI valued at US$1,103.2 million in 166 projects contributed to 49.6 per cent of investment and 33.1 per cent of projects in this period, respectively. This new JDI increased both the number of projects and amount of investment as many Japanese SMCs emerged as new investors together with bigger Japanese MNCs. In the past, growth in the amount of investment was rarely accompanied by a disproportionately high increase in the number of projects. Clearly, JDI after the *endaka* has been led by the electrical/ electronics industry; MNCs in the industry established new export platforms or enlarged existing export bases. This not only stimulated other MNCs, but also SMCs, mostly subcontractors, to invest in Malaysia, creating a 'bandwagon effect'. The Promotion of Investments Act and deregulation of foreign equity ownership guidelines, coupled with the strong yen, encouraged them to invest in Malaysia.[6]

This historical review has shown that JDI developed in response to changing industrialization policies in Malaysia. The Government indicated preferred industries to foreign investors with fiscal incentives under the

Pioneer Industries Ordinance (1958), the Investment Incentives Act (1968), and the Promotion of Investments Act (1986). These were clear signs to Japanese companies identifying industries in which to invest. In addition to these pull factors, push factors, such as the changing economic environment in Japan, e.g. increasing wage levels and the yen appreciation and changing company strategies, encouraged JDI. As a host country eager to attract foreign direct investment (FDI), and recognizing the strategies of MNCs and smaller investors, the Malaysian authorities provided an attractive institutional and physical environment for JDI and Japanese companies were encouraged to establish subsidiaries in Malaysia.

Equity share strategies

The equity shares of Japanese manufacturing companies changed considerably after the yen appreciation, reflecting the Malaysian Government's new guidelines as well as company interests and strategies. Generally, Japanese companies had previously preferred joint ventures in Asia.[7] In the import-substitution stage in the 1950s and 1960s, Japanese companies invested in joint ventures, partly because of shortcomings of their financial resources under the foreign exchange restrictions in Japan and partly to make use of the local marketing networks of their partners. In some cases, *sogoshoshas* were also involved as investment partners, making a peculiar feature of JDI.[8] From the 1970s, import-substituting companies were generally not permitted to establish wholly foreign-owned subsidiaries. They invested mainly to expand and protect their market shares behind tariffs. Those companies which had been exporting their products had direct business contacts with local wholesalers or indirect contacts through *sogoshoshas*. In the former cases, they established joint ventures with local partners, and in the latter cases, with *sogoshoshas* and local partners. It was beneficial and advantageous for Japanese import-substituting companies to have Malaysian partners, in order to utilize their business contacts, decrease financial exposure, and reduce management risk.

Almost all Japanese import-substituting companies in Malaysia have been joint ventures, while Japanese export-oriented companies prefer to establish wholly Japanese-owned subsidiaries to run them based on global strategic consideration without interference by local partners. In Singapore, for instance, because of the very small domestic market, most of the Japanese companies in Singapore have been export-oriented. Thanks to almost no restrictions on foreign equity ownership in the manufacturing sector in Singapore, most of the Japanese manufacturing companies have been wholly Japanese-owned subsidiaries, showing evidence of the preference of export-oriented Japanese companies for establishing wholly owned subsidiaries.

Table 3.5 shows that of the 134 companies in Malaysia as of 1985, 74 companies, or 55.2 per cent, chose to be minor shareholders, with most being import-substituting companies. On the other hand, 31 companies, or 23.1 per cent, were wholly Japanese-owned, most of which were export-oriented and located in FTZs or set up as companies which obtained Licensed Manufacturing Warehouse (LMW) status.

For Japanese companies in Malaysia as a whole, joint ventures were more common before the yen appreciation, compared with the USA and European subsidiary companies which generally chose to establish wholly foreign-owned companies.[9] Next to Singapore in the ASEAN region, there are more wholly Japanese-owned subsidiaries in Malaysia, mainly because of the favourable attitude of the authorities towards export-oriented companies, even before 1986. However, especially after the yen appreciation and the relaxation of foreign equity ownership guidelines under the Promotion of Investments Act, more Japanese companies preferred to establish wholly Japanese-owned subsidiaries. Moreover, under the Promotion of Investments Act, those exporting indirectly by supplying export-oriented companies in FTZs and LMWs, were also recognized as export-oriented companies, making it easier to establish wholly Japanese-owned subsidiaries. As seen in Table 3.5, of 229 companies investing after 1986, 143 companies, or 62.4 per cent of the total, were wholly Japanese-owned. The change after 1986 is remarkable. It can be inferred that most recent investors have been export-oriented companies. With such favourable conditions, export-oriented companies preferred to establish wholly Japanese-owned subsidiaries. The strong yen as well as accumulated

Table 3.5 Japanese equity in Malaysian manufacturing sector

Equity share	Companies established up to 1985	Companies established from 1986	Total
0–24%	14	11	25
	(10.4%)	(4.8%)	(6.9%)
25–49%	60	30	90
	(44.8%)	(13.1%)	(24.6%)
50%	3	9	12
	(2.2%)	(3.9%)	(3.3%)
51–74%	10	24	34
	(7.5%)	(10.5%)	(9.8%)
75–99%	16	12	28
	(11.9%)	(5.2%)	(7.6%)
100%	31	143	174
	(23.1%)	(62.4%)	(47.8%)
Total	134	229	363
	(100.0%)	(100.0%)	(100.0%)

Source: Calculated from Toyo Keizai Shinpo-sha, *Kaigai Shinshutu Kigyou Souran 1993* (List of Japanese Companies in Operation Abroad in 1993), Toyo Keizai Shinpo-sha, Tokyo, 1993.

information and experience in managing foreign subsidiaries also encouraged them to have wholly Japanese-owned subsidiaries.

After the yen appreciation, two specific changes with regard to equity strategies emerged. First, more than one Japanese company has combined with or without *sogoshosha* involvement, to establish wholly Japanese-owned companies. Such cases were also found in the past, but they are now less exceptional. It seems that some Japanese SMCs which still do not have enough management or other resources to run businesses abroad prefer Japanese to Malaysian partners. Secondly, Japanese subsidiaries in Singapore, Hong Kong, and Taiwan have also invested in Malaysia as part of their regional strategies. Subsidiaries in Singapore have, of course, been most prominent in this regard because of their geographical proximity to Malaysia and their closer business networks with subsidiaries in Malaysia.

With regard to the equity strategies of Japanese companies, it should be pointed out that only 18 Japanese companies have been listed on the Kuala Lumpur Stock Exchange (KLSE), even though Prime Minister Mahathir has urged them to go for a listing on the KLSE. Japanese companies' reluctance to list is reportedly due to their fear of losing control.[10]

Markets and procurement

Research conducted by the Japanese Chamber of Trade and Industry, Malaysia (JACTIM) and JETRO in 1990[11] and the Japan Embassy/JETRO in 1987[12] shows market and procurement data for Japanese manufacturing companies in Malaysia. In 1990 JACTIM/JETRO recognized 283 such companies in operation, of which 119 companies responded to questionnaires about their markets and sources of production materials.

In 1989, 39.0 per cent of their products were sold in the domestic market and 61.0 per cent exported. The largest industry selling products on the domestic market was transport equipment, followed by electrical/ electronics, and iron/non-ferrous metals. On the other hand, the largest exporter was electrical/electronics, contributing nearly 80 per cent of total exports by Japanese companies, followed by textiles and iron/non-ferrous metals. Before that, the proportion of exports by Japanese companies had risen rapidly after the yen appreciation from 45.4 per cent in 1985 to 50.7 per cent in 1986, 59.3 per cent in 1987 and 61.7 per cent in 1988. The main foreign markets in 1989 were Japan (26.7 per cent), the USA (22.9 per cent), and Singapore (15.4 per cent). Compared with the corresponding figures for 1986, it was observed that exports to Japan and the USA increased most.

Since this survey, no data have been published regarding the amount or percentage of exports or production for the domestic market. However, the 1992 JETRO survey[13] found that of 197 company respondents, 78 exported 100 per cent of their products, and 47 exported more than 80 per cent of their products, indicating that more than 60 per cent of the total were quite export-oriented. Thirty-eight companies exported less than half their products and 21 did not export directly, but supplied export-oriented companies. Only five companies replied that they did not export at all.

Among export markets, 56 companies responded that Japan was the largest market, 50 identified ASEAN as the largest, and for 24 companies, the USA was the largest market. The second largest market for 29 companies were the Asian NIEs; for 27 companies, it was the EC; for 25 companies, it was ASEAN; while for 24 companies, it was Japan.

In 1989, 49.3 per cent of production materials were imported from Japan, and of these, 36 per cent were imported from the parent companies in Japan. Procurement from the domestic market was only 26.6 per cent, of which procurement from Malaysian companies came to 13.4 per cent, while procurement from Japanese companies in Malaysia came to 8.1 per cent. Imports from third countries came to 24.1 per cent, of which more than half originated from Singapore (see Table 3.6). Since this data is from 1989, i.e. after the *endaka*, one can infer that Japanese companies purchase more from local markets and import more from third countries to avoid the high costs of importation from Japan, as discussed later.

The 1992 JETRO survey[14] also revealed that roughly 70 per cent of the companies still depended mostly on imported materials. The remaining 30 per cent depended mostly on locally supplied materials. The motivations analysed previously suggest that an increasing number of Japanese companies have invested in Malaysia at the request of, or to retain supply contracts with, assemblers.

The 1992 JACTIM survey[15] of 26 major assemblers of electrical and transport equipment found evidence of increasing local content. For seven

Table 3.6 Procurement by Japanese companies in Malaysia, 1989 (million ringgit)

Imports from Japan	2,864	(49.3%)
(from parent companies)	(2,094)	
Imports from third countries	1,399	(24.1%)
(from Singapore)	(714)	
(from Taiwan)	(111)	
From within Malaysia	1,546	(26.6%)
(from Japanese companies)	(470)	
(from local companies)	(776)	
Total	5,809	(100.0%)

Source: Teranishi Takehide, 'Nikkei Seizogyo no Doukou ni Tuite (The Trend of Japanese Manufacturing Companies)', *JACTIM Kaihou* (JACTIM Bulletin) No. 34, July, Kuala Lumpur, 1990.

companies, the local content ratios exceeded 50 per cent, with two companies even exceeding 70 per cent. Six companies responded that their local content ratios fell in the range from 40 to 50 per cent. Half purchased materials from domestic sources, both Malaysian and Japanese companies. The factors cited as discouraging procurement from domestic sources were low quality (47.3 per cent), inefficient delivery (20.0 per cent), and high prices (10.0 per cent). Next to quality, delivery is becoming more important than prices for assemblers.

Research by the author in 1989 revealed changes in Japanese companies which started operating before 1985, caused by the yen appreciation. Table 3.7 breaks down the companies researched by industry, while Table 3.8 sums up their activities. In spite of the limited sample size, it gives us some indications for analysing the impact of the *endaka*. Among the 19 import-substituting companies, six had increased exports to Japan, four had increased exports to third countries, while for eight others, the situation remained unchanged. Of 14 export-oriented companies, eight had increased exports to third countries, while four had increased exports to Japan.

Several import-substituting companies became export-oriented with the stronger yen, as reinforced by the 1992 JETRO survey. From the viewpoint of global logistics strategies, some import-substituting companies have changed their functions. Instead of establishing new export platforms, some Japanese companies chose to make use of existing plants in Malaysia. These plants were originally domestic market oriented, and their production facilities may not be large enough to either enjoy scale economies or be completely export-oriented. Hence, for the time being, it seems that they will be marginal exporters. With decreasing domestic demand due to the recession of 1985–86, some were forced to develop export markets for survival.

With regard to the procurement of materials for production, both

Table 3.7 Surveyed companies by industry

Industry	EO	IS	Total
Electrical/electronics	8	4	12
Chemicals	2	4	6
Transport equipment	0	4	4
Precision	3	0	3
Textiles	1	2	3
Food	0	2	2
Others	0	3	3
Total	14	19	33

Source: Author's survey.
EO: export-oriented companies; IS: import-substituting companies.

Table 3.8 Market and procurement changes

Market	EO	IS	Total
Increased exports to Japan	4	6	10
Increased exports to third countries	8	4	12
Increased supply to domestic markets	2	3	5
No changes	1	8	9
Subtotal	15	21	36

Procurement	EO	IS	Total
Purchased more from local companies	4	8	12
Purchased more from Japanese companies in Malaysia	6	3	9
Decreased imports from Japan	5	6	11
Increased imports from third countries	7	10	17
No changes	3	5	8
Subtotal	25	32	57

Source: Author's survey.
EO: export-oriented companies; IS: import-substituting companies. Some companies had multiple responses.

import-substituting and export-oriented companies have increased imports from third countries and decreased imports from Japan. Purchases from local sources differ depending on the nature of the company. Import-substituting companies increased purchases from Malaysian companies, while export-oriented companies purchased more from Japanese subsidiaries in Malaysia, partly because import-substituting companies generally had long-standing transactions as well as wider and deeper business networks with Malaysian companies. Having Malaysian partners may have contributed to developing such business networks. In addition, most local materials suppliers were less competitive. Developed initially to supply the protected domestic market, such materials are not necessarily competitive internationally, in terms of quality, price, and so on.[16]

Export-oriented companies depended heavily on materials imported from Japan enjoying duty-free importation for FTZ and LMW companies. With these privileges, they sometimes preferred to import from third countries, particularly Singapore. Also, their products always faced tough competition in world markets; thus, production materials had to be competitive in terms of both quality and price. Narrow manufacturing bases and inadequancies caused by protection for import-substitution made it difficult for many local companies to supply products to export-oriented companies.[17]

Geographical distribution

The 360 Japanese manufacturing companies in Malaysia were distributed as follows: 134 in Selangor, 62 in Penang, 60 in Johore and 29 in Kuala Lumpur. Since Kuala Lumpur was part of and is surrounded by the state of Selangor, altogether 45.3 per cent of these companies were in operation in this central region.[18] The remaining companies were also to be found in the more developed states such as Perak (18 companies), Kedah (17 companies), Melaka (13 companies), and Negri Sembilan (14 companies) on the West Coast of Peninsular Malaysia. The Government used to encourage companies to locate in less developed areas by providing fiscal incentives under the Investment Incentives Act, as this was thought to help correct income differentials among states. However, the Japanese companies have found it more advantageous to locate in the more developed states where commercial and physical infrastructure is better. Most of their customers and local suppliers can also be found in these areas, as well as other foreign and large Malaysian companies.

A new phenomenon has been observed with recent JDI, which may be considered to be a 'spillover effect' caused by geographical concentration. The rapid growth of manufacturing investments has made it harder to find well-located factory sites, especially in big cities and their vicinity, with Japanese investors competing with an increasing number of other foreign companies e.g. from Taiwan and Singapore, as well as local companies. Most of the better located industrial estates and FTZs are fully occupied and newcomers have to go elsewhere.[19]

For instance, in the Klang Valley, the early developed industrial estates in Petaling Jaya and Shah Alam have been fully occupied for some years. Companies intending to locate near the capital city of Kuala Lumpur have to set up their factories in less conveniently located industrial estates, Batu Caves, Bangi and Kelang, though such areas offer more relatively cheap labour. The situation is similar in Penang, where the Bayan Lepas and Prai industrial estates and FTZs are almost fully occupied, and new Japanese companies are to be found in neighbouring Kedah. In Johore, Johore Bahru and its vicinity and the Pasir Gudang area cannot provide enough industrial sites and/or labour, with Batu Pahat and other areas emerging as alternatives.

In the past, centripetal forces worked and well-supplied industrial estates and FTZs developed by state economic development corporations (SEDCs) enabled Japanese companies to locate in better factory sites in big cities and their vicinity. Rapid industrial development and FDI have caused centrifugal forces or spillover effects. More and more Japanese companies have begun to locate further from big cities and even in the less developed areas or states on the East Coast of Peninsular Malaysia and in Sabah and Sarawak to ensure availability of cheap labour.

Table 3.9 Problems encountered by Japanese companies in Malaysia

Industry	A	B	C	D	E	F	G	H	I	J	K	L	M	Total
Problems														
Personnel	2	9	4	9	1	4	8	7	2	45	4	7	26	128
Rising wages	2	5	2	8	1	3	7	9	2	43	1	2	21	106
Financing	1	3	2	4	1	3	3	8		24		2	15	66
Quality control	1	2	3	2	1	1	6	10	1	22	1	1	13	64
Infrastructure		3	3	4	1	1	4	5		27	1	1	9	59
Visas/work permits	1	1	1	3		2	2	5	2	28		1	8	54
Competition with other companies	2			6			6	6		20	2		11	53

Source: Same as Table 3.2.
Industries are the same as for Table 3.2.

Problems encountered

Problems faced by Japanese companies were also revealed by the 1992 JETRO survey (see Table 3.9). Of 202 companies, 128 (63.4 per cent) cited personnel problems, including difficulties in recruitment, job hopping, and trade unions. Of these, the most serious was staff recruitment, both relatively cheap unskilled labour as well as skilled and professional such as engineers, technicians and managers. A second problem is rising wages, mentioned by 106 companies (52.5 per cent). For labour-intensive industries such as electrical/electronics and textiles, shortfalls in labour supply and rising wages are serious problems to cope with.

Other major problems cited include financing (66 companies, or 32.7 per cent), quality control (64 companies, or 31.7 per cent), infrastructure (59 companies, or 29.2 per cent), visas or work permits (54 companies, or 26.7 per cent) and competition with other manufacturers (53 companies, or 26.2 per cent). Compared with the previous survey in 1991, financing and infrastructure problems appear to have become more serious, reflecting higher interest rates, domestic borrowing restrictions, electricity supply problems and shortage of telecommunication lines.

NEW JAPANESE COMPANY NETWORKS[20]

Intra-company networks

The yen appreciation has also forced Japanese companies to drastically restructure their global management strategies. Changes have been observed in their logistics strategies, which in turn determine FDI patterns and intra-company networks. In Malaysia JDI should thus be understood in the context of Japanese companies' global, or at least regional, strategies in ASEAN. The economic policies of neighbouring countries, of course, also affect JDI in Malaysia. Particularly, the spillover effect from Singapore will be emphasized in this section by examining the interrelationship between the changing logistics strategies of Japanese companies and Singapore's economic strategies.

In the ASEAN region, Singapore has developed and retained an important position in the regional strategies of the Japanese companies due to its good infrastructure and efficient financial, commercial, and service sectors. Singapore, being the most developed country in the region, is the business centre in ASEAN, and its economic strategies cannot be ignored in investigating Japanese MNC strategies in the region. Its proximity to Malaysia has also influenced Malaysia's industrial policies and FDI in Malaysia. Singapore's new economic strategy since 1986 has, for instance, been embodied in the new fiscal incentives for Operational Headquarters (OHQs),[21] aiming to enhance its function as a regional headquarters (RHQs) for MNCs with subsidiaries in ASEAN. Being a small nation whose open economy and outward-looking economic policies depend greatly on MNCs, Singapore has been very sensitive to such company strategies

Before the *endaka*, only a limited number of large Japanese MNCs, mainly in the electrical/electronics industry, had their own intra-company networks and regional strategies in ASEAN or in Southeast Asia. The strong yen not only caused these MNCs to restructure their regional strategies,[22] but also forced other MNCs and even SMCs to develop regional strategies, especially for logistics and intra-company networks among subsidiaries. With the new company strategies, and Singapore's institutional development based on its new economic strategy, relocation of existing production facilities from Singapore has taken place. This relocation has promoted the restructuring of their subsidiaries in the region based on the comparative advantages of the countries, with JDI in Malaysia very much affected by such relocation.

The new logistics strategies were initially reflected by the relocation of their production facilities from Singapore to Johore. Reconstitution of these regional logistics strategies around Japanese subsidiaries in Singapore accelerated after 1986, coinciding with Singapore's strategy to relocate labour-intensive manufacturing, owing to high wage levels, and to stimulate high value-added manufacturing as well as financial, commercial, and service sectors. This strategy was subsequently reflected in the form of the 'Growth Triangle Plan'[23] between Johore, Singapore and Batam (Riau) in Indonesia, first announced by then Deputy Prime Minister Goh Chok Tong in December 1989.

After 1986, but prior to the announcement of the 'Growth Triangle Plan', many Japanese companies in Singapore had begun to relocate their production facilities in Johore. Some only relocated labour-intensive production processes while others relocated most of their production facilities. As Johore is geographically close to Singapore and still has a relatively cheap labour force and available factory sites, this was the preferred destination of Japanese MNCs in Singapore. Meanwhile, more capital or technology-intensive production processes were left in Singapore, where engineers and technicians were available, with offices for administration and support services. Such relocation has been favourable for both Japanese MNCs and Singapore. Japanese companies have reduced production costs, while Singapore has succeeded in displacing labour-intensive production processes while retaining higher value-added activity in Singapore.[24]

Of 72 Japanese manufacturing companies in Johore, at least 34 had affiliate subsidiaries in Singapore at the end of 1990, implying expanding intra-company regional networks. It has been pointed out that most Japanese companies in Johore have business relations, whether intra- or inter-company, with Japanese companies in Singapore.[25] Those which invest directly in Johore from Japan have also taken easy access to Singapore into consideration. They often establish Singapore offices while building factories in Johore. In some cases, Japanese subsidiaries in Singapore establish new subsidiaries in Johore. In other cases, they partner the Japanese parent companies. Being located near Singapore has been a great advantage for the state of Johore, and the recent rapid increase of FDI in Johore is largely due to this.[26]

In addition to the high wage levels and the limited supply of new factory sites in Singapore, the imposition of a 40 per cent ceiling on the number of foreign workers who may be employed by a company in October 1987, the increase in the foreign worker levy in 1988 and the appreciation of the Singapore dollar against the Malaysian ringgit have encouraged the relocation of factories from Singapore.[27] Deregulation favouring export-oriented companies in Malaysia has, undoubtedly, also reinforced this trend.[28]

As companies relocating in Johore began to face labour shortages, especially of young female production operators, Singapore announced the 'Growth Triangle Plan', ostensibly promoting regional cooperation among three ASEAN members involving comparative advantage based on different factor endowments. It seems that this plan emerged in response to the labour shortage in Johore to provide new alternatives for companies planning to relocate their factories in Singapore or to reconstruct their logistics strategies in ASEAN from the city-state. For instance, Sumitomo Electronics was the first to make use of the 'Growth Triangle Plan' effectively, with factories in both Johore and Batam. The subsidiary in Singapore imports materials for production from Japan, which are then distributed to the factories in Johore and Batam; After processing, they are sent back to Singapore for re-export to Japan.[29]

The 'Growth Triangle Plan', however, has also created new competition to attract FDI within the region. The development of Batam island and industrial estates such as Batamindo Industrial Park[30] has attracted new investment which might otherwise have gone to Malaysia. Likewise, competition among ASEAN countries to attract FDI is still growing. The new international division of labour, or specialization, is taking place in ASEAN and the East Asian region. Japanese companies now have more alternative destinations for investment besides Malaysia, which is losing its earlier comparative advantage in labour-intensive industries.

New inter-company networks[31]

In this section I investigate inter-company networks following the preceding analysis of Japanese MNC regional strategies and intra-company networks. The establishment of inter-company networks in Malaysia has been promoted by the rapid growth of JDI in the electrical/electronics and other industries after the *endaka*.

Inter-company networks among Japanese companies

More detailed analysis of the process of making inroads into Malaysia has revealed that soon after the yen appreciation, existing Japanese companies increased their investments to enhance their production facilities.[32] Subsequently, many Japanese MNCs in the electrical/electronics industry have established new export platforms, mainly located in FTZs or with LMW status. They have been forced to purchase less from Japan to reduce material costs. Multinational corporations' measures in response to the high yen have company specific aspects. Some expanded in-plant production of parts in Malaysia, while others established subsidiaries supplying parts and components. In addition, their supporting industries rushed to Malaysia, as part of the 'Third Wave' discussed earlier.

The Japanese electrical/electronics industry is one of the most competitive internationally along with the transport equipment industry, both of which have been predominant in Malaysia's manufacturing sector. The specific features of these industries can be summarized as follows: (a) under the umbrellas of a few large assembling MNCs, there exist many subcontractors supplying parts and components; (b) these subcontractors also belong to pyramidal hierarchies; (c) there is tough competition among subcontractors; (d) there is both cooperation and competition between MNCs and subcontractors.[33] It has been argued that subcontractors in Japan have reduced costs, enhanced flexiblility, e.g. in response to fluctuations in demand, and made best use of their specialized know-how, with the last factor more emphasized recently.[34]

Subcontracting or inter-company networks are not, of course, limited to the electrical/electronics and/or transport equipment industries. Those companies in the other industries, such as plastics, metal and so on, can also be subcontractors of MNCs in the electrical/electronics and transport equipment industries. Other developed country MNCs generally prefer in-plant production of parts and components to subcontracting and their suppliers are rarely organized. The rapid and massive relocation of Japanese electrical/electronics MNCs into Malaysia has encouraged their subcontractors to invest in Malaysia, reflecting the strong backward linkages caused by them. The transport equipment industry has also encouraged their subcontractors to invest in Malaysia.

Had they remained in Japan, subcontractors would have faced decreases in demand since exports from Japan have been encountering growing difficulties; thus, they have been forced to follow their principals. Furthermore, competition among subcontractors has been encouraged by their principals to maintain low prices and raise quality. Hence, several subcontractors supply the same parts or components to the same principal. Generally, they are afraid of losing business opportunities by not following the behests of their principals. The just-in-time (JIT) system employed by principals has forced subcontractors to follow them. The system works effectively only if subcontractors can supply their products and change technical specifications quickly in response to their principals' requests. To cut down inventory, it is important for subcontractors to be located near their principals.

Institutional developments in Malaysia, such as the relaxation of guidelines on foreign equity in 1986, have helped encourage investments by these subcontractors, mostly SMCs.[35] These SMCs running businesses abroad with limited management resources and experience prefer not to have local partners as most of their customers are Japanese companies in Malaysia and neighbouring countries, particularly Singapore. Instead, some prefer to invest with Japanese partners, which may be *sogoshoshas* or other manufacturers.[36] This is one way to reduce each SMC's risks and to compensate for management resource shortages. These SMCs often need assistance by MNCs, *sogoshoshas*, and public authorities, like JETRO, to invest in Malaysia. Sometimes MNCs have urged Japanese subcontractors to follow them to Malaysia, promising a minimum volume of transactions. *Sogoshoshas* have assisted the SMCs through financing and other services and by becoming partners. JETRO, for instance, has a scheme to help Japanese SMCs invest in Malaysia.[37]

Table 3.10 surveys Japanese subcontractors in Malaysia, showing the importance of Japanese subcontractors to their principals, particularly in the electrical/electronics industry, which accounted for 23 of 40 Japanese principals. Moreover, they tend to have more Japanese subcontractors; exclusively accounting for those with more than 11 subcontractors, of which three had more than 50 Japanese subcontractors.

Table 3.10 Japanese subcontractors in Malaysia

Industry	A	B	C	D	E	F	G	H	I	J	K	L	M	Total
Subcontractors:														
1–5							1	3	1	14	3	1	4	27
6–10						1					2		1	4
11–20										4				4
21–30										1				1
31–50										1				1
51–100										3				3
Total						1	1	3	1	23	5	1	5	40

Source: Same as Table 3.2.
Industries are the same as for Table 3.2.

The emergence of the subcontracting system among Japanese MNCs and subcontractors in Malaysia has also promoted the construction of new networks. Japanese SMCs first began by supplying their affiliated MNCs, and have later also supplied their products to other MNCs, with whom they had not had transactions in Japan. With introductions by affiliated MNCs or other Japanese business networks, they have enhanced their business in Malaysia. These developments have witnessed the flexibility of the Japanese subcontracting system due to the fact that rapidly growing demand by MNCs, especially for parts and components for the electrical/electronics industry, has made it impossible for them to procure enough materials only from their own subcontractors in Malaysia.

Inter-company networks between Japanese and local companies

The JETRO survey of 1992 also gives us information on subcontracting systems. The breakdown of subcontractors, including Japanese subcontractors, is shown in Table 3.11. Of 82 companies which had subcontractors, 55 (67.1 per cent) procured from one to five subcontractors. Four companies, three in electrical/electronics and one in transport equipment, had more than a hundred subcontractors each. A comparison of Table 3.10 with Table 3.11 suggests that we can find more local than Japanese subcontractors.

Japanese principals have subcontractors in Malaysia to reduce costs by replacing imported materials, to save delivery time, and to increase the local content ratio. Parts and components with sophisticated technology still need to be imported, mainly from Japan. As long as subcontractors can supply the required parts and components without delay, it should not matter whether they are Japanese or local companies. Japanese subcontractors nevertheless have certain advantages, because of their

Table 3.11 Total subcontractors by industry

Industry	A	B	C	D	E	F	G	H	I	J	K	L	M	Total
Subcontractors														
1–5	1	4	2	1			3	4		28		2	10	55
6–10								2		2				4
11–20								1		1	2	1		5
21–30									1		1		3	5
31–50						1				4	1			6
51–100										3				3
100-										3	1			4
Total	1	4	2	1		1	3	7	1	41	5	3	13	82

Source: Same as Table 3.2
Industries are the same as for Table 3.2

technological superiority and easier access to Japanese principals. However, increasing domestic demand for parts and components has provided more opportunities for local companies to supply their products to Japanese companies as Japanese subcontractors alone cannot supply enough. Advice by the Malaysian Government to Japanese companies to increase procurement from local companies has also encouraged them to enhance inter-company networks with local companies.[38] As discussed above, local companies which can supply import-substituting companies have better prospects than those hoping to supply export-oriented companies. However, the rapid growth of demand for parts and components in the export-oriented electrical/electronics industry has made it possible for more local companies to be engaged in subcontracting networks.

Out of 40 non-Japanese subcontractors sampled,[39] 21 companies supplied parts and components to the automobile industry while 12 companies supplied plastic products to the electrical/electronics industry.[40] The average number of principals was 2.25, while 13 companies had four principals and 11 companies supplied their products to two principals. The most important reasons for starting transactions were to increase sales (60 per cent) and in response to requests by Japanese companies (60 per cent). Other reasons included introducing technology (28.6 per cent) and stabilizing transactions (23.5 per cent). Malaysian suppliers point out that increasing local content and developing supporting local industries have been important reasons for Japanese MNCs to have local subcontractors. There have been two main ways for obtaining information on Japanese companies, namely personal relations and recommendation and/or mediation by a person from the same industry.

To continue transactions with Japanese companies, it has, of course, been important to keep competitive prices. In addition, delivery on schedule for the Japanese JIT system has been as crucial as pricing. Two-thirds of local subcontractors have been requested to improve the quality of their

Table 3.12 Development measures for subcontractors

Industry	A	B	C	D	E	F	G	H	I	J	K	L	M	Total
Measures														
Visiting	1	4		1			6			37	5	1	7	62
Dispatching engineers						1	5			20	2	2	3	33
Lending machinery and equipment				1	1		3			21		2	3	31
Organize subcontractors association									1	9	1		1	12
Sending representatives to Japan										2				2
Others										2				2

Source: Same as Table 3.2
Some companies cited several measures.
Industries are the same as for Table 3.2

products.[41] More than half local subcontractors have been receiving technical assistance from Japanese companies, mostly by dispatching engineers to local subcontractors. Table 3.12, indicating development measures for local subcontractors by Japanese companies, reveals that 62 companies visited subcontractors frequently to provide technical assistance. Thirty-three companies dispatched engineers and 31 even lent machinery and equipment.

Other research suggests that Japanese principals are eager to support their local subcontractors and up-grade the quality of their products through technical assistance.[42] Inter-company technology transfer which may be as important as in-house technology transfer in Japanese subsidiaries will thus be promoted, contributing to the further development of the Malaysian manufacturing sector. In some cases, Japanese principals urge local subcontractors to make technical contracts with Japanese companies. To a lesser extent, the management know-how transferred has been recognized as important for local subcontractors.

Malaysian companies have to make more and better use of the backward linkages brought about by Japanese companies through the subcontracting system to progress and develop additional demand.[43] Through such inter-company networks, local products are indirectly exposed to international markets and local companies are encouraged to increase competitiveness. Here again, technical support or assistance can help them. If more local companies can utilize the externalities generated by Japanese companies, it can contribute to widening Malaysia's manufacturing base as well as strengthening linkages among such companies.

With the rapid growth of JDI in the electrical/electronics industry, Malaysian manufacturers have more opportunities to establish inter-company networks with Japanese companies. However, the increasing number of Japanese subcontractors in Malaysia and their expanding production volumes suggest that it seems possible for them to displace local subcontractors and establish more exclusively Japanese inter-company networks in Malaysia. Some MNCs have established distribution companies for their parts and components in Malaysia in addition to their international procurement offices (IPOs) and the OHQs in Singapore, thus vigorously moving into supporting services. Increasing control of parts and components distribution by the IPOs and OHQs in Singapore may also have a negative effect on Malaysian subcontractors by preventing them from entering these networks. If Japanese companies establish closed or exclusive networks among themselves, these networks will reduce backward linkages to local companies. Whether or not Japanese companies can establish open networks including local companies remains to be seen. Through such open networks, they can promote localization and contribute to the diffusion of technology and other management know-how, thus enhancing the business opportunities and competitiveness of local companies.

CONCLUDING REMARKS

The yen appreciation caused drastic changes in JDI bringing about the so-called 'Third Wave' of Japanese investments in Malaysia. This has mainly involved a huge inflow in the electrical/electronics industry, involving both MNCs and SMCs. This chapter has emphasized that JDI should be understood as the result of both industrial development policies in Malaysia (pull factors), as well as the strategies of Japanese companies in response to the changing economic environment in Japan (push factors).

Second, JDI in Malaysia should be seen in the context of the global or regional strategies of Japanese companies, particularly logistics strategies or intra-company networks in ASEAN. They have been restructuring or constructing intra-company networks based on the changing comparative advantage of ASEAN member countries. In this regard, the RHQs or OHQs in Singapore have begun to play more important roles. Proximity to Singapore has encouraged relocation of Japanese companies in Malaysia, particularly to Johore. With its 'Growth Triangle', Singapore has been eager to develop Batam island which might compete with Malaysia in attracting FDI.

The concentration of JDI in the export-oriented electrical/electronics industry has involved supporting industries, resulting in the relocation of inter-company networks or subcontracting systems from Japan into Malaysia. With the development of inter-company networks involving local companies, inter-company technology transfer, both in hardware and software (management), has taken place. However, an increasing number of Japanese companies may establish more closed inter-company networks of Japanese companies.

NOTES

1 The definition of a manufacturing SMC in Japan is one with capital of not more than 100 million yen, or not more than 300 employees.

2 The rapid JDI inflow, especially after 1988, was called the Third Wave, following the First Wave during 1973–74 involving light manufacturing, and the Second Wave during the early 1980s involving construction.

3 From 1987 to 1989 and in 1991, Japan was the largest investor in terms of approved projects.

4 JETRO KL Center, *NIES, ASEAN ni okeru Nikkei Seizougyou Kigyou no Katudou Joukyou – Malaysia* (The Activities of Japanese Manufacturing Companies in NIES, ASEAN – Malaysia), JETRO, Kuala Lumpur, 1992.

5 For instance, Matsushita Industrial Corp., Matsushita Electronic Components, Tamura Electronics and Toko Electronics in the Sungai Way FTZ, Toshiba Electronics (Malaysia) in the Telok Panglima Garang FTZ.

6 Indirect exports, i.e. supplying products to FTZs and to LMWs, were also recognized as exports; this made it possible for the suppliers to establish wholly foreign-owned subsidiaries.

7 For instance, M.Y. Yoshino, *Japan's Multinational Enterprises*, Harvard University Press, Cambridge, 1976.

8 *Sogoshoshas* enhanced their businesses by exporting machinery and production equipment before starting operations and supplying materials for production thereafter. They also made use of their business networks in the host country.

9 Even in joint ventures with minority Japanese shares, it is often possible for Japanese to control the subsidiaries through loans, technology contracts and sales arrangements provided by parent companies.

10 For instance, Shukri Rahman, 'Going Public', *Malaysian Business*, 16–31 January 1993, pp. 14–16.

11 Teranishi Takehide, 'Nikkei Seizougyou no Doukou ni Tsuite (The Trends in Japanese Manufacturing Companies)', *JACTIM Kaihou* (JACTIM Bulletin) No. 34, July, Kuala Lumpur, 1990.

12 Hosono Tetsuhiro, 'Zai Mareisia Nikkei Seizougyou Kigyou no Jittai (Present Conditions in the Japanese Manufacturing Sector)', *JACTIM Kaihou* (JACTIM Bulletin) No. 18, July, Kuala Lumpur, 1987.

13 JETRO, op. cit.

14 Ibid.

15 Ohtsubo Kiyoshi, 'JACTIM Boueki Tohshi Iinkai Report (Report of the Trade and Investment Committee of JACTIM)', *JACTIM Kaihou* (JACTIM Bulletin) No. 42, June, Kuala Lumpur, 1992.

16 In the import-substituting stage, companies were protected by tariffs and not exposed to tough competition, often encouraging inefficient production systems and making their products less competitive due to low quality and/or

high prices. This was enhanced by lack of business experience and economies of scale.

17 FTZ companies could not purchase materials from local companies because they were not produced in Malaysia, were of low quality, had delivery problems, and also high prices.

18 Calculated from Toyo Keizai Shinpo-sha, *Kaigai Shinshutu Kigyou Souran 1993* (List of Japanese Companies in Operation Abroad in 1993), Toyo Keizai Shinpo-sha, Tokyo, 1993.

19 See, for instance, Riduzuan Mohd Akil, 'The Spatial Aspects of Economic Planning and Development in Malaysia', paper presented at Eleventh Economic Convention of the Malaysian Economic Association, in Kuala Lumpur, 24–26 September 1991.

20 For more information on networks, please see, Aoki Takeshi, 'Japanese FDI and the Forming of Networks in the Asia-Pacific Region: Experience in Malaysia and Its Implications', in Tokunaga Shojiro (ed.), *Japan's Foreign Investment and Asian Economic Interdependence*, University of Tokyo Press, Tokyo, 1992.

21 In 1986, the Economic Committee published a report prescribing Singapore's future economic development. The report emphasized the promotion of high value-added manufacturing as well as non-manufacturing activities, particularly the commercial, financial and service sectors. (See The Economic Committee, *The Singapore Economy: New Directions*, Ministry of Trade and Industry, Singapore, February 1986.) In line with this policy, new fiscal incentives for OHQ were introduced for those companies which controlled subsidiaries in Southeast Asia in 1986. By the end of 1992, 42 companies obtained OHQ status including eight Japanese subsidiaries, namely Asia Matsushita Electric (S), Fujikura Asia Limited, Fuji Xerox Asia Pacific, Hitachi Asia, NEC Electronics (S), Omron (S), Sony International, and Toshiba Electronics Asia.

22 The regional logistics strategies base on the subsidiaries in Singapore can be typically observed in the cases of Sony, Matsushita, Hitachi, Toyota and so on.

23 So far, only Singapore and Indonesia have made an agreement to develop Batam island. For more on the Growth Triangle plan, see Lee Tsao Yuan (ed.), *Growth Triangle: The Johore-Singapore-Riau Experience*, Institute of Southeast Asian Studies and Institute of Policy Studies, Singapore, 1991. Anazawa Makoto, 'Nikkei Takokuseki Kigyou to Seichou no Toraianguru' (Japanese MNCs and the Growth Triangle), in Kohama Hirohisa (ed.), *Chokusetu Tousi to Kougyou-ka Nihon, NIES, ASEAN* (Foreign Direct Investment and Industrialization: Japan, NIES, ASEAN), JETRO, Tokyo, 1992.

24 Many Singapore companies migrated to Johore in the 1980s to make use of the cheaper labour there. Proximity to Singapore has been a great advantage to Johore.

25 Based on the author's interview in Johore.

26 Johore was the second largest FDI-receiving state after Selangor in the latter half of the 1980s.

27 See, for instance, Hui Weng Tat, 'Singapore's Immigration Policy: An Economic Perspective', in Linda Low and Toh Mun Heng (eds.), *Public Policies in Singapore: Changes in the 1980s and Future Signposts*, Times Academic Press, Singapore, 1992.

28 The relocation of Japanese companies from Singapore to Johore was observed. In addition, some companies migrated to Selangor, Penang, and even to Thailand and Indonesia.

29 Economic Development Board (Singapore), *Singapore Investment News,* December 1990.
30 At the end of 1992, Batamindo Investment Corp. developed 116 hectares (ha) of Batam Industrial Park (Phase 1). Thirty-five companies were in operation and twelve thousand people were employed. Of these companies, 14 were Japanese.
31 Inter-company networks not only involve transactions, but also technical or managerial cooperation; in this section, industrial subcontracting within the national border will be emphasized.
32 JETRO, *JETRO Hakusho* (JETRO White Paper), JETRO, Tokyo, 1987, p. 135.
33 The subcontracting system is also called vertical *'keiretsu'* (affiliate relations). Japanese subcontractors are becoming more independent by diversifying their principals. Only 17.3 per cent of subcontractors relied on one principal, while 36.2 per cent of them had more than six principals. Japanese MNCs have many subcontractors in Japan. For instance, Matsushita has more than one thousand subcontractors, while Toyota has about 200 direct subcontractors.
34 See, for instance, The Medium and Small-Scale Enterprise Agency, *Chu-sho Kigyou Hakusho* (White Paper on Medium and Small-Scale Enterprises), Government Publication, Tokyo, various issues.
35 In 1991, 48 Japanese manufacturing SMCs invested in Malaysia.
36 Normally, they establish wholly Japanese owned subsidiaries with one or two Japanese partners.
37 JETRO provides assistance for companies in targeted industries to invest in Malaysia.
38 For instance, Sharp-Roxy Appliance Corp. was appointed by MITI as an anchor company to help develop local small and medium scale industries; it identified three *Bumiputera* firms to supply electronic and other components to its subsidiaries (*Business Times*, 26 August 1992).
39 Toh Kin Woon and Yeoh Kok Kheng, 'The Role of Japanese Direct Investment in Malaysia' in Institute of Developing Economies, *The Role of Japanese Direct Investment in Developing Countries: Malaysia, China, Korea*, Institute of Developing Economies, Tokyo, 1992, p. 158.
40 Of 40 companies, 27 were wholly Malaysian-owned, while the remaining 13 were joint ventures with non-Japanese foreigners.
41 Many Japanese managers claimed that inconsistency in product quality was very serious.
42 Ohtsubo Kiyoshi, op. cit., and the author's own survey support these results.
43 Only about 25 per cent of large local firms offered subcontracting work to SMCs. (Fong Chan Onn, 'Industrialization in Malaysia: Role of Small and Medium Scale Industries', in Ambrim Buang (ed.), *The Malaysian Economy In Transition*, INTAN (National Institute of Public Administration), Kuala Lumpur, 1990, p. 123.)

4

JAPANESE INDUSTRIAL INVESTMENTS AND TECHNOLOGY TRANSFER IN MALAYSIA

Anuwar Ali

This chapter will examine the impact of Japanese foreign direct investments (FDI) and technology transfer in Malaysia's industrialization. Given that Japan has been one of the major players in the industrial development of the country, right from the import-substitution phase beginning in the late 1950s right through until the current export-oriented phase, there have been many expectations of its role in technology transfer to domestic industries. Since Malaysia needs to upgrade its industrial base and technological capability, the extent of technology absorption and assimilation is indeed critical. Further, the Japanese industrial experience itself has often been looked upon to be emulated by Malaysia.

In the following section, the importance of FDI in Malaysia's industrial expansion will be highlighted; FDI is sought with the expectation that it will expand employment opportunities in the manufacturing sector and enhance the country's technological capability. While the issues pertinent to both FDI inflows and technology transfer from Japanese companies will be the main theme, the nature of technology transfer into domestic enterprises in Malaysia as well as the technology absorptive capacity through human resource development will also be dealt with.

Since an important aspect of this transfer involves formal agreements between domestic licensees and Japanese technology licensors, the institutional framework within which the Malaysian government tries to ensure that such transfer will benefit domestic industries will also be highlighted. The last section of the chapter will highlight some policy initiatives to enable Malaysia to benefit more fully from rapid industrial expansion.

Technology transfer into an economy like Malaysia generally involves the transfer of written information, human-embodied skills, know-how and the adaptation of production processes by technology suppliers. Such transfers involve a variety of different modes, the principal being the purchase of technology through licensing agreements, imports of machinery and equipment, technical assistance contracts and turn-key arrangements. While options chosen vary from industry to industry and from firm to firm, choices are generally influenced by the objectives and capacities of users as well as the desire of the supplier to extract maximum rent from the provision of its technology.

One can also distinguish between what has generally been referred to as 'packaged' technology transfer on the one hand and 'unpackaged' technology transfer on the other. The former refers to an arrangement whereby technology is purchased as an important component of an investment package to be complemented by management, marketing services and equity participation. However, the drawback of this approach is that it tends to perpetuate technology dependency upon industrial countries and creates bottlenecks which can hamper the pace of industrial growth in a developing economy. Depending on their respective technological capabilities, many developing countries try to 'unbundle' technology packages to facilitate separate treatment of the different components offered such as management, production methods, marketing strategies and control systems.

The other common method of technology acquisition is through licensing, involving 'pure technical collaboration agreements' which exclude foreign equity participation. In fact, Japan's early industrial development and South Korea's experience since the 1960s have mainly been explained by their respective technological capabilities in acquiring and adapting technologies from more industrialized countries in this way. However, the effectiveness of this approach greatly depends upon both the industrial infrastructure and science and technology capabilities in the national economy.

Malaysian manufacturing enterprises have resorted to most of the above methods to acquire technologies from more industrialized countries. However, given the country's narrow industrial base and the dominance of FDI in key industries, technology acquisition and assimilation has been all the more difficult. A number of other factors have to be considered when a domestic industry acquires technology, including the willingness of foreign investors, mainly multinational companies (MNCs), to transfer their technologies, the appropriate price of such technologies as well as domestic absorptive capacity.

INDUSTRIAL GROWTH AND FOREIGN DIRECT INVESTMENT SINCE THE MID-1980S

Foreign direct investment inflows into Malaysia have grown markedly since the 1985–86 economic recession, after which, according to the Sixth Malaysia Plan, 'there was a remarkable increase in proposed foreign capital investment from about RM1,000 million (Malaysian ringgits) in 1985 to more than RM18,000 million in 1990. Apart from efforts by the government to enhance greater FDI, the nation has also benefited from the relocation of industries from the industrialized countries, notably Japan, South Korea and Taiwan as a result of rising costs of production and appreciation of currencies in these countries. Malaysia has, therefore, positioned itself favourably to take advantage of these opportunities' (Malaysia, 1991: 132).

In approved projects during the 1985–90 period FDI amounted to RM34,908 million, out of which Japan's share was highest with 25.7 per cent of the total. During the Sixth Malaysia Plan period (1991–95), it is projected that RM80,000 million will be invested in the manufacturing sector, of which RM33,000 million will be FDI. The government has long encouraged as much FDI inflow as possible. This thrust seems to be fully supported by the Federation of Malaysian Manufacturers (FMM), which represents most of the large manufacturing firms in the country. As emphasized by the FMM, 'a liberal policy which will encourage greater inflow of foreign capital, technology and expertise, and more reinvestments on the part of exisiting investors, will enable the country to be better prepared to face any economic conditions and situations arising from the current global restructuring' (Federation of Malaysian Manufacturers, 1990: 3–11).

Since the late 1950s, when Malaysia initiated its industrialization programme, imported technologies from industrial countries, including Japan, have been dominant, the consequence of FDI inflows. When export-oriented industrialization became the policy objective from the early 1970s, the importation of technologies was as important as in the preceding import-substitution phase, but more selectively, depending on the needs of the industries promoted, while a few indigenous technologies appeared in some established industries. During this phase, Free Trade Zones (FTZs) were established to encourage the relocation in Malaysia of MNC activities, particularly in electronics and textiles.

Since then, FDI has been dominant in export-oriented activities. Since 1989, for instance, foreign-controlled firms have accounted for more than 90 per cent of the export sales of the electronics industry and the machinery and electrical appliances industry. They also dominated the export of rubber products, basic metals and metal products, textiles and garments, and food, beverages and tobacco. Overall, they account for nearly 55 per cent of manufactured exports in 1989 (Bank Negara Malaysia, 1991: 51). Such foreign domination also prevails in some other countries in this part of the world, especially Singapore, where FDI participation is regarded as critical for the establishment of high-technology industries as well as for market penetration of the industrial countries (Parry, 1988: 95–128). Malaysia has also been dependent on industrial countries including Japan for international demand for manufactured exports such as electronics and textiles. In fact, the success of export-led growth in newly industrializing countries depends on the capacity of industrial countries to absorb imports from countries such as Malaysia (Thurow, 1992: 62).

As implied above, Malaysia's industrialization programme has been dominated by FDI, right from the early import-substitution phase up to the current export-oriented phase. Since 1987, the FDI presence has become more apparent, especially as a consequence of the liberalization measures to encourage foreign equity participation in 1986 with the Promotion of Investment Act. As indicated in Table 4.1, the share of proposed foreign capital investment in newly approved manufacturing projects increased substantially after 1986, reaching a peak in 1989, with 70.8 per cent of total proposed capital investment.

Apart from responding to the more open and liberal investment climate in Malaysia, the recent substantial investment inflows are also a reflection of the changing pattern of investments by firms in Japan and the East Asian newly industrialized countries (NICs). In view of their changing comparative advantage, the NICs, especially Taiwan and South Korea, have been forced to relocate industries in lower labour-cost countries such as Malaysia and its neighbours (Chen and Wong, 1989: 204–39; Tsuruoka, 1990: 87–8). In addition to the increasing domestic labour costs in Taiwan and South Korea, exacerbated by the appreciation of their currencies, such relocation has also been driven by their desire to upgrade domestic production into higher value-added and knowledge-intensive industries, especially in electronics (see Organisation for Economic Cooperation and Development, 1988: 82).

During the 1985–91 period, Japanese FDI flow has been a major source of capital for Malaysia's domestic industries. Table 4.2 shows that Japan's significance in this respect and its share of total FDI has always been very high, surpassing all other investing countries, except in 1986, 1990 and 1991. In 1986, Malaysia was experiencing an economic recession while in 1990 and 1991 Taiwanese investments overtook Japanese inflows as the latter directed greater investments to North America and Europe in anticipation of greater protection there.

Despite the recent significance of Taiwanese investments, Japanese FDI undoubtedly still has the biggest cumulative impact on the country's industrialization. This is illustrated in Table 4.3, which shows proposed capital investments in approved projects during the 1980–92 period. Japanese FDI was most dominant in the electrical and electronics industry, which accounted for 43.7 per cent of the total, followed by the chemical and chemical product industries with only 13.8 per cent. Other relatively important industries in terms of Japanese FDI include the non-metallic and basic metal products, the machinery industry, and transport equipment.

Substantial Japanese participation in these industries is largely an extension of its comparative advantage in these areas. Increasing Japanese FDI by major manufacturing firms dominance has been reinforced by the inflow of investments by Japanese small and medium-scale industries, to supply and support their larger counterparts. This has also been a consequence of increasing production (labour and inventory) costs in Japanese industry and yen appreciation, forcing such industries to relocate their manufacturing facilities in lower wage economies such as Malaysia (George, 1988: 84–6; Kosaka, 1989: 52).

While FDI inflow has contributed to relatively more rapid growth of the manufacturing sector, such inflow provides substantial opportunities for Japanese industries to increase their exports of intermediate and capital goods to Malaysia (Nakanishi, 1990: 49–53). At the same time, they also encourage greater investments by related Japanese industries, particularly by supporting or small and medium-scale enterprises. The close links between these industries and their parent industries in Japan via sub-assembly and subcontracting systems have encouraged them to expand their activities to overseas locations more effectively to supply and support their parent or core companies' requirements (Go Iwaki, 1992: 309–51). Thus, according to Masayoshi Ikeda (1991: 132–47), 'while the production processes are conducted outside, they work as one synchronisation as exemplified by the processes which are interlinked with the parent company'.

While the Malaysian government is promoting the development of small and medium-scale enterprises as supporting industries, Takeshi Aoki (1992: 73–110), in his study of Japanese investment in Malaysia, concludes that 'the enterprises that have contributed to this most effectively are affiliates of Japanese firms that have shifted their production facilities and established factories in Malaysia'. This, of course, has important implications for long-term industrial expansion as such a phenomenon

Table 4.1 Proposed capital investment in approved manufacturing projects, 1985–90 (RM million)

	1985	1986	1987	1988	1989	1990
No. of projects	625	447	333	732	792	906
Potential employment	53,597	40,230	60,068	142,875	176,628	169,764
Malaysian capital investment	4,727.6 (83.1)	3,475.3 (67.3)	1,873.9 (47.6)	4,215.9 (46.4)	3,562.7 (29.2)	10,539.0 (37.4)
Foreign capital investment	959.3 (16.9)	1,687.9 (32.7)	2,060.0 (52.4)	4,878.0 (53.6)	8,652.7 (70.8)	17,629.1 (62.6)
Total	5,686.9	5,163.2	3,933.9	9,093.9	12,215.4	28,168.1

Source: Malaysian Industrial Development Authority (MIDA).
Figures in parentheses are percentages of total capital investment in that year.

106

Table 4.2 Major sources of foreign investment in approved projects, 1985–91 (RM million)

	1985	1986	1987	1988	1989	1990	1991
Japan	264.4	116.3	715.1	1,222.0	2,690.4	4,212.6	3,157.7
	(27.6)	(6.9)	(34.7)	(25.1)	(31.1)	(23.9)	(19.8)
Taiwan	31.9	10.8	243.0	829.6	2,159.9	6,339.1	3,548.4
	(3.3)	(0.6)	(11.8)	(17.0)	(25.0)	(36.0)	(22.2)
Singapore	100.2	183.7	258.5	419.6	914.7	895.3	1,026.9
	(10.4)	(10.9)	(12.5)	(8.6)	(10.6)	(5.1)	(6.4)
UK	26.9	49.5	76.8	196.5	764.1	867.2	538.4
	(2.8)	(2.9)	(3.7)	(4.0)	(8.8)	(4.9)	(3.4)
USA	11.9	53.6	162.7	535.1	320.8	567.3	1,724.3
	(1.2)	(3.2)	(7.9)	(11.0)	(3.7)	(3.2)	(10.8)

Source: Malaysian Industrial Development Authority (MIDA).
Total foreign investment (RM million): 1985 – 959.3, 1986 – 1,687.9, 1987 – 2,060.0, 1988 – 4,878.0, 1989 – 8,652.7, 1990 – 17,629.1, 1991 – 15,956.0.
Figures in parentheses are percentages of total investment in that year, including other unlisted countries of origin.

will inevitably stifle domestic entrepreneurship and enterprises and the potential for inter-firm linkages involving Malaysian industries.

TECHNOLOGY TRANSFER AND HUMAN RESOURCE DEVELOPMENT

Industrial progress would inevitably require the promotion of high-technology or knowledge-based industries. However, the development of such industries ought to be initiated by domestic capital, supported by an abundant supply of highly skilled labour as well as substantial increases in research and development (R&D) and technical training expenditure. With both R&D and in-service training, it is equally important to stress the role of the private sector. It is therefore crucial that human resource development be focused to develop both the critical skills needed by industry and, more important, labour's capacity to innovate. There is little doubt, as suggested by the experience of industrial countries as well as newly industrialized countries, that innovative capacities will ultimately determine the economy's competitiveness.

Basically, existing human resource development does not really emphasize the capacity to innovate. The lack of funds for R&D purposes is indeed an important constraint in this respect, while domestic industries are too reluctant to allocate substantial funds for this purpose in view of the high risks involved. Furthermore, the development of local venture capital to encourage such activities is still in its infancy in Malaysia. But equally important, FDI preferences and existing investment incentives generally

Table 4.3 Proposed Japanese capital investment in approved projects, 1980–92
(RM million)

Industry	Number of projects	Potential employment	Capital investment	% of Total
Food manufacturing	27	3,165	112.6	1.8
Textiles	33	5,059	51.4	0.8
Leather products	3	650	1.9	–
Wood products	46	15,267	186.7	3.0
Furniture and fixtures	12	1,771	30.5	0.5
Paper and printing	15	1,139	26.5	0.4
Chemicals	63	4,239	848.4	13.8
Petroleum	5	302	15.4	0.3
Rubber products	31	3,152	48.6	0.3
Plastic products	54	4,039	251.7	4.1
Non-metallic products	77	10,719	458.1	7.5
Basic metal products	75	6,687	414.8	6.8
Fabricated metal products	62	5,267	165.0	2.7
Machinery	60	10,100	292.7	4.8
Electrical and electronics	373	114,740	2,680.8	43.7
Transport equipment	86	13,658	253.7	4.1
Scientific equipment	15	4,032	134.8	2.2
Miscellaneous	21	1,822	31.7	0.5
Natural gas	1	570	126.4	2.0
Total	1,059	206,378	6,130.7	100

Source: Malaysian Industrial Development Authority (MIDA).

encourage the importation and adoption of highly capital-intensive equipment and technology packages from the industrial countries. This not only discourages the adoption of more appropriate and indigenously developed technologies, but also undermines the capacity to innovate as the dependence on imported technologies is perpetuated.

Foreign direct investment in general thus tends to discourage meaningful technology transfer and development of domestic innovative capacity. Furthermore, most foreign-owned firms, particularly Japanese companies, do not view technology transfer as a priority in choosing to locate their manufacturing facilities in Malaysia, since their main rationale for establishing such facilities is to take advantage of cheap labour in the country (Fong Chan Onn, 1992: 193–217).

If there is any transfer at all, it is normally between the principal licensor or investor and its subsidiary or affiliate established in Malaysia. Technology transfer is thus internalized within the context of the transnational foreign firm's global production system. There is also a general reluctance on the part of most foreign firms to allocate R&D funds to their overseas subsidiaries, let alone affiliates, since most of these activities are controlled by their head offices in the industrial countries where R&D facilities have already been established in close consultation. As such, the technology linkages between FDI and locally owned enterprises are not as fully developed as in Japan (see Anuwar Ali and Muhd. Anuar Adnan, 1990: 151–71; Fong Chan Onn, 1990: 254–84; Ozawa, 1982: 7–53).

The availability of qualified and technically experienced scientists and engineers is an important determinant of the establishment of R&D facilities. As these personnel are scarce in Malaysia, the top management of foreign MNCs tends to perform mainly managerial and organizational, rather than innovative functions, unlike their counterparts in Japan or other industrialized countries. This has a stifling effect on the development of domestic entrepreneurship. Nevertheless, in an industrializing economy, it is vital for domestic entrepreneurship to take initiatives which will ensure that capital formation is directed to manufacturing activities.

However, this situation creates an industrial structure which leaves domestic entrepreneurship in areas such as services, including finance, trading, and small-scale manufacturing utilizing low-level technologies which contribute little towards a more independent industrializing process. This tendency is reinforced by other structural features characteristic of skewed, open economies like Malaysia, where high demand for luxury consumer goods tends to ensure that the most profitable areas of economic activity, to which domestic entrepreneurs are attracted, are commercial activities related to consumption. At the same time, the recent influx of FDI, including small and medium-scale Japanese enterprises, puts considerable pressure on domestic capital, crowding out enterprises, especially the weaker ones (Lim, 1990: 39–46).

In theory, technology transfer basically involves the purchase of technology from another country based on the mutuality of interests. For the importing country, there is a price to be paid for the technology import; hence, domestic industries need to assess whether the technology transferred is suitable in relation to their own technological capability and the actual technology components made available. The other costs of such transfers, including the indirect costs imposed by the technology supplier and opportunity costs, also need to be considered.

As mentioned earlier, an important rationale for encouraging FDI is the expectation that it would facilitate technology transfer. Technology acquisition is perceived as a crucial component in ensuring rapid economic growth and industrial progress, especially for the transformation of the economy into one with a larger industrial base. The flow of technology to domestic industries, as measured by the number of formal contractual agreements, has increased rapidly in recent years. However, one must note that these numbers are but a crude indicator of technology transfer, and may not reflect the actual extent of technology acquisition within domestic industries. It is difficult to measure with any certainty the complex nature of technology transfer. The increase in technology contracts may also reflect the strengthening of intellectual property rights in the last decade and greater attempts at enforcement as well as the increased significance of rent outflows in this connection.

During the 1980–92 period, the Ministry of International Trade and Industry (MITI) scrutinized and approved a total of 1,655 agreements. The number of such agreements averaged more than a hundred annually, except in 1982 and 1985; it reached a peak of 198 agreements in 1989. The trend suggests increasing reliance on foreign technology and FDI inflows into the manufacturing sector.

Slightly over half of all agreements approved since 1980 were in the form of technical assistance and know-how agreements, and another 17.0 per cent involved management and joint venture arrangements (see Table 4.4). While this suggests that considerable technology imports were needed by manufacturing enterprises, it also shows a shift away from the 'packaged' type of FDI and technology acquisition process, particularly apparent after 1985 when the number of trademarks and patents agreements increased substantially so that the share of such agreements was 17.2 per cent of the total by mid-1992.

Japan has contributed significantly to FDI inflow into Malaysia, accounting for the highest proportion (39.0 per cent) of all agreements signed during the 1985–92 period. In fact, the numbers increased substantially after 1987, partly owing to greater relocation of Japanese small and medium-scale enterprises. The other countries that were relatively important were the United Kingdom and the United States, accounting for 11.3 per cent and 10.8 per cent of the total respectively (see Table 4.5). The importance of Japan as a technology supplier is further reflected in the import of capital equipment or machinery. Since the mid-1970s, between 35 and 40 per cent of local machinery needs have originated from Japan. Only the United States appears to challenge the position of Japan in this respect. Even then, its share has been well below that of Japan. However, capital equipment or machinery alone does not constitute technology, representing as it does only that part of a technology embodied in hardware, while the remainder comprises disembodied knowledge which should best be acquired through enhancing indigenous technological capability.

Most of the agreements approved during 1980–92 were in the electronics and electrical industries (20.2 per cent), chemical industries (13.8 per cent) and transport equipment industry (10.6 per cent). Japanese investments in the transport equipment industry have been more visible during the last few years, growing in tandem with the ancillary industries stimulated by the national car project. These three industries account for more than 40 per cent of all agreements approved, thus reflecting the great need for technology transfer in these industries (see Table 4.6).

Under the Industrial Coordination Act of 1975, all manufacturing firms

Table 4.4 Types of technology agreements approved, 1980–92

Type of technology agreements	1980	1981	1982	1983	1984	1985	1986	1987	1988	1989	1990	1991	1992[b]	Total	%
Technical assistance and know-how	57	64	48	61	71	51	50	53	67	77	84	103	54	840	50.8
Management	13	6	10	13	10	6	10	5	7	12	5	6	1	104	6.3
Joint venture	14	22	14	14	17	9	19	11	11	15	15	11	5	177	10.7
Services	6	7	2	7	2	1	1	1	2	12	6	4	4	55	3.3
Trademarks and patents	4	8	8	7	1	19	33	30	44	53	36	37	5	285	17.2
Turn-key and engineering	5	5	4	4	6	—	1	—	1	—	1	1	—	28	1.7
Others[a]	15	19	8	25	12	10	9	10	18	29	8	3	—	166	10.0
Total	114	131	94	131	119	96	123	110	150	198	155	165	69	1,655	100.0

Source: Malaysian Industrial Development Authority (MIDA).
[a] Others include supply and purchase, sales, marketing and distribution.
[b] Figures for 1992 are for January–July only.

requiring project approval by the Ministry of International Trade and Industry (MITI) are also required to submit any agreement signed with any foreign company for approval. The main objectives of MITI are: first, to ensure that the agreements will not be prejudicial to the national interest; second, to ensure that the agreement will not impose unfair and unjustifiable restrictions on the Malaysian party; third, to ensure that the payments of fees, wherever applicable, will be commensurate with the level of technology to be transferred and will not have adverse effects on Malaysia's balance of payments; and last, to ensure a meaningful transfer of technology.

Even if the direct costs of technology transfer were not excessive, Malaysian-owned or managed firms might still be disadvantaged substantially if restrictive conditions are imposed by their technology suppliers. Restrictions on export outlets, the level of technology transferred, and domestic R&D activities are often observed. In view of the negative impact of such restrictions, MITI tries to minimize them to allow domestic manufacturers flexibility to expand their operations and become less dependent on their technology suppliers in the long run. For instance, if the licensors insist on export restrictions, MITI will demand that consent for sales outside the restricted territories should not be unreasonably withheld.

There have been cases in which the technology licensors insist on fixing the prices of the licensed products, while others insist that the local licensees purchase all material inputs and components from them at prices fixed by them. The second restriction appears to be more common. Such tie-in purchases undoubtedly strengthen the position of the technology suppliers, enabling them to maximize their gains by selling overpriced components, intermediate inputs, capital equipment and spare parts, thus creating opportunities for transfer pricing. Additionally, the obligation to purchase key inputs from the technology licensor enables the latter to monitor the activities of the local licensee, by constantly checking the production volume of the licensee, mainly for the purpose of determining royalty or technical fees.

In order to minimize both direct and indirect costs to local licensees, MITI has laid down a number of guidelines for the purchase of components or intermediate inputs. First, wherever possible, the licensee should determine alternative sources of supply, which obviously requires a reasonably high level of technology competence within domestic industries, to be acquired through more in-service training and R&D allocations. Second, any clause binding the licensee to purchase all imported components and supply through the technology supplier should be avoided. Third, if such a provision cannot be avoided, the licensee should stipulate that the prices are to be based on internationally competitive prices.

Table 4.5 Technology agreements by country of origin, 1980–92

Country	1980	1981	1982	1983	1984	1985	1986	1987	1988	1989	1990	1991	1992[a]	Total	%
Japan	32	35	33	46	39	33	38	37	54	87	82	92	37	645	39.0
UK	20	17	6	19	11	14	21	17	17	21	8	14	2	187	11.3
USA	11	14	10	18	12	13	12	12	22	23	10	18	4	179	10.8
India	5	4	4	4	2	6	1	—	2	2	1	1	1	33	2.0
West Germany	9	11	10	2	2	3	2	5	5	6	8	5	4	72	4.4
Australia	10	5	6	2	5	3	9	3	16	2	7	4	1	73	4.4
Hong Kong	9	2	3	2	7	4	7	7	5	9	3	6	2	66	4.0
Singapore	4	7	5	3	8	2	3	4	4	3	6	4	1	54	3.3
France	—	7	—	4	—	—	4	3	2	4	—	6	1	32	1.9
Italy	2	—	—	—	—	2	1	1	—	3	3	—	1	13	0.8
Panama	1	—	1	—	—	—	5	1	—	—	—	—	—	8	0.5
Switzerland	—	3	1	2	2	1	1	1	3	2	1	1	1	19	1.1
Norway	1	—	2	1	2	5	—	2	1	—	1	1	2	18	1.1
South Korea	—	—	2	4	6	1	3	1	—	3	10	2	7	39	2.3
Others	10	26	11	24	22	9	16	16	19	33	15	11	5	217	13.1
Total	114	131	94	131	119	96	123	110	150	198	155	165	69	1655	100

Source: Malaysian Industrial Development Authority (MIDA)
[a] Figures for 1992 are for January–July only.

Table 4.6 Technology agreements by industry groups, 1980–92

Industry	1980	1981	1982	1983	1984	1985	1986	1987	1988	1989	1990	1991	1992ᵃ	Total	%
Electronics and electrical	19	16	19	15	21	20	12	29	37	40	41	45	20	334	20.2
Fabricated metal	6	14	7	12	3	9	22	21	17	7	4	13	1	136	8.3
Chemical	11	21	5	15	17	16	15	18	29	27	24	21	10	229	13.8
Transport equipment	10	11	11	22	17	20	15	4	1	15	18	16	16	176	10.6
Food	14	15	4	21	6	10	8	8	16	21	4	6	1	134	8.1
Textiles	8	5	2	5	6	1	7	2	6	4	7	6	3	62	3.7
Basic metal	7	10	13	5	5	1	1	2	—	6	4	7	—	61	3.7
Wood and wood product	—	—	4	1	6	—	4	1	—	—	6	5	—	27	1.6
Pulp, paper, printing and publishing	—	—	—	—	—	3	4	1	3	—	4	4	—	19	1.1
Rubber and rubber products	8	14	2	7	5	4	13	8	22	18	8	10	4	123	7.4
Non-metallic mineral products	5	4	16	9	17	7	7	12	4	10	7	7	3	108	6.5
Hotel & tourist complex	4	2	4	8	7	4	4	1	2	6	3	8	1	54	3.3
Plastic	5	6	1	2	7	—	4	—	2	6	5	6	5	49	3.0
Others	17	13	6	9	2	1	7	3	11	38	20	11	5	143	8.6
Total	114	131	94	131	119	96	123	110	150	198	155	165	69	1,655	100.0

Source: Malaysian Industrial Development Authority (MIDA)
ᵃ Figures for 1992 are for January–July only.

Despite all the above stipulations, MITI's experience suggests that it is difficult to ensure effective technology transfer given the Ministry's lack of experience, expertise and capacity to assess the 'technology content' imparted to domestic licensees or local personnel, not to mention the meticulous task of trying to keep track of the increasing number of technical assistance or joint venture agreements submitted for approval.

As in most developing countries, technology transfer regulations in Malaysia have not been utilized to screen for more 'appropriate technologies', partly because technology transfer arrangements are monitored and processed by administrators lacking the necessary technology background (also see Segal, 1987: 1–32). Nevertheless, even if the authorities are able to minimize the imposition of formal controls by the technology supplier, the latter may still be able to enforce restrictions under informal agreements with the local licensee (see MacBean and Balasubramanyam, 1978: 224). It is therefore critical that the country's technology assessment capability be upgraded to ensure that the negative effects of technology transfer arrangements can be minimized (Malaysia, 1991: 193).

The extent of technology transfer to domestic industries is largely influenced by the bargaining strengths of the foreign technology licensor and the local company or subsidiary or joint venture partner, and to a certain extent, MITI. Each of these parties has its own perception of the value of the technology and the method of transfer. MITI, reflecting the government's intention to ensure effective technology transfer to local companies, is desirous that technology be acquired at the lowest possible cost, basing its calculations on its perception of the long-term national interests, rather than immediate returns to either firm. Such calculations consider the social costs and benefits of each technology, linkages with other industries, use of domestic resources, the direct costs of technology (for example, royalties) as well as hidden costs, such as possible over-pricing by the technology licensor to the local licensee.

While this is the stated objective of the government, in practice, it invariably has to balance the desire for technology acquisition at the lowest possible cost and the need to attract FDI into the country. This has been the dilemma of many developing countries, where options are really limited. To a large degree, the fixing of royalty payments by MITI has been flexible in its attempt to encourage FDI into domestic industries and to accommodate the increasingly technological needs of these industries in the form of machinery, equipment and processes as well as managerial expertise and marketing know-how. With growing industrialization, this is inevitable because of the need for economic diversification and production of more technologically advanced products, for which the availability of technology is relatively scarce and costly. In such cases, technology suppliers are generally quite reluctant to transfer their technology under the recipient country's terms of technology regulations, particularly if they are accompanied by controls over FDI, including local equity conditions.

Technology payments required for new and increasingly complex technologies may have to be significantly higher than the maximum rates generally approved by MITI. The effective absorption of more complex technologies may also require longer periods, which may exceed the durations prescribed in the MITI guidelines. While regulatory controls continue to be applied for relatively mature and standardized technologies, the acquisition of the latest techniques in high-technology areas and special priority sectors is increasingly being encouraged and promoted through various incentives, including exemptions from regulatory norms and guidelines.

JAPANESE FOREIGN DIRECT INVESTMENT AND TECHNOLOGY TRANSFER

Despite the rapid pace of technological progress and global commercialization of technologies since the early 1970s, the actual choices open to locally owned enterprises as far as applied technologies are concerned may be rather limited. The bulk of imported technologies has its origins in large firms in a relatively small number of industrial countries, including Japan, which claim proprietary rights, and thus can impose obligations and restrictions upon locally owned and managed firms that utilize these technologies.

Such a high concentration of technology-generating capacity exists because most R&D activities are being undertaken by large firms in the industrial countries. Japan is one of those countries which has advanced rapidly in this regard during the last two decades. Although the international patent system was intended to protect inventors and thus encourage innovations, the system seems to work against the interests of firms in developing countries (see World Bank, 1979: 65–6). In such a scenario, it is certainly difficult for domestic industries in Malaysia to catch up with their counterparts in the industrial countries on the technological ladder. Most domestic firms have instead become increasingly dependent upon technology suppliers in the industrial countries for the supply of both mature and new technologies and technological enhancement, for both product and process development.

It must also be noted that technology transfer transactions, which take place under very imperfect market conditions, generally favour the technology suppliers of the industrial countries. This is even more true of transactions between the MNC technology supplier and its subsidiary or joint venture partner in Malaysia. This has become even more significant since 1986, with the increased pace of Japanese FDI flows, including those related to Japanese small and medium-scale industries. Apart from the

116

oligopolistic nature of technology supply, the ability to assess the appropriateness of technology and assimilate imported technologies has generally been constrained by the lack of indigenous technological capability, particularly in locally owned or managed firms.

With a few exceptions, most domestic manufacturing firms lack sufficient knowledge of the technologies they hope to acquire from their potential suppliers because of the limited pool of suitably skilled personnel or expertise available. Furthermore, this has been complicated by the fact that the demand for highly skilled manpower in recent years has put the generally smaller, locally owned firms at an added disadvantage. Technology suppliers are reluctant to disclose full information about their products or processes to potential buyers until all transactions are completed to protect their proprietary value. Valuable technological knowledge is therefore not readily given away, but has to be purchased at a cost. Thus, local firms lacking technical expertise will generally agree to purchase technology without sufficient knowledge of its eventual functional value and actual performance.

The cost of purchasing a particular technology may also reflect the lack of the technical, legal and commercial expertise required to acquire relevant information on the technology and for evaluating the various options which may exist. This disadvantage is particularly felt by small and medium-scale enterprises, although their larger counterparts tend to have greater access, either because of their better organizational capacity or because they are in better bargaining positions *vis-à-vis* their technology suppliers.

The terms and conditions attached to a particular acquisition of technology are generally restrictive to local licensees on matters pertaining to export outlets, purchasing and pricing policies, technology diffusion and in-house R&D. One of the most common restrictions is prohibiting exports of goods produced under licensing or technical assistance agreements. There are also cases where licensees are prohibited from producing competitive products. Usually, they are required to secure prior approval from their Japanese licensors before they can sell intermediate products also covered under such agreements. There are cases where the licensees are required to sell their products only through marketing firms appointed by the licensors.

As indicated earlier, domestic firms are often also required to purchase materials from the licensors, which has significant implications for efforts to broaden the country's industrial base. According to the central bank's Survey of Private Investment in 1989, on average, 65 per cent of the total expenditure of manufacturing firms was incurred on the purchase of raw materials. Of this, a high proportion, averaging 53 per cent, represented imported materials (Bank Negara Malaysia, 1991: 47). For several industries, the import content of their raw material requirements was even higher, reaching 97 per cent for the electronics industry, 82 per cent for the paper products and printing industry, and 63 per cent for the transport equipment industry.

This is also a reflection of the fact that very few inter-firm linkages have developed between the FTZs and the rest of the national economy. Another consequence is that the possibilities for transfer pricing are great, thus negating the positive impact of FDI inflows (Bank Negara Malaysia, 1992: 60). In this regard, Takeshi Aoki (1992: 73–110) noted that:

> Foreign-owned firms operating in FTZs originally procured almost all their parts and materials from abroad. The ratio of local content in the electronics and electrical equipment industry was only 2 per cent, and in the textile industry only 0.5 per cent. Although FTZ firms contributed to the Malaysian economy in terms of expanded production, exports and job creation, they had almost no linkage with local firms in terms of procurement. FTZs were sometimes referred to as 'export-enclaves' or 'tenant industries'. From the standpoint of the input–output structure, firms in FTZs were independent, which means that they did not procure materials from other firms. This situation changed rapidly in the latter half of the 1980s, when more foreign-owned firms established operations in Malaysia.

The supplier–buyer relationship in international technology purchases can also be viewed as a 'bilateral monopoly', where the price is largely determined through a series of negotiations between the two parties assumed to be of equal strength. If this is true, then the final negotiated price should be reflective of a price in a competitive market. However, if one party is in a weaker bargaining position, as is often the case for Malaysian firms, the final negotiated price would deviate from the competitive one in favour of the stronger party. Thus, where a licensee has less than sufficient mastery of and knowledge about the technology, the licensor is usually able to extract larger economic rents from the technology transaction.

In Malaysia, the largest proportion of technology transfer payments made by firms involves payments for new machinery and equipment. These purchases are normally made through the parent companies of foreign-controlled firms. While royalties are a popular mode of payment for contracts involving continuing technical assistance or the use of patents and trademarks, they are generally fixed within a range from 1 to 5 per cent of net sales. Lump-sum payments are also utilized for the payment of technology purchases, although this has not been encouraged by MITI. Another expense for technology transfer among Malaysian firms is the cost of overseas training for local staff, found to be common among Japanese firms.

In the event that a Malaysian firm lacks the necessary technical, financial and commercial expertise in technology transfer negotiations, it can be subjected to very disadvantageous terms or may pay unreasonably high prices. This appears to be the case among many small and medium-scale firms in Malaysia known to pay royalties even for expired patents. Thus, there is a clear need for programmes to educate small firms on various aspects of technology sourcing, purchase and negotiation. Although the recent launch of the Industrial Technical Assistance Fund (ITAF) to upgrade technological capabilities within domestic small and medium-scale enterprises is a step in the right direction, this fund has not been fully utilized by such firms.

The constraints faced by local firms are reinforced by other factors such as the Japanese companies' inherent strengths and their considerable negotiating and bargaining skills built up through extensive experience in selling technology. Hence, the bargaining position of Japanese companies tends to be greater at the beginning of a relationship, when the need for their resources and expertise is most critical. Once the manufacturing facilities are established, the recipient enterprise becomes more adept, while the services of the Japanese counterpart then become less indispensable. In such a situation, there could be a shift in the relationship in favour of the local enterprise. Even then, when Japanese interests maintain equity and management control, the relationship may not be so straightforward, as Japanese companies generally tend to have a higher proportion of Japanese personnel working in Malaysia relative to other comparable foreign companies.

Equity ownership by local capital in companies where FDI participates does not necessarily mean management control. With few exceptions, most FDI operations appear to be effectively controlled by the expatriate personnel from the parent companies. This is particularly apparent in companies dependent on foreign partners to provide technical know-how as well as market access. Thus, modest foreign equity participation may not fully reflect actual foreign control of and influence over domestic industries.

The indigenization of management, particularly at the second echelon, in some companies involving foreign FDI has been observed. Although most key posts are still usually held by expatriates, efforts have been made to Malaysianize the next most senior positions. However, this process is generally more advanced among US and European-based foreign firms, perhaps to minimize the costs of employing expatriates. In contrast, there is a tendency among Japanese companies to retain a higher proportion of expatriates at the senior level, partly to ensure that technological processes originating from the parent companies are well guarded (Fong Chan Onn, 1992: 193–217).

This can also be related to the extent of local decision-making autonomy vis-à-vis the global strategic framework of FDI operations generally. This issue has a crucial bearing on FDI investment and operating behaviour. Obviously, FDI with relatively centralized systems of decision-making will be less susceptible to leverage by local factors than those which practise more decentralized styles of management.

Parent companies generally make decisions or give technical advice to local operations on matters of technology identification and the sourcing of capital equipment and machinery. It is obviously in the interest of parent companies to maintain this type of relationship, as in some cases, the parent companies are also the technology suppliers. This situation may also apply to local subsidiaries at the initial stage, when they still lack the expertise to determine their need for technology, capital equipment and machinery.

Also, a very significant proportion of international trade is intra-firm, where technology transfer offers more opportunities for transfer pricing manipulations. Vertically integrated firms (i.e. where the various stages of production from raw materials into finished goods are undertaken by the same firm or its subsidiaries) relocate their profits internationally by using transfer pricing, i.e. underpricing goods for export while selling them at market prices in foreign markets. Such behaviour seeks to minimize global tax burdens and avoid political risks. Thus, although technology may be transferable to a domestic enterprise, the costs can be very substantial. Such costs will, to a large extent, be determined by the technological gap between the foreign technology supplier and the domestic enterprise, and the socio-economic environment in the receiving country.

In such a situation, the pricing of the technology, or its components and peripherals, may not reflect competitive market prices, but may instead be dictated by transfer pricing considerations to minimize taxation on corporate income. Thus, in a country like Malaysia, where the withholding tax rate on repatriation of royalty payments under technical or licensing agreements is lower than the corporate profit tax rate, technology transfer may be overpriced to reduce such tax liabilities.

Malaysian firms' bargaining positions *vis-à-vis* Japanese technology suppliers with respect to technology transfer have tended to weaken in recent years due to intensifying competition among developing countries for FDI in general and 'high-tech' investments in particular (Djeflat, 1988: 149–65). In addition, 'sun-rise' industries characterized by rapid technological changes are unable to catch up, and as such, are much more vulnerable and dependent upon the Japanese MNCs to provide the latest improvements.

The existence of in-house R&D activities, as an indicator of a firm's technological capability, also presents one of the most effective opportunities for upgrading technical skills within such a firm. Generally, subsidiaries of foreign MNCs, including Japanese ones, which benefit directly from R&D conducted at parent companies, do not initiate substantial R&D locally. The subsidiaries simply took whatever product

120

specifications and technology that were felt to be appropriate by the parent company. Most basic research, product design, product development and process development are conducted by the parent companies. One can only observe some product adaptation activity in some local subsidiaries. Local firms have also been lacking in R&D resources, although a few of the larger ones have small R&D units engaged in quality control or product and process adaptation.

In Malaysia, Japanese firms tend to rely more than their non-Japanese counterparts, on their parent companies for basic research and new product designs. Possible explanations for the lack of R&D in the Malaysian electronics industry (especially in the semiconductor industry), for example, are the following: the short product life-cycle, the high costs and economies of scale required for R&D, highly competitive prices, and the small domestic market. However, in domestically oriented firms, the Japanese companies have tried to diversify their R&D activities through process alteration, raw materials substitution, marketing research and product design. Although this is by no means conclusive, it seems that the R&D activities of domestically oriented import-substituting firms may, in the long term, contribute to technological independence.

ENHANCING DOMESTIC TECHNOLOGICAL CAPABILITY

The above observations suggest that Japanese FDI control production methods, leaving local subsidiaries or joint venture partners very limited control over technology. Most Japanese subsidiaries are technologically dependent on their parent companies for their requirements such as machinery, equipment, parts and components. Expenditures for such purchases usually constitute a large proportion of the costs of technology transfer, apart from other payments such as royalties and fees for foreign technical assistance and expertise.

Very little R&D is carried out by local subsidiaries as such activities are usually only conducted by parent companies, ostensibly to avoid duplication and to ensure economies of scale. Consequently, parent companies are usually the major, if not exclusive source of technical information and assistance. Such technological dependence is believed to be more pronounced among the subsidiaries or affiliates of Japanese MNCs compared with, say, American companies, e.g. in the electronics industry.

Given the increasing assymetric dependence of the ASEAN economies in general, and the Malaysian economy in particular, on Japan, it is in the long-term interest of Japan to create an environment that would make Japanese firms more responsive to the needs of Malaysian firms by enhancing the latter's capacity to absorb Japanese technology and by ensuring that technology transfer from Japan is less restrictive.

Domestic industries, on the other hand, must play an important complementary role, providing a more conducive environment for effective technology transfer. Another bottleneck is the relatively under-developed science and technology (S&T) infrastructure in Malaysia. For example, there is generally little interaction between industry and the universities and research institutes. Improved relations leading to a more productive, interdependent system require substantial planning and government initiative, involving the creation of a more supportive environment for creativity and innovation, making possible greater interaction among industrial entrepreneurs, scientists, technologists and researchers.

In Malaysia, policies on technology transfer, adaptation and development, especially in relation to FDI, are vague, involving exhortation, rather than implementation. Specific guidelines should be formulated to reduce ambiguity and to facilitate the concentration of scarce resources in priority areas of technology development. Technology agreements must be closely scrutinized to minimize restrictive clauses and to induce technology licensors to develop real technological capacities. Such capacity is indeed crucial to enhance the industrial base of the economy, and will require more positive contributions from Japanese and other foreign technology licensors.

Relevant policy-makers must specify priority industries and even types of firms for technological upgrading and development. Scarce resources cannot be spread too thin over too many sectors. Implementation of the Action Plan on Industrial Technology Development should concentrate efforts on target sectors, especially industries with potential comparative advantage. Focus must shift to potentially internationally competitive industries even if only of medium or small-scale and still domestic market-oriented, especially if resource-based. This should include specific measures to enhance development of new-technology based firms.

The weakness of the existing education system is considered a primary factor contributing to low technological capability in domestic industries. It has long been recognized that the constraints related to technology absorption capacity stem from this weakness as well as the limited in-house training available to Malaysian industrial labour (Svennilson, 1964: 405–28; Edwards, 1992). The reorientation of technical and vocational schools as well as university curricula and training are urgent necessities as industry needs have changed and become more complex with rapid technological progress. There is also a significant shortage of skilled middle-level human resources, requiring major reforms in Malaysian schooling to reduce the supply gap. A key problem has been the poor linkages between various academic institutions and local firms, although there seem to be numerous obvious opportunities for mutually beneficial collaboration. The government should therefore encourage such linkages by inducing joint ventures between private firms and state institutions involved in training and R&D.

Alternative schemes for expanding technical training must also be promoted. This may include provision of incentives, and perhaps even subsidies for training programmes in priority industries, besides expanding the supply of qualified personnel to disseminate skills to the industrial work force. Additionally, there must be more publication and wider dissemination of technical textbooks, handbooks and manuals, which can be important components of skill development and technology transfer processes.

Malaysian enterprises may initially have to depend on imported technologies, rather than be expected to develop their own know-how, but can subsequently proceed to develop appropriate adaptations. Adaptive activity may in turn encourage enterprises to establish in-house R&D facilities, thus generating their own technological capabilities. Technical progress can thus be either externally induced or achieved through 'learning by doing', which involves labour accumulating experience at the firm level. This process already takes place in Malaysian industries, although it is not widespread, and mainly involves the technically skilled. However, the occupational structure of the manufacturing sector hinders such technical progress since the semi-skilled and unskilled account for a large proportion of the Malaysian manufacturing labour force (Anuwar Ali, 1984: 44–59).

On-the-job training must therefore be emphasized as the primary mode for building a firm's capacity to apply new technologies. Foreign firms should also try to run their training programmes in Malaysia rather than at their parent-company headquarters as having such training on-site encourages testing and adaptation of the technologies to suit local requirements.

Fiscal incentives should be provided and improved to encourage technology transfer and R&D activities in Malaysia. These may include: special promotional incentives for foreign firms to be tied to a definite plan for technical human resource manpower development and skills upgrading; government subsidy for R&D projects on condition that the beneficiary firms initiate the projects, specify their needs and contribute a portion of the investment required for the R&D project; reduction of import duties on laboratory equipment and offering tax credits for investments or expenditure for R&D work in Malaysia; and to establish common user R&D facilities which firms in Malaysia could use. Such a facility would even permit small firms to use equipment which would normally be beyond their means, paying according to the extent of their usage.

It will be critical for Malaysian manufacturing enterprises to catch up with their counterparts in the more industrialized economies. This will pose a formidable challenge in the years ahead as, according to Freeman (1988: 67–84):

Catching up and overtaking established technological leaders could pose formidable problems for imitators and aspirants for leadership, since they must aim at a moving target. It is no use simply importing today's technology from the leading countries, for by the time it has been introduced and efficiently assimilated the leaders have moved on and the relative position of the various countries may be unchanged or even worsened from the stand point of the followers.

CONCLUDING REMARKS

This chapter has identified and highlighted the major issues relating to FDI flows and technology transfer by Japanese firms in Malaysia. However, it is important to emphasize that, though the problems are due to the country's nascent industrial and technological base and the under-development of its human resources, they are also related to factors associated with the behaviour of capital and technology-exporting firms and countries. After spending substantial effort and investment on R&D and technology improvements, manufacturing enterprises expect to more than recover their costs to capture a certain economic rent. In this sense, the activities of Japanese FDI in Malaysia, or for that matter elsewhere, are logical extensions of their long-term strategic objectives to maximize profits and expand market control.

While it is crucial for Malaysia to try to reduce such problems with appropriate strategies as well as effective policy planning and implementation, it is equally important that advanced industrial countries like Japan also appreciate aspirations for technological enhancement. While the amount of FDI may be important to induce economic growth in the short term, the quality, type or nature of foreign investments will be crucial from a long-term perspective. This means that investments made by Japanese firms, for instance, must be viewed in terms of their impact on Malaysian technology acquisition and enhancement as well as inter-industry linkages within the domestic economy.

This would also mean that FDI must be selectively encouraged so that it will not stifle domestic investments or enterprises. The experiences of Japan and South Korea, for example, suggest that FDI was discouraged in favour of licensing arrangements for the purpose of domestic technological enhancement, as domination by foreign capital would have been detrimental for the development of domestic industrial enterprise (see Wade, 1988: 129–63; Amsden, 1989: 20–2).

REFERENCES

Amsden, A.H. (1989) *Asia's Next Giant: South Korea and Late Industrialization*, Oxford University Press, New York.
Anuwar Ali (1984) 'The Need for Technical Skills and Innovative Capacity: The Case of Manufacturing Industries in Malaysia', *Akademika*, 25.

Anuwar Ali and Muhd Anuar Adnan (1990) 'Technological Acquisition and Absorption Via Multinational Companies: The Malaysian Experience', *Jurnal Fakulti Ekonomi*, 21, 22.

Aoki, T. (1992) 'Japanese FDI and the Forming of Networks in the Asia-Pacific Region: Experience in Malaysia and Its Implications', in Shojiro Tokunaga (ed.), *Japan's Foreign Investment and Asian Economic Interdependence*, University of Tokyo Press, Tokyo.

Bank Negara Malaysia (1991) *Quarterly Bulletin*, Vol. 6, No. 1, March–June.

Bank Negara Malaysia (1992) *Annual Report, 1991*, BNM, Kuala Lumpur.

Chen, E.K.Y. and Wong, T. (1989) 'The Future Direction of Industrial Development in the Asian Newly Industrialized Economies', in Suh Jang-Won (ed.), *Strategies for Industrial Development: Concept and Policy Issues*, Asian and Pacific Development Centre, Kuala Lumpur and Korea Development Institute, Seoul.

Djeflat, A. (1988) 'The Management of Technology Transfer: Views and Experiences of Developing Countries', *International Journal of Technology Development*, Vol. 3, Issue 23.

Edwards, C. (1992) 'Foreign Investment and Industrialization in Malaysia', Paper presented at ISIS-HIID Conference on the Malaysian Economy, Kuala Lumpur, 1–3 June.

Federation of Malaysian Manufacturers (1990) 'Memorandum on National Economic Policy After 1990', *Forum 1990*, The Annual Economic and Business Journal of the Federation of Malaysian Manufacturers, Kuala Lumpur.

Fong Chan Onn (1990) 'Multinational Corporations in ASEAN: Technology Transfer and Linkages with Host Countries', in Soon Lee Ying (ed.), *Japan's Foreign Investment and Asian Economic Interdependence*, University of Tokyo Press, Tokyo.

Fong Chan Onn (1992) 'Foreign Direct Investment in Malaysia: Technology Transfer and Linkages by Japan and Asian NIEs', in Shojiro Tokunaga (ed.), *Japan's Foreign Investment and Asian Economic Interdependence*, University of Tokyo Press, Tokyo.

Freeman, C. (1988) 'Technology Gaps, International Trade and the Problems of Smaller and Less Developed Economies', in C. Freeman and B.A. Lundvall (eds.), *Small Countries Facing the Technological Revolution*, Pinter, London.

George, R.L. (1988) 'Potential NICs Move Upmarket', *Asian Finance*, Vol. 14, No. 11, 15 November.

Go Iwaki (1992) 'SMI Development and the Sub-Contracting System in Japan', in Kim Seung Jin and Suh Jang-Won (eds), *Co-operation in Small and Medium-Scale Industries in ASEAN*, Asian and Pacific Development Centre, Kuala Lumpur.

Ikeda, M. (1991) 'A Comparative Study of International Subcontracting Systems: The Automotive Parts Industries of the USA, the UK, France and Japan', in K. Shibagaki, M. Trevor and T. Abo (eds), *Japanese and European Management: Their International Adaptability*, University of Tokyo Press, Tokyo.

Kosaka, M. (1989) *Japan's Choices: New Globalism and Cultural Orientation in an Industrial State*, Pinter, London.

Lim Imran (1990) 'A Domestic Investment Initiative: Justifications and Strategies', *Forum 1990*, The Annual Economic and Business Journal of the Federation of Malaysian Manufacturers, Kuala Lumpur.

MacBean, A.I. and Balasubramanyam, V.N. (1978) *Meeting the Third World Challenge*, Macmillan, London.

Malaysia (1991) *Sixth Malaysia Plan, 1991–1995*, Government Printers, Kuala Lumpur.

Nakanishi, H. (1990) 'Japan's Trade in the Asia Pacific Region', in Susumu

Awanohara (ed.), *Japan's Economic Role in the Asia Pacific Region*, Centre for Asian Pacific Studies, Hong Kong.

Organisation for Economic Cooperation and Development (1988) *The Newly Industrializing Countries: Challenge and Opportunity for OECD Countries*, OECD, Paris.

Ozawa, T. (1982) 'The Role of Transnational Corporations in the Economic Development of the ESCAP Region: Some Available Evidence from Recent Experience', in ESCAP/UNCTC Publication Series B, No. 2, United Nations, Bangkok.

Parry, T.G. (1988) 'The Role of Foreign Capital in East Asian Industrialization, Growth and Development', in H. Hughes (ed.), *Achieving Industrialization in East Asia*, Cambridge University Press, Cambridge.

Segal, A. (1987) 'Learning by Doing', in A. Segal (ed.), *Learning by Doing: Science and Technology in the Developing World*, Westview Press, Boulder, Colorado.

Svennilson, I. (1964) 'The Transfer of Industrial Know-How to Non-Industrialized Countries', in K. Berril (ed.), *Economic Development: With Special Reference to East Asia*, Macmillan, London.

Thurow, L. (1992) *Head to Head: The Coming Economic Battle Among Japan, Europe and America*, Nicholas Brealey, London.

Tsuruoka, D. (1990) 'Taiwanese Investors Flock to Low-Wage Neighbours', *Far Eastern Economic Review*, 19 April.

Wade, R. (1988) 'The Role of Government in Overcoming Market Failure: Taiwan, Republic of Korea and Japan', in H. Hughes (ed.), *Achieving Industrialization in East Asia*, Cambridge University Press, Cambridge.

World Bank (1979) 'International Technology Transfer: Issues and Policy Options', Staff Working Paper No. 344, July, Washington DC.

5

JAPANESE MULTINATIONAL INTRA-FIRM TRADE TRANSFER PRICING PRACTICES IN MALAYSIA

Anatory Marappan and Jomo K.S.

The practice of transfer pricing by multinational corporations can be detrimental to a country by disguising capital outflows and reducing tax revenue. This empirical study was done by analysing data collected from two Japanese multinational corporation (MNCs) operating in Malaysia for more than two decades.

METHODOLOGY

Data was gathered for this study through an examination of documents from the Royal Customs and Excise Department, as well as interviews and discussions with personnel from the MNCs and government officials from a number of relevant departments. The main basis for this research is the examination of Customs documents and interviews with personnel from selected firms.

Except for one study on the car assembly industry in Malaysia (Lall, 1977), there seems to be no literature on transfer pricing practices by MNCs in Malaysia. Lall used the directly comparable uncontrolled price method to check for transfer pricing of completely knocked down (CKD) and completely built up (CBU) units in the car industry.

Other authors (Vaitsos, 1974; Rahman and Scapens, 1986) have also used this method, where the transfer prices declared for the goods under study were compared with the prices of similiar products on the open markets (or world prices).

The problem with this method is that it often happens that such evidence is not available, or it is impractical to collect it all or there is a doubt as to whether the prices quoted are comparable or the goods and services are not available in the open market.

Other methods suggested (OECD, 1979) to carry out research on transfer pricing and MNCs are the 'resale price' and the 'cost plus' methods. With the resale price method, the price at which goods are sold by the reseller (who could be an affiliate member) to independent customers is taken as the starting point. From this price, a mark-up is subtracted to arrive at the arm's length price for sale by the original vendor. The mark-up subtracted comprises the reseller's cost and a margin of profit.

In the cost plus method, the original vendor's cost is added to an appropriate mark-up to arrive at the arm's length price for sale by the vendor to the reseller. These two methods also have their drawbacks in that the addition or subtraction of appropriate costs and profit mark-up will require detailed financial data from the MNCs involved, as well as detailed knowledge of the accounting methods and conventions followed by the MNCs in pricing their goods as well as appropriate mark-up values.

In view of all these difficulties with the various methods, a combination of methods might well offer the best results in a study of transfer pricing among MNCs.

This direct comparable uncontrolled price method was also chosen for this research for three main reasons: first, the accessibility of various business documents made available by the Customs and Excise Department, second, time and resource constraints, and third, the obtainable price information closely approximating arm's length prices, since the transfer prices are negotiated prices.

Attempts were made to check prices quoted in invoices, bills of transfer, and contractual documents against prices declared to the Customs Department on sales to and purchases by affiliated parties. These were then checked against prices quoted on sales and purchases to independent parties. The prices quoted to independent parties will be deemed to be 'arm's length prices'. These prices will be used as reference prices to establish whether over- or under-pricing is being practised by the MNCs under study.

The pertinent point in this study is the 'arm's length principle', which should be followed by the MNCs for proper evaluation of prices for goods and services, for tax purposes. Following this principle, prices paid for goods transferred between associated enterprises should be those which would have been paid between unrelated parties for the same or similar goods under the same or similar circumstances (OECD, 1979).

Unrelated parties in this regard are deemed to be enterprises that do not hold any equity in each other and do not have any control whatsoever in each other's operations. Same or similar goods are taken to be final or intermediate goods having the same identification number (if it is from one supplier to a number of purchasers) and used to manufacture the same or similiar final products. In cases where the goods are the same or similar, but different identification or part numbers are used to describe them, then attempts were made to establish their similarity and then compare their transfer prices (in transactions between one supplier and many purchasers, the goods are marked differently according to purchasers' specifications).

Same or similar circumstances for the purposes of this research are deemed to be situations in which the goods are imported or purchased from one enterprise, either in the principal's or affiliate's country, and transferred to many buyers within a country, preferably within a certain location (e.g. the Kelang Valley). The mode of transport, port of embarkation and port of offloading will all have to be similar so that these factors can be disregarded when transfer prices are compared. The time frame for each investigation should be reasonably short so as to minimize the effect of fluctuations in exchange rates, inflationary tendencies and demand and supply scenarios.

SAMPLE

As is well known, there are a large number of MNCs operating in Malaysia, producing a vast array of products for local consumption as well as export. Ideally, the MNCs chosen for study should be either producing goods or importing inputs which are general in nature, i.e. the goods produced or imported cannot be differentiated from one MNC to another. In this situation, the open market values or world prices can easily be obtained from various business publications.

Examples of such goods and industries would be the primary commodities (wheat, barley, etc.) or the pharmaceutical industry. But, as mentioned before, due to data availability, time and resource constraints, the samples were taken from the electrical and electronic consumer products from Japanese MNCs. The choice of MNCs was influenced by a number of considerations, i.e. the geographical location of the production facility (i.e. easy access) and the availability of the necessary data (invoices, bills, contracts, declaration forms, etc.). Another consideration was the chance to compare the 'Japanese system' of procurement and sales with other systems. The large number of affiliates established by these MNCs, both locally and internationally, involve a large volume of inter-firm trade with an intra-firm trade character.

RESEARCH PLAN

A preliminary study was carried out to see whether the necessary data could be obtained, and to ascertain the extent of cooperation likely to be forthcoming from the MNCs. This was carried out with the help of staff of the Royal Customs and Excise Department and through discussions with some MNC personnel.

Once the feasibility of the research had been established, the structures of the MNCs were studied. Structure here refers to both managerial as well as operational structure. Equity holdings and management control were investigated, and then operations (i.e. purchases, production and sales) were studied to establish how pricing, purchases, production volume and sales decisions are arrived at, and who makes these decisions. The extent of the international spread will also be looked into to get an idea of the markets available to the MNCs for their products. The incentives and reasons why these MNC affiliates practise transfer pricing and the implications of government policies for it are also looked into. Do existing government policies and incentives curb transfer pricing or do they encourage this practice? Information on the structural aspects of the MNCs and incentives to transfer price were obtained from interviews with MNC personnel as well as from available documents.

To establish arm's length prices, sale prices to independent parties of similar goods by a vendor over a period of time were taken and the prices averaged to arrive at the arm's length price for those goods.

This price was then compared to prices of sales to affiliated parties by the vendor to draw conclusions on the existence of transfer pricing within the MNC concerned. To ensure the economic comparability of the markets in which the goods are sold, only transactions within the Kelang Valley and nearby are considered. This helped establish similar economic conditions for all buyers. Using the comparable uncontrolled price method also requires fulfilling comparable market level criterion. It is therefore necessary to compare goods sold at the same point in the chain from producer to consumer. This is a tough criterion to fulfil, unless it can be established that the main vendor sells goods to a purchaser who is the manufacturer of consumer goods. To fulfil this criterion, only bills, invoices, contracts and other documents contracted between a vendor and the manufacturers of similar consumer goods were taken into consideration. The consumer goods selected for this study are washing machines, television sets and refrigerators. The goods purchased by manufacturers are major components that go into manufacturing these items. Examples of such components are blower wheels, motors, compressors, welded bundy tubes, copper tubes for airconditioners and refrigerators, deflection yokes, integrated circuits, electrolytic capacitors and transformers for televisions.

The main factors examined and compared were the component description by name and identification number, the currency of transaction, the mode of transport, including shipping points, and the volume of the transactions. These data were extracted, tabulated and then analysed to draw conclusions.

Due to the confidential nature of the information contained in the documents examined and the sensitivity of the MNCs, the identity of the MNCs cannot be revealed. One Japanese multinational in Malaysia will be designated as AM and its subsidiaries as AM 1, AM 2 or simply 'an AM', while its parent in Japan will be designated as AP. If it has a subsidiary in Singapore, then that subsidiary will be AS. Similarly, the other Japanese MNC in Malaysia is designated as BM, its subsidiaries in Malaysia as BM1, BM2 and so forth, the subsidiary in Singapore as BS and the parent in Japan as BP.

STATISTICAL METHODS

In the research carried out on transfer pricing, the most commonly used statistical method is the average or mean prices method (Vaitsos, 1974; Lall, 1979; Rahman and Scapens, 1986). Other statistical techniques – e.g. chi square tests, t-tests, and linear programming – have been used to compare the extent of transfer pricing between two or more entities, but not to establish whether or not transfer pricing is being practised. Bearing this in mind, the method used here was the averaging method. In arriving at the arm's length price, the average (and not the lowest) of available quotations and sale prices to unrelated parties was computed. This was then compared to the average of available quotations and sale prices to related parties for a particular item, to estimate the extent of overpricing or underpricing. The following simple formula to estimate the extent of overpricing or underpricing was used in this study:

$$\frac{(P_R - P_u) \times 100}{P_u} = \% \text{ over- or underpricing}$$

where P_R stands for average sale price to related parties and P_u stands for average sale price to unrelated parties.

Corrections for differences in transportation costs, insurance costs and the time factor were not carried out since, as already mentioned, these can be disregarded by choosing transactions which occur within a short span of time and the same ports of loading and unloading. A margin of error is allowed for exchange rate fluctuations when the need arose (fluctuations in the exchange rates within a short span of time are not usually significant enough to affect the overall results much). The figures obtained were rounded off to two decimal points to make comparisons and calculations easier.

FINDINGS AND ANALYSIS

MNC Characteristics

The Japanese parent

This is a very large and internationally widely spread MNC, manufacturing many kinds of electrical and electronic items based in Japan, with subsidiaries in the Association of Southeast Asian Nations (ASEAN)

131

region, Taiwan, Hong Kong, Australia and the Americas. Its assets run into hundreds of billions of dollars worldwide and its reserves amount to billions of dollars. This AP MNC is not a single firm, but a conglomerate consisting of a publicly listed holding company, with numerous affiliates and subsidiaries in Japan. This industrial MNC was formed after the Second World War and was centred around a Japanese bank and the bank's trading companies (Buzzel and Quelch, 1988). This AP MNC is organized along product lines as well as functional lines. This MNC's organizational structure is outlined in Figure 5.1.

The products manufactured are finished consumer goods as well as components for these consumer goods. As such, a lot of intra-firm trade takes place among its subsidiaries. Components not manufactured by any of the subsidiaries are sourced from other suppliers by the purchasing

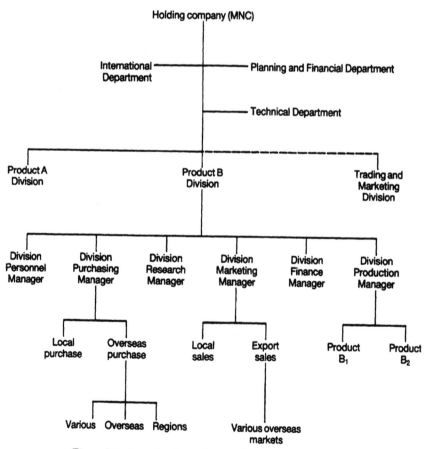

Figure 5.1 Organization of a multinational corporation.

division, with the approval of the holding company's planning and financial department.

The prices of purchases are subject to negotiations between the various parties concerned and is normally subject to the rule that 'each centre tries to obtain the best deal possible and to maximize profits', according to a senior executive of a Malaysian subsidiary. The volume to be produced and the minimum sale price for a product are set by the planning and financial department of the MNC. Overall, the operation and structure of the MNC are highly centralized and its operations integrated to facilitate planning and administration.

The trading arm's main function is to handle all the export and import business of the MNC. It acts as the agent in Japan for all its subsidiaries worldwide in the purchasing and rebilling of goods from both affiliated and non-affiliated companies. An interview with a senior Malaysian executive of the company revealed that purchases by the trading arm are negotiated with the purchasing section of a product division which places the order to an overseas subsidiary. The purchases are then made in Japanese yen and the trading arm rebills the purchases in US dollars after adding on a certain mark-up as the buyer's commission.

The amount of the mark-up 'depends on the country to which the goods are to be consigned'. If the overseas subsidiary is not satisfied with the price, then the price is renegotiated with the parent product division subject to approval by the trading arm. The process of supplying an overseas subsidiary is as shown in Figure 5.2.

A few points to note in this process of fulfilling an order is that prices are not fixed for every consignment. Prices for (common usage) goods of a general nature are fixed once or twice a year. The factors taken into account for costing are the prices of inputs, including labour, the country from which the order originates and the minimum profit level required.

Currency conversion depends on the strengths of the currencies involved. When it is favourable to the MNC, the currency of transaction is left in Japanese yen (with a mark-up) by the trading arm. This was

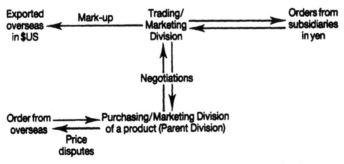

Figure 5.2 The process of supplying an overseas subsidiary.

133

confirmed by checking available invoices from the MNC's trading arm to one of its subsidiaries for the period 15 October 1986 to 16 December 1988. For example, an invoice for electrolytic capacitors dated 15 October 1986 was made out in Japanese yen, as was an invoice for similar goods dated 26 July 1988. But an invoice dated 20 November 1987 for similar goods was made in US dollars. Similarly, invoices dated 11 August 1988 and 16 December 1988 billed refrigerator parts in Japanese yen, but the grand total of the invoices, including freight charges, was added up in US dollars, with the exchange rate from Japanese yen to US dollars specified in the invoices. Payment for the goods had to be made in US dollars or Japanese yen, whichever appeared as the grand total in the invoices, according to an interview.

Checking invoices of independent suppliers of refrigerator metal tube parts, it was found that payment was demanded by one supplier in US dollars, while another supplier wanted it in Japanese yen. Of the many intra-company invoices checked for the period studied, the majority (21 out of 25) involved payment in US dollars, while the rest were in Japanese yen. The conditions or circumstances in which either Japanese yen or US dollars were demanded could not be ascertained.

Checking on the order dates, filling of orders, invoicing, and the delivery of goods to consignees, it was found that the process took between one and three months by ship. Payment for goods had to be made within 30 or 60 days of receipt, as agreed upon by both parties. As such, a period of at least four months passed from the order date to the payment date. So which exchange rate is used in intra-firm trade? Is it the rate prevailing when the order is received, or when the invoice is made out, or when payment is made? As mentioned before, the exchange rate is specified in the invoices (i.e. the yen price is also quoted in US dollars) and the payee might gain or lose depending on the exchange rate on the date of payment. For example, an invoice dated 14 January 1988 specified the exchange rate of one US dollar to 141.20 yen, but at the time of delivery of goods at Port Kelang, the prevailing rate was one US dollar to 124 yen.

The matter is further complicated when the Malaysian ringgit (RM) is brought into the picture. In such a situation, does the MNC as the consignor use forward rates to invoice, or the spot rate prevailing, or a fixed rate specified for a certain period? Most large firms regard foreign exchange trading as part of their total banking relationship, and foreign exchange trading profits compensate the banks for their other services rendered (Eiteman and Stonehill, 1986). The banks most used by the Japanese MNC for these transactions are the Bank of Tokyo and the Mitsui United Bank. To quote from a letter dated December 1986, written by the Malaysian branch of the Bank of Tokyo to vouch for a subsidiary applying for a licence under the Promotion of Investments (Amendment) Bill 1986, '. . . The company is an affiliate of (the MNC) of Japan, the largest manufacturer of electrical appliances, and maintains an active and satis-factorily conducted account with credit facilities of large means granted . . .'. The size of the credit facilities and its nature were not mentioned, though, from the business documents checked, payments were made via letters of credit. With this kind of close relationship between the banker and the client, and considering the size of the client, the bank would or could advise and guide the MNC in its dealings with various overseas affiliates.

The bank can provide foreign currencies, projected future exchange rates to the MNC as part of its service, and these can be used to try to reduce the risk of exposure to foreign exchange fluctuations as well as to shift foreign reserves to more favourable 'parking' locations. The extent of such activities is difficult to determine.

Another interesting aspect of this intra-firm trade is the flow of physical goods compared with business documents and payments. The purchase order is forwarded to the trading subsidiary in Singapore (AS), which acts as the regional purchasing and marketing agent. The AS then places the order in Japan, which then supplies the goods, as described before. The goods are supplied directly to the purchaser by the trading arm of the Japanese MNC, while the invoices for the goods are forwarded to the AS in Singapore, with a copy extended to the AM for port clearance. The invoices are marked 'for the account of AS, Singapore'. The AM then pays the AS, which charges a buyer's commission for the services provided. At no point does AS take delivery of the physical goods since the route of the goods is from Kobe to Port Kelang, where they are off-loaded. An executive explained that AS acts as the regional consolidation centre for purchasing and marketing as well as the collection centre for bills.

This roundabout way is to facilitate the smooth flow of business since the AP is such a large organization. Each subsidiary is given a code number for quick and easy identification and to facilitate book-keeping by the AP.

Another fact which emerged from this interview is that the AP's trading arm makes forward contracts with the AP's supplying subsidiaries. These forward contracts can run for three-month, six-month or one-year durations depending on the business situation, business forecasts and exchange rate conditions.

Dealings with other MNCs

Do all Japanese MNCs of a similar nature practise this form of trading or is it just practised by the MNC under study? To answer this question, contractual documents between the MNC studied and other MNCs established in Malaysia were examined. Three such agreements, in which the MNC undertook to manufacture consumer goods for other MNCs, were examined. In all three agreements, the terms and conditions were similar.

With regards to the purchase price of the final products, the wording was 'The supplier and purchaser do hereby mutually agree that the prices for products for the duration of one year from the signing of their agreement shall be as set forth in the Schedule (price list). The prices are subject to revision after mutual agreement between the purchaser and supplier in the event the Government changes any existing levy or customs duties on the products, there are abnormal price changes in the raw materials or there are undue fluctuations in the foreign exchange markets'. On the purchase prices of spare parts, the agreement states that the 'price of the spare parts to be purchased by the purchaser shall be at the negotiated and agreed prices between both parties'.

From these agreements, it can be concluded that the prices agreed upon are fair prices since the deals are between independant MNCs. In negotiating an agreement, the purchaser MNC strives to strike the best deal possible and not be shortchanged by the supplier MNC. The actual prices charged could not be compared because the price lists of both the final goods and the spare parts were not provided together with the agreements. However, the prices charged varied from one MNC to another.

If the price lists of the inputs – as negotiated and agreed upon by the MNC with other MNCs – had been available, then direct comparison could have been made to establish the 'fairness' of the prices charged by the MNC to its subsidiaries. Unfortunately, not even a single list was forthcoming from the MNC's companies, and none were found in the files of the Customs Department. Another difficulty encountered was that practically no independent manufacturer bought directly from any of the parent divisions of the MNC.

As such, price comparisons, to ascertain fair deals, were difficult to make. Overall, it can be said that the MNC is both vertically as well as horizontally integrated, and the degree of autonomy allowed to its various holdings is limited. The prices charged varied depending on the purchaser and other factors.

The Japanese MNC in Malaysia

In Malaysia, the MNC has a total of 15 holdings, which can be categorized into three main types:

1 A publicly listed holding company with a wholly owned subsidiary manufacturing components for electrical consumer products, and an associated company in which the holding company holds a minority 40 per cent equity interest; the principal activity of the associated company is to sell consumer products, home appliances and batteries.
2 Firms which manufacture electrical and electronic components situated in the various Free Trade Zones (FTZs) around the country, which are

mostly wholly owned by the Japanese MNC (i.e. 100 per cent equity held by AP) and enjoy all the benefits accorded to firms situated in Malaysian FTZs, deemed to be situated outside the principal customs area of Malaysia, including pioneer status, duty free imports and exports of capital equipment, inputs and final products.

3 Firms which have licensed manufacturing warehouse status (LMW), which, for all intents and purposes, is similar to firms in FTZs; they enjoy similar benefits, i.e. duty-free imports, pioneer status and so on, are deemed to be situated in the principal customs area and have to adhere to certain rules and regulations laid down by the relevant authorities.

This category of firms are either wholly owned or majority owned by the MNC, with the Japanese MNC having around 90 per cent equity in these firms. The organization of all three categories of firms is shown in Figure 5.3.

The chairman of the subsidiary is usually a titled Malaysian, the managing director a Japanese, and the various directors either Japanese or Malaysian depending on the age and nature of the subsidiary. In the early stages, the works director, accounts director and export director are Japanese, while the personnel director is local. The managers are Malaysians, but with Japanese advisors appointed for various functions. For example, the post of products manager is held by a Malaysian, with a Japanese appointed as manufacturing advisor. Similarly, the post of quality control and design executive is held by a local, with two Japanese advisors for quality control and design respectively.

In the case of the publicly listed company, the post of accounts director was handed over to a local after some time. For the other two categories, the posts have been maintained as at the outset. For these two categories, when applying for manufacturing licences, the MNC categorically stated

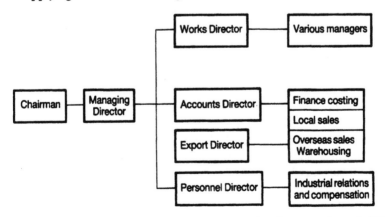

Figure 5.3 Organization of the Malaysian multinational corporation subsidiary.

that a key condition for investing in the project was official approval for a number of key posts to be held by Japanese throughout the duration of the investment as well as provision for 12 to 18 posts to be held by Japanese on a rotation basis. The key posts to be held by Japanese in perpetuity were the posts of managing director, works director, accounts director and export director, while the rotating posts were those for the various advisors. Other key provisions applied for were 10 years' pioneer status, 5 per cent royalty payable to AP of Japan, and 100 per cent equity to be held by AP of Japan in perpetuity. From interviews and published documents, it was found that most of these demands were granted, except for the duration of pioneer status which is shorter, but subject to re-application and re-negotiation when the period ends. This kind of organization plus the concessions granted to these subsidiaries enable these firms to be tightly controlled by the parent MNC in Japan.

Historically, the MNC started off in Southeast Asia on a small scale as a trading company based in Singapore. In 1965, it was incorporated in Malaysia under the Companies Ordinance, 1940, to manufacture electrical appliances, and in 1966, it became a public company by a special resolution of its board of directors. With the introduction of the FTZ concept in Malaysia, the Japanese MNCP established manufacturing subsidiaries in these FTZs to take advantage of the various concessions as well as the cheap labour force available in Malaysia. The business strategy of these establishments in the FTZs is growth by expansion. A manufacturing subsidiary starts off by manufacturing a product and its major intermediate inputs. As demand and – as a consequence – production increase, and as the pioneer status period comes to an end, the subsidiary 'splits'. Separate establishments are set up to manufacture the major components and fresh pioneer status obtained for these new subsidiaries. In this manner, the period of pioneer status granted for the component almost doubles, and in some cases, more than doubles when pioneer status is further extended for some reason or other. For example, the first holding in an FTZ was set up in 1972, and enjoyed pioneer status (after an extension) until 1981. Then, two separate companies (wholly owned by the Japanese MNC) were set up to manufacture a number of major components in the same FTZ as well as in another FTZ. Pioneer status for a further seven years was granted to these new subsidiaries.

According to a senior manager of the first holding, this firm had not paid any income tax as of 1990, and was not expected to pay any tax for at least the next two to three years. Such tax avoidance was possible because, besides pioneer status, capital depreciation allowances usually cancel out whatever taxes may be payable. Overall, it can be said that once established, an AP subsidiary in a FTZ enjoys pioneer status for 7 to 10 years, and avoids paying income tax for a period of about 12 to 15 years, depending on its capital outlay.

Similarly, subsidiaries with LMW status could use the same strategies to enjoy long tax holidays, and when the situation allows, they can 'split' and carry on having pioneer status for new establishments manufacturing old components. Another feature in this 'split and expand' strategy is that the top management of the various subsidiaries in the FTZs as well as the LMWs are the same. For example, the financial director for a subsidiary in the Sungai Way FTZ and an LMW in Shah Alam is the same person, while the two subsidiaries have common accounts. Except for the publicly listed company and its subsidiaries and affiliates, all the other subsidiaries share common top management and accounts.

Purchases, sales and pricing in the Malaysian subsidiaries

The transactions of the publicly listed company, which has no interests in the other Japanese MNC subsidiaries, has to be distinguished from the transactions of the FTZ and LMW subsidiaries. In placing a purchase order for inputs not available from local suppliers, the publicly listed company's product divisions places the order with the MNC's trading company in Singapore. The Singapore Subsidiary then forwards the order to the parent division (which manufactures the particular product) in Japan. The order is then filled, as explained earlier. Only when the quantity ordered is large enough, does the product division place an order directly with the parent division in Japan.

As explained by a costing executive, 'small orders will not be entertained by Japan, so we have to go through Singapore, which collects orders from all the subsidiaries on a regional basis and forwards them to Japan'. On setting prices for the purchases, the executive explained that the Japanese advisors will negotiate with the parent division in Japan, which in turn sets prices, as explained earlier. In fixing prices for general inputs, prices are discussed and fixed during the periodic visits of the advisors to Japan and during management meetings between subsidiaries and parent divisions. During the course of the research, it was found that the Malaysians appointed to the board did not have much say in negotiating the prices of inputs from Japan. A director explained that he and his costing and purchasing staff appointed local suppliers and negotiated the purchase prices of local supplies upon the advice of the resident Japanese advisor. As far as inputs from Japan were concerned, he did not have much knowledge of the pricing mechanism and process, and left it to the Japanese advisors and the holding company's financial section to make the deals. He has set up a committee, comprising costing personnel and purchasing executives, to study sourcing from other suppliers of inputs presently being bought from Japan.

If cheaper sources are found, without compromising quality, then the committee is empowered to recommend that source to the management.

One of the committee members interviewed explained that the committee can only purchase limited amounts from other sources, even if the prices are cheaper. This committee was established to give locals greater autonomy in managing the company, but he noted that the autonomy was limited, and major purchasing decisions were still decided by the advisors.

Television components

The pricing of the completely manufactured product is done by the top down method of costing, as shown in Table 5.1. This costing is then submitted to the Customs authorities for approval. As such, the ex-factory prices of these products are negotiated prices. In some situations, the ex-factory prices submitted for approval are raised by between one to two per cent by the authorities to cover for missing factors in the costing procedure. An example of an application for approval by the authorities – of a home appliance model – is shown below, though the figures are not the actual prices.

Table 5.1 Valuation method for tax purposes

Description of the item: *Model ABC*

Parts	Part no.	Supplier	Value (RM)
Switch	ST20	AP, Japan	14.00
Electrolytic capacitor	ET11	AP, Japan	25.00
Integrated circuit	AK60	AM, Sg. Way	30.00
Other items			307.00
		[SUBTOTAL]	376.00
Other imports			250.00
Import duties			130.00
Local inputs			95.00
Labour			20.00
Overheads			15.00
Administration			40.00
Interests			12.00
Royalty			40.00
Sales expenses			20.00
Profit			200.00
Ex-factory		[SUBTOTAL]	1198.00
Agency uplift 12.5%			149.75
Open market value		[SUBTOTAL]	1347.75
Excise duty 10%			134.78
Sales tax 10%			148.25
Sale price		TOTAL	1630.78

Major imported items and major locally purchased items are listed, and invoices provided to substantiate the price claims. The rest of the items are lumped together as 'other imports' and 'other local inputs'. To these figures, other costs – like customs duties, labour, overheads, royalty and loan interest – are added, together with a percentage for profit. These amount to the ex-factory price of the good. If the authorities are satisfied with the costing, then the ex-factory price is raised by a factor of 12.5% to arrive at the open market value for tax purposes. This percentage is deemed to be an 'agency uplift', since the sale is to a related party, i.e. to the marketing arm of the MNC in Malaysia. This agency uplift is allowed by international trade practice to arrive at an open market value or fair price. It has to be noted that agency uplifts are variable and reflect the relationship between the selling subsidiary and the purchasing subsidiary. The cost declared by the MNC is scrutinized by the Customs' Valuation Department to determine what is to be considered a fair uplift to be levied on the MNC. If the MNC feels that the quantum of the uplift is too high, it can appeal – with supporting documents – to have the quantum reduced.

These prices can also be verified by checking prices at retail outlets in Malaysia as well as Singapore. Another factor that promotes fair prices for goods sold locally by the MNC is the competition provided by other MNCs in the market.

The main points at which transfer pricing (under- or overpricing) can be practised by this MNC are when it is importing components from its overseas subsidiaries or from its subsidiaries in the FTZs and LMWs. Whether they do or do not practise transfer pricing in components trading was investigated by researching the information contained in invoices from Japan as well as from the subsidiaries in the FTZs and LMWs. To check for this practice, a number of components for household electrical goods commonly imported from the AP were identified and the invoiced prices extracted for a number of importations from Japan. These prices were obtained from invoices provided to the Customs Department for valuation purposes, and as such, full compatibility for the periods under comparison could not be achieved. These invoices were provided to the authorities by the local subsidiaries only as and when deemed necessary.

The components chosen for the research were: (i) electrolytic capacitors (ECs); (ii) integrated circuits (ICs); (iii) flyback transformers; (iv) copper tubing; and (v) resistors. As an example, the data were extracted and compiled as in Table 5.2, to facilitate analysis and to obtain average prices. The results of the preliminary compilation are shown in Tables 5.3, 5.4 and 5.5. The currency of transaction was also noted to establish the role of exchange rates in the trade. The prices were all standardized to FOB or CIF prices to facilitate comparison and analysis.

In the first exercise, involving television components, the average prices for the period studied in Tables 5.3 to 5.5 were RM17.36 for flyback

Table 5.2 Importing subsidiary: AM (television manufacturer)

Date of invoice	Part name	Part no.	Price (FOB)	Supplier
2.1.88.	EC	XYZ	RM12.00/pc	AM
6.2.88.	IC	ABC	US$6.00/pc	AP
7.2.88.	Copper tube	CD-22	US$800.00/ 12,000 pc	AP

Table 5.3 Import prices for flyback transformer (part no. TF4695F1) supplied by AM (FTZ, Johor Baru) to the importing publicly listed television manufacturer subsidiary

Date of invoice	FOB price/pc (RM)
16.10.87.	16.92
20.10.87.	16.92
20.11.87.	16.92
11.12.87.	16.92
27.1.88.	16.92
11.7.88.	17.00
14.8.88.	17.00
11.6.89.	20.12
6.10.89.	17.43
13.10.89.	17.43
Average	17.36/pc

Table 5.4 Import prices for integrated circuit (part no. MN1514 EAI) supplied by Japanese parent firm in Osaka to the importing publicly listed television manufacturer subsidiary

Date of invoice	FOB price/pc
20.11.87.	[a]US$2.77 = yen 332
14.1.88.	yen 332
16.7.88.	yen 343
20.8.88.	US$2.95 = yen 416
21.11.88.	yen 332
2.5.89.	yen 332
21.8.89.	yen 332
6.10.89.	US$2.46 = yen 305
10.10.89.	US$2.46 = yen 305
28.12.89.	yen 356
17.1.90.	yen 356
Average	yen 313/pc

[a] US$ conversion rate to yen is as stated in the invoices.

Table 5.5 Import prices for deflection yoke (part no. TLY259F) supplied by AM (FTZ, Sungei Way) to the importing publicly listed television manufacturer subsidiary

Date of invoice	Price (RM)
25.9.87.	9.43
14.1.88.	13.90
26.1.88.	13.90
27.1.88.	13.90
25.5.88.	13.90
16.8.88.	14.32
13.6.89.	14.32
6.10.89.	14.32
Average	13.45

transformers, 313 yen for integrated circuits imported from Japan, and RM13.45 for deflection yokes bought from subsidiaries in Malaysian FTZs. With this price information, attempts were made to find independent purchasers of these components from the Japanese MNC as well as the Malaysian subsidiaries.

These attempts proved futile because no documents or other evidence could be found showing the sale of these components to independent parties. Hence, no conclusions as to whether or not transfer pricing was being practised could be made. Nevertheless, in the course of the exercise, a few observations were noted, namely:

1 Payments were mainly in US dollars to the account of the marketing arm in Singapore for all imports from the AP.
2 The exchange rate from US dollars to Japanese yen was specified in most of the invoices from the Japanese MNC. Usually these exchange rates did not tally with the exchange rate prevailing at the time of the goods entry into Malaysia.
3 In purchase and supply contracts, in case of big fluctuations in the exchange rate, provisions were made for prices to be re-quoted.
4 Most of the major components, accounting for 60 per cent of all inputs, were from related companies.

Refrigerator components

When this exercise failed to confirm whether or not transfer pricing was being practised, another Japanese MNC manufacturing refrigerators was studied. The components studied were copper tubing and related parts imported from the parent MNC in Japan. There are two ways for this component to be imported by the MNC subsidiary in Malaysia. One way is direct importation from Japan, and the other method is to import the component through the Singapore trading arm. The data obtained is shown in Table 5.6.

The consignments were usually in lots of about 700 to 1,200 pieces per part per consignment, but prices per piece were worked out for easy comparison. The average price was US$ 0.71 per piece for direct imports by the Malaysian subsidiary, while imports through Singapore averaged US$ 0.61 per piece. The direct imports were thus overpriced by 16 per cent compared with imports via the Singapore account. The Singapore subsidiary earns a buyer's commission of 2.5 per cent of the sales value. Even taking this into consideration, the direct sales were still overpriced by about 14 per cent. This overpricing does seem difficult to explain since goods delivery in both cases is directly from Kobe to Port Kelang, the quantities ordered are similar, and the final purchaser is the Malaysian subsidary manufacturing refrigerators. In fact, if pricing is fair then importation via the Singapore account should be higher due to the 2.5 per cent buyer's commission charged.

The reason that prices are lower for orders via Singapore could be because the trading arm receives quantity discounts since it acts as the regional trading centre for the Japanese MNC. These quantity discounts could reduce the price in spite of the buyer's commission. Another reason could be that the Singapore trading arm is a better bargainer than its Malaysian counterpart.

Also, the Malaysian associated company in this case is a publicly listed company, and the locals hold a substantial amount of shares in it, while the Singapore trading arm is a wholly owned subsidiary of the Japanese MNC.

Table 5.6 Importation of refrigerator copper tubes

Part name	Part no.	Price (US$) per piece direct imports (11.8.88.)	Price (US$) per piece imports Singapore account (16.2.88.)	Difference
Copper tube	T.00100	0.81/pc	0.77/pc	0.04
Copper tube	T.00380	0.56/pc	0.43/pc	0.13
Copper tube	T.00510	0.55/pc	0.38/pc	0.17
Copper tube	T.8680	0.53/pc	0.37/pc	0.16
Pipe dryer	4950	0.48/pc	0.47/pc	0.01
Suction pipe	5220	0.41/pc	0.39/pc	0.02
Av. price		0.71/pc	0.61/pc	

$$\text{Overpaid by:} \quad \frac{0.71-0.61}{0.61} \times 100 = 16\%$$

Hence, the Japanese MNC tends to extract higher prices from the publicly-listed Malaysian associate (indirectly affecting profitability and local shareholders' profits) compared with its wholly owned subsidiary. Invoices for imports by wholly owned subsidiaries in the FTZs and the LMWs were not available to make further comparisons and conclusions.

Another possible reason for the price differential could be the differences between corporate tax rates in Malaysia and Singapore. Profits originating in Malaysia and remitted to Japan are not subject to any withholding taxes on dividends remitted, but are liable to a 20 per cent tax on interest earned from financial institutions, and then remitted abroad. Similarly, there is a 15 per cent withholding tax on royalties remitted abroad by MNC subsidiaries in Malaysia. Singapore does not impose many of these taxes on MNC subsidiaries on the island, while taxes levied are very much lower after discounting incentives and subsidies. Very little or no tax liability arises when a Singapore branch remits profits to its head office, according to the 1990 International Tax Handbook. These factors could cause an MNC to charge higher prices for goods sold directly to Malaysia to compensate for the lower profits forthcoming. For example, the total volume of imports of DC motors into Malaysia from Japan in 1989 amounted to about RM40 million (*Annual Report 1989*, Royal Customs and Excise Department). If the MNC overpriced these imports by, say, 16 per cent, then the amount overpaid would be RM5.52 million. If all imported components are considered, then the excess paid would run into hundreds of millions of ringgit.

Another aspect of the operations of the Malaysian subsidiary studied was the sale of components between various subsidiaries within Malaysia. For this exercise, a subsidiary manufacturing electrolytic capacitors in a FTZ

Table 5.7 Sale prices of electrolytic capacitor from a Japanese MNC subsidiary to sister companies and independent buyers

Month of invoice	Part no.	Price to buyers	
		Sister companies (RM/12,000 pieces)	Independent buyers (RM/12,000 pieces)
Jan. 1991	470B	1200.00	985.20
Dec. 1990	101B	877.20	810.00
Dec. 1990	2R2B	634.00	516.00
Dec. 1990	R47B	634.00	516.00
Dec. 1990	471E	1512.00	1132.00
Dec. 1990	770E	1104.00	1033.20
Nov. 1990	330B	636.00	516.00
Nov. 1990	3R3B	546.00	490.00
Average price		892.90	749.80

was studied. This subsidiary sells its products to its sister companies in Malaysia and overseas, as well as independent buyers. The data compiled are shown in Table 5.7.

The sale prices to sister companies are very much higher than to independent buyers. A senior financial executive of the manufacturing subsidiary was interviewed regarding these differences in prices. He claimed that due to stiff competition from other manufacturers, the prices to independent buyers had to be kept low. If this is the case, then it can be concluded that the price to independent buyers is an arm's length price, while sales to sister companies are transfer priced at inflated prices. This high transfer price would actually adversely affect the publicly listed Malaysian associated company in the long run, since the other subsidiaries are wholly owned by the Japanese MNC parent. With this high price, the profits of the publicly listed Malaysian associate would be reduced, with local shareholders receiving less than would otherwise be due to them. The manufacturing subsidiary makes extra profits, which can be used for further expansion and remittances abroad to its Japanese parent company. In this case, the overpricing to subsidiaries averaged 19 per cent.

What would the supplying Malaysian subsidiary and eventually, the Japanese MNC gain by overpricing sales to other subsidiaries? The component-manufacturing subsidiary manufactures major components used in final consumer goods manufactured by other subsidiaries. These goods are only exported via the Singapore trading arm, and via the local sales and service arm for local sales. Export sales prices for these consumer goods are not scrutinized by the Customs Department since no export duties or taxes are due. In this kind of an environment, the subsidiaries in the LMWs and FTZs can transfer their final goods at whatever price they see fit. Even the publicly listed company can export its goods at convenient transfer prices without being queried by the authorities. Only for sales to the local market (except for Labuan, Langkawi and to PERNAMA – a marketing organization set up for the Armed Forces in Malaysia) is the price negotiated with the Customs' authorities since excise and sales tax have to be paid. As such, with high sale prices of components to other subsidiaries and high sale prices of final goods for export sales, the MNC gains handsome profits. The higher the transfer price at each stage of manufacture, the higher the profits reaped for exported items by the MNC via its marketing arm in Singapore. This strategy is feasibly possible in Malaysia because the MNC's position in this particular industry is virtually monopolistic. The situation is such that some other large Japanese MNCs have ceased manufacturing some of their own products, and have signed contracts with this MNC to manufacture some of their goods for them. These goods are then labelled with the other MNCs' respective trademarks for sale in the market. Documents examined show that six large Japanese

MNCs and an American MNC have contracted with this MNC to manufacture goods for them.

Finally, the prices of finished consumer goods were checked to see whether this MNC practises transfer pricing. These goods fall into two categories for Customs' purposes. One category of goods is liable for excise duty and sales tax, while the other only incurs sales tax. These duties and taxes apply only to sales in the local market, and not to goods exported or sold to PERNAMA (for Armed Forces personnel). Two washing machine models and a refrigerator model manufactured by a subsidiary were selected, and the FOB or FOR (free on road) prices at which the units were sold to a number of buyers was checked. The results are summarized in Tables 5.8 and 5.9. Taking the price to other Japanese MNCs as the FOR arm's length price, the price differences to various buyers were calculated to determine whether transfer pricing was being practised (Table 5.9).

From these results, it can be seen that sales to the local sales subsidiary are almost at arm's length prices. This can be attributed to the fact that local sales prices are prices negotiated with the Customs Department (i.e. valuation and costing are agreed upon between the Malaysian subsidiaries and the Department). The small differences can be attributed to the competitive forces involved. The model ABC is the leading and main model, and as such, prices are kept lower than for other Japanese brands (some of which are manufactured by the same MNC in any case) to ensure a price advantage.

The lowest price was for sales to the parent firm in Japan with a difference of −32 per cent for model ABC; the next lowest price was −23

Table 5.8 FOB or FOR prices to various purchasers

Customers/ destination	Washing machine model ABC (RM)	Washing machine model XYZ (RM)	Refrigerator model MN (RM)
Local sales arm	320.00	644.00	450.00
Singapore sales arm	260.00	n.a.	n.a.
Japanese parent	yen 10742 = 230	n.a.	n.a.
Japanese independent (one sale in 1990)	281.00	n.a.	n.a.
PERNAMA	387.00	750.00	524.00
Middle East (via Singapore)	285.00	n.a.	n.a.
Latin America (via Singapore)	311.00	n.a.	n.a.
Pacific Islands (via Singapore)	285.00	n.a.	n.a.
Local independent (arm's length price)	336.00	627.00	435.00

The prices are an average for the years 1990 and 1991.

Table 5.9 Percentage transfer pricing to various purchases

Customers/ destinations	Model ABC	Model XYZ	Model MN
Local sales arm	−5%	+3%	+4%
Singapore sales arm	−23%	n.a.	n.a.
Japanese parent	−32%	n.a.	n.a.
Japanese independent (one sale only)	−16%	n.a.	n.a.
PERNAMA	+15%	+20%	+20%
Middle East	−15%	n.a.	n.a.
Latin America	−7%	n.a.	n.a.
Pacific Islands	−15%	n.a.	n.a.
Local independent (arm's length price)	0	0	0

Note: Sales to the Japanese independent, Middle East, Latin America and Pacific Islands were through the Singapore trading arm.

per cent to the Singapore sales arm. The lower transfer price to the Japanese parent MNC could be because the Singapore trading arm does not take its usual commission for such sales. As explained earlier, it is the Japanese MNC that advises the Malaysian subsidiaries on how much to produce for export sale and at what price. Similarly, it is the Japanese parent that advises the Singapore trading arm on prices for various purchasers in different countries. So, it is not surprising that sales to itself carry the lowest prices. Sales to independent Japanese purchasers do not tell us much since only one sales document, dated mid-1990, was found.

Sales of model ABC to the Middle East, Latin America and the Pacific Islands were under transfer priced at between −7 per cent to −5 per cent. This can be explained because these sales were not direct but via the Singapore trading arm. These transfer prices could be manipulated by the trading arm with the actual supply price charged being higher. The only higher transfer price for model ABC discovered, was for sales to PERNAMA. The prices to PERNAMA were between 10 and 24 per cent higher than prices to the local sales arm. From these figures, it can be seen that there is a hidden profit flow through lower transfer prices from local subsidiaries to the Singapore trading arm and the parent firm in Japan.

To see whether other Japanese MNCs practise this kind of strategy, another Japanese MNC manufacturing television sets in a LMW was studied. The sale prices of a number of television models for export via a Singapore trading arm and to the local market via another local subsidiary were analysed. The results are shown in Table 5.10.

As can be seen, the transfer prices were between 8 to 17 per cent lower for the Singapore trading arm, suggesting that it acts as the profit accumulation centre for the region. The price lists provided by the

Table 5.10 Sale prices to Singapore and Malaysian trading arms and percentage differences

	Transfer price per TV set for 1991 (RM)		
Models	*Singapore*	*Local*	*% Difference*
8441GB	572.88	619.99	−8
8441NA	494.92	550.16	−10
8461MT	605.12	671.30	−10
8461GT	1095.56	1237.45	−12
8491GT	661.49	738.04	−10
5312MT	874.88	973.02	−10
8412MT	768.32	855.25	−10
8412MT/6	709.16	855.25	−17
Av. price	722.79	812.56	−11

Malaysian marketing subsidiary clearly state that the prices are transfer prices. A company executive interviewed claimed that price differences were due to the moulds supplied by the Singapore subsidiary; in lieu of payment for the moulds, the manufacturing subsidiary reduced prices to the Singapore subsidiary in countertrade. The moulds supplied by the Singapore subsidiary were between RM250,000 to RM350,000 per piece; two moulds per model are needed each year according to the import/ export manager. This works out to an average of RM600,000 per television set model, amounting to about RM4.8 million for the eight models sampled. The production figures extracted from financial documents show that 70,000 sets of 12 models are produced per month; this figure, which works out to 840,000 sets per year, was confirmed in the interview. Taking the average prices to Singapore as RM722.79 (refer Table 5.10) and to Malaysia as RM812.56, according to the financial documents and interviews with Malaysian subsidiaries, the Singapore subsidiary paid RM47,748,000 less than the Malaysian subsidiary would have paid if the sets had been sold locally.

The total value of moulds supplied by the Singapore subsidiary amounts to RM5.4 million, undermining the 'explanation' by the executive that sets are sold cheaper to the Singapore subsidiary to pay for the moulds supplied free. The Singapore subsidiary pays about RM42 millon less than Malaysian subsidiaries would have to pay even after the moulds are fully paid for. This points to a profit outflow from the local manufacturing subsidiary to the MNC's Singapore trading arm which, for all intents and purposes, is just an extension of the parent MNC in Japan. If the MNC's six other manufacturing subsidiaries in Malaysia practise the same kind of transfer pricing, then the volume of profit outflow would be enormous.

A further exercise was carried out to check whether the manufacturing subsidiary would sell its product to independent buyers. For this exercise, the help of a locally owned and registered trading company was sought. This company enquired about purchasing the product for export to Europe. All necessary documents – letters of credit, purchase intentions, quantity and specification, duration of purchase (contracts) and country and port of destination – were provided to the manufacturing subsidiary's management. The quantity and amount involved were quite substantial since the local company actually wanted to purchase the product for export to some European countries. The manufacturing subsidiary's reply was that 'their manufactured products for export were 100 per cent sold to the Singapore trading subsidiary and sales to other parties for export were totally prohibited by the (MNC parent firm) of Japan'. It further explained that the Malaysian manufacturing subsidiary acted solely as a production unit, while other business transactions (i.e. export, pricing, international marketing, appointment of distributors worldwide, supply of components, transportation and insurance) were handled by the parent in Japan.

With such tight control over the manufacturing unit, it would not be surprising if the Japanese MNC and, for that matter, other MNCs, set transfer prices to draw profit from Malaysia to Singapore. According to Lall (1977), the Singaporean authorities thought then that profits were being shifted to the island, rather than away from it; this analysis suggests that they were probably right then as well as now.

This flow of profits away from the Malaysian subsidiaries does not mean that these firms run at a loss, but only that they suppress profits. The balance sheets of the publicly listed Malaysian associated company discussed earlier and the manufacturing subsidiary producing television sets show that profits after taxation were RM9.92 million for 1987 in the first case and RM2.57 million for the month of March 1990 in the latter case. The actual profits could have been very much higher, especially in the latter case, if fair trading and pricing policies were adopted instead. MNCs may disclose low levels of profits locally in some countries to maximize net global profits, as suggested by Booth and Jensen (1977).

SUMMARY AND CONCLUSION

Summary

The main objective of this study has been to find out whether MNCs in Malaysia practise transfer pricing. The knowledge gained by this study can be used by the authorities to plug loopholes in the flow of profits from the country as well as to check the trade practices of the MNCs.

From the data collected and analysed, it can be concluded that both the MNC subsidiary manufacturing electronic products in the FTZ, and the MNC subsidiary producing washing machines practise transfer pricing. The

FTZ subsidiary practises transfer pricing for sales to its affiliates, while the other subsidiary practises transfer pricing for sales to the MNC's Singapore marketing arm and to the parent firm itself. Both these practices result in profit accumulation in wholly owned pioneer status firms or the wholly owned trading subsidiary. As such, we can conclude that the MNCs studied practised transfer pricing as and when it suited them.

But monopolistic pricing should also not be left out of the analysis. By virtue of their status as MNCs with huge resources backing them and their domination of the market, it would not be surprising to find that these prices are actually monopolistic prices as well. As explained earlier, the MNCs, especially the Malaysian manufacturing subsidiaries, manufacture household electrical goods for other MNCs as well on a contract basis. This arrangement makes it easy for the Malaysian manufacturing subsidiaries, and indirectly, for the parent firm in Japan, to set prices, not only for their goods, but also for the other MNC goods. Large scale production can push down production costs but sale prices can still be maintained at previous levels, especially for goods sold locally and to contractors. Goods exported can be transfer priced at cost, and the benefits of large scale production gained by others. In this situation, the MNCs make use of market conditions and their product popularity to fix prices to their advantage and maximize profits locally as well as offshore.

As noted in a proposal submitted to the authorities to open a FTZ plant in 1987, of the proposed authorised capital of RM20 million, paid-up capital of RM20 million was to be remitted by the parent MNC and not to be contributed by the Malaysian subsidiaries and associated companies, with a further RM25 million forthcoming from offshore loans. Of course, the RM20 million remitted by the parent could actually be from accumulated profits in Malaysia and the further RM25 million could be from profits accumulated in Singapore from regional operations, though no hard evidence exists to support these conjectures.

One reason these profits may have been accumulated in Malaysia and in Singapore is that all sources of income, wherever they arise, are taxed on an effective rate of 51 to 53 per cent in Japan, while such income in Malaysia is tax free (owing to pioneer status), while the effective rate in Singapore is well below 32 per cent, after taking into consideration all the incentives given (1990 International Tax Handbook). One of the industries for which 50 per cent of foreign income is tax-exempt is the warehousing and servicing industry in Singapore. Dividends paid out of exempted income are free of tax. Combined with other incentives, the effective rate is then around 10 per cent in Singapore. If the industry is granted pioneer status, it enjoys tax holidays for up to 15 years. With this kind of tax environment, the MNC would be foolish indeed to remit all its profits to Japan, where it would be heavily taxed.

One reason for transfer pricing and profit accumulation offshore is that there are no exchange controls that hinder the flow of funds. Singapore and Malaysia have very liberal exchange control policies. These facilitate the transfer of funds to any part of the world, as desired and without interference from the governments.

Tariffs and quotas do not seem to have much significance for transfer pricing practices while exchange rates may play a role. A financial statement for a Malaysian subsidiary of a Japanese MNC shows that foreign exchange trading gains amounted to RM33,000 for March 1990 and to RM179,000 for the years 1988, 1989 and 1990. This acknowledgement of foreign exchange gains or losses in financial statements was discontinued after March 1990. Another statement during the same month indicated the existence of a Tokyo fund with RM797,000 but the meaning of this statement was not clear as it could be merely the total foreign exchange gains from selling intermediate goods to the subsidiary.

Conclusions

Because successful pricing is a key element in achieving profits, transfer pricing strategies are inevitably corporate secrets. The information available, though meagre, suggests that some MNCs probably practise transfer pricing to a greater extent than others, though few, if any, abstain from it totally. Some MNCs may maintain a 'flexible' transfer pricing policy, by complying with tax and customs authorities' rulings on a case-by-case basis. To overcome the problem of transfer pricing and to avoid excessive disguised profit outflows, the government must improve methods of information gathering and investigation. Such systematic gathering and use of information will require greater co-ordination among the departments concerned with transfer pricing, i.e. Income Tax, Customs, Bank Negara, Statistics, MIDA and MITI in the case of Malaysia. To date, very few laws have provisions to check the pricing policies of MNCs. The Customs Act, the Excise Act, the Sales Tax Act and the Income Tax Act seem to be the few Acts with specific sections pertaining to fair or arm's length prices; these particular Acts and sections should be strengthened and enforced vigorously, but judiciously.

BIBLIOGRAPHY

Booth, E.J.R. and Jensen, O.W. (1977) 'Transfer Prices in the Global Corporation Under Internal and External Constraints', *Canadian Journal of Economics*, IV, 3, August, 434–46.

Buzzel, R.D. and Quelch, J.A. (1988) *Multinational Marketing Management: Cases and Readings*, Addison Wesley for Harvard Business School, Reading.

Eiteman, E.K. and Stonehill, A.I. (1986) *Multinational Business Finance*, Addison Wesley, Reading.

Horwath International, CCH International (1990) *International Tax Hand Book*, CCH Australia, Sydney.

Lall, S. (1977) 'Transfer Pricing in Assembly Industries: A Preliminary Analysis of Issues in Malaysia and Singapore', Commonwealth Secretariat, London.

Lall. S. (1979) 'Transfer Pricing and Developing Countries: Some Problems of Investigation', *World Development*, 7: 59–71.

OECD (1979) *Transfer Pricing and Multinational Enterprises*, Report of the OECD Committee on Fiscal Affairs, OECD, Paris.

Rahman, M. Zubaidur and Scapens, Robert W. (1986) 'Transfer Pricing by Multinationals: Some Evidence from Bangladesh', *Journal of Business Finance and Accounting*, 13, 3, Autumn, 383–91.

Vaitsos, C.V. (1974) *Inter-Country Income Distributions and Transnational Corporations*, Clarendon Press, Oxford.

6

A JAPANESE FACTORY IN MALAYSIA

Ethnicity as a management ideology

Wendy A. Smith

By the end of the 1970s, Japanese foreign investment in Malaysia approached the RM1 billion mark, spread over 368 firms. Of these, 43 per cent were directly involved in manufacturing, predominantly in electronics, chemicals, wood products and textiles, with over 60 per cent of these having a workforce of over one hundred employees.[1] In dealing with manufacturing firms of this size, subject to Japanese managerial control, the issue of Japanese corporate paternalism[2] becomes important. From this starting point, i.e. the significance of the Japanese cultural presence, a case study of a Japanese joint venture in Kuala Lumpur,[3] which employed 241 workers, was conducted.

In studies of Japanese-owned or managed companies overseas, there is always a tendency to exaggerate the 'Japanese-ness' of the venture. Reports of the success of the Japanese managerial style in the United States and United Kingdom,[4] themselves suffering from the effects of late capitalism, have heightened this tendency to explain in terms of a Japanese stereotype. In this chapter, I will examine the issues of Japanese cultural homogeneity and the Japanese management system in the light of the ethnicity vs class debate. I will show that the 'Japanese' identity functions in the Malaysian venture, as it does elsewhere, as an ethnicity-based ideological resource. The 'paternalism' associated with the Japanese managerial style is also an ideological form,[5] supposedly a hang-over from pre-industrial Japanese society.[6] Although there is no demonstrable historic continuity, the vertical patron–client type relationships of a 'feudal'[7] era, between lord and retainer, landowner and tenant, function similarly to mystify economic realities for those in subordinate class positions.[8]

In fact, the ideal model of paternalism is shown to be a lie as the extent of its practice varies historically and with economic circumstances. In contemporary Malaysia, this is especially true, as local legislation and other circumstances prevent or render unnecessary the practical application of the paternalist system *in toto*. But still the Japanese image is promoted within the venture and to society at large through seminars and training schemes.[9] Coupled with the ethnic diversity of the labour force itself, and subsequent status group[10] type affiliations which obscure the class basis of relations of production – hence functioning to benefit management – we can see the consistent role of ethnicity as a basis for mystification.

Within the Malaysian venture, some features of the paternalist model are present, usually those which are the least financially demanding. To prove that the structural forces of productive relations within the venture are not uniquely Japanese, but are subject to economic determinants like any other, I will examine the responses within the company's organization to the problems of industrial production under monopoly capitalism.[11] Although solved in a different way, the problems are still the same. To quote Moore, reviewing explanations of the Japanese model, 'the Japanese employment system, in inspiration and practice, has been far less a Japanese creation than a capitalist creation'.[12]

This paper will outline the ideal model of Japanese company organization; discuss ethnic factors and their influence within the venture; evaluate to what degree features of the Japanese model are actually present, and by their absence, further demonstrate its ideological role; show ways in which the Japanese organizational stereotype, to the degree that it is present, is consistent with the organization of monopoly capitalism.

THE JAPANESE MANAGEMENT SYSTEM

The ideal model of the Japanese management system[13] in Japan itself may be described as follows:

The company is staffed according to a system of 'lifetime employment' (*shushinkoyo*) in which employees are recruited directly from school or university. This managerial policy is based on the assumption that it will be easier to instil a sense of company loyalty in employees who have no previous work experience. In return for their loyalty, as expressed by devoted and productive service to the company in a way which often forces them to put family life in second place, the employees[14] (*shain*) are assured of lifetime job security. The company will never retrench them, but will manipulate the parallel systems of contract and temporary labour to cope with economic recession. The generalized, as opposed to specialized, job function of the worker and the common use of horizontal transferring complement this system. Promotion is based on a 'seniority system' (*nenkojoretsu*), in which selection of individuals for higher positions takes place within the cohort of all those who entered the company in a particular year.

This system functions to cross-cut and hence dilute other hierarchical distinctions within the employment system,[15] such as educational status, which forms the justification of the manager–worker hierarchy in Western enterprises, and hence validates their relative class positions, based on individual merit.

The company operates a comprehensive system of benefits which includes annual wage revision, and an annual bonus from between six and nine months' wages. Other benefits include free housing, recreation facilities both within the company grounds and at country resorts, and subsidized meal and transport costs. These all demonstrate to the worker that he has access to the company profits.

Perhaps the most striking feature of the Japanese model is the enterprise union, which operates on the principle that its bargaining power depends on the prosperity of the company, hence encouraging cooperation between workers and management. This is further reinforced by forces promoting an egalitarian perception of the relationship between superior and subordinate on the shop floor as noted above. There is willingness for managers to get their hands dirty fixing machinery, which again reflects the principle of flexibility in job function and the ultimate goal of group advancement.

Finally, Japanese organizations are characterized by the low status of women, who are expected traditionally to retire on marriage, or first pregnancy at the very latest, in more liberal cases. Here discrimination against women is used as yet another criterion to produce flexibility in the company organization. Given the high resignation rate of female employees, intake of the female labour force can be regulated to suit economic conditions and hence make up for the rigidity of the commitment to 'lifetime' employees, who are usually men. Hence the female labour force functions in the same way as contract or temporary labour, as a 'reserve army'.

It is important to note however that these features are not a hangover from a more traditional era, but are a product of specific circumstances in the history of the development of Japanese capitalism. Sumiya[16] has shown that the lifetime employment system and the comprehensive benefits enjoyed by Japanese workers were a product of the shortage of skilled labour during Japan's early industrial development and came into being after a period of well-organized labour unrest in the 1920s.

Similarly, in ventures owned or controlled by the Japanese in Malaysia, the degree of importation of this model of company organization will not be due to the mere fact of cultural contact, but will be dependent on the specific economic and political factors operating in Japan and Malaysia at the time. We cannot assume the automatic transfer of paternalist labour relations to Malaysia. Paternalism in labour relations is itself a historical product. Paternalism obscures the basic nature of productive relations by fragmenting the working class into individuals standing in a vertical relationship, akin to patronage, with their masters. The Japanese management system performs this ideological function.

However, paternalism has no material base in the Japanese joint venture in Malaysia to the degree that it may have in the organization of the parent company in Japan. In Malaysia, it serves as a way in which the Japanese express their ethnicity in the foreign venture. It has the potential to be used by all participants as an ideological resource in handling the advantages or disadvantages of their relative class positions. Specifically, it is used by Japanese management to co-opt productive labour from the Malaysian employees without giving them the comprehensive benefits provided for the employees in the parent company. Small tokens may be given, such as birthday presents, but there is no comparison with the food, travel, housing and leisure subsidies given in Japan, which constitute expenditure by the parent company for the reproduction of labour. The greater exploitation of relatively lowly paid workers in the overseas subsidiaries, producing for the export market, may actually be subsidizing the high level of benefits enjoyed by workers in the parent company.[17]

Ironically, the system with all its benefits has been exported with great success to industries of the West because Japanese manufacturers in those economies have to compete for better paid skilled labour in a context of institutionalized labour relations. But a paternalist system is not necessary in most of Asia, where a ready workforce can be easily assured in the general climate of unemployment and underemployment and government legislation and other controls over labour. In fact, there are many aspects of national industrial development policies[18] and the complementary set of labour laws[19] in Malaysia limit some features entirely, for instance, bonus levels.

Nevertheless, Japanese staff in the Malaysian venture studied continue to idealize the Japanese system and express regret and indignation when Malaysian workers are not as loyal and dedicated to work as their Japanese counterparts in the parent company, despite the lack of commensurate benefits. Instead, they may use the job to gain some experience or skill before leaving for a more highly paid position.

However, I observed positive responses to Japanese management ideology by a few individual workers. This phenomenon can be seen as a crucial element in their strategy for personal advancement. So, in this analysis, I emphasize the innovative potential of the individual in a society subject to the drastic effects of industrialization, especially one in which class boundaries are still in a state of flux.

It remains to be explained why the Japanese staff of the venture express as their aim, the desire to create a Japanese-style situation of employee loyalty and dedication to work, while continuing to pay workers wages and bonuses which are dictated by government policy and local industrial environment, yet which are still proportionately very low compared with the benefits received by the Japanese company employee, and also barely adequate to meet the daily needs of workers who must participate in the urban economy of Kuala Lumpur.

I explain this not merely as a practical aim to make the company function more efficiently, by motivating workers to be company-oriented, as opposed to self-oriented. Companies in the West also issue ideological appeals to company identity and solidarity to achieve the same end. Ironically, implementation of the Japanese system tended to retard cooperation and cohesion in the factory.[20] On another level, however, the constant expression of Japanese work norms by the Japanese managers to themselves and to willing listeners may be explained as a system of meaning which they need to maintain, to explain to themselves and to the top levels of Malaysian management, the various contradictions inherent in their situation in Malaysia, that is, as the only available ideology of the dominant group.[21]

As individuals back home, the Japanese staff in Malaysia are merely middle management, or they may even be unionized employees. The previous general manager returned to the parent company to become a *fukubucho*[22] (deputy chief) of the International Department (*Kokusaijigyobu*). Two of the technical managers in the Malaysian venture were still union members back in Japan. Yet in Malaysia, all the Japanese expatriate staff are accorded instant high status, on par with the indigenous elite. They rent houses in the best residential areas, drive Mercedes Benz, and are members of the most prestigious golf clubs. This high status is supported by Japan's economic power in Southeast Asia. Yet the Japanese individual, an ordinary employee at home, has to justify this prestige to himself and to his subordinates. He does this by bringing to the Malaysian work context, and reasserting as an ideal, the model of Japanese company organization, raising it to the level of an ideology. This model was constantly described as ideal to observers such as myself, and to receptive individuals in the workforce, despite the fact that the model is beginning to crumble in Japan as economic circumstances change.[23]

THE CASE STUDY: A JAPANESE JOINT VENTURE IN MALAYSIA

The company under study was set up in 1964 as the third overseas investment of the parent company in Japan, a leading company in its field of manufacturing. The original parent company was set up by one of Japan's big business families (*zaibatsu*) during the Meiji era and expanded production to China and Taiwan during the Japanese rule of those countries. After the Second World War, the *zaibatsu* were officially dissolved, but the company continued in the hands of the original founding family, and it is only recently that the presidency of the company was given to an employee who came up through the ranks, with members of the original family continuing to hold directorships. After the Second World War, the company resumed its policy of overseas investment to secure overseas markets. Following the pre-war pattern, it was one of the first Japanese companies to set up factories in Asia, beginning with Thailand and the Philippines in the early 1960s, then Malaysia and Indonesia. As a part of a more general trend, now that its production centres are established in Asia, the latest factories are opening in South America. Exports and sales centres have diversified, but the core of the market remains in Asia. Sales networks have normally been established before the factories have been set up, so the company has advanced largely in the context of local Chinese commercial networks in Southeast Asia, as they provided both capital and entrepreneurial skill for setting up sales networks and also a ready market for the product in the early days. This Chinese bias has brought about some difficulties for the internal organization of the firm today.

In Malaysia, the company is producing one highly specialized product, although there are plans to diversify. Production is highly technical in nature, involving a series of continuous chemical reactions. This requires only a small workforce, in relation to the quantity and value of the product: primarily unskilled and semi-skilled male workers, organized in three shifts over twenty-four hours to regulate and observe the ongoing production process, a smaller group of female packers, who work only a day shift, and the necessary maintenance, administrative and sales staff, who also work ordinary daily office hours. Since 1969, total employment has remained stable, yet production has increased sevenfold, showing the emphasis placed on technological development.

The workforce is characterized by a high ratio[24] of Japanese staff to local employees due to the capital-intensive nature of production, hence, the need to supervise technical aspects of production and also to protect the capital invested. The Japanese at present occupy six positions: General Manager/Managing Director, Administrative and Accounting Manager, Factory Manager, Technical Manager, Engineering Development Manager and Production Control Manager. Hence, there are four Japanese staff in technical roles and two in administration. The first four positions are classified as 'line', i.e. in the line of authority of various Departments. The last two positions are 'staff', i.e. having a consultative capacity only. These posts – previously held by Japanese – were handed over to local staff in 1976. In accordance with government policy to repatriate all but key expatriate staff in foreign enterprises by 1980, the Japanese in the Engineering, Production and Technical Departments were training their local counterparts to be self-reliant, leaving Japanese only in the three key posts permitted by Malaysian government policy: General Manager, Administrative Manager and Factory Manager.

Ethnic factors

The ethnic balance of the Malaysian workforce in the company reflects the national population percentages; 54 per cent Malays (53.5 per cent in Peninsular Malaysia), 37 per cent Chinese (35.3 per cent), 9 per cent Indians and others (11.3 per cent), but there is a predominance of Chinese in the management, especially at senior executive level. This is one of the major sources of conflict in the firm. Although management has attempted to balance ethnic ratios at all levels since the introduction of the New Economic Policy in 1971, they have encountered difficulty in recruiting and securing Malays with technical qualifications for the higher managerial levels.

Their concern was increased by the promulgation of the controversial Industrial Coordination Act of 1975. Under this Act, all manufacturers must apply for a licence, which must be renewed annually, on condition that their operations are 'in the national interest' and are seen to 'promote the orderly development of manufacturing activities in Malaysia'. The criteria of *national interest* are not specified, but ethnic composition of the workforce at all levels of organization is known to be a key factor. The licence can be revoked at any time.

In this company, the only Malay Manager was the Personnel Manager. Two Malay section chiefs in the Engineering Department had been recruited and had resigned within a year. There were three Malay junior executives on the production side, all of whom rose from the ranks – two operators and a former driver. This reflects the Japanese policy of promoting from within, rather than going outside the company to fill vacancies.

This imbalance is explained as a result of the lack of Malay science graduates, especially those willing to work in private industry, during the selection of the first batch of trainees sent to Japan for training in 1964, and who now hold senior managerial posts: this, despite the fact that the company advertised at the time specifically for *Bumiputera* recruits. Secondly, as explained to me, the early Japanese managers' feelings of affinity with the more business-like, urbane background of the Chinese, with their common cultural roots in Confucianism, and the Chinese ability to flatter the Japanese on their own terms, led to favouritism in promotion, ostensibly on the grounds of perceived superior ability.

It is significant that all the early Chinese recruits now holding top management positions are Chinese-educated rather than English-educated. For Chinese-educated Chinese, who took higher degrees in Nanyang University in Singapore, or in Taiwan, and whose English is comparatively less fluent, the Japanese firm presents the best-paying alternative short of going into private business. It is more difficult for them to get positions in

European firms, and if they were to seek employment in a Chinese-owned company, they would probably receive lower wages.

In contrast to Chinese dominance at the executive level, at the level of unionized workers, Malays predominate. Malays make up 56 per cent, Chinese 35 per cent and Indians 9 per cent. While these figures do not vary significantly from those of total employment, the Malay percentage greatly increases in the lower unskilled male grades, with fourteen Malays and no Chinese in the lowest category of 'General Worker' (Division 10). These are recruits with Primary Standard 6 education. The Division 10 jobs are the most unpleasant in the factory; the main one for males consists of tipping bags of powdered raw material into vats of water to form a solution. The room is extremely humid and smelly, and the workers become coated with the white powder. The task could be performed mechanically, but it is left as a job which initiates young rural Malays into the labour process. As the toughest and most ill-paid job in the industry, tipping bags constitutes an entry point into the internal labour market, a reservoir of first-time wage labourers who may go out to fill vacancies that occur higher up in the organization. It also disciplines and prepares workers for industrial labour, weeding out those who fail to demonstrate a 'rules' orientation. Hence the entry points into the internal labour market are at the lowest levels of the organization, Divisions 9 and 10, for process jobs. The entry point is higher for trade jobs such as boilerman, mechanic, and electrician. The standard method of recruitment is the posting of notices within the factory, advertising for friends or relatives of existing employees.[25] The management has steadily refused to be put on the books of employment agencies. The 'friends or relatives' policy provides the first stage of a screening process since new recruits have a ready communication channel for learning what the work is all about. Once they are inside the company, they will be under obligation to the employee who introduced them.

While there is no contracted guarantee of permanent employment, the company's Collective Agreements include a 'last hired first fired' clause for 'those employees whose services are terminated by reason of the construction or reorganization of the Company or change in the Company's business, trade or work'. In fact, the company's steady growth has allowed it to avoid layoffs.

General characteristics of the labour force

Over 50 per cent of the labour force were recruited before 1969 in the first five years of operation. They were employed as young, single men and women. The men were usually in their first job after leaving school, or else employed for the first time in a large corporation, after having some experience of contract labour. However, having a steady job did not give these workers the financial basis to get married immediately. It was generally only in the mid-1970s, at an average age of 25, that they began to marry and have children. Local managers see this maturing process in a relatively stable labour force, in terms of turnover, as contributing to greater stability in attitudes to work. But the workers complain that the shift work which they did not mind too much as bachelors is troublesome for the families. Also, and more importantly, it prevents them from seeking extra qualifications.

The position of women

Of the 241 employees, 66 are women, the majority of whom are in the lowest salary grade, Division 10. There is only one woman at the management level. Her position as Section Chief in charge of the laboratory is a terminal category, i.e. closed to further promotion. She is the only Section Chief whose prospects are limited in this way, and it is entirely on account of her sex, although she successfully completed a science degree, unlike some of her male managerial colleagues.

In relation to women employees in general, Japanese management has attempted to transplant the Japanese system of treating women as expendable elements of the labour force.

In the early days of recruitment, when the company was not sure how successfully they could develop a market for their product, most male and female workers were employed on a temporary basis, with a renewable contract of six months. Later, after receiving confirmation of permanent status, they were again subjected to reduced security under the 'Short Term Employment Scheme'[26] in the late 1960s, but this was duly abolished without ever being implemented. However, women have been subject to additional discrimination in the labour contract – they have been subject to an early retirement age, which was raised gradually from the initial 25 years, reflecting the Japanese case, to 35 years and then to 45 years, as at present, while men retire at 55 years of age. Women were also kept on daily rates for three years, until this system was abolished for all workers by the Collective Agreement of 1977.

Unable to retire women through the pressures of custom or legislation,[27] the management has been forced to accommodate a permanent and ageing female labour force. The majority of women packers have married and have taken maternity leave several times. Five have married fellow workers. In fact, a system whereby women are forced to retire on marriage would produce great strains on the economic viability of urban working class families. Nevertheless, the women of this factory are unionized, unlike many other foreign industrial ventures employing many women where the turnover of young women workers has tended to be relatively high, probably as a result of poor work conditions, including shift work and occupational hazards, e.g. permanent damage to eyesight after four or five years using a microscope in the silicon-chip industry.[28]

In my study, the turnover of female workers was not high, and because of management's reluctance to retrench, there is now a slight surplus, measured in terms of maximum production efficiency. But sick leave and pregnancies are a major problem for management, and this 'surplus' will be reduced by half on any given day.

The General Manager of a Japanese electronics factory whose workers were members of the national union, explained how his company overcame the problems of an ageing female labour force. First, he explained that the concentration and speed of older women on the production line was low because of pregnancies or pre-occupation with sick children or other family problems. Absenteeism was also much higher because of family commitments, so much so that the women could not be relied upon to be present in sufficient numbers to run the conveyor-belt production line each day. The Japanese solution was to create a piece-work section making spare parts for the main process, so the women could proceed at their own pace, presumably with appropriate wage adjustments. This solution is entirely consistent with the Japanese model: treatment of women as expendables, akin to contract labour, and the use of horizontal transfer within the organization for organizational flexibility.

In the company under study, formerly there were few promotion incentives for women, as they were limited to positions in Division 10, the lowest division on the salary scale. But more recently, one woman was promoted from the ranks to become Packers Supervisor, i.e. into Division 9A, a terminal category. A major battle of the Collective Agreement negotiations of 1977 was to have her placed in Division 8, this despite the large number of employees she was supervising – 49. While most workers agreed with the basic principles involved in the case, the Japanese staff and non-Malay union members remarked cynically that the case was fought so strongly because the Packers Supervisor was then the fiancee of the Secretary of the Works Committee.

Labour turnover

The workforce is now fairly stable. Annual turnover has gone down from over 15 per cent in the early 1970s, to below 10 per cent in the last few years. Following the employment system of Japan, the Japanese appear reluctant to retrench. However, this apparent ideological commitment has not yet been fully tested in the Malaysian venture, as there has been no large drop in sales so far which would necessitate retrenchment.

Employees stay on despite dissatisfaction with wages and conditions, for a number of reasons. They recognize the flexibility and laxity of discipline in the shift system as administered by Japanese management and realize that conditions in other firms, especially those with US or European management, may be tougher. By manipulating the shift schedules with the aid of sympathetic foremen,[29] they are able to conduct side businesses. At the same time, though, the ultimate uncertainty of the shift system prevents them from attending any regular courses which would help them to increase their qualifications and thus get a better paid job.

The skills attained by workers who have been with the company for any length of time are mainly firm-specific. Only those with trade certificates, such as boilermen, electricians and mechanics, are relatively mobile.

Other factors which mitigate against workers resigning are as follows: they are reluctant to leave the friends and associates they have at the factory, whom they both live and work with, and who make up the cooperative networks which are substitutes for kinship. This is strengthened by the fact that vacancies are advertised among 'relatives and friends' of employees, so most have a tie with another worker as the basis for their recruitment. Second, the factory, which needs a special water supply, in the form of a large mining pool, is isolated from the large industrial estates in Petaling Jaya, Sungei Way or Shah Alam. Hence there is little direct contact around the workplace with other workers or comparative knowledge about working conditions or wages which might encourage mobility. Furthermore, most workers have moved to nearby housing estates or squatter *kampung* or are living in Kuala Lumpur proper, or the Kampung Pandan side of town, so that communications with the newly developed industrial areas along the Federal Highway are inconvenient.

For *Bumiputera* workers who have outside offers, there is pressure from families to stay in a stable position rather than chance a new situation where the permanency of their job tenure is untested. Often this family pressure is a result of commitments to make installment payments for the purchase of household appliances or furniture. Workers are also obligated to send remittances to relatives in the village on a regular monthly basis.

The Chinese workers are more restricted in their opportunities, given the policies stressing *Bumiputera* employment. However, for many of the Chinese workers in my sample, working in the company was not their prime interest; it was seen as a source of secure income. They preferred a job in which they could coast along; meanwhile devoting all their creative energies to side business, which ranged from market gardening, mee stall owner, electrical repair business, and inter-state food cartage contractor.

Labour control

Within the happy picture painted so far of worker conformity to the labour process, the productive relations of which have been conveniently obscured by a management ideology which creates vertical status group structures in the workers' consciousness, we ask: is this enough to control workers' performance for the interests of the company?[30] Are the small self-interested manipulations workers are able to make within the system, sufficient to blind them to their fundamental class disadvantage and hence guarantee their cooperation with the goals of management? While concluding that ultimately it is the organization of relations within the work place which guarantee consent to the labour process, there are, at the same time, formalized disciplinary measures within the organization.

Disciplinary measures for such offences as misoperation, lateness, chronic absenteeism, sleeping on the job, etc., take the form of a series of warning letters and corresponding suspension of the annual wage increment for several months. Cases of dismissal are rare and are usually for theft or gross insubordination. Since the production process (apart from packing and warehouse) involves regulation rather than constant labour, e.g. checking an automated switchboard, periodically opening and closing valves and taking control samples, the work does not demand full time concentration or activity, and sleeping on the job is a major problem especially on the second and third shifts (3.30–11.30 p.m., 11.30 p.m.–7.30 a.m.). Misoperations generally occur on the latter half of the third shift, early morning, when most workers are dozing. There is a small sleeping room of wooden benches where workers take turns to sleep at night, but 'falling asleep at the wheel' also occurs. In 1972, both local and Japanese senior staff instituted a programme of raids to be carried out by them from 2 to 5 a.m. They consistently caught so many asleep that the project was abandoned. Even during the day when the factory is noisy, hot and humid, sleeping is a problem. Some control rooms are air-conditioned, but this is for the recording machines, not for the workers.

Japanese staff over the past few years have come to realize that the best method to prevent misoperation and inattention is to teach the operators the basic meaning of their process work: why they must open a certain valve at a certain level. Hence the Japanese have been lecturing the section and unit chiefs, who have in turn been lecturing their foremen and chargehands. This is the basic principle followed in the Japanese company at home, where the education level, level of knowledge of the process and loyalty to the company are much higher. For instance, a Malaysian trainee sent to the parent company in Japan observed that Japanese workers from the third shift seemed to be in no hurry to get home, but stayed behind late to hold a meeting with first shift workers to tell them what had happened to the process during the night.

It is in the company's interests to retain employees, since skill in handling the chemical process is largely acquired through on-the-job training and experience. The process involves regulation rather than constant labour,[31] e.g., checking an automated switchboard, periodically opening and closing valves, taking control samples. Concentration and intimate knowledge of the states of the various chemical reactions are required, as a mis-timing in the operation can reduce the yield of the product considerably. To encourage understanding of the overall process and appreciation of the importance of each task within it, the Japanese give lectures to section and unit chiefs. They in turn lecture foremen and chargehands.

This on-the-job training is reinforced by rotation at intervals of approximately two years around the various units of the production process,[32] although usually only within one section. The process is divided into a number of stages, each under the care of a 'unit'. The first three units form one 'section', the other two units another, while packing and warehouse make up a third. This horizontal transfer system, so typical of the Japanese model, both educates workers into generalized work roles and enhances their knowledge of the total process. Frequent transfers around all units of a section signal that a worker is about to be promoted. The promotion from Foreman to Assistant Unit Chief, i.e., from unionized worker to junior managerial level, is preceded by a period of three to six months' training in the parent company in Japan. Male workers who fail to show aptitude in acquiring a scientific knowledge of the process are often transferred into the warehouse and packing section.

The main thrust of Braverman's work[33] on the changes in the labour process under monopoly capitalism has been to emphasize the degradation of work, i.e. the separation of the worker's knowledge from his activity, or of 'conception from execution'. Hence, domination is not external to the technical arrangements of production, i.e. a feature of the relations *of* production, but rather is actively located within the relations *in* production, inherent in the division of labour characterizing the production process itself. Hence, by limiting the workers' awareness of their contribution to production, the socially fragmented technological arrangements of the labour process serves to subordinate and atomize them. Hence, the workers' attention is diverted away from the external domination inherent in relations *of* production in the classical sense. They exert their individual energies to maximize advantage by manipulating relations *in* production, by participating in the games[34] made possible by management, and hence, by consenting as individuals to the 'rules' of the labour process.

How does this fit in with the Japanese managerial preference for educating their workers to take pride in the technological success of production? This must be understood in the light of two related aspects of the Japanese employment system – life-time employment and the insistence on generalism in job function. In Japan, all workers are expected, within reason, to perform the tasks of others in the event of absenteeism, etc. This principle operates both horizontally and hierarchically. We have seen that generalism is an indispensable principle in the context of life-time employment in order to create flexibility in the workforce in the face of changing economic circumstances. In the context of the current discussion, it also functions to diffuse skills, so that no one worker can bargain on the basis of his individual skill and hence partial control of the production process. Hence, the Japanese system has an in-built feature which functions similarly to those which have evolved under monopoly capitalism in the West.

Despite the attempts to motivate and hence discipline workers through these educational measures, misoperations do occur. The disciplinary measures mentioned above are implemented in a lenient manner. Often, the individual's role in the mishap is subsumed under group responsibility.

Disciplinary measures, apart from warning letters issued by the Factory Manager, are implemented along the 'line', with the offender's immediate supervisor investigating the incident and talking with him (her) first. However, there have been discrepancies in the practice of disciplinary measures, and recently matters have been referred to the Personnel Officer as the absolute authority. However, as is the case with the Personnel Section in Japan, the Japanese still see him as 'staff' rather than 'line', i.e. as an advisor only in factory matters; hence, he has been struggling to gain more power while seeing through the implementation of his decisions, which are sometimes overruled by local managers on the factory side. In fact, there is a real tension between the Malay Personnel Manager and the Chinese managers on the Production and Engineering side, despite the fact that they are all members of the first batch sent for training in Japan before the factory was set up. The source of tension is in the growing appreciation of, and hence power given to, the production side by the Japanese. Once again, this is entirely consistent with Japanese practice, and more than personal or inter-ethnic rivalries are at issue, despite the fact that this is how the situation is perceived. If the Personnel Manager were to consolidate real disciplinary power in his hands, as would be the case in a Western enterprise, this would mean the establishment of a direct relationship between himself and individual workers. The emphasis thus placed on their individual responsibilities and skills would upset the group solidarity and generalism being built up within the 'line' organization of production, of which the local Production and Engineering Managers are part.

Unionism and class consciousness

The workers were unionized at the national level in 1973 under a union which is unique for the degree of Malay representation at the national executive level. The entire National Executive Committee is Malay, except for the Treasurer and one other committee member who are both Chinese. This control of the union set a precedent in the Malaysian trade union movement, which has been dominated by Indian leadership, especially from the plantation sector. At the time of study, the company had negotiated two collective agreements – on 12 July 1974 and 12 July 1977. The Company

Works Committee consisted of seven members, a president and a secretary. It is significant that in the last election held early in 1977, which elected the second committee since the formation of the union, an all-Malay committee was elected. There were accusations from the Chinese and Indian candidates, who dominated the first committee after forming an alliance against the Malays to contest the election, that there was foul play with the ballot papers at the national headquarters. Their suspicions were strengthened by the fact that all the office bearers of the National Executive are Malay, except the Treasurer. I have no evidence of the truth of these accusations, but mention them as evidence of the tendency of members of the union to perceive issues in ethnic terms.

Before the formation of the union, there were a series of Joint Consultative Committees and Works Committees. The formation of the union and the negotiations for the first collective agreement were accompanied by some industrial unrest, which the Japanese staff explain as representing the national state of unrest prevailing at the time. There was little organized action in this company, however. Discontent was expressed by sporadic acts of sabotage, rather than strikes, even when the leader of the early movement, an Indian production worker, was dismissed for negligence and insubordination.

When early attempts failed to contain workers' moves to organize, many Japanese companies in Malaysia, including the company under study, tried to establish enterprise (in-house) unions. None were successful then due to national government policy.[35] Given the effectiveness of in-house unions in Japan itself, it is perhaps understandable that Japanese expatriate managers in Malaysia tried to prevent the registration of their employees with industry-wide unions. This conservatism was based on a false fear of the 'power' of unionism. The establishment of collective bargaining and grievance machinery gives the firm political mechanisms for jurisdiction over its own problems. 'Consciousness raising' at the point of production can atomize as well as collectivize, as workers become preoccupied with using the grievance mechanism to satisfy their immediate situational grievances, rather than attempt fundamental structural changes. Class struggle can be contained within the parameters of capitalism if workers are able to extract concessions which make it tolerable. Only one Japanese manager I talked to recognized this potential for organization and control through the affiliation of his workers with the national union. Significantly, he was the manager of a larger Japanese electronics firm, whose production-line type of technology is least amenable to granting 'concessions' to workers. In Japan, the enterprise union works because the ideology of paternalism incorporates workers vertically within the capitalists' interest structure.

Negotiations for the second collective agreement reached an early settlement after only eight sittings. This was explained to me as a result of the timing of the negotiations. Hari Raya, the most festive annual event for Muslims, was coming, and the Malays were anxious to receive the new pay scale plus arrears, which would have helped to finance the occasion.

Present at the negotiating table on the Management side were: the Administrative Manager, a Japanese directly answerable to the General Manager in administrative matters, and himself a labour leader in his younger days in the parent company (he acted as the spokesman for the management side); the Factory Manager, a Japanese whose role was to provide information and the viewpoint of the factory side, (he is comparatively poor in English and remained silent most of the time); the Personnel Manager, a Malay who was in the most difficult position of having to juggle the interests of the Japanese with his understanding of what his fellow countrymen really want, while having no authority to push through his opinions.

On the union side was the Executive Secretary (a Malay), a professional negotiator and the spokesman; the President (Malay) and Secretary-General (Malay) of the National Executive Committee; the Company Works Committee President (Malay), Secretary (Malay), and two Malay Works Committee members.

The negotiations extended into Ramadhan, the Muslim fasting month before the Hari Raya festival, at which time the Japanese Factory Manager refrained from his chain smoking and no drinks were served in the room.

Very few innovative benefits were given in the new collective agreement. The rise in salary scales was low to average compared with similar industries, i.e. either Japanese or foreign, in the KL region, or of a related industrial type. The main criterion for the Japanese management in the fixing of wage levels was that they should be on par with those of other major Japanese enterprises in the KL region.[36]

Most striking by their absence from the labour contract are the comprehensive benefits received by Japanese workers in Japan, such as free housing and transportation, and extensive recreational facilities, including company guest houses at resort centres. In Malaysia, there is no need to bind workers to the company with a display of paternalism. As Moore demonstrates, 'welfare capitalism' is not unique to Japan, but also existed in the USA under historically specific conditions.[37] In this company, as we have seen, worker mobility is limited by a number of other factors, and labour turnover is not great. What benefits Malaysian workers receive to subsidize their basic wage are provided mainly within the context of government labour legislation: the Cost of Living Allowance (COLA), participation in the Employees Provident Fund (EPF), and free medical treatment by the company doctor. The bonus level is also strongly influenced by government policy. As private companies are subject to taxation on annual bonus payments exceeding two months' wages, under the 1977 Collective Agreement, the company set its bonus award at this amount. Two sets of uniforms are supplied per year. As the company is isolated from the public transport network by several miles, a company bus ferries workers to and fro during shift change intervals. Workers receive a monthly book of tickets to subsidize the purchase of one meal at the company canteen per day. Recreation facilities are minimal, although a recreation club organizes worker participation in a range of sports and finances their uniforms, equipment and transport to competitions. The recreation club also organizes an annual company dinner, a great source of discontent, as workers are not permitted to bring spouses or partners. Restriction of activities to the work group alone is typically Japanese, but very unusual in terms of the Malaysian concept of entertainment.

From observation of the union's performance, it can be seen that their inexperience in negotiating wages and other benefits, and the general level of understanding of their class position, are quite undeveloped. Major issues raised by the union throughout the year were: improvements in architecture of the canteen, bringing partners to the annual dinner, getting more free samples and merchandise at staff price, attendance at Friday prayers for Muslim workers, etc., and they are obsessed with finding cases of favouritism against Malay workers in promotions. They are relatively unconcerned with such major issues as shorter working hours, shift allowances and improved safety conditions. Non-Malay members accuse the union of selling them out on the wage increase issue in the negotiations in order to get immediate benefits for Malays at Hari Raya.

Overall, the union fails to unite the workers on a class basis, and actually further divides them on the basis of their perceived ethnic rivalries. Secondly, the union has little bargaining power with the Japanese management who, they acknowledge, treats them leniently in matters of discipline, i.e. sleeping on the third shift, changing shifts to suit personal arrangements, etc.. The nature of the production process, which requires on–off vigilance, means that constant disciplinary measures have been very difficult to enforce. Hence, because of this relaxed situation, the workers explain that they cannot fight too strongly for higher wages, because they know that whereas wages may be higher in a US firm, they would also have to work much harder. Here consent to the labour process due to the granting of concessions is clear.

The Japanese complain that it is difficult to run the factory because of ethnic rivalries; yet they benefit from the situation. In the collective agreement negotiations, they gained advantage from the fragmented nature of the union in that they knew the non-Malay workers would blame the Malay union leaders for not securing higher wages. More specifically, the timing – with the meetings beginning in late July and extending into the first two weeks of Ramadhan – allowed the Japanese the alternative of trying to tempt the union with the small bait of a two or three per cent wage increase above the previously bargained figure, then standing firm, knowing fully well that the union did not want to go into strike action or picket with Hari Raya coming, but instead wanted an early settlement to get their arrears in time.

The Japanese may reject proposals for general improvements in work conditions, and innovations in schemes of reward: they say 'But if we do that, surely it will be taken by the Malays that we are favouring the Chinese' (or vice-versa). In fact, this is an excuse for not doing anything to improve the lot of the workers in general.

From this picture of the overwhelming ethnic definition of the labour situation, we may ask: What is the level of class consciousness among workers, and to what degree do they perceive the class position of their Japanese management?

Firstly, I wish to stress that I do not consider 'the level of class consciousness' to be the most important indicator of class relations in production. In fact, the very presence of ethnic cleavages to this pronounced degree reflects attempts by workers to maximize their personal interests by pledging individual allegiance to vertically structured groups which promise more immediate upward mobility in the form of promotions, distribution of rewards, or cooperation and personal support to members.

On the contrary, class action, based on an accurate understanding of class position, is unusual in the face of the individual need to survive in Third World situations.[38] There is nevertheless evidence of very sound class awareness in the factory.

Historically the most active in the union movement in Malaysia, Indians are few in number in the company, but most likely to express their grievances in class terms. One young Indian worker – who had the clearest understanding of the consequences of foreign investment of all interviewed in the factory – stood for Deputy Secretary in alliance with a Chinese candidate for Secretary, in the last Works Committee elections. He failed to be elected because the Malay front was stronger. He has become rather bitter, and says resignedly, 'Let them (i.e. the Malays) try, and see how difficult it is'. But the attitude of the unelected Indian and Chinese candidates, who had, by far, a better grasp of the principles of unionism, is also quite pragmatic. The Malay Works Committee and National Executive of the union may be able to deal more effectively with the Malay elite in power, and hence secure privileges for the union on a patron–client, or common status-group, basis.

Other workers, too, were aware of the sale value of their product, and with their knowledge of annual output, were able to calculate total sales value and to compare it with their wages. Although they did not talk in terms of surplus value, they were obviously indignant at the result of their calculations. But the possibility that this might be translated into a class consciousness inspiring organized action was squashed under the weightier preoccupation with ethnic rivalries.

Similarly, there was a lack of real concern for the class position and interests of the Japanese management. The Japanese were viewed as a discrete cultural group; any antagonism was directed towards them as 'Japanese', rather than as 'managers'. There were complaints that the Japanese, because they were 'Japanese', were 'mean with money' for things like worker canteen or recreational facilities, or the venue of the Annual Company Dinner. (American companies which staged elaborate events in the best hotels met with their approval.) The Japanese involved themselves in work 'below their level' or outside their area of expertise; they reprimanded workers directly in front of colleagues, without going through the 'proper' channels, i.e. down the 'line' from superior to subordinate; they tried to transfer workers outside their designations to meet temporary labour shortages. All these things were 'bad' because they were 'what the Japanese did'. In fact, they represent an accurate perception of the characteristics of the Japanese model as implemented in the Malaysian venture, but the workers, understandably, perceived only the epiphenomena and did not analyse the structural causes.

Japanese management

Since the company's establishment, the Japanese management has been able to incorporate a number of Japanese features into the organization of work, as noted above. However, they have been unable to use the process of personal communication to influence workers to accept some more overt behavioural features of the system, such as temporary transfers between sections or egalitarian behaviour between superior and subordinate. In fact, there is little personal contact between Japanese staff and unionized workers below shift supervisor level. It is the local management who are most likely to be influenced in thought and behaviour by the Japanese managerial style. The workers are shielded to a significant extent by their participation in the national union and the context of Malaysian labour legislation.

In previous years, the Japanese technical staff used to wander around the factory, speaking to individual workers, correcting them in certain aspects of the work. They offended on three counts here. Given the understanding of the formal organization of the factory by the workers, they would expect to be reprimanded only by an immediate superior. If a person of higher rank wants to comment on their work, he should transfer the point 'down the line'. Secondly, the linguistic encounter with the Japanese tended to be most unpleasant for the worker; he had difficulty in understanding what was being said and the abrupt English and blunt statements of the Japanese tended to have insulting connotations. Thirdly, it is considered generally insulting, particularly by Malays, to be reprimanded in public.

The Japanese managers stopped addressing workers in the factory about work matters after the workers requested the union secretary to complain on their behalf. He spoke to the Personnel Manager, who explained the situation to the Japanese.

By speaking directly to a lowly worker on the job, and other acts, the Japanese show their basic concern for the success of the organization over and above individual interests. This demands flexible principles of organization if the individual is not to feel threatened. The generalized nature of job functions in the Japanese organization is not reflected in Malaysia, where high unemployment leads everyone to guard his own special function jealously. The only way the Japanese can achieve some level of generalized skill among workers is through the practice of extensive horizontal transferring, but this is usually limited to units within one section.

Anything more overt is immediately suspect. A former Japanese member of staff once asked a group of workers whose section was closed during the annual shutdown, to come and help him with maintenance in the engineering section. This incident almost led to strike action. Another incident occurred when the Engineering Manager, to demonstrate by example that workers should be proud of their company and keep it as attractive and pleasant as possible, went around cleaning the toilets and clipping rose bushes and hedges in the factory. This was seen as a highly provocative action since it implied that the cleaners and gardeners were not doing their jobs well, hence threatening their job security. However, the engineer is unable to restrain his gardening instincts, and it is arranged that he can clip the hedge at lunch time.

The Japanese management have no institutionalized system for gathering information about Malaysian workers' social expectations or legal position. Convinced that their system is the best as it works so well for company prosperity in Japan, they initially ran the venture by a process of trial and error, leaving major errors to be sorted out by the Personnel Manager. It is significant that the position of Personnel Manager is always one of the first to be given to local management and this position in Japanese factories is usually given to a Malay. This reflects the need to boost the number of *Bumiputeras* in management to conform to government policy, and also the realization on the part of the Japanese that Malay values are much harder for them to understand than those of the Chinese, who share a common cultural tradition.

Japanese in Southeast Asia have been characterized as culturally inept in relating to indigenous workers and the general society surrounding their overseas ventures.[39] The Japanese behaviour of 'not getting to know the locals' seems to be based more on a strategy of maximizing the use of their resources to meet the most pressing substantive needs of the situation. Despite the fact that the venture is an independent legal entity and not a subsidiary, their position overseas is an official posting (*shutcho*) from Japan; they never relinquish their position in the parent company. Although their names may be temporarily removed from the organization chart of the parent company and placed under the Malaysian venture, they are still very much in the line of promotion and competing by the very fact of being away. More recently, overseas postings have been short, from three to five years, although there have been some moves in the more 'progressive' companies to lengthen this. Hence, a Japanese individual's main concern during this period is to last it out, without making any bad mistakes. Implementing all kinds of managerial policies which provide for the welfare of the local workers would be viewed as wasteful by head office, who do not know the local scene well, and whose prime concern is the level of profit. Hence Japanese personnel put their efforts into raising profit levels by known methods, e.g. technology improvement, and retreat from the 'labour relations' area of the venture.

The desire of Japanese investors to be well represented in the management of the foreign venture in areas relating to finance, long-term planning and technology, and to leave labour management to local staff, has been noted in a comparative study by Sim[40] of the differences in management style of a number of foreign ventures in Malaysia. He also argues that the Japanese ventures are the least 'decentralized' or autonomous of all the foreign investors, which would confirm the above description of the tight organizational control the Japanese parent company has over the careers of its expatriate staff.

Malaysian management

The smooth running of the venture depends, primarily, on the efforts of senior and junior Malaysian management to comprehend and implement the expectations of their Japanese superiors in a way acceptable to their own countrymen in the worker ranks. Realizing the important intermediary role[41] local management plays, the Japanese select and train a group of local managers whom they believe they can trust to carry out their policies. In my experience, these people were selected primarily for their weaknesses, i.e. lack of bargaining power, and were trained in a way to make them familiar with Japanese values. This was done by sending the initial batch to Japan in 1964 for over a year of initial training. Today, most of this original group are still with the company, and fill the most senior managerial posts open to local management, i.e. Personnel Manager, Production Manager, Engineering Manager, Sales Manager and Laboratory Section Chief. A period of technical training in Japan, now reduced to a period of four to six months, is obligatory for all local managerial staff, both senior and junior, and a promotion from the ranks to Unit Chief is usually followed by a stay in Japan.

The trainees do not gain a very good understanding of Japanese society in general, because language is a problem. However, as Third World Country citizens, they are impressed with the level of Japanese technological development and so believe that Japanese management – seen as the means of achieving this – must be good. Some realize that there are defects in the Japanese system if applied within the Malaysian context and come back with an ambivalent attitude, but they usually stay on in the factory because they have been chosen initially for their career vulnerability and would have difficulty finding a job elsewhere. Such vulnerability includes: failure to get a university degree though the person attended university (in the case of one local Manager and one Assistant Manager); being a Chinese-educated Chinese (three local Managers are in this position).

Such individuals, once employed in the Japanese company, see conformity to Japanese rules as a strategy for career advancement and security. One Chinese manager went so far as to adopt the Japanese 'egalitarian' generalist approach of placing the good of the company before his own personal status. He rolled up his trousers and started sweeping out the drains in an effort to show the workers, by example, what they should be doing. It was remarked to me by many workers that such a job was beneath his status, and by doing so, he lost their respect, apart from the fact that they felt he was insulting them by implying that they could not do the job properly.

Even after promoting the first batch of 1964 trainees up to managerial status in 1976, the Japanese Factory Manager expressed doubts as to their capability to run the factory properly. He constantly used the term *sodateru* (which means to socialize a child) in talking about the process of training he felt they still needed. This suggests that he still considers them to be inept in Japanese ways. This lack of confidence is reflected in the lack of any actual authority delegated to local managers. They have no information about the financial structure of the company, or its long-term development planning. They complain that they are invited to discuss matters in a token fashion at meetings with the Japanese, but all issues are decided in a Japanese-only meeting which takes place separately afterwards.

It is also common for Japanese companies to exploit the fact of marriage between local men and Japanese women. Several leading Japanese firms have one high-up local executive, the General Manager's 'right hand man', who is a Chinese educated in a Japanese university and who married a Japanese girl during his studies. These couples are in a special position. The local Japanese wife has no social intercourse with the wives of Japanese staff who are here on a temporary basis. The avoidance is mutual. The regular Japanese wives look down on one who has married a Southeast

Asian. The wife, on the other hand, may have married a foreigner as a radical act of rejection of her own society. Given the male bias in Japanese kinship organization, she is considered to have 'married out', into her husband's family, and if he is a foreigner, she has turned her back on Japan.[42] She usually speaks English and the Chinese dialect of her husband fluently. She complains about the way the Japanese company has turned her non-Japanese husband into a Japanese, in the way he must stay late at the office, attend numerous dinners and bow to the Japanese General Manager, whereas most Chinese would prefer to be their own boss in a small family business.

The husband is in a difficult position also. He resents the way the Japanese exploit his knowledge of them, yet do not give him the authority he deserves in his own society. He expresses the desire to leave, but never does. He was probably a young Chinese-educated boy who had a choice of going to Singapore, Taiwan or Japan[43] for tertiary education. He chose Japan, and was snapped up by the Japanese company planning to invest overseas, perhaps before he even finished his training. At first, the prospects seemed good, but at the peak of his career, he finds he has reached the end of the road in a powerless advisory liaison post between General Manager and local staff. He does not stay on in the Japanese company because of his wife's nationality: far from it, as the company has ignored her completely, and only exploited her patience as a Japanese wife who will acquiesce to the demands made by overtime work on her husband. But he stays put because it may be too late for him to find other opportunities and he certainly does not have the time to set up his own business. Such individuals are the keys to the success of Japanese investment in Malaysia.

The Malay Personnel Manager also plays a key role as cultural interpreter, and is the main channel for worker–management communication. He knows the Japanese way, but he does not accept it. He understands the Japanese language, but does not try to speak it, nor does he speak it well. The Chinese managers, on the other hand, are sensitive about their English speaking ability. One of them found it more comfortable to speak to me in Japanese than in English. He also submits his reports to the General Manager in written Japanese. The Personnel Manager appears very lazy to the Japanese because he insists on leaving the office at 4.30 p.m. each day. They showed their lack of appreciation of his conduct by giving him a slightly lower bonus than the Chinese managers, his contemporaries. However, it is largely due to his efforts after hours that the labour relations in the factory run smoothly. He is a personal friend of the Malay union secretary. Even though his status and his salary are now much higher, he takes pains to maintain the relationship. But the Japanese do not recognize this role and give him no credit for his efforts. He also makes personal loans to workers, which are often unrecoverable. The existence of such informal patron–client type links is not perceived by the Japanese, and they are more impressed by the behaviour of a Chinese manager, who always stays back late at work and is seen to be constantly busy on the job. He has not established vertical personal links with workers, even the Chinese, and is regarded by them as being tight-fisted because he rarely lends them money. They expressed the opinion that he was of good character, but had gone over to the Japanese side. However, this manager is himself quite frustrated that there is no real authority delegated to him and this makes him lose face in front of the Malaysian workers.

Hence, there is a strong perception of the features of the Japanese management model on the part of local management. However, as middle-management,[44] they stand in an ambivalent position *vis-à-vis* their Japanese superiors and fellow Malaysian workers. They adopt the Japanese model to varying degrees. The strategy they choose is highly innovative and based on an individual choice of whether to maximize career chances in the company, despite the frustration of lack of authority and the disadvantage of heavy demands on their private time with comparatively little financial reward, or to maximize their interests outside the company, in family, private business or social activities.

CONCLUSION

I have shown how the Japanese management system operates to generate workers' consent to the extraction of surplus value from their labour. The Japanese model does this particularly well in Japan by obscuring the class position of workers and linking them, through corporate paternalism in personal relationships of a vertical, patron–client nature, to their superiors and the company.

In Malaysia, too, the Japanese system is implemented, but only partially, due to Malaysian government policy constraints and the lack of a need to grant substantial benefits to workers who have little to bargain with in terms of labour rights and alternative employment opportunities.

In Malaysia, as elsewhere, the Japanese investors benefit in that their class position is mystified by the notoriety value of their ethnic identity. Similarly, ethnic cleavages within the Malaysian labour force preoccupy workers and mitigate against a realization of their common class position. Hence, the ideological role of ethnicity obscures the class positions of those engaged in the relations of production.

NOTES

This chapter is the revised version of a paper presented at the Asian Studies Association of Australia Malaysia Society's Third Colloquium, 22–24 August

1981, University of Adelaide. Although the fieldwork for this chapter was carried out in the late 1970s, no comparable work has been undertaken since.

1 Chee Peng Lim and Lee Poh Ping, *The Role of Japanese Direct Investment in Malaysia*, 1979, Institute of Southeast Asian Studies, Singapore, p. 17.

2 A huge debate surrounds the concept of Japanese 'paternalism', beginning with the study by J.G. Abegglen, *The Japanese Factory*, 1958, Glencoe. Paternalism has been termed 'familialism' (Chie Nakane, *Japanese Society*, 1970, Weidenfeld and Nicolson, London, pp. 18–19), and 'welfare corporatism' (Ronald Dore, *British Factory–Japanese Factory*, 1973, George Allen & Unwin, London, p. 370), but these terms all describe a system in which individual workers' interests are linked directly with those of the company. In the work of uncritical contributors to the debate, an explanation of this phenomenon is usually linked with the view of Japanese society as 'unique', e.g. as expounded by Nakane, op. cit.

3 I conducted the study from January 1977 to February 1978, and hence this paper is based on data from that period. To protect the anonymity of individuals mentioned, I do not reveal the identity of the company.

4 See articles such as 'Management: the Japanese Touch', *Newsweek*, p. 47, 8 July 1974, and 'An Attractive Japanese Export', *Time*, p. 56, 2 March 1981. Also 'The zippy "cycle of goodness"', *Far Eastern Economic Review*, p. 75, 25 April 1980.

5 See the definition of managerial ideologies by Reinhard Bendix, *Work and Authority in Industry – Ideologies of Management in the Course of Industrialization*, 1963, Harper and Row, New York, p. 2: 'All ideas which are espoused by or for those who exercise authority in economic enterprises, and which seek to explain and justify that authority, are subsumed under this phrase'. See also a more recent article by Reginald Whitaker, 'Scientific Management Theory as Political Ideology', *Studies in Political Economy*, Ottawa, Autumn, 1979, pp. 75–108, in which he ties the ideological role of 'scientific management' to the need to mystify material changes in capitalist production during the Taylor era and hence legitimize capitalist hegemony (p. 80).

6 See the work of Abegglen, op. cit., as discussed in Joe Moore, 'The Japanese Worker', *Bulletin of Concerned Asian Scholars*, 6, 3: 35–47 (Sept.–Oct. 1974).

7 Ellen Kay Trimberger, 'State Power and Modes of Production: Implications of the Japanese Transition to Capitalism', *The Insurgent Sociologist*, 6, 4: 85–98 (1976), argues convincingly against the use of the term 'feudal' to characterize Japan's *Tokugawa* period, preferring the implications of the 'tributary mode of production' terminology. I retain the popular usage of 'feudal' for simplicity. In either case, the structural argument applies.

8 See an excellent statement on class relations in Japanese history in Perry Anderson, *Lineages of the Absolutist State*, NLB, London, Note on 'Japanese Feudalism', pp. 435–61, and Trimberger, op. cit.

9 See papers of the workshop on 'Business Opportunities and Management Techniques in Japan', 29 Nov.–1 Dec. 1979, organized by the National Institute of Public Administration Malaysia (INTAN) and an article by Mohammed Salikon Sarpin, 'Konsep Pengurusan di Jepun – Keuntungan Dicari, Kemanusiaan Dikekalkan', *Dewan Masyarakat*, 15 January 1980, pp. 36–40.

10 The very facility of ethnic explanations should tempt us into an analysis of the underlying structural forces which have pushed them into prominence. In all societies penetrated by capitalist forms of production and exchange, ethnic or similar divisive categories, such as tribe, race, gender or religious belief, are emphasized and function to obscure the prior fact of class relations created by

colonial penetration. Immanuel Wallerstein argues for the usefulness of the concept of 'status group' in the class analysis of multi-ethnic or tribally divided post-colonial societies. Here 'status group', in the Weberian sense, typifies the above categories, which are found invariably to be ordered hierarchically within the social system in terms of their members' access to power, privilege or prestige. Status group affiliations, although highly visible, are not 'given', but are a resource used by individuals or groups in their strategies for coping with class relations. Many phenomena of present-day Malaysian society can be seen in this light – the intensification of Islamic belief among Malays, the conversion of some Chinese to Islam as an entrepreneurial strategy, or the development of a Malay-controlled union in the factory I studied. Status group affiliations also function to conceal the reality of class difference, hence benefitting the dominant class, i.e. as an explanation or justification of the on-going system, they function as ideologies. See Immanuel Wallerstein 'Social conflict in post-independence Black Aftrica: the concepts of race and status group reconsidered', in *The Capitalist World-Economy – Essays by Immanuel Wallerstein*, 1979, Cambridge University Press, Cambridge, pp. 169, 176–7, and Gerth, H.H. and Mills, C. Wright, (eds), *From Max Weber: Essays in Sociology*, 1970, Routledge & Kegan Paul, London, pp. 180–4.

11 See Harry Braverman, *Labour and Monopoly Capital – the Degradation of Work in the Twentieth Century*, 1974, Monthly Review Press, New York.

12 Moore, op. cit., p. 41. Moore has given an excellent summary and critique of the debate available in English on this subject. I found that many of the insights which emerged from my fieldwork had already been stated by Moore in his critical review of the literature.

13 See Abegglen, op. cit., Mikio Sumiya, *Social Impact of Industrialization in Japan*, Tokyo, Japanese National Commission for UNESCO, 1963, and Dore, op. cit., to name a few.

14 *Shain* is a special term for employee in Japanese used to designate the permanent employees of large companies, i.e. the recipients of paternalist benefits. It would not be used to refer to temporary or contract workers in these companies, nor to employees of small industries. Hence the so-called 'Japanese' model applies only to permanent employees of large companies (*daikigyo*) with over 100 employees; in other words, to only 30 per cent of the total Japanese labour force.

15 Dore, op. cit., p. 263, as emphasized in Moore, op. cit., p. 39.

16 Sumiya, op. cit.

17 Moore, op. cit., p. 43.

18 For instance, the government's 'restructuring' policy at management level has meant that Malay technical staff who are in short supply have a very high degree of mobility between companies and the public and private sector. This has hampered Japanese attempts to set up a permanent workforce with close personal links between superior and subordinate.

19 See the *Employment Ordinance, 1955* and the *Employment (Amendment) Act, 1971*.

20 For example, employees rejected the morning assembly with company anthem and exercises. They also rejected generalism in work roles and egalitarianism in work relationships.

21 See Whitaker, op. cit., for a discussion of this phenomenon in the USA during the era of Taylorism; e.g. the ambiguous position of efficiency engineers in the class structure (p. 80).

22 The Japanese managerial ranking system is as follows:
Shacho company president, *Senmu Torishimariyaku* managing director,

Torishimariyaku director, *Bucho* department chief, *Kacho* section chief, *Kakaricho* unit chief.

These classifications are retained in the overseas venture.

23 Robert E. Cole, 'Permanent Employment in Japan: Facts and Fantasies', *Industrial and Labour Relations Review,* Oct 1972, pp. 615–30.

24 This is typical of most Japanese companies in Malaysia. See A.B. Sim, 'Comparative Management Practices and Performance of American, British and Japanese MNCs in Malaysia', Paper presented to the Malaysian Economic Association Seminar on 'Foreign Investment: Benefits and Responsibilities', 10 July 1978, Kuala Lumpur.

25 See A. Halim Ali, 'The Adaptation of Rural Migrants in Urban Factory Employment – a Case Study of a Malayan Factory', Paper presented to the 1978 Conference of the Australian Anthropological Society, August, for a lengthy discussion of this phenomenon and its implications as a management strategy.

26 This scheme, if implemented, would have replicated the flexibility in the system of hiring temporary or contract labour along with permanent employees in large companies in Japan.

27 See *Employment Ordinance*, op. cit.

28 'Women's Place in the Integrated Circuit', *Pacific Research*, 9, 5–6: 11 (July–Oct, 1978).

29 Foremen may promote the individual interests of workers or workers may cooperate among themselves because of patron–client relationships, kinship links or outside business partnerships.

30 This is the central theme of Michael Burawoy's book, *Manufacturing Consent – Changes in the Labour Process Under Monopoly Capitalism,* 1979, University of Chicago Press, Chicago; also stressed by Moore, op. cit., in reviewing Robert E. Cole, *Japanese Blue Collar,* 1971, University of California Press, Berkeley and Los Angeles.

31 See T. Nichols and H. Beynon, *Living with Capitalism,* 1977, London, pp. 19–21, for a discussion of the tensions inherent in 'control room' labour in the chemical industry.

32 Thirty per cent of all workers have experienced a horizontal transfer, 7 per cent more than once. Among production workers alone, 74 per cent have been transferred.

33 Braverman, op. cit.

34 Burawoy (op. cit., pp. 77–94) shows how, depending on the type of technology used, workers may be offered a 'bait' of limited freedom in their attempts to adapt the labour process to their best advantage. Rules may be instituted by management, but these also function to constrain managerial intervention. So long as a small but crucial degree of choice is available to workers, they can constitute the labour process as a 'game'; their very 'consent' to these rules, which offer the small carrot of choice, obscures the fact of their loss of control over the labour process and reduces their sense of deprivation. Burawoy illustrates this with the example of 'rate-fixing', 'banking' and 'chistelling', i.e. the games played by individual workers in the piece-rated machine tooling shop. This same flexibility is inherent in the continuous process type of technology, which calls for twenty-four hour shift-work, with on-off vigilance and long periods of inactivity. The potential for 'games' is less, by comparison, in the conveyor-belt type production of the electronics industry.

35 See *Lapuran Tahunan,* Pejabat Pendaftaran Kesatuan Sekerja, for legislation and official guidelines relating to trade unionism in Malaysia.

36 Comparable with the process of decision-making in Japan itself. See Dore, op. cit., pp. 138, 218.

37 See Stuart D. Brandes, *American Welfare Capitalism*, 1976, University of Chicago Press, Chicago.

38 Peter Lloyd, *Slums of Hope?*, 1979, Penguin Books, Ringwood, p. 225.

39 Yoshi Tsurumi, *The Japanese are Coming: A Multinational Interaction of Firms and Politics*, 1976, Ballinger, Cambridge, Mass. See especially Ch. 10 'The "Ugly Japanese" and their Dilemma Abroad'.

40 Sim, op. cit.

41 This is the theme of a paper by Edith C.C. Yuen, 'The Management Problems of a Japanese Factory in Australia', presented to the 1978 Conference of the Asian Studies Association of Australia, University of New South Wales, 14–19 May 1978.

42 For an analysis of Japanese attitudes to Southeast Asia, see Wendy A. Smith, 'The role of cultural factors in Japanese investment in Southeast Asia', *Industrial Policies, Foreign Investment and Labour in Asian Countries – Proceedings of the 1977 Asian Regional Conference on Industrial Relations*, 1977, Tokyo, pp. 131–45.

43 Until recently, degrees from Japanese universities were not recognized in Malaysia, and a Malaysian graduate of a Japanese university, subsequently employed in a Japanese company in Malaysia, may experience the irony of working side by side with Japanese expatriate staff who graduated from the same university, yet receive far less pay than the Japanese because he is not recognized by the company as a 'graduate'.

44 The Production Manager was insulted when he found that the training seminar he attended in Japan was for 'Middle Management'.

7

MALAYSIAN FORESTS, JAPANESE WOOD

Japan's role in Malaysia's deforestation*

Jomo K.S.

Tropical rainforests are the earth's most diverse biological habitats. Covering a mere 6 per cent of the world's surface, they contain over half the species of animal and plant life found on this planet. They are of vital importance to global ecological processes, as basic as converting carbon dioxide, the major cause of global warming, into oxygen, necessary for all forms of life. They hold the key to the discovery of new foods and medicines: 40 per cent of all drugs prescribed in the USA are derived from rainforest plants, while it is estimated that only 2 per cent of species have been screened for their medicinal properties. They are home to more than 100 million people, who, having lived in them for thousands of years, naturally depend on them for their continued survival. They are crucial to maintaining the ecological balance of local environments by preventing flooding, soil erosion and changes in climate. And yet, worldwide, 11 million hectares of rainforest are logged each year, and if present rates of deforestation continue, there will be little left by the turn of the century (Hurst, 1990).

The size and complexity of Sarawak's rainforest have inspired many scientists to devote their lives to studying it. According to a professor of dendrology who lived in Sarawak for several years, 'It can be said, without any reasonable doubt, that the northwest part of Borneo, including the whole of Sarawak, is the richest forest in terms of trees in the world', (quoted by Sesser, 1991: 46). Sarawak's nearly fifty thousand square miles of rainforest is said to contain some twenty thousand species of flowering plants, several thousand species of trees, hundreds of species of butterflies, a hundred and eighty species of mammals, and more than a hundred kinds of fruiting trees. Thirty birds, thirty-nine mammals, and a third of all plant species are endemic to Borneo. In a twenty-five acre sample plot, the Royal Geographical Society identified nearly eight hundred species of trees – twenty times the number of native species in all of Britain. Sarawak's several thousand tree species, in a rainforest that may be ten million years old, include some that are a hundred and fifty feet tall. Borneo is the last spot on earth in which substantial growths of dipterocarps remain. This family of trees, yields very durable wood for the construction of houses and furniture, and for other objects. Dipterocarps have provided half the hardwoods used worldwide in the last thirty years (Sesser, 1991: 46).

Japan has had a significant role in Malaysian deforestation. Japan currently imports approximately 64 per cent of its tropical hardwood logs from Sarawak, Malaysia. With only some 2 per cent of the world's population, Japan imports 30 per cent of all tropical timber, and half of all tropical hardwood logs traded internationally. Tropical sawnwood production in International Tropical Timber Organization (ITTO) nations fell 16.5 per cent in 1991 to 32.9 million cubic metres. Tropical hardwood veneer production increased by 12.7 per cent to 1.5 million cubic metres in 1991, while tropical plywood production increased by 3.7 per cent in 1991 to 12.8 million cubic metres. Malaysia has substantial new plywood and veneer capacity and will continue to account for a large proportion of aggregate increases in these categories in 1994. Log exports by ITTO producing members totalled 23.9 million cubic metres in 1991, 5.7 per cent less than 1990 exports of which Malaysia accounted for 81 per cent. Tropical sawnwood exports were 7.3 million cubic metres in 1991, (with Malaysia accounting for 67 per cent), increasing by 7.6 per cent in 1992. Veneer exports, also led by Malaysia, increased by 23 per cent to 0.83 million cubic metres in 1991. Tropical plywood exports continued to grow in 1991, rising by 7.5 per cent from 1990 levels to 10.5 million cubic metres, with the increases in the near future largely accounted for by Malaysia, with Indonesia's share falling to 80 per cent in 1993. Tropical hardwood log imports by ITTO consumers came to 22.9 million cubic metres in 1991; 45 per cent of this total went to Japan, though Japanese consumption dropped by 8 per cent in 1991. Japan also dominates the international import market for tropical sawnwood, accounting for almost a fifth of total ITTO consumer imports of 5.5 million cubic metres in 1991. Japan is also the dominant tropical hardwood veneer importer, accounting for 677,000 cubic metres in 1991 from total imports of almost 1.2 million cubic metres. Japan is also, by far, the largest market for tropical plywood, taking 2.9 million cubic metres of total consumer imports of 8.1 million cubic metres in 1991 (ITTO, 1993). Many Japanese claim that such criticism stems mainly from jealousy of Japan's economic might, i.e. Japan-bashing. It is often also claimed that such timber extraction constitutes or contributes to economic development, and the improvement of Malaysian welfare. It is usually also stressed that logging practices and timber exports are in accord with Malaysian government policy.

By looking at Japan's tropical timber trade and *sogoshosha* trade practices, we will examine how intense commercial logging has given rise to more widespread deforestation. An analysis of Japan's official Development

Assistance (ODA) will show how development projects also contribute to the destruction of the rainforest.

As local communities, especially in Sarawak, see their ancestral lands handed out in concessions to loggers, they have been forced to take what measures they can, e.g. in the form of blockades across logging roads to protest. Largely ignored or accused of being subversive, 'anti-development' or worse, they have had no real recognition of their situation. Some have warned that they will defend themselves to the death with their spears and blowpipes, because they know that the disappearance of the forests means their own extinction, and so have nothing to lose by fighting for their lives. It is indeed ironic that some of the least 'developed' communities, considered by many to be uncivilized and backward, are reminding the modern world of the importance of maintaining man's sensitive balance with nature. As the world's leading importer of tropical hardwood, Japan has the responsibility to put the considerable economic power at its disposal to effective use in saving the rainforests.

JAPAN'S TIMBER INDUSTRY

Why Japan has come to require a third of the world's tropical timber

Wood has always been extremely popular in Japan. With two-thirds of the country covered in forest, it is one of its only natural resources, and has become an integral part of the Japanese way of life. The Japanese still greatly cherish the atmosphere created by wooden rooms and houses. But more important, in the construction of concrete housing or office blocks, the amount of wood used is considerable. This is because plywood is used for moulding concrete: for every square metre of floor area, 4 square metres of plywood are required, and each time, 44 per cent of the plywood is new. In other words, plywood used in this way is rejected after only two or three uses (Nectoux and Kuroda, 1989: 58). This concrete panelling (or *kon-pane*) accounts for nearly 30 per cent of plywood consumed in Japan (the other major end-use being furniture), and in 1986, 96 per cent of all plywood was made from tropical hardwood (Nectoux and Kuroda, 1989: 46). In 1992, 75 per cent of the 111.2 million cubic metres of wood used in Japan was imported (Friedland, 1993). In 1986, tropical hardwood imports accounted for 16 per cent of timber requirements in Japan, softwood imports from North America and the USSR for a further 50 per cent with the remaining third coming from domestic supplies. Plywood can be made from temperate softwoods, and as the sources of tropical timber run out, the plywood manufacturing industries will have to adapt to alternative materials. In view of the ecological importance of rainforests, both locally and globally, the switch to softwoods must happen before the rainforests are more or less totally destroyed.

Japan has not always relied so heavily on imported timber. Whereas Japan was formerly able to satisfy demand with domestic supplies from the extensive wood reserves found all over the country, since the war, a situation has developed where imports now account for nearly two-thirds of requirements (Nectoux and Kuroda, 1989: 5). The 1930s were a time when Japan was eager to compete with the other industrialized nations, but lack of sufficient natural resources encouraged Japan to invade the Asian continent and establish colonies. Manchuria, Korea and Sakhalin nearly doubled the area of commercial forest available to Japan. However, during the Second World War, Japan was less able to rely on the resources from its colonies, and was forced to return to its own forests for supplies. The high demands of the war effort led to desperate overlogging, and serious depletion of national reserves followed, which continued even after the war, as the costs of reconstruction took their toll. During this period, Japan did not have the financial means to import on a sufficiently large scale, and was forced to rely solely on domestic forests.

The effect of such acute increases in demand for a dwindling resource is obvious enough. The 1950s saw a 60 per cent price rise in domestic timber, causing the government huge problems in dealing with the massive costs of reconstruction. To try and stabilize the price, supply had to be increased, and so, domestic logging of national forests – as opposed to private forests – was stepped up, and imports from the USSR and North America were introduced. But despite these efforts, supply still fell short of demand, and further action had to be taken by the government. At the beginning of the 1960s, as the economy started to take off, national expenditure grew, followed by a 26 per cent increase in the number of new houses built between 1960 and 1961 (Nectoux and Kuroda, 1989: 32). The already intensified logging of the national forests had to be supplemented by mass imports, as it was no longer economically viable to rely on the now very expensive domestic stock. High labour and other production costs, a rising yen and increasingly difficult access to the mountainous forests rendered domestic timber non-competitive to imports.

Sarawak's hardwoods provide a beautiful, durable wood, resistant to warping, with a smooth, defect-free surface. Why is this wood used for disposable plywood? The answer is that it costs less to cut down a tree and ship it to Japan to make plywood than to make plywood from an inferior Japanese softwood tree because workers in Japan earn far more than in Sarawak. But also the Sarawak rainforest is considered free; no compensation for the use of the land is factored into the cost of the tree. The government gives out the concessions instead of charging for them, and the forest people get nothing or a pittance. In the system of politically motivated concessions, the actual worth of the raw material becomes irrelevant. This triggered and has sustained the 'logging boom' in Southeast Asian countries, which has continued until the present. The continued availability of relatively cheap tropical timber from abroad has discouraged less wasteful uses of timber as well as substitution by other materials.

Tropical plywood has become so much a part of the Japanese construction industry that building contractors will not consider anything else. Some plywood also goes to make cheap furniture, so little valued that it is often discarded when people move house.

In fact, Japan had already been importing tropical hardwood from the Philippines during the 1950s, but on a small scale, for the production of high-quality plywood to be exported to the USA. The valuable dollars earned from this earned the timber industry a distinguished position in the Japanese government's eyes, and so it received substantial official support for modernization and development. The government policies encouraging imports, combined with the rapidly expanding economy during the 1960s, meant a sudden rapid growth of the timber industry. From 1960 to 1963, log imports more than doubled, and tropical log imports rose by 70 per cent. Total demand went on to peak in 1973 at ten times the 1960 level; for tropical hardwood, demand increased by six times (Nectoux and Kuroda, 1989: 34).

This boom had a serious impact on the forests of the Philippines, Japan's main supplier until 1971, when large scale logging switched to Indonesia. Gradually, all the easily accessible forest areas in the Philippines were exhausted; the remaining sources were not only more expensive to extract, but also of lower quality. So, after 1973, tropical log imports fell by nearly half for two main reasons. First, the effects of unrestrained logging in the Philippines had become apparent, and in 1974, the Southeast Asian Lumber Producers Association was formed to strengthen the position of the exporting countries. Changes in trade practices were made to restrict, and eventually ban the export of raw logs, to encourage processing within the producing country into higher-value products, such as plywood, before export. This meant that the producing countries could get more money for less wood extracted from the forests, and further develop their own timber-processing industries. At the same time, it was hoped that this would reduce demand on forests to supply large quantities of raw logs. Second, in the early 1970s, the number of houses being built in Japan fell by 31 per cent, directly affecting the consumption of wood products. Although consumption recovered in the late 1970s, the world economic slump of 1980–81 once again brought imports down. Between 1979 and 1985, total log imports fell by 35 per cent, while tropical log imports dropped by 29 per cent (Nectoux and Kuroda, 1989: 34).

It appears that the behaviour of Japanese companies in the timber-producing countries of Southeast Asia has changed very little since the 1960s when the mass imports first began. Having invested heavily in logging in the Philippines, once there was no more wood available for commercial extraction, instead of reviewing operations, similar direct investments were then made in Indonesia, with similar effects, until the Indonesians banned the export of logs, fearing a repetition of the Philippines experience. Indonesia banned the export of logs in 1986, to try to slow down the rate of deforestation and increase revenue from higher value-added exports by encouraging wood processing industries; it has since developed the world's largest plywood industry. Once this happened, the investments moved to Malaysia, particularly to the states of Sabah and Sarawak. In other words, Japan has been ignoring the adverse effects its overseas investments have been having on the local people and environment. At the same time, the host governments have largely colluded by turning a blind eye to the problems encountered by the people affected by the logging, in favour of short-term economic gain, usually referred to as economic development. For example, the government sees the tribal people in the rainforests of Sarawak as an embarrassment, as primitives in need of development and 'civilization'! Meanwhile, hundreds have been arrested for protesting against the logging, by barricading the logging roads as the loggers advance further into their domain.

The late 1980s saw a recovery of tropical hardwood imports into Japan, but it was not as significant as those of temperate softwoods. This suggests that in recent years, actions taken by producing countries, such as the Indonesian and Peninsular Malaysian log-export ban, have made it difficult for importers to continue the practices of the 1960s and 1970s. Hence, softwoods are beginning to replace tropical hardwoods. However, at present, Japan still imports 29 per cent of the world's rainforest hardwood (Nectoux and Kuroda, 1989: 5), and wood and paper consumption in general remains high. For example, the average Japanese uses more than twice the amount of paper and paperboard per year than the average European, reflecting the widespread throwaway attitude in Japan (Nectoux and Kuroda, 1989: 25). Japan uses most of its imports of tropical hardwood for the production of plywood, but because tropical hardwood is so cheap, there is no economic imperative to seek alternatives to the use of hardwood in plywood production and the use of plywood. Hence, tropical hardwood imports remain high. Indeed, demand increased in the mid-1980s when housing starts increased from 1.14 million in 1983 to 1.37 million in 1986, and again sharply to 1.67 million in 1987, to a level roughly double, per thousand inhabitants, of that in the USA and Europe (Nectoux and Kuroda, 1989: 55).

Malaysia provides four-fifths of the 10 million cubic metres of tropical hardwood logs used by Japanese plywood manufacturers (Friedland, 1993). Three-quarters of Japan's hardwood imports come from Borneo, logs from Sarawak and Sabah, and plywood from Indonesia. If the rate of deforestation continues, soon there will be none left for export, as has happened in other former log exporting countries. In fact, it has been estimated that Sarawak will have to start importing in several years at current levels of deforestation. It is clearly in Japan's interests to see that the forests are managed properly for sustainable, continued timber production and supply, but this reasoning is not necessarily shared by individual importing companies. There has been little or no change in attitude by the companies involved in logging, as they shift their attention from place to place, as timber reserves become more difficult to reach and extract, and as an area's commercial value declines. The consequence is the gradual disappearance of the rainforests, which not only threatens the livelihood of the indigenous tribes who live in them, but also the stability of the global climate. Furthermore, producing countries have come to rely heavily on the export of raw materials such as timber as a major source of revenue. In 1990, timber export earnings amounted to 11.3 per cent of Malaysia's total export proceeds (Jomo, 1992: 1). Clearly, the loss of the rainforests will eventually result in economic and other difficulties for the producing countries, but such medium- and long-term considerations are not of much concern to governments and businesses with short-term priorities and considerations.

SOGOSHOSHA TRADE PRACTICES

How Japanese companies have secured control of the resource base

Having established that there is a huge demand for timber products in Japan, the companies responsible for importing the timber, and their methods of conducting the trade, should be examined. All along the line, from the forests in the producing countries to the depots in the harbours of Japan, it can be seen that Japanese companies have in many ways been taking advantage of the weaker bargaining position and inexperience of the timber exporters, reducing their profit from the trade, and frequently ignoring social problems arising from logging activities. The result is that the local environment, i.e. the rainforests and their inhabitants, all suffer and gain little, with most of the profits from logging going to local politicians who are concession-holders, the mainly Chinese loggers, and the mainly Japanese controlled companies which import and process the logs.

Japanese *sogoshoshas*, or general trading houses, organize the imports of tropical timber. In the early 1980s, the top nine *sogoshoshas* accounted for 30 per cent of Japan's gross national product (GNP), falling more recently to about 25 per cent (Nectoux and Kuroda, 1989: 63). They conduct all sorts of commercial and financial operations, being closely associated with large city banks (Dai-ichi Kangyo Bank, Sanwa Bank and Fuji Bank) and often affiliated to the large industrial groupings (Mitsui, Sumitomo and Mitsubishi). Competition among the *sogoshoshas* is fierce, with their profitability relying on large transaction volumes, rather than profit margins. This means profits are mainly gained from business conducted

Table 7.1 Imports of tropical timber by major consuming countries

Country	1988	1989
Japan	18,383,644	23,939,512
South Korea	6,008,160	6,027,300
USA	5,122,450	3,605,848
UK	2,859,822	2,586,634
Netherlands	1,984,686	2,350,914
France	2,076,242	2,249,956
Italy	1,623,764	1,860,012
Germany	1,597,052	1,738,320
Spain	1,085,660	1,165,400

Source: Japan Tropical Forest Action Network, 1991.
Unit: cubic metres of roundwood equivalents.

on a large scale. In recent years, competition has increased among the *sogoshoshas* because, as manufacturing conglomerates grew, they increasingly bypassed the *sogoshoshas* and marketed their products themselves. As these companies grew more independent of the *sogoshoshas*, they increasingly financed themselves, further weakening their ties with the *sogoshoshas*. Consequently, the proportion and relative importance of their remaining commodity transactions have grown. However, primary commodity prices fell in the early 1980s and remained low thereafter, further undermining the *sogoshoshas*. In the case of timber, Japan's share of the Southeast Asian exports is so important that prices have come to be determined by demand in Japan, weakening the bargaining power of the producers and their influence on prices.

The top 15 *sogoshoshas* are important dealers in tropical timber, with the ten biggest being: C Itoh & Co., Marubeni Corp., Yuasa Sangyo, Sumitomo Forestry, Ataka Mokuzai, Nissho Iwai Corp., Nichimen, Mitsui & Co., Mitsubishi Corp. and Tomen. Together, these companies imported over half the tropical logs into Japan in 1987 (Nectoux and Kuroda, 1989: 65).

The *sogoshosha* role in the tropical timber trade is crucial because they involve themselves in all levels of activity: extraction, processing, importing and distribution, both domestically and abroad. Two practices employed by the *sogoshosha* have greatly facilitated imports into Japan, with dire effects on the environment. The first has been to loan capital and equipment to timber merchants who organize the logging. The *sogoshosha* may then also sell or lease the necessary heavy equipment to the loggers for their operations. Repayments for the loans may be required in log-shipments, thus guaranteeing the supply of logs. The second has been to engage in joint ventures with local companies which are often required by government policy to put up 60 per cent of the initial investment to retain local control. All too often, the Southeast Asian side has been unable to raise the required funding, so the Japanese company may advance the rest (sometimes up to 30 per cent of the total for the project) in uninsured, back-door dealings (Nectoux and Kuroda, 1989: 68).

Under pressure from market forces, these practices put huge pressure for the logs to be extracted as quickly as possible. In the first, the growing debt servicing requirements put pressure on the loggers' side. In the second system, concern over uninsured funding pressures the Japanese side. Either way, the loggers are rushed, giving rise to numerous problems.

Meanwhile, sometimes unaware of the economic, social and environmental consequences of the logging of rainforests and often benefitting from low tax rates, the authorities usually do not tax the logging companies enough to cover the real costs of reforestation and enforcement of logging and other related regulations, let alone maximize resource rent capture by the state. With few taxes to pay, and poor enforcement, the loggers cut down the forests to maximize short-term rather than long-term returns for themselves and the usually politically connected concession holders. Having no stake in the forest's regeneration, the loggers have largely been oblivious to the importance of long-term management. Much illegal logging follows as a result, with logging companies often disregarding the restrictions for selective felling in order to maximize profits in the short-term. Under-declaration of the wood extracted and exported from a concession is common, while accounts are often 'fiddled'. This allows exporters to pay less to the government in royalties and tax, while concealing illegal profits. As governments realize that timber revenues have been well below what they should be, taxes have been raised, but often only leading to further tax evasion. The statistical discrepancies suggest that more wood arrives in Japan than has been declared as exports from the country of origin (Nectoux and Kuroda, 1989: 72). Much of such illegal activity has been ignored by the Japanese companies importing the timber.

As the forest area disappeared in the Philippines, Japanese interests carried on with the same sort of investments in Indonesia during the 1970s,

Table 7.2 Imports of tropical timber by major Japanese *sogoshoshas*

Company	1988	1989	1990
Mitsubishi Corp.	1,256,580	1,455,292	1,253,752
Nissho Iwai	1,358,715	1,591,081	1,261,158
Marubeni	1,393,934	1,502,534	1,153,887
C. Itoh & Co.	1,292,288	1,690,203	1,237,119
Sumitomo Forestry	1,505,424	1,542,734	1,134,710
Nichimen	903,295	1,025,004	1,038,858
Mitsui & Co.	694,123	826,028	719,225
Sumitomo Corp.	549,181	713,659	529,817

Source: Japan Tropical Forest Action Network, November 1991.
Unit: cubic metres of roundwood equivalents.

and Malaysia (especially Sabah and Sarawak) in the 1980s. The late 1980s saw important changes in these patterns, at least in neighbouring Philippines and Indonesia. The changes have been initiated and implemented by the producer countries, in response to the serious consequences of the timber trade, and not by Japan. Since President Marcos of the Philippines was ousted in 1986, there have been efforts by the government to enforce logging rules and to collect taxes more efficiently, but unfortunately, it seems that this has come too late, for there is little timber of much commercial value left. In the case of Indonesia though, the ban on log-exports in 1986 has meant that domestic processing industries now export higher-value products such as plywood, making the illegal trade in logs much more difficult, and at the same time increasing government revenue.

As the Japanese have gone from one Southeast Asian country to another in search of tropical hardwoods, Malaysia, particularly Sarawak, have proved to be very accommodating. As early as 1966, a Malaysian government timber official wrote, 'It is incumbent upon us to open an area for exploitation irrespective of whether this area is adequately stocked with the requisite regeneration or not. . . . Inadequacy of stocking before felling should not be allowed to hinder the progress of exploitation' (quoted by Sesser, 1991: 46). However, Malaysia, too, was forced to impose restrictions. Realizing that the peninsula's timber supply was rapidly running out, the federal government limited logging from 1978, reducing the annual rate of cutting by more than 60 per cent in six years, and banning the export of logs.

The Sarawak state and Malaysian federal governments seem determined to continue exporting logs, in spite of the now much reported popular local native resistance to the logging. On the other hand, there is no reason to expect the Japanese authorities to require the Japanese timber industry to ensure that the logs are extracted at a sustainable rate with greater benefit to the Malaysian economy and the local populations adversely affected. Instead, in 1988, two shipments of 38,500 cubic metres of logs were made from Brazil (where, in fact, log exports have been officially banned since 1973), suggesting that Japan is perfectly aware that supplies are diminishing in Southeast Asia, and alternative sources must be secured (Nectoux and Kuroda, 1989: 30).

JAPANESE OFFICIAL DEVELOPMENT ASSISTANCE AND THE ENVIRONMENT

Japan is the biggest donor to 29 developing countries, many of which have endangered forest resources. The number of ODA projects aimed at developing the forestry sector has been small, which may seem surprising in Japan's case, in view of the size of its timber industry. Even these projects have often tended to be primarily inventories of forest resources, which may well encourage and facilitate future logging. So far, they have not been concerned with reviewing logging practices known to be environmentally destructive. Official development assistance projects involved more directly in logging have seen the introduction of unsustainable logging techniques – incredibly considered 'technology transfer'! All too often, Japanese techniques are unsuitable for successful tropical forest management, making use of heavy machinery which causes considerable damage to smaller trees and the forest floor during the extraction process. Lack of information about the ecological importance of rainforests is reflected in the common belief among Japanese and Malaysian officials that, for example, plantations are adequate replacements for virgin forests, when in fact, they cannot begin to approach the ecological value of rainforests (Forrest and Harago, 1990: 4).

However, some of the projects which have had the most adverse effects on the rainforests have not been targeted at the forestry sector at all, but rather on infrastructure, agriculture and mining development. These account for nearly 40 per cent of the projects. Environmental impact assessments (EIAs) prior to the start of projects are not usually required for Japanese ODA projects, often with disastrous consequences. Dam construction displaces communities, floods large areas of farmland and forest with reservoirs, and totally changes the natural environment and ecosystems further down the valley. Roads open up the forests to landless farmers who convert logged-over land into agricultural land; without them, the farmers would not be able to penetrate the forest. Similarly, agricultural expansion means that logged-over areas will never be allowed to regenerate though it could reduce pressure on remaining forest land. Finally, power stations, metal refineries and factories pollute the air and rivers, affecting the local habitat of plants and animals on which local people depend for food, drinking-water, medicines and other necessities.

A disturbing aspect of Japan's ODA is how tied aid turns the funds into profits for private Japanese companies. The system operates in such a way that once a request for aid is accepted by the government in Japan, the funds are provided, and then alloted to the company which gets the contract, all too often a Japanese company. This is because if the recipient country agrees to have a Japanese company carry out a project, it is more likely that the Japanese government will agree to put up the funds for it. In the past, much of Japan's aid to developing countries was 'tied' to Japanese private companies. In other words, Japanese taxpayer money went straight into the pockets of these companies, supposedly for the benefit of the Third World.

Like many of the other major aid donors, Japan hardly deserves credit as the world's top foreign aid donor since the main consideration behind much of its ODA is to provide business for and to otherwise support and favour the business interests of its private companies. Many projects still end up being means for Japanese companies' business growth. For example, logging roads funded by Japanese ODA are said to be for the use of the local people as well, but in fact, they are usually cut where they are most useful for loggers, and are rarely maintained after the logging finishes. In spite of growing recognition of the role of logging and infrastructure (especially roads) on deforestation, there are still projects put to the World Bank which the Japanese feel happy about funding, e.g. a road construction project in Sarawak scheduled for 1993, where 'the roads are to be used for local traffic, for bringing in people and goods, and for exporting logs. . . . Japan Technical Assistance Grant Facility support of 64 million yen will be provided for environmental studies and project design'. Greenpeace has listed a number of concerns about the project. The project also violates the new World Bank forest policy 'which prohibits the World Bank from facilitating logging and states the goal of World Bank policy to preserve primary moist tropical forests'. This project is reckoned to be part of a larger project to link Sarawak and Sabah by road, thus opening large tracts of land to logging and colonization (Batker, 1992). It is clear that many of the pledges by Japanese officials to make sure that Japanese funded development projects do not damage the environment have been forgotten.

Japan's ODA projects are largely channelled through the Japan International Cooperation Agency (JICA), which mainly provides technical aid, and the Overseas Economic Cooperation Fund (OECF), which provides funding. There are fundamental problems within the administration of these two bodies, which have been important causes of environmental damage related to ODA. In 1985, the Development Assistance Committee (DAC) recommended EIAs for all projects. Only in 1989, did the Ministry of Foreign Affairs in Japan insist that no project be carried out without the necessary environmental impact research having taken place; in the same year, JICA finally set up an Environmental Unit for this purpose. There are only three part-time staff manning the unit, and eight other staff who liaise with the unit. It has no budget of its own, and no authority to stop a project from going ahead on environmental grounds (Forrest and Harago, 1990: 6). Furthermore, bureaucrats in the Japanese government are usually rotated from section to section every four years, meaning that there is little accumulation of experience and expertise in environmental matters within the unit, though this may be overcome by recruiting directly from specialized government agencies. Above all, so keen is the government to disperse impressive amounts of money, often for large-scale infrastructure, that alternatives to a project are rarely considered. In other words, the emphasis is on growth rather than conservation, e.g. a project to build a power station or dam to provide electricity is usually considered of more importance than proposals for energy conservation.

The OECF is similarly understaffed in environmental issues. One individual from the Japan Environment Agency (JEA) works as an advisor on the environmental aspects of a project. Guidelines are laid out for the recipient country, but these do not follow the standards which Japanese see fit for their own country, claiming that if Japanese standards were to be applied, the costs of the projects would be dramatically increased, which would jeopardize their implementation (Forrest and Harago, 1990: 9). Instead of setting a good example to developing countries, Japan has instead developed environmental double standards by externalizing many of its environmental problems including deforestation to meet domestic timber requirements.

THE JAPANESE RESPONSE

Many Japanese try to defend their country when the destruction of the rainforests in Southeast Asia is blamed primarily on Japan. Some feel that they are merely scapegoats for international environmentalist groups to bring the plight of tropical rainforests into the open. Since Europe imports roughly equal amounts of tropical timber as Japan, it seems unfair to direct all the attention to the Japanese trade. Furthermore, only 4.5 per cent of the total wood extracted from tropical forests around the world is exported, the rest being consumed within the country of origin (Arafune, 1991: 14). From this standpoint, it would seem that the producing countries themselves are to blame in view of their high levels of consumption. However, in Malaysia, where Japanese involvement in logging is high, exports constitute an important part of the total wood extracted. In particular, roughly two-thirds of the wood extracted from Malaysia was exported; if fuelwood gathered from forests is discounted, leaving only commercial timber, then the percentage exported rises to over 80 per cent (Nectoux and Kuroda, 1989: 21); 63 per cent of logs exported from Malaysia went to Japan in 1989 (Jomo, 1992: 2). In any case, the figure of 4.5 per cent is misleading because only a small portion of the wood extracted globally is of any commercial value. When measuring the volume of wood extracted, domestic consumption appears high, but this is because local people collect firewood from the forests, scraps from the forest floor or debris left behind after logging. In doing so, they certainly do not damage the forest as logging practices do.

Japan provides a market for high-quality hardwood, and secures control of the resource base via methods employed by the *sogoshoshas* which put pressure on the loggers to work as fast as possible, and practices employed by loggers which are highly destructive. In a survey of commercial logging operations in Malaysia, extraction of only 10 per cent of the trees in a specific area resulted in an additional 55 per cent being damaged or destroyed in the process (Arden-Clarke, 1990: 5). The heavy equipment provided by Japan for this extraction has been estimated to leave up to 40 per cent of the area bare (Chin, 1992: 59). These areas consist of severely compacted sub-soil, where natural regeneration of the forest is almost impossible. Logging roads alone may amount for a further 14 per cent of the area cleared by logging activity (Nectoux and Kuroda, 1989: 20).

The long-term impact on the forest due to logging is less obvious. By removing all the largest trees during logging, the shade from the sun is lost, and the complex eco-systems of the forest floor, unable to survive the increase in temperature, gradually decline and die out. Also, without the shelter of the taller trees, the rain washes the soil away, while logging roads turn into rivers of mud after rain. Finally, the forests are cleared when 'slash and burn' farmers move into the forest, after the loggers have left, and convert the old forest floor into exhausted wasteland within a few years.

It has often been argued that shifting cultivation is the major cause of deforestation. In an attempt to defend themselves against accusations that their involvement in commercial logging has been partly responsible for forest destruction, Mitsubishi has published a comic-book (or *manga*) claiming that 'slash and burn' farmers are primarily to blame. What Mitsubishi failed to admit is that this form of agriculture has been practised in the tropics for hundreds of years, and if it really destroyed the forests, they would have disappeared long ago. The fact is that this is a potentially sustainable method of agriculture, provided the population density is low enough and the forest is allowed to regenerate before being cultivated again.

One reason why shifting cultivators are blamed is because they may make use of new roads, particularly logging-roads, to penetrate deep into the forest, to gain access to new areas of land. Such migration is often a problem stemming from over-population coupled with resource deprivation and the fact that the best land has been taken for plantations, leaving farmers to fend for themselves, often forcing them to return to previously cultivated land before it has had time to recover. In other words, although the direct effects on the forests from commercial logging are considerable, the damage done following logging, or which develops ecologically as a result of logging, can be far greater.

If the demand for tropical timber is reduced, the producing countries would have a greater chance of managing their rainforests sustainably. In 1987, Sabah, Sarawak, and Papua New Guinea provided 96 per cent of Japanese tropical hardwood imports (Nectoux and Kuroda, 1989: 5); most of this (96 per cent in 1986) is processed into plywood, the major end-uses for which were in construction (55.4 per cent) and furniture (30.2 per cent). In 1986, the number of housing starts per thousand inhabitants in Japan was double the number in the USA, and more than double that in the EC.

There is evidence to suggest that the Japanese have privately recognized that changes are required. The timber importers in Japan agreed to cooperate in reducing imports for 1992 by 15 per cent from 1991 levels, and plan to reduce imports by 35 per cent over the following five years, perhaps due to declining demand and in an effort to try to raise timber prices. Moreover, companies like Marubeni, Komatsu, and C. Itoh have pledged to help promote development in the producing countries by building processing plants and paper factories, in order that the producing countries' revenue from exports is increased. Efforts to promote international afforestation projects are also underway. Finally, the association of plywood manufacturers is tackling the issue of using temperate softwoods instead of tropical hardwoods (*Nihon Kogyo Shimbun*, 23 March 9191).

There are arguments which suggest that the tropical timber trade is too important to the producing countries' economies, and that by stopping logging, the people will be forced to exploit them in some other way, for instance by clearing them for farming or grazing (Arafune, 1991: 14). But with efficiently enforced, sustainable forestry techniques, the forests could be harvested, not only for timber, but also other 'secondary forest products' such as fruits, nuts and oils. A rainforest community in Indonesia makes high-quality perfume from just these sorts of products (Nishimura, 1990: 37), while rattan cultivation in forests appears commercially feasible in Malaysia. At the moment, the emphasis remains exclusively on the extraction of timber, with the damage to the forest which goes with it. More research into sustainable exploitation could encourage local people to realize the potential long-term value of rainforests, rather than concentrating on logging and agriculture. But until the supplies of cheap high-quality tropical timber diminish sufficiently for softwood to become economically competitive, the construction industry in Japan will continue to use hardwood plywood, and may eventually divert its attention to other suppliers when Malaysia becomes unable to meet Japanese demand.

In light of this, a code of conduct should be drawn up for the international timber trade, restricting exports to sources which are managed sustainably. Problems arise, however, when defining sustainable forestry, and in finding methods for enforcement of the regulations. Independent organizations, such as non-governmental organizations (NGOs), may have the capability of solving both of these. Producing countries may be forced to respond positively since they would be unable to sell their wood if extracted unsustainably. 'Good' wood is, of course, going to be more expensive, and while it is this which causes companies to turn a blind eye to unsound logging techniques, it could compensate for the lower output levels. The real costs of forest management, i.e. including the enforcement of logging regulations and reforestation, need to be recognized, with the full resource rent captured by the state and utilized to compensate victims of past and ongoing deforestation. But in Japan, public support for such reforms is still weak. Financial contributions per capita average US$0.9, against US$9.2 for the USA or US$11.3 in Germany (FAIR, 1991: 11).

An important development has been the establishment of the International Tropical Timber Organisation (ITTO). Following the signing of the International Tropical Timber Agreement (ITTA) in 1985, which aims to achieve sustainable management of tropical forests by the year 2000, most of the producer and consumer countries came together to form the ITTO. Japan, as the world's leading importer, agreed to set up and support the head office in Yokohama, with the first head from Malaysia, the biggest exporter. Japan has been the largest contributor of funds to the ITTO, totalling US$42.2m by late 1991 (*Yomiuri Shimbun*, 5 December 1991). By monitoring the levels of trade in tropical timber, and the resulting deforestation, it is now broadly acknowledged that the current levels of consumption are unsustainable. The ITTO has also been encouraging producer countries to develop their processing industries to reduce the number of logs extracted from the forests.

In the half-decade after the establishment of the ITTO, 85 million hectares of rainforest have been lost. Indeed, this brings into question the whole effectiveness of the organization itself, highlighting its contradictory role of promoting the timber trade while ostensibly balancing sustainable use and conservation of rainforests. One problem with the ITTO is that it focuses primarily on timber as the only economically viable forest product, while the commercially ambiguous ecological value of virgin tropical forests in the short run is overlooked. The Japanese government, in efforts to promote a 'green' image, has been the main provider of funds to the ITTO, but what this has actually achieved is far from clear. The 1992 announcement that log production would be reduced from September and quotas of 1.4 million cubic metres per month could be introduced was held up by Sarawak Chief Minister Taib Mahmud and other politicians as proof of Sarawak's commitment to the ITTO recommendations. However, total official log production in 1992 of about 19 million cubic metres is still well in excess of the ITTO recommendation. Sarawak has also failed to implement other crucial ITTO recommendations, and to address the land rights claims of the indigenous people. This only underlines the ineffectiveness of the ITTO to see its recommendations carried out.

Further, there are conditions laid down in the General Agreement on Tariffs and Trade (GATT) which inhibit efforts towards sustainable forest management. It is already clear that if the producing countries developed their processing industries, the same amount of or more revenue could be gained from exporting higher-value goods, rather than by relying on the export of larger volumes of cheap, unprocessed logs. But the introduction of bans on exports of logs, as in the Philippines, Indonesia and Thailand, are said to be protectionist, and hence, directly contravene the GATT, unless restrictions on domestic production and consumption are applied.

Another problem with the GATT is that it is illegal to impose trade restrictions on a product according to the method of production. In other words, importing countries cannot limit or ban the import of unsustainably produced timber in favour of sustainably produced timber, as Austria sought to begin doing with eco-labelling from late 1992, much to the displeasure of the Malaysian government. Furthermore, if a producing country wants to provide incentives to promote sustainable management by introducing subsidies to the industry, these too would be illegal under the GATT. These economic restrictions with adverse environmental consequences will have to be amended. At the moment, the GATT trade regulations make it illegal for any industry to be subsidized so that it can be more environmentally responsible. With the rise in concern for the environment in recent years, such terms are becoming outdated and ecologically destructive, and should be amended.

What is really required is a reduction, if not a ban on the use of tropical timber in plywood production, especially for *kon-pane* in the construction industry, thereby dramatically reducing consumption for this wasteful end-use. Too much is now known about this matter for Japan to continue to ignore this problem, and to side-step responsibility. In fact, it presents an ideal opportunity for Japan to take on a more responsible position internationally, and to lead the world, not just economically, but also in the increasingly important environmental issues for the future. Unfortunately, Japan's failure to take the initiative and global leadership at the June 1992 United Nations Conference on the Environment and Development (UNCED), or Earth Summit, in Rio de Janeiro suggests that it lacks the commitment, political will and moral vision to transcend national interests as determined by big business.

MALAYSIAN TIMBER

Timber has been Malaysia's second largest export earner, after petroleum, since the early 1980s, greatly exceeding palm oil (except in 1984, an exceptional year) and rubber. In 1990, for instance, export earnings from timber and timber products amounted to RM8.9 billion (Malaysian ringgit) – or 11.3 per cent of total export proceeds – compared with RM10.6 billion for petroleum, RM4.4 billion for palm oil and RM3.0 billion for rubber. Malaysia's impressive economic growth record and official efforts to promote industry have obscured the significance and vulnerability of continued reliance on primary commodity exports, albeit more diversified, particularly the increased contribution of depleting resources such as petroleum and timber. While forestry is theoretically renewable, those familiar with logging activities in the Malaysian jungle and the country's track record – especially in the eastern or Borneo (Kalimantan) states of Sabah and Sarawak – have no illusions about this.

198

The problem was exacerbated by the general decline in primary commodity prices during the early and mid-1980s, encouraging compensatory increases in production volumes, especially of petroleum, gas and timber. Hence, despite some earlier half-hearted efforts at forest conservation, mainly in Peninsular Malaysia, until fairly recently, logging interests in Sabah and Sarawak have faced few constraints other than local community resistance and international disapproval. The pillage of Malaysian forests – primarily for export to Japan from Sabah and Sarawak – will probably come to an end by the end of this decade, when there will be little left to export if current levels of output continue in the interim. Already, the Philippines and Thailand have been virtually logged out, with Indonesia fast moving in the same direction. Before 1992, rising prices – due, for example, to declining log supplies – only accelerated the felling rate in Malaysia, thus containing timber price increases for over a decade.

In the early 1970s, an average of 70,000 hectares were cut in Malaysia annually. In 1975, 8.5 million – or 44 per cent of the 19.2 million cubic metres logged – were exported, yielding RM670 million. By the early 1980s, however, timber prices had more than doubled and the logging pace had more than tripled to 240,000 hectares per annum, yielding over 30 million cubic metres of logs yearly, of which over 60 per cent has been exported as logs. For some time now, Malaysia has been the world's leading exporter of tropical hardwood, in addition to palm oil, rubber, tin and pepper. By 1983, Malaysia accounted for 58 per cent of world tropical log exports and 81 per cent of Asian exports, exporting 18.7 million cubic metres in that year alone. As log prices rose by 47 per cent between 1985 and 1989, timber export earnings rose to RM7.3 billion in 1989; the 21.1 million tonnes of saw logs Malaysia exported yielded RM4.4 billion. In 1989, 63 per cent of Malaysian log exports went to Japan, 15 per cent to South Korea and 12 per cent to Taiwan. Meanwhile, Malaysia's sawn timber exports of 5.1 million tonnes in 1989 – mainly to Singapore, Holland and Thailand – fetched RM2.9 billion. Official statistics suggest that sawn timber exports to Europe have declined in recent years, probably due to successful pressure exerted by anti-tropical timber logging lobbies.

By the end of the 1970s, diminished available forest resources and heightened public awareness of its grave environmental consequences reduced logging in Peninsular Malaysia, but this has been more than compensated for by increased timber production in both Sarawak and Sabah. Annual timber output in Sarawak rose from 2.5 million cubic metres in 1975 to 12 million in 1985 and 18 million in 1990. Between 1963 and 1985, 30 per cent of Sarawak's total forest area was logged. In 1989, Japan's imports of Sarawak logs rose by 27 per cent, accounting for 53 per cent of total Japanese imports. Half of Sarawak's logs went to Japan, with the balance going elsewhere in Asia. In 1990, Sarawak also accounted for 18.8 million, or 47 per cent of the 40 million cubic metres logged in Malaysia. At this rate, an average of 1850 acres was being logged out in Sarawak every day!

As Malaysia entered a deep recession in 1985–86, it became even more dependent on export earnings from exhaustible natural resources such as petroleum and timber. However, dramatic economic growth since the late 1980s has not resulted in a corresponding reduction in timber export earnings, as one might have hoped. Despite increased international concern about Malaysian overlogging, especially in Sarawak, timber production was stepped up in the late 1980s. In Sarawak, log output rose by 64 per cent from 11.5 million cubic metres in 1986 to 18.8 million cubic metres in 1990, with the greatest increases occurring in 1987 (19 per cent) and 1989 (26 per cent), when log prices rose by an average of 20 per cent and 19 per cent respectively. Meanwhile, saw log exports rose by 55 per cent in volume, but by 123 per cent in value – from 10.2 million cubic metres worth RM1,291 million in 1986 to 15.9 million cubic metres worth RM2,883 million in 1990!

Sarawak and Sabah only joined the Malaysian federation in 1963, as Britain tried to ensure that its lucrative colonial possessions in Southeast Asia passed into safe hands as decolonization became inevitable. From 1933, no logging had been allowed in Sarawak unless an area had sufficient stock for regeneration. According to the official Sarawak Timber Museum in Kuching, 'Up to 1961, hill forest logging operations were very limited. . . . Timber harvesting was limited to a very few species which were mainly consumed by the local building industry. In the early days, logging was carried out with simple tools – axes and saws – while elephants and water buffaloes were used for log transportation . . . . From 1962 onwards, logging operations steadily increased. This was largely due to the entry of Japanese buyers'.

The two Borneo states secured some special prerogatives not available to the other eleven states of Peninsular Malaysia as compensation for giving up alternative options, including independence. 'In part because of British fears that the federation would imperil native land rights, Sarawak was accorded the power to set its own land policies. That arrangement proved no insubstantial irony . . . later, when state officials began to plunder the forests' (Sesser, 1991: 45). From 1963 – the year of Malaysia's incorporation of Sabah and Sarawak – to 1985, 2.82 million hectares, or about 30 per cent of Sarawak's forest land, had been logged. By the end of 1984, an additional 5.8 million hectares, or another 60 per cent of Sarawak's forest land, had been given out as timber concessions. Of the 3.4 million hectares in the Fourth Division, i.e. the Baram river basin, where popular resistance to logging has been greatest, 2.46 million hectares – or 72 per cent – had been given out by 1984.

The political economy of timber has shaped and animated Malaysian state-level politics, especially in Sabah and Sarawak, at least over the last two decades. Hence, timber concessionary rights have become the much coveted prize for political office and power, engendering a vicious cycle of timber politics, which only comes into the public eye when politicians fall out in the intensifying scramble for the diminishing and increasingly inaccessible resource.

If state governments either take direct control, or give concessions directly to those involved in downstream processing, or at least give them directly to those with proven logging experience, unnecessary subcontracting, corruption, payment of under-the-counter money, illegal logging and inefficiency could be reduced, while generating more money for the state governments. Currently, timber concessions given to politicians, their families, cronies, or to royalty are in turn subcontracted – a system which encourages corruption and illegal logging owing to the lack of accountability on the part of the concessionaires and loggers. Industry experts claim that if the present system is terminated, most of the ills facing the timber industry would be cured (*Business Times*, 1 February 1993). The logging concessions controlled by Sarawak Chief Minister Taib Mahmud have been established to be worth about RM10 billion (Sesser, 1991: 62).

The most powerful logging operator is reputedly Senator Tiong Hiew King. Also owner of the largest circulation Chinese language daily in Malaysia, the *Sin Chew Jit Poh*, his family timber company does about half a billion ringgit worth of business yearly. Raphael Pura of the *Asian Wall Street Journal* (February 1990) reported, 'Sen. Tiong's 800,000-hectare (1,970,000-acre) timber empire of concessions and logging contracts includes the forest that Uma Bawang's rebel farmers are struggling to retain. His partners in that concession are Tan Sri Taib's sister, the Sarawak government, a private Islamic foundation and a second influential senator'. How much the timber operators pay the concessionaires to get the logging contracts varies, but figures of up to fifty million ringgit for a single contract are not unusual.

Datuk ('Tengku') Wong, a close associate of the Pahang royal family, has been accused by Primary Commodities Minister Lim Keng Yaik of illegally logging in Pahang. Newspapers have reported that Wong was paid RM140 million by logging contractors in advance of logging concessions given to the Pahang royalty to be sold by Wong. Contractors 'buying' the concessions claim to have been 'overcharged', in one reported case by almost twice the going rate. Keng Yaik himself stated that the 37,000 hectares given to the Pahang royal family could yield timber valued at RM270 million (*New Straits Times*, 22 January 1993). Meanwhile, Pahang is, besides illegal logging, officially logging 16,000 hectares per annum – 4,000 hectares above the quota set by the National Forestry Council. Other states have also reported similar pressure from royalty to be given timber concessions.

Not unlike the Archipelago timber shipping monopoly for the Japanese

Nanzai Freight Association (NFA) in Sabah – run by Tan Sri Wong Chek Lim – which charged US$1.55 per cubic metre ostensibly on 'behalf of Malaysian politicians', Archipelago Shipping in Sarawak – managed by the Chief Minister's brother – runs similarly lucrative monopoly operations. Despite the Federal Government's supposed commitment to deregulation, there is strong evidence that powerful federal politicians have colluded to maintain these monopolies. Malaysians also have no illusions that there is considerable underdeclaration of timber production and exports – partly reflected, for example, by the inconsistencies in official timber statistics – to facilitate tax evasion and capital flight.

Even logging's contribution to Malaysian growth is limited. Reflecting the rentier nature of their wealth, most of the beneficiaries did not even reinvest within the country, let alone in Sarawak. The ecological, economic, social and cultural damage it causes, especially to poor rural communities, basically means that logging constitutes devastating, albeit indirect exploitation of nature and people. Despite the considerable profits from logging, the government gets little. Timber companies pay income tax, but their financial statements show losses or small profits. According to Pura, between 1976 and 1987, Rimbunan Hijau had more than two billion ringgit in revenues, but paid the federal government less than five million in taxes. The state government collects a modest royalty on each ton of logs, amounting to barely 1 per cent of the timber price. The massive scale of the logging, however, means this revenue provides nearly half of the Sarawak state budget.

Another factor encouraging increased logging has been the federal–state division in the Malaysian tax revenue system. Most tax revenue is collected and controlled by the federal government, with the state governments constitutionally only allowed to collect resource related revenue, including timber export duties. Ostensibly to encourage Malaysian timber manufacturing, higher export duty is collected on saw logs than on sawn timber. But to maximize such revenues, the state governments, especially in Sabah and Sarawak, have preferred to maximize log – rather than timber – exports, thus encouraging more logging, but less timber processing, let alone wood-based manufacturing. Thus, the revenue system undermines the economic case for greater forest conservation with more limited and selective logging, as well as the development of wood-based manufacturing – rather than log exports – to increase domestic value-added and employment generation by the Malaysian timber industry.

The pillage of Malaysian forests will probably come to an end by the end of this decade, when there will be little left to take if current levels of output continue. However, the high profile the Mahathir administration took before and at the June 1992 Rio Summit, has introduced a new silver lining to the deteriorating situation earlier. After taking the high moral ground on environmental issues at various international fora since the 1989

Langkawi Declaration of the Commonwealth Heads of Governments Meeting (CHOGM), Mahathir apparently then felt obliged to try to put Malaysia's 'house in order', at least in order to stand up to the greater international scrutiny anticipated after Rio, and directed government officials to act accordingly. Only more careful analysis can ascertain whether these measures are adequate or 'too little, too late'. And it seems that political considerations, more than anything else, will probably determine whether such efforts will be sustained, and whether ecologically, economically and socially acceptable 'sustainable logging' will ever be achieved in Sarawak before it is too late.

Sarawak state officials claim that their system of selective logging harvests only the largest trees, leaving others to grow and the forest to regenerate around them. 'We take only two or three trees an acre; that's not much. There's no clear-cutting, as in America' (quoted in Sesser, 1991: 48). While logging is selective, what is selected is every tree with profit potential, while the remaining forest is seriously damaged in the process of getting those trees out. Even the ITTO, with its headquarters in Yokohama, and dominated by timber-consuming governments condemns Sarawak's logging practices. The Sarawak forestry department is too understaffed to enforce regulations, hence rules to safeguard watershed areas are regularly violated, as untrained logging workers ignore selective-cutting regulations, while concession owners and logging companies 'plan their operations so as to get the maximum possible output with the minimum possible fixed investment in plant, roading, training, safety, or infrastructure'.

Primary Industries Minister Lim Keng Yaik proposes changes to the National Forestry Act 1984 to increase maximum fines for illegal logging from RM10,000 to RM100,000 and jail sentences from a year to a new maximum of 5 years. Meanwhile, the Sabah state government has recently amended its own forestry laws to allow for a seven-year jail sentence for illegal logging. The support of the army and police in combating illegal logging is also to be enlisted. A *New Straits Times* editorial (21 January 1993) fully supports the measures, adding 'it is to be hoped that this directive (to curb illegal logging) will be faithfully implemented, as timber, being a particularly profitable proposition, has been a murky territory for quite a long while, where personal greed has more often overtaken national interest; illegal logging is not merely theft, but wanton destruction of the country's national heritage'. Existing government regulations are routinely ignored. Officials have never suspended, let alone revoked, a company's licence for destructive logging practices. Between 1988 and 1991, the Forestry Department only took 39 out of 1,769 cases of illegal logging to court, citing the difficulty of producing evidence. Some paid compound fines, a mere pittance compared with the values of the trees taken. Even the proposed RM100,000 fine is considered by many to be still too small, given the vast amounts of money being made.

According to Sesser (1991: 48): 'many who have witnessed the logging operations come away shocked. "There is no management of the logging procedure in the upland forest of Sarawak that I'm aware of", says an American botanist who has spent considerable time doing research in Sarawak. "The road building and the methods of extracting the logs are said to be extremely damaging. The people who man the bulldozers are paid piece rates. They're given no map; they just go into the forest looking for suitable trees. When the trees are cut down, they don't cut them in any particular direction. Then the skidders go in and look for these cut trees with no idea where they are. There's no plan. The companies just go in and take what they can as quickly as they can". Skidders are four-wheel tractors with grapples that drag the logs down to logging roads. The combination of bulldozers plowing their way to each tree that's going to be cut and skidders dragging the tree out – not to mention the haphazard felling of the tree, which takes others with it when it falls – means that ten trees can be lost for every one actually logged. These damaged, crushed, or buried trees add to the damage previously created by the bulldozing of roads, skid trails, log-storage areas, and logging camps, which together can occupy up to forty per cent of the area to be logged. Then, day after day, come the heavy rains, sometimes in torrents. The thin layer of topsoil from the skid trails and other bulldozed areas washes away, eventually turning the rivers muddy brown and – along with pollutants from the logging camps and diesel fuel from barges and other operations – killing the fish. With the tree cover gone and the topsoil washed away, the sun bakes the bare earth, making it inhospitable for all but scrub growth.'

The timber concession system encourages getting as many logs as possible out of the rainforest as quickly as possible. The politicians face an election every four or five years, and if they lose, the concessions could be revoked. Timber merchants get paid by tonnage, so a tree left represents foregone profits. And speculation that the government might be forced to impose restrictions, as in March 1991 and August 1992, only accelerates logging. Feverish efforts to cut down trees to beat deadlines become so intense that work continues through the night. The director of the Forestry Department, Datuk Leo Chai, described a 'mad rush' to cut down trees in August 1992, following the announcement that the reduction in logging would come into force on 1 September. He stated that in that month, production doubled the monthly average.

In September 1992, the Sarawak Government's Director of Forestry announced a programme to reduce significantly – some critics would argue inadequately, owing to the high rates prevailing and the damage already done – logging output by 60 per cent.

In December 1992, Lim Keng Yaik, Malaysia's Primary Industries Minister, temporarily banned log exports only from Sabah state – held by the opposition United Sabah Party (PBS) – ostensibly to ensure timber supplies for local processors said to be operating at only half capacity. Sabah Chief Minister Joseph Pairin Kitingan claimed the ban was politically motivated and discriminatory, alleging that the local wood-processing industry was inefficient. In May 1993, Kitingan announced a permanent ban, which Keng Yaik then claimed was politically motivated to embarrass him as he had promised Japanese importers that he would lift the ban to export due to an alleged over-supply of Sabah timber of two million cubic metres – precisely the amount exported to Japan in 1992!

Keng Yaik has revealed that export dockets he has seen indicate that the average value of exported logs was US$125 per cubic metre, whereas the FOB going rate then was US$210. Disputing figures given by the Sabah state government which claimed that 4 to 6 million cubic metres were logged in 1992, Keng Yaik claimed the figure to be closer to 11 million. A letter to the *New Straits Times* (29 January 1993) welcomed the Sabah initiative, but went on: 'Why the Ministry has to wait so long to do something about it, one cannot really understand. As the Minister has admitted, Malaysia has been deprived of earnings running into millions of ringgit because of this (corrupt practice), it is common knowledge that in Sarawak, log exporters have over the past 15 to 20 years hived off considerable profits by manipulating prices and downgrading the various species at the export point'. The letter went on to say that the Inland Revenue Department should conduct an audit exercise going back 15 years 'if the minister is indeed serious'.

For reasons which are not quite clear, tropical timber prices rose sharply during 1992. While the price increase in the last quarter might be attributed to the Sarawak authorities' September announcement of cuts in permissible logging after years of domestic opposition and international criticism, the earlier rise is more difficult to explain. Presumably, the Indonesian Plywood Association, Apkindo's success in marketing 95 per cent of its total Japanese sales (accounting for 30 per cent of Japanese use) through an affiliated company, Nippindo, at prices comparable to those charged by Japanese manufacturers, had also helped. Happily, for the business interests concerned, Tokyo timber price increases have more than compensated them for the loss of earnings due to the reduced volume of output and exports. Sarawak logs – the benchmark for tropical hardwood prices in Japan – rose by over 110 per cent in the year since, despite recessionary conditions in Japan, especially affecting construction start-ups.

The irreparable and irreversible consequences of logging for the equatorial forest ecosystem and its resources are increasingly studied and known. More importantly, rural Malaysians – especially those with the most intimate relationship with the forest – are well aware of some of the environmental consequences, especially those which impinge upon and undermine their way of life. It is not in the least bit surprising that it is those who live closest to the forest, who are most threatened by the wanton

JOMO K.S.

destruction of the forest which accompanies logging. Hence, it is precisely those with the simplest of lifestyles, and who are closest to nature – like the hunting and gathering nomadic Penan of Sarawak – who have been in the forefront of the resistance to logging. It may nonetheless seem ironical that those whom many consider 'primitive', 'wild' and 'uncivilized', are unselfconsciously reminding the modern world of the urgent need to protect man's delicate balance with nature.

APPENDIX

Table A7.1 Malaysian wood exports to Japan and furniture imports, 1962–91 (RM million)

| | Exports to Japan | | | Furniture | | |
Year	Saw logs	Sawn timber	Total exports	Exports to Japan	Total imports	Imports from Japan
1962	0.012	0.023	3.21	–	3.87	0.29
1963	0.95	0.13	4.02	–	4.93	0.31
1964	0.30	0.11	4.66	[RM 96/-]	3.42	0.24
1965	–	0.04	4.94	–	3.84	0.27
1966	3.10	1.46	3.93	–	3.69	0.39
1967	315.98	5.48	3.25	0.0006	6.04	0.82
1968	335.88	9.70	1.72	0.0004	5.22	0.78
1969	357.54	11.53	1.62	0.0012	4.42	0.67
1970	362.75	19.73	1.70	0.0072	4.54	0.74
1971	349.57	17.11	2.21	0.0008	4.26	0.75
1972	338.05	18.88	2.26	0.005	5.04	0.69
1973	653.87	42.60	4.45	0.084	5.84	0.75
1974	735.13	55.74	4.86	0.31	7.44	0.78
1975	444.03	10.85	9.61	2.08	8.46	0.56
1976	1,061.65	24.22	18.02	5.82	5.68	0.73
1977	109.88	33.65	16.36	4.84	6.41	0.95
1978	1,215.82	35.21	22.81	5.40	9.65	1.65
1979	2,140.88	64.42	33.68	6.84	12.87	2.17
1980	1,762.00	83.95	36.73	7.55	20.77	3.17
1981	1,483.94	51.79	38.75	4.33	23.90	3.99
1982	2,126.28	75.42	23.52	0.26	32.07	6.04
1983	1,783.88	64.37	21.65	0.18	34.81	7.70
1984	1,817.66	77.29	25.07	0.074	44.83	8.65
1985	1,824.98	108.16	29.92	0.65	46.78	9.31
1986	1,895.77	89.60	45.64	2.54	30.81	7.97
1987	2,771.65	180.38	86.35	3.94	37.5	10.94
1988	2,478.11	256.35	165.34	11.15	45.02	20.92
1989	2,738.28	450.07	306.12	25.75	65.16	34.79
1990	2,315.66	516.05	459.48	66.76	107.37	66.09
1991	2,223.03	526.16	740.00	133.26	147.70	90.18

Source: Department of Statistics, *External Trade Statistics*, various issues.

Table A7.2 Malaysian timber export duty revenue, 1968–91 (RM million)

Year	Federal	Sarawak	Sabah[a]
1968		2.24	2.02[b]
1969		1.08	1.52[b]
1970		0.50	2.02
1971		62.40	1.84
1972	14.99	n.a.	1.23
1973	11.40	n.a.	0.83
1974	9.54	5.42	1.0
1975	5.74	3.88	1.6
1976	5.52	11.73	0.39
1977	3.51	13.49	0.45
1978	1.89	16.20	0.03
1979	3.66	40.04	0.1
1980	3.45	60.91	0.75
1981	2.81	80.50	0.08
1982	3.64	124.30	0.09
1983	3.50	118.50	0.09
1984	0.93	130.35	0.15
1985	0.28	136.77	0.15
1986	0.29	128.27	0.15
1987	0.93	192.15	0.16
1988	1.02	186.52	0.2
1989	0.54	22.85	0.4
1990	0.46	0.02	1.5
1991	81.80	[RM 82/-]	0.55

Sources:
1. Malaysia, *Belanjawan Persekutuan: Anggaran Hasil dan Perbelanjaan*, Percetakan Negara, Kuala Lumpur.
2. Sarawak, *Estimates of Revenue and Expenditures*, Government Printer, Kuching, various issues.
3. Sabah, *Estimates of Revenues and Expenditures*, Government Printer, Kota Kinabalu, various issues.
[a] Estimates.
[b] Inclusive of forest produce.

Table A7.3 Exports of gas (natural and manufactured) – SITC 34

Year	Exports (RM million)
1962	0.053
1963	0.021
1964	0.067
1965	0.81
1966	1.22
1967	1.97
1968	2.64
1969	0.63
1970	2.10
1971	1.15
1972	0.66
1973	0.05
1974	0.18
1975	0.48
1976	0.01
1977	0.001
1978	0.002
1979	0.002
1980	0.015
1981	0.001
1982	0.03
1983	831.30
1984	1,774.73
1985	2,356.39
1986	1,933.52
1987	1,827.86
1988	1,909.24
1989	2,149.92
1990	2,731.89
1991	3,448.0

Source: Department of Statistics, *External Trade Statistics*, various issues. Ministry of Finance, *Economic Report*, 1992/93.

Table A7.4 Contribution of petroleum to government revenue (RM million)

Year	Petroleum income tax	Export duty revenue	Royalty	Excise duty and revenue
1963				16.63
1964				68.87
1965				76.40
1966				89.06
1967				100.24
1968				113.53
1969				120.96
1970	–		7.30	118.57
1971	4.0[a]		6.05	144.88
1972	–		22.67	189.62
1973	27.0[a]		25.12	194.45
1974	144.0[a]		46.22	201.30
1975	322.0[a]		78.43	216.77
1976	322.0[a]		83.98	291.31
1977	776.0[a]		110.79	344.44
1978	771.0[a]		116.16	389.96
1979	829.0[a]		165.90	410.17
1980	1,736.0[a]	723.98	345.29	333.43
1981	1,978.0[a]	1,240.80	417.0	280.07
1982	2,075.0[a]	1,351.45	425.26	309.0
1983	1,998.0[a]	1,476.70	491.0	438.36
1984	2,570.17	1,629.40	580.95	489.57
1985	3,130.27	1,639.31	619.30	427.37
1986	3,072.27	1,076.50	548.58	737.20
1987	1,533.0[a]	1,170.14	410.28	691.24
1988	2,208.0[a]	1,149.29	499.38	752.57
1989	1,847.0[a]	1,431.61	509.08	795.07
1990	2,644.0[a]	1,910.03	626.86	671.53
1991	4,051.74	1,899.75	875.31	1,011.83

Source: Belanjawan Persekutuan, *Anggaran Hasil dan Pekerjaan*, Percetakan Negara, various issues.
Excise duty revenue is from locally refined petrol, locally refined heavy and fuel oils, liquefied petroleum gas, diesel and kerosene.
[a] Data from Ministry of Finance, *Economic Report*, various issues.

*NOTE

Much of the material in this article was previously presented in Brandt (1992) and Jomo (1992). The author would like to acknowledge the assistance of Christopher Brandt in research for this chapter.

REFERENCES

Arafune, K. (1991) 'Japan as an Environmental Pariah', in *Economic Eye*, The Global Environment, Winter.

Arden-Clarke, C. (1990) *Conservation and Sustainable Management of Tropical Forests: The Role of ITTO and GATT* (November), WWF, London.

Asahi Shimbun (9 May 1991), '"Kankyo" jushi e keizaikai ga henshin'.

Asahi Shimbun (17 October 1991), 'Kankyo suwappu ishin'.

Batker, D. (21 January 1992), 'Briefing on Sarawak Roads', World Bank Project Proposal, World Bank.

Brandt, C. (1992) 'Japanese Companies and South East Asian Tropical Rainforests', Dissertation for the Faculty of Oriental Studies, University of Cambridge, Cambridge.

Business Times (1 February 1992), 'Overhaul Timber Concession System'.

Chin S.C. (1992) 'Shifting Cultivation and Logging in Sarawak', in Jomo K.S. (ed.) *Logging Against the Natives of Sarawak*, second edition, Institute for Social Analysis (INSAN), Kuala Lumpur.

Colchester, M. (1992) *Pirates. Squatters and Poachers*, second edition, Survival International, London and INSAN, Kuala Lumpur.

Forrest, R. and Harago, Y. (1990) *Japan's Official Development Assistance and Tropical Forests*, WWF, Tokyo.

FAIR (Foundation for Advanced Information and Research), (1991) *A Guide to Japan's Grant Aid and Technical Cooperation*, FAIR, Tokyo.

Friedland, Jonathan (1993) 'Meany Greenies: Japan Faces Soaring Cost of Imported Timber', *Far Eastern Economic Review,* 4 March.

Fujibayashi, K. (1990) 'ODA to kigyo shinshutsu' in *'No' to iwareru Nihon*, Nihon Shohisha Renmei; Gakuyo Shobo, Tokyo.

Hasegawa, J. (1989) 'Japan's ODA and an Analysis of the Macroeconomic Effect of Aid', US–Japan Relations Occasional Papers, Harvard University, USA.

Hurst, P. (1990) *Rainforest Politics*, Zed Books, London.

ITTO (1993) 'Elements for the 1992 Annual Review and Assessment of the World Tropical Timber Situation', International Timber Trade Organization, Yokohama.

Jomo K.S. (1992) 'The Continuing Pillage of Sarawak's Forests' in Jomo K.S. (ed.) *Logging Against the Natives of Sarawak*, second edition, Institute for Social Analysis, Kuala Lumpur.

KEIDANREN (1991) 'An Environmental Charter for the Business World', in *Economic Eye*, The Global Environment, Winter.

Mitsubishi (1991) *For GAIA*, Environmental Affairs Department, Mitsubishi Corporation, Tokyo.

Nature (1992) 'Malaysian Take-Away', BBC, London.

Nectoux F. and Kuroda Y. (1989) *Timber from the South Seas*, WWF, Tokyo.

Nihon Kogyo Shimbun, (23 March 1991), 'Nettai urin o sukue! Nihon kigyo ga taidodanketsu'.

Nishimura, T. (1990) 'Nettairin ga hakai sareteiru' in *'No' to iwareru Nihon*, Nihon Shohisha Renmei; Gakuyo Shobo, Tokyo.

Sesser, Stan (1991) 'Logging the Rain Forest', *The New Yorker*, May 27: 42–68.

Yomiuri Shimbun (5 December 1991) 'Lumber Importers Issue Rainforest Guidelines'.

Part II

8

IN-HOUSE UNIONS
'Looking East' for industrial relations*
Peter Wad and Jomo K.S.

From an initial, somewhat diffuse focus on Japanese (and South Korean) work ethics, management style and technology as the primary factors behind rapid late industrialization in East Asia, the Malaysian Government under Mahathir Mohamad elaborated and enlarged upon its policy of 'Looking East'. In 1983, therefore, the 'Look East' policy was more closely related to other official policies of 'Malaysian Incorporated', 'Privatization' and 'Leadership by Example' as well as 'in-house' or 'enterprise unionism', which is the subject of this chapter.[1]

MAHATHIR'S LABOUR POLICIES

While there were occasional government efforts during the 1960s and 1970s to portray itself as a neutral arbiter standing above and mediating between management and employees, the Mahathir administration has, by and large, overtly favoured employers over labour. This is reflected in the various amendments to the labour laws as well as the government's role in industrial relations and labour policy. Since the 1980s, the anti-labour character of the state has become even more apparent as evidenced in the following survey of more recent labour policies.

With the rapid economic growth of the 1970s, especially the expansion of labour-intensive, export-oriented manufacturing and the public sector, unemployment declined, raising real wages within the country. It also saw pockets of labour scarcity emerging, mainly in activities offering low wages and poor working conditions. To offset wage pressures and overcome labour shortages, the Government unofficially sanctioned illegal labour immigration, primarily from Indonesia, Southern Thailand (especially to the northern States of Peninsular Malaysia), and the Southern Philippines (to Sabah). The magnitude of such illegal labour immigration is difficult to measure, with estimates varying from one to two million by the early 1990s – an astonishingly high figure given a national population of barely nineteen million and an official labour force estimate slightly exceeding seven million.[2]

The recession as well as government attempts to freeze and reduce the size of the public sector after the early 1980s resulted in rising unemployment and concurrent downward pressures on wages. Tacit official approval of the massive labour immigration further adversely affected wage levels, especially for the mainly Malay and Indian unskilled and semi-skilled workers. Despite this apparent consequence, the rationale behind the immigration policy is said to be politically justified as a move to meet the supposed need for the Malay-dominated government to strengthen itself demographically by increasing the number and proportion of ethnic Malays, through immigration and assimilation of foreign labour, especially of Muslim Indonesians.

Soon after Mahathir's ascendance to the prime ministership in mid-1981, he announced his 'Look East' policy. This policy was initially widely believed to refer to changing Malaysia's orientation in a variety of foreign economic matters. 'Looking East' seemed not only to refer to efforts to emulate specific aspects of the Japanese and South Korean economic miracles, especially late industrialization (e.g. by state intervention to develop heavy industries), but also to efforts to establish Japanese-style *sogoshosha* trading agencies as well as improved relations between the public and private sectors ('Malaysia Incorporated') and privatization. For a time, 'Looking East' was also believed to mean favouring Japanese and South Korean firms bidding for Malaysian government tenders, a view reinforced by such examples as the six billion ringgit worth of construction projects given to such companies in the early 1980s.[3]

Criticism, not least by those who stood to lose from the new policies, and some very costly failures (e.g. the heavy industries and Malaysian *sogoshosha* experiments) forced the government to backtrack a little. Mahathir claimed that the main purpose of 'Looking East' was to introduce Japanese-style work ethics in Malaysia, mainly through efforts to increase work productivity and quality through propaganda campaigns, company welfarism, in-house unions, harder work, greater loyalty to company management, incentive payments, wage flexibility, and cutting losses (with measures such as quality control circles and zero defect groups). Although these Japanese 'achievements' have evolved along with complex, culturally and historically rooted systems of material incentives, which include guaranteed life-long employment and seniority wage systems, Malaysia's 'Look East' policy has been selective in its main emphasis on the virtually costless promotion of 'proper' work ethics, quality control circles (QCCs) and in-house unions.

In 1983, the government announced that it would officially encourage the growth of in-house unions as part of its 'Look East' policy. In support of this, the RTU claimed that such unions would produce leaders who are much more aware of their companies' needs, thus facilitating effective introduction of improved productivity programmes.[4] Further, in-house unions would be less able to compare wages and other work conditions offered by different employers within an industry, thus reducing pressure on companies with a lower capacity-to-pay to match the higher wages and/ or better conditions provided by other employers.[5]

Two in-house unions were registered in 1983, both in industries where national unions for the workers already existed.[6] However, two other in-house unions were refused registration because existing unions had already organized the majority of the employees concerned.[7] The seemingly arbitrary nature of these decisions suggests that future expansion of existing unions into previously unorganized workplaces could be limited by the Registrar of Trade Unions (RTU) in favour of in-house unions. The government's encouragement of in-house unions can work to further fragment the position of national unions, thus undermining the collective strength of workers. Recognizing this, some employers have even initiated the formation of in-house unions to pre-empt their workers' involvement with stronger, more-established national unions.[8]

This policy of promoting in-house unions over national, industry-wide unions represented a significant departure from previous labour policy. In-house unions have existed in Malaysia for some time, mainly in the statutory bodies. In the mid-1970s, the Government intervened on behalf of management to facilitate the establishment of an in-house union for employees of United Motor Works (UMW), although many of the workers involved had already joined another union – not unlike what happened a few years later with Malaysian Airline System (MAS) employees. Despite ostensible government support for in-house unions, few new enterprise unions have been registered where no unions existed before, except for several in the electronics industry. Instead, in-house unions seem to be encouraged to displace 'troublesome' national (industry-wide) unions already in existence. This government encouragement of in-house unions for the private sector has implications for undermining the already weak trade union movement in the country.

In his 1987 Budget speech delivered in October 1986, the Finance Minister called for a voluntary wage freeze for the next three years. The Government made no commitment, however, to freezing prices, nor did it try to explain why such a freeze was needed for three years. Instead, a mandatory wage freeze was threatened if the official call for an ostensibly voluntary freeze was not heeded. In the context of the then rapidly rising prices and productivity, the official wage freeze recommendation enabled employers to increase profits in the ensuing boom at labour's expense. However, the tighter labour market conditions subsequently succeeded in pushing wages up.

Cuts in public spending and a package of new amendments to existing labour legislation were introduced in 1988 after the recession of 1985–86. Some of the inducements introduced in the 1980 legislation, notably higher remuneration rates for overtime work, were reduced while other amendments were designed to encourage the establishment of in-house unions and to facilitate the introduction of more flexible wage systems. Coming after the 1985–86 recession and the economic liberalization policy reforms of that period, the 1988 labour legislation is generally perceived as intended to enhance labour flexibility and to strengthen management prerogatives and control over labour without significantly protecting labour's interests.

With the trade union movement divided and weakened by a combination of government manipulation and cooptation, management intransigence, and petty personal rivalries among unionists, there was little organized resistance to the new legislative changes. The 1988 reforms were justified by invoking the supposed requirements for economic recovery after the recession and high unemployment of the preceding years. They also clearly reinforced the economic policy reforms by the Malaysian Government from the mid-1980s.[9] However, since managerial prerogatives were already so established and so difficult to challenge, such legislative reforms may have made very little difference in practice, only officially reflecting the bias of the government.[10]

IN-HOUSE UNIONS

According to the ideology underlying the 'Look East' policy, enterprise unionism is presented as a key factor underlying the Japanese miracle. Hence, after propagating work 'ethics' without any great success, the Government announced its intention to promote enterprise unionism, ostensibly in the cause of national development.

Such a strategy, declared the Prime Minister, would not be carried out at the expense of the supposedly Western, mainly national, industry-based trade unions in Malaysia inherited from the late British colonial period. These would continue to co-exist with the supposedly Japanese in-house unions for 'it was not the government's intention to negate the work of trade unions as it was well aware of the need for trade unions to protect the legitimate rights of workers in the country'. But what was equally important, he continued, was the 'national interest and the need for a successful system suited for Malaysia in its development efforts. . . . There is therefore a need for Malaysia . . . to look into a new concept like in-house unions that have been used successfully by the Japanese "who have easily beaten the West" which practises the old system of trade unionism'.[11]

The government interest in enterprise unionism, he further explained, followed from its acceptance of wage differentials between enterprises with different productivities and profitabilities. He claimed that in-house unions were more conducive to raising productivity and promoting smooth labour–management relations within a context of company, instead of class solidarity. Such a system of industrial harmony at the enterprise level would clearly benefit capital, labour and the state:

> Some of our companies . . . have just been set up and are coming up, but if forced to pay the same benefits as the more successful ones, will definitely not succeed. Hence . . . it would be more meaningful for these firms, especially the new ones, to have in-house unions which have proved to be a big success in Japan . . . by having a union within a firm, the union could negotiate with the management concerned, while taking into consideration the various circumstances. And with workers totally involved in the company, which would result in increased productivity and higher profits, all sectors would benefit, including the Government through revenue. It would therefore be more meaningful . . . for the thousands of workers in firms, and not represented by unions, to have in-house unions.[12]

Clearly, this endorsement of enterprise unionism represented a significant shift by the Prime Minister away from the wholly negative stance he had developed towards all trade unionism during his previous spell in politics in the 1960s. In 1970, he had declared: 'In a scheme to force Malay labour into the competitive field of skilled and semi-skilled work, trade unionism can find no place. Absolute security and good working conditions are not the aims. . . . Trade unions are therefore superfluous'.[13]

In brief, the New Economic Policy (NEP) and other development policies succeeded in creating a larger working class with a higher proportion of Malays. Both the state and capital became increasingly aware of the considerable threat that the organization of workers into effective unions – willing to strive for greater material benefits and industrial rights – could become to their interests. More important, the new labour policy sought to shift the very basis of trade unionism away from the collective representation of workers to new relations which should ensure their systematic cooptation, not only to contain their discontent, but also to render them more pliable and committed to the achievement of employer objectives.

This, it would seem, was the general aim. However, lest it generate too hostile a response, enterprise unionism has not been imposed by law (although this could still happen, as was the case in South Korea in 1981).[14] Rather, the state has sought to avoid confrontation with existing national industrial unions by simply bypassing them. The policy seems primarily intended to accommodate new demands for unionization by the more than 80 per cent of the wage workforce, mainly in the private sector, which remains unorganized. The main targets of the new model seem to be the workers in the relatively recently established, large factories which have been set up in Malaysia since the 1970s. The main intended beneficiaries of enterprise unionism, in other words, are the big industrial employers, mainly transnational corporations (TNCs) and public enterprises. More specifically, the policy actually caters primarily to Japanese employer preferences since American employers generally seem more antagonistic to any kind of unions, including the in-house variety, while European employers appear more tolerant of national unions. It should also be noted that some employers have not been averse to taking advantage of the new official policy to undermine 'difficult' national unions by encouraging in-house unionizing efforts, though the Government has remained more discreet in endorsing such efforts compared with the 1970s when in-house unions were set up in UMW and MAS after national unions supported industrial actions by their members in their employ.

The object here is to analyse the contemporary struggle surrounding enterprise unionism to assess the strategies adopted by trade unions for their survival under the 'Look East' policy and the appropriateness of conventional approaches for analysing enterprise unionism.

CONTAINMENT AND CONTRADICTION

Enterprise unionism in Malaysia has a history which long predates the 'Look East' policy, having previously been associated with public enterprises, especially statutory bodies, and to a lesser extent with employers seeking to undermine or pre-empt national trade unions. Further, employers' resistance to national trade unions has greatly benefitted from the sympathetic RTU. The RTU did not allow the emergence of a single national union for textiles and garments workers from the late 1960s, endorsing only five regional unions instead. In 1974, the RTU prohibited a regional textile union from unionizing a locally owned plant despite the fact that at least 50 per cent of employees clearly chose such an affiliation. In-house unions were established at quite a number of TNCs, including the British-controlled Perak Hydro, the US-owned Union Carbide battery factory and the Japanese Malayawata steel mill. In some cases, divisions within existing unions were manipulated by the management in their favour. For example, when the National Union of Employees in Companies Manufacturing Rubber Products split, an Malaysian Trade Union Congress (MTUC) official was suborned into withdrawing the Dunlop plant collective from the national union.[15]

Attempts by management to secure company unions have not always gone smoothly; in a number of cases, workers have struggled hard and long to establish their own autonomous organizations. At the Malaysian-owned UMW, for example, the Transport Equipment and Allied Industries' Employees Union (TEAIEU) attempted to organize, but the sixteen members of its initial committee were dismissed the moment management discovered the plan. Subsequently, attempts by the union to picket the company with supporters from other plants were thwarted when management resorted to strong arm tactics and called in the police. A yellow ('stooge') enterprise union was then established by the company in a bid to demobilize the workforce, only to see workers transform the new union into their own instrument of struggle. After failing to buy over the union leadership, the company then opted for mass retrenchment of unionists. And when this too failed, management subcontracted work in sections where key unionists were employed. Although this went a long way in reducing the autonomy which the in-house union had acquired, UMW has nonetheless had to adopt a rather less antagonistic labour strategy. Its expansion and diversification into a high tech, capital goods producer has required it to deal with a more skilled labour force.[16] In sum, while enterprise unionism has made important inroads among some large firms in the private sector even before the announcement of the 'Look East' policy, even the constrained in-house unions have been utilized by some workers to resist managerial domination.

Following the adoption of the 'Look East' policy, however, the entrenchment and promotion of in-house unions have been transformed into a coherent strategy of enterprise unionism, albeit by administrative means and facilitated, but not enforced by law. Within this context, enterprise unionism is usefully analysed in relation to (a) industrial unions, (b) Japanese TNCs, (c) the response of established unions towards the 'Look East' policy.

THE ASSAULT ON NATIONAL UNIONS

Officially, the 'Look East' policy is said to promote enterprise unions without adversely impinging upon the activities of industrial unions. However, it has become apparent that the objective is to cut the ground from under the feet of existing unions as far as possible. In particular, the intention is to contain the emergence of autonomous organizations among workers in relatively recently established industries with many employees. What this has meant in particular is that registration has generally been denied to new national industrial trade unions except in exceptional circumstances.

Consideration of a number of cases may serve to illustrate the general trend. In October 1983, for example, a claim by the National Union for Petroleum and Chemical Workers (NUPCW) for recognition – instead of the already registered in-house union – on the grounds that it had obtained majority support among the four thousand workers at the Petronas plant, was rejected out of hand. The NUPCW subsequently accepted this decision without any further struggle and decided to direct its organizing efforts elsewhere.[17]

In another case, workers at Tanaka Sdn Bhd (a subsidiary of the Dragon and Phoenix garment factory in Penang) had previously been organized by the Penang Textile Workers' Union (PTWU). The union branch was deregistered after its members took part in an illegal strike in 1979. A subsequent bid by the PTWU to represent the mainly female workforce was turned down. Although the PTWU then took this up through the MTUC, the Textile Workers' Asian Regional Organization and the International Textile, Garment and Leather Workers' Federation, such action failed to secure a reversal of the RTU's decision. Subsequently, plans to amalgamate the five regional textile unions in Peninsular Malaysia into a single national union were abandoned for a more defensive strategy of maintaining the *status quo*, though a national federation was eventually formed in the late 1980s.[18]

Meanwhile TEAIEU, which had successfully organized all nine pre-existing car assembly plants, has been blocked from recruiting workers at the new Proton plant belonging to the Malaysian Government-owned Heavy Industries Corporation of Malaysia (HICOM) in partnership with Mitsubishi.[19] The relatively militant TEAIEU has thus lost much of its membership base. The Malaysian car market – of about 150,000 new cars sold annually – is relatively small. The car assembly industry then was already overcrowded with considerable surplus capacity. On the other hand, Proton enjoys extensive state support through heavy tariff protection and other measures. The TEAIEU has therefore been forced to fall back on the more difficult task of organizing the relatively smaller non-automotive vehicles and the subcontracting companies making transport equipment components.

There have also been a few instances where industrial trade unions have successfully resisted attempts to displace them. At the Dragon and Phoenix garment factory, for example, the RTU refused in 1983 to register an in-house union which had been formed after the PTWU had already organized a majority of the workers and applied to the company for recognition.[20] Similarly, the RTU ultimately rejected an application in June 1983 to register an in-house union at ITT Transelectronics – a factory in the Penang Free Trade Zone with a thousand workers – as a result of a determined struggle by the Electrical Industry Workers' Union (EIWU) to organize the largely female workforce. This case saw the government sorely embarrassed by the widespread publicity it generated internationally as an example of a gross violation of the right to organize.[21]

In sum, both capital and the state are determined to contain resistance among the industrial workforce by accommodating enterprise unions when forced to allow unionization or to undermine existing national trade unions. However, they have generally hesitated to face the possible consequences of total suppression of existing national trade unions. The current policy and its implementation suggest a less confrontational strategy of encircling existing national unions with restrictive laws and regulations, besides preventing their further expansion.

JAPANESE TNC PRACTICES

The labour practices of Japanese TNCs in Malaysia are clearly crucial to the entire 'Look East' project, for if they fail to practise enterprise unionism successfully, others can hardly be expected to do so. Notably, the only known survey on the subject found that the personnel policies of Japanese TNCs were generally more centralized – allowing local subsidiaries' managements less room for manoeuvre – than those of their US and UK counterparts.[22] Japanese managements are said to have made determined efforts to transplant some aspects of the Japanese industrial relations system to Malaysian subsidiaries. This includes the notion of the company family, productivity drives (via quality control circles and suggestion boxes), cost reduction campaigns, morning exercises, company songs and recitation of company principles – all of which are designed to promote company loyalty and reduce conflict between the company management and workers.[23]

Despite such initiatives, however, the indications are that wholesale Japanization is neither possible nor intended. In the first place, the sharp differentiation of workers into permanent and temporary staff – which is a principal feature of the industrial relations system in Japan – was not very acceptable to the Malaysian labour authorities until relatively recently, with the pronounced current trend towards greater labour flexibility, especially in the manufacturing sector. Under Malaysian law, after six months on the job, a probationary employee acquires normal rights and duties. This does not extend to a life-long guarantee of employment (as in Japan), but to indefinite employment which may only be terminated subject to previously generous retrenchment benefits, which were reduced in 1988. In essence, it is clear that even Japanese employers in Malaysia do not offer their Malaysian employees life-long employment guarantees, seniority wage systems or other significant pecuniary benefits designed to inculcate company loyalty among Japanese workers. Although little used in manufacturing, a sector where Japanese capital is concentrated, contract labour is used extensively in land development, plantations, construction and lowly-skilled services. However, there is considerable evidence of significant casualization of labour since the mid-1980s in the manufacturing, plantation and services sectors as well as in the public sector.[24] Furthermore, the wage system in the private sector is not based on seniority as much as on job ratings and credentials.

Secondly, the Japanese company world in Malaysia is dualist, with one culture for Japanese management and another for the (often multi-ethnic) employees. Such a divide severely inhibits the development of Japanese-style company norms, thereby impeding the evolution of enterprise community consciousness, company loyalty and reciprocal obligations, and a consensual system of decision-making. The replication of Japanese company (rather than state) welfarism in Malaysian subsidiaries of Japanese firms is highly unlikely, given the fact that they are often motivated to invest in Malaysia to cut production, especially labour costs. Unattractive working conditions and remuneration, especially in a tight labour market, have encouraged a relatively high labour turnover, resulting in 'chicken and egg' or vicious circle-type consequences. The very different lifestyles of Japanese managers on the one hand and Malaysian workers on the other, and some legal restrictions on foreign companies (such as limitations on their right to buy land, which would preclude the provision of company housing for employees by the exceptionally few employers who might be inclined to do so, have been advanced as explanations for the failure of Japanese employers in Malaysia to offer terms and conditions of employment comparable to those offered to workers in Japan).

In brief, besides still being influenced primarily by national industrial unions where they exist, the relationship between management and the shop-floor is located in a very different social and cultural context in Malaysia compared with Japan. Hence, not surprisingly, the much vaunted family spirit which Japanese capital boasts of at home is rarely found in Malaysian subsidiaries of Japanese TNCs. Extensive passive – and sometimes not so passive – resistance by workers has limited replication. In any case, Japanese TNCs themselves have not proved to be automatic conveyors of ostensibly Japanese-style industrial relations, which are reputedly declining in significance in Japan itself. They do not seem to have acted significantly differently from their Western counterparts in retrenching Malaysian workers during slumps, and have generally ignored practices such as housing their employees, which is said to occur in Japan. As far as Japanese TNCs are concerned, the Japanization of Malaysian industrial relations is clearly a partial, rather than a total process, whose development is subject to considerations of cost and prevailing practices, nicely legitimized as deferring to Malaysian conditions.

UNION RESPONSES

When the Malaysian Government first attempted to promulgate Japanese work ethics and the ostensibly Japanese model of management-labour cooperation, it was generally quite well received by the MTUC and the older, larger, more conservative unions. They welcomed the prospect of the benefits Japanization might bring, including life-long employment and the seniority wage system. On the other hand, smaller unions in the fast expanding manufacturing sector tended to be more critical from the outset, with the TEAIEU arguing, for instance, 'that Japan lags behind many other industrial nations in the West, especially on human rights and social welfare. It has to be realized that the vast majority of Japanese workers do not enjoy security of tenure, housing facilities and other welfare benefits.

Discrimination against female workers is also rife'.[25] However, whatever the attitude, there was widespread scepticism that the so-called Japanese model could be easily adapted to the very different Malaysian context.

Subsequently, as the threat to national trade unions mounted with the concerted effort to promote enterprise unionism, the Japanization initiative met with increasing resistance among private sector unions. Compared with CUEPACS, the MTUC adopted a more hostile attitude towards the whole concept of enterprise unionism: 'It is simply another weapon which can be used to weaken and dismember an already sickly union movement. The collective strength of workers in one industry will be broken into separate house unions in each factory, where union leaders will be dependent on the goodwill of their bosses, and unable to champion the workers' interests'.[26]

Notwithstanding this belated opposition, the MTUC until 1992 was strongly criticized by more militant unions like the TEAIEU for having failed to provide the necessary leadership to counter the long-term consequences of the new labour policies and legislation adversely affecting the working class. But if, as the TEAIEU alleged, the MTUC proved inadequate to what should have been its task, how will enterprise unionism affect workers' struggles in the years ahead, and what is labour's most appropriate strategy for survival?

UNIONIZING ELECTRONICS WORKERS

Currently, the most well-known and blatant case in which the RTU has exercised his powers to prevent unionization involves workers in the electronics industry. In 1974, the EIWU began organizing electronics workers, but the RTU objected on the grounds that the 'electrical' and 'electronics' industries were different despite their common classification in official industrial statistics. In 1978, the MTUC applied for the registration of a National Union of Electronics Workers. This was finally rejected by the Registrar in 1989. Many electronics industry employers, especially those from the USA, have openly opposed the unionization of their workers.[27] This, together with the fear of the potential size of an electronics workers' union (about 130,000 predominantly female workers in 1992),[28] probably influenced the Registrar's decision to delay the unionization of these workers for as long as possible.

On 22 September 1988, then Minister of Labour Lee Kim Sai unexpectedly announced that the electronics industry was 'strong and stable enough' to allow the formation of trade unions. Since workers in the industry as well as others in the labour movement had long campaigned unsuccessfully for unionization, it is generally agreed that the announcement was precipitated by preceding international developments. In late 1987, after over a hundred social, political, and other activists were arrested and detained without trial under the Internal Security Act (ISA), the conservative, powerful and influential AFL-CIO (American Federation of Labor-Congress of Industrial Organizations), together with another labour rights support group, petitioned the United States Congress to withdraw Malaysia's lower import duty privileges under the General Agreement on Tariffs and Trade (GATT) Generalised System of Preferences (GSP) because of the Malaysian Government's violation of workers' rights. This action came after the Malaysian Government had been receiving adverse publicity in international forums, particularly the International Labour Organization (ILO), over the Malaysian Government's adamant refusal to allow workers in the electronics industry to unionize. The threat to the Malaysian economy's international competitiveness – posed by the possibility of GSP status withdrawal – finally forced the Government to allow the unionization of workers in the electronics sector. This was a landmark decision, given that of all the manufacturing industries, the electronics industry employs the greatest number of workers directly. (It has been claimed that the textile and garments industry employs about two hundred thousand, many indirectly, on a putting-out basis.)

However, less than three weeks later in the first half of October, after loud protests, especially from US firms in the American-dominated semiconductor industry, the Minister announced that only in-house or company unions would be allowed. This came five days after the MTUC-supported National Union of Electronics Workers (NEW), applied for registration to the RTU, as required by law. Asked as to whether his stipulation contravened the Trade Union Act, the Minister replied that it 'may appear to contradict the law, but it is policy'. Although the Minister's revised position did not completely satisfy the US electronic firms which had threatened to leave the country if unions were allowed, the Malaysian Government's capitulation to the foreign investors was clear. Ironically, however, the decision of the NEW and MTUC leaderships to continue to try to establish a national industry-wide union may unwittingly serve the preferences of both the Government and the foreign employers, as the following experience of the RCA workers' effort to set up an in-house union seems to suggest.

With its application for registration arriving soon after the Minister's announcements, the Director-General (previously the Registrar) of Trade Unions (DGTU) was obliged to register the in-house union at RCA Sdn Bhd. Two factors apparently influenced this union's decision to 'go it alone' despite the ongoing effort to organize nationally. Firstly, the MTUC and NEW organizing efforts had mainly focused on a few free trade zones, neglecting others, including the Ulu Kelang zone, where the RCA factory was located. Secondly, the December 1988 takeover of the GE Solid State electronics group – which owned RCA – by the Harris Corporation heightened concerns of mass lay-offs at RCA after almost a thousand employees were made redundant when Advanced Micro Devices and

Monolithic Memories Incorporated merged earlier in 1988. There was also ominous talk of duplication between the RCA plant and the neighbouring Harris factory, which had a reputation for retrenching workers.

In January 1989, the RCA Workers Union (RCAWU) was registered by the RTU, but not recognized by the RCA management as representing the workers. Considering the exigencies of the situation, the MTUC decided to forego its opposition to the formation of in-house unions in the electronics industry and threw its support behind the RCA workers' initiative. The labour centre was rewarded by a unanimous vote at the first general meeting of the RCAWU to affiliate with the MTUC. However, the DGTU later ruled that with the employer's name change from RCA Sdn Bhd to Harris Solid State (M) Sdn Bhd, the RCAWU could no longer represent the workers. The union then changed its name to reflect the company name change, after which the management formally transferred all Harris Solid State workers, except the union leadership, to employment in the neighbouring Harris factory without any real relocation or reorganization of production operations. After thus isolating the union leadership from its membership, RCA/Harris used various ways and means to rid the company of these union 'troublemakers' while trying to create the public impression that the workers did not want a union. The fate of the RCAWU and its leadership sent the clear message to the rest of the industry that efforts to emulate the RCA workers' initiative were likely to fail.

The protracted saga of this union's struggle for survival and recognition exposed the actual management attitudes of US electronics firms to unionization of any kind, including the in-house variety. These attitudes seem to vary among employers by national origin, with European firms generally less resistant to trade unions, and Japanese firms accepting the establishment of in-house unions. These differences seem to reflect the different industrial relations cultures existing in their own home countries.

While other US electronics firms were constrained from publicly applauding the RCA management's handling of the new union, RCA received discreet support in private meetings of American electronics industry firms in Malaysia and in those involving the US Embassy's Labor Attache. They all watched developments affecting the RCAWU with considerable interest in what was generally seen as a test case affecting the prospects for unionization in the industry. In response to the Minister's first announcement allowing electronic industry workers to unionize, managements introduced new carrots as well as sticks to discourage their employees from joining as well as forming unions. This is borne out by a report prepared in 1990 by the International Labour Rights Education and Research Fund (ILRERF) which was submitted in the USA under GSP procedures. It cited evidence of how 'the Malaysian American Electronic Industry (MAEI) has systematically pursued a policy of intimidation and coercion in order to persuade the Malaysian government to protect the electronic industry from unions'. The report contains telexes, memos and other evidence to show how the MAEI pressured the government to control unionization. It is now evident that the US managements' fear of unionization were greatly exaggerated, as the outcome of the RCAWU saga suggests.

In 1990, the ILO Committee formally asked its Governing Body to approve the following recommendation:

a) The Committee asks the Malaysian government to take the necessary steps to amend Sections 8 and 12 of the Trade Unions Act 1959 so as to bring them into conformity with the principles of freedom of association,

b) The Committee regrets that the Director-General of Trade Unions has seen fit to reject the application for registration submitted by the National Union of Electronic Industry Workers on grounds which are not compatible with the principles of freedom of association. It expresses the hope that this decision will be reversed on appeal.'

However, the government has done neither and does not seem to have any intention of doing so.

The embarassment to the Malaysian Government at international labour forums, such as ILO meetings, owing to its refusal to allow a national union for electronics workers has been blamed on the supposedly 'anti-national' lobbying efforts of 'irresponsible' labour leaders. The MTUC leadership and the Malaysian affiliates of the International Metalworkers Federation (IMF), particularly the EIWU and the MIEU, have been the main targets of this counter-attack. Meanwhile, the leaderships of the other labour centres patronized by the Government have been watching awkwardly from the sidelines, trying to seek advantage for themselves whenever and wherever possible while trying to retain some minimal credibility for themselves. In an attempt to defuse the charges, the Human Resources Minister, Lim Ah Lek, has actually encouraged the formation of several in-house unions, especially in Japanese electronic factories. The credibility of his efforts, however, have been undermined by the continued refusal of American electronic firm managements to recognize even in-house unions allowed by the government for collective bargaining purposes.

International support for Malaysian labour demands, particularly those for the electronic workers' right to form a national union, has prompted the Malaysian Government to denounce and attempt to discredit the Malaysian unionists in the forefront of such efforts as well as their foreign allies. However, the wrath of the authorities has primarily been vented against the MTUC-associated unionists as they are unable to respond effectively to the criticisms and to do much about its foreign critics who lie beyond the bounds of Malaysian Government jurisdiction.

WORKER'S RESPONSES

Since trade unions are class organizations which have historically embodied workers' aspirations under capitalism, conventional theorization has inevitably viewed company or enterprise unionization as primarily a managerial strategy for imposing hegemony over workers and containing more radical actions by the workforce. Certainly, there can be little quarrel with this perception when company unions clearly operate to ensure the effective subordination of labour to management, and develop no independent initiatives of their own. However, it is suggested here that rather than dismissing company unionism in all circumstances, there is an increasing need to analyse it as a growing labour phenomenon which needs to be dealt with. In the first place, enterprise unionism has been put forward as a major factor behind the Japanese miracle, and as such, it becomes important to understand the forms of coercion and hegemony over workers that it entails, and whether or not it is a principle of managerial domination which is particularly rooted within a peculiarly Japanese-style of capitalism. Second, and of rather more importance here, is the fact that like it or not, enterprise unionism is quite widespread and for one reason or another, defines the context within which many disadvantaged workers must struggle.

It must be recognized at the outset that enterprise unionism in Japan is not quite the docile creature it is commonly alleged to be. Hence, although the exclusion of non-permanent employees from the benefits of unionization, company employer influence on union policy and union integration into company personnel strategies are all legitimate reasons for concern, these are not problems exclusive to Japanese, or in-house unions. By strictly economistic criteria, Japanese unions do not compare unfavourably with trade unions in a number of OECD countries (Organization for Economic Development and Cooperation) in terms of the proportion of the labour force organized, the wage gains they have made and the militancy they exhibit and express.[29] In addition, although many features of Japanese unions must necessarily be related to Japan's rapid economic growth, the long-term rise in life-long employment in earlier times may be regarded as something of an important achievement. In sum, whatever the final judgement, the Japanese situation is much more complex than Western mythology generally admits.

In much of the world, meanwhile, enterprise unions have often been contemptuously pushed aside by workers upon whom they have been foisted. But it should be noted that even when initiated by management or where the state has intervened to support them, militant activity on the shop floor has not always been contained. In Chile, for example, where the Labour Law of 1924 was instrumental in impeding the development of genuine national unions until the late 1960s, the working class was nonetheless able to forge a united and radical trade union movement in close cooperation with left-wing labour parties. This was a key factor in the later election of the Allende government to office in 1970.[30] Indeed, even in Japan, radical and militant tendencies have struggled with reactionary and conformist influences within the dominant enterprise unions for some time. This can be seen in the rise of the communist Sanbetsu grouping between 1945 and 1950, the militant economistic struggles of 1955–62 (involving the *shunto* or Spring Offensive strike waves every year), and the subsequent rivalry between the Sohyo and Domei federations. This rivalry represents a struggle between economistic militancy and economistic corporatism before the eventual ascendance of the latter with the restructuring of the 1980s, beginning with the formation of the united private sector federation (Zenmin Rokyo) in 1982 and the Rengo mutations of the late 1980s expanded into the public sector as Sohyo strength waned.[31]

What, then, are the prospects for enterprise unionism in Malaysia, and how is it likely to impinge upon working class struggles? In so far as the imposition of Japanese industrial relations forms on Malaysian labour is intended to contain shop floor struggles and pre-empt independent, let alone militant organization by the emergent working class in the rapidly expanding manufacturing sector, it represents a major threat to the trade union movement. The historical development of the trade union movement in Malaysia from general unions to national industrial unions, then regional unions and now enterprise unions[32] has been continuously channelled by the state towards subordinate and controllable forms. Yet, that said, it may be argued that the current official strategy may have contradictory results.

First, it appears unlikely that Malaysian industrial relations will not be easily Japanized, even to the extent desired by the Government. For one thing, non-Japanese TNCs remain largely unfamiliar with Japanese management styles. Furthermore, even large Japanese TNCs have proved reluctant to lead the way towards a holistic Japanization of Malaysian industrial relations (see Chapter 6 in this volume). In Japan, the cooperation of enterprise unions with management is generally secured by the allegiance of those in white collar and supervisory grades to the management and the exclusion of a significant fraction of blue collar workers. Existing unions in Malaysia generally do not preclude largely unskilled, blue collar labour. While this has often resulted in large unions with unwieldy bureaucracies that have been highly susceptible to corruption and impervious to union democracy, the other side of the coin is that the currently enforced fragmentation of much of the union movement in Malaysia may, by that token, actually assist in the widespread development of workplace-based, grassroots control over union policy. Ironically, therefore, enterprise unionism may democratize the decision-making process within worker organizations by removing it from trade union bureaucracies and encouraging shop-floor activity. Whether this will actually materialise remains to be seen. Finally, voluntary enterprise unionism can only be pre-empted by greater union democratization and accountability, thus preventing local enterprise-rooted grievances against union bureaucracies from becoming demands for in-house unions.

If enterprise unionism is the only path that workers are allowed to pursue by the authorities, then the possibilities for struggle that emerge within the confining constraints of enterprise unionism will eventually require the evolution of coordination among such in-house unions. This is currently provided for under existing labour laws, by provisions for trade union federations. Were enterprise unions then to develop their muscle, despite the best efforts of the government and employers, then it is likely that they can and will take up issues at the industry level. Indeed, although the Japanese 'Spring Offensives' (*shunto*) are a unique phenomenon, greater labour pressures upon employers may well become possible with the emergence of a stronger, shop floor-based enterprise unionism in Malaysia.

A further dilemma for the government is that a fragmented union movement is an unwieldy, if not clumsy instrument for the pursuit of any form of administratively directed incomes policy, requiring institutions for centralized collective bargaining, as suggested by the 1993 Budget Speech's announcement of an impending National Wage Council. The existence of trade union centres and large union bureaucracies opens the way for co-opting labour into the framework of corporatist development policy. Indeed, with ethnic Malays now in a majority in terms of union membership, this option might become increasingly realistic and attractive, especially for a post-Mahathir administration which does not inherit his personal prejudices in such matters. Already, this has been partly realized in the public sector through the Congress of Unions of Employees in the Public and Civil Services (CUEPACS) and is potentially embodied in the MTUC's commitment towards a tripartite corporatist relationship with the state. However, if the government enables or allows enterprise unions to develop links and form federations, it might set in train the emergence of a more grassroots-responsive and re-invigorated industry-oriented unionism.

Thus, while the attempted Japanization of the Malaysian trade union movement undoubtedly represents a concerted threat to workers' collective organization, it simultaneously opens the door to new possibilities. In seeking to contain the trade union movement, the government may find that the enterprise unions fostered under the 'Look East' policy may yet give rise to a more vibrant, accountable and responsive workers' movement built on the very enterprise unions set up to pre-empt this.

*NOTE

This is a considerably revised and updated version of Peter Wad (1988) 'The Japanization of the Malaysian Trade Union Movement' in R. Southall (ed.) Trade Unions and the New Industrialization of the Third World, Zed Books, London, pp. 287–305.

NOTES

1   First announced by then Information Minister Adib Adam, *New Straits Times* (*NST*), 24 January 1983. An enterprise union is defined here as a trade union constituted at the plant or company level, and is synonymous with 'in-house', 'house' or 'company' union.
2   *New Straits Times*, 12 June 1992.
3   Chang Yii Tan (1985) 'Tilting East', in Jomo (ed.) *The Sun Also Sets: Lessons in 'Looking East'*, second edition, INSAN, Kuala Lumpur, 1985.
4   Registrar of Trade Unions, 'Trade Unions Malaysia' (unpublished, 1983), pp. 12–13.
5   Ibid.
6   An in-house union for Petronas workers was registered although the workers could have joined the National Union for Petroleum and Chemical Workers. Similarly, an in-house union was registered for the textile workers at Tanaka Sdn. Bhd. in Penang, although they could join the Penang Textile and Clothing Workers' Union. KCTSU could have registered as a branch of the NUCW; Shell employees disaffiliated from NUPCIW to form an in-house union. It might be mentioned, however, that unions do have to come up with pretexts as to why affiliation to an existing body is untenable, though the DGTU seems to accept just about any rationale. Since KCTSU was receiving help from the MTUC, it did not want to join the NUCW since the latter was not an MTUC affiliate at the time; Shell felt that the NUPCIW was dominated by poorly paid chemical workers more likely to make greater demands for wage increases.
7   Applications for in-house unions at the ITT electronics factory and the Dragon and Phoenix garment factory were rejected as the workers had been organized by the Electrical Industry Workers' Union and the Penang Textile and Clothing Workers' Union respectively.
8   In the case of the Tanaka workers, the union was established by management through company supervisors. See *The New Straits Times*, 12 March 1984.
9   Jomo K.S. (1989) *Beyond 1990: Considerations for a New National Development Strategy*, Institute for Advanced Studies, University of Malaya, Kuala Lumpur.
10 Standing, Guy (1991) 'Structural Adjustment and Labour Flexibility in Malaysian Manufacturing: Some Post-NEP Dilemmas', in Lee Kiong Hock and Syamala Nagaraj (eds), *The Malaysian Economy Beyond 1990: International and Domestic Perspectives*, Malaysian Economic Association, Kuala Lumpur, 1991.
11 *NST*, 6 March 1983.
12 Ibid.
13 Mahathir Mohamad (1982) *The Malay Dilemma*, Federal Publications, Kuala Lumpur, p. 108.
14 Michael A. Lanius (1984) 'The State and Industrial Labour in South Korea', *Bulletin of Concerned Asian Scholars*, vol. 16, no. 4, p. 5.
15 R. Sielaff (1976) *Malaysia: Gewerkschaften, Wandlungen im Selbverstandnis einer Gessellschaftlichen Gruppe*, Friedrich Ebert Stiftung, Bonn, pp. 21–2.
16 Interviews with a former UMW unionist and current UMW leaders, 1984.
17 *NST*, 12 March 1984.

18 Personal communication from the General Secretary of the PTWU in 1984. Later, an offensive to amalgamate into a national (Peninsular Malaysian) union was reopened (*Asian Workers Solidarity Link*, Malaysia, vol. 2, no. 1, 1985).

19 On the Malaysian car project, see the relevant article in this volume and Chee Peng Lim (1985) 'Malaysian Car Dream: Need for Reconsideration', in Jomo K.S. (ed.), *The Sun Also Sets*, second edition, INSAN, Kuala Lumpur, 1985: pp. 329–31.

20 *NST*, 12 March 1984, and *Suara Buruh*, December 1982.

21 Arne Wangel (1988) 'The ILO and Protection of Trade Union Rights: The Electronics Industry in Malaysia', in R. Southall (ed.), *Trade Unions and the New Industrialization of the Third World*, Zed Books, London, 1988: 287–305.

22 A.B. Sim (1978) 'Comparative Practices and Performance of American, British and Japanese MNCs in Malaysia', Malaysian Economic Association seminar, Kuala Lumpur.

23 Experiences from a study trip to Malaysia in 1984.

24 For example, see Guy Standing (1993) 'Structural Adjustment and Labour Flexibility in the Malaysian Manufacturing Sector' in Jomo K.S. (ed.) *Industrialising Malaysia: Policy, Performance, Prospects*, Routledge, London, 1993; and Siti Rohani Yahya (1993) 'Fleksibiliti Buruh Di Semenanjung Malaysia' (Labour Flexibility in Peninsular Malaysia), PhD thesis, University of Malaya.

25 Syed Sharir bin Mohamed, Transport Equipment and Allied Industries Employees Union (TEAIEU) and Mohan, V.C., Sahabat Alam Malaysia (SAM), *Country Report on Malaysian Workers Reality*, Asian Workers Solidarity Links (AWSL), Penang, Document 8, undated: p. 2. See also Arokia Dass, *Not Beyond Repair*, Hong Kong, 1991: 153–65.

26 *NST*, 12 March 1984, and *Suara Buruh*, April 1983, May 1984.

27 *The New Straits Times*, 9 March 1983, reported that 'the management of most factories are not in favour of a union for the electronics industry'. *The Star*, 5 July 1983, reported that the managing director of the Hewlett-Packard factory in Penang, Dan Nelson, stated: 'Corporate officials would probably hesitate to invest further in Penang if unionism proves to be successful in electronics factories'.

28 Mohd. Kadir, then acting Registrar of Trade Unions, estimated that there were about 90,000 workers in the electronics industry in an interview on 28 January 1984.

29 Therborn G. (1984) 'The Prospects of Labour and the Transformation of Advanced Capitalism', *New Left Review*, 145: 5–38.

30 A. Angell (1972) *Politics and the Labour Movement in Chile*, Oxford University Press, Oxford, 1972.

31 Iwao F. Ayusawa (1966) *A History of Labor in Modern Japan*, East West Center Press, Honolulu; Okochi Kazuo, B. Karsh and S. Levine (eds) (1973), *Workers and Employers in Japan*, University of Tokyo Press, Tokyo; Muto Ichiyo (1984) 'Class Struggle on the Shopfloor – The Japanese Case, 1945–1984', *Ampo*, vol. 16, no. 3: 38–49.

32 Jomo K.S. and Patricia Todd (1994) *Trade Unions and the State in Peninsular Malaysia*, Oxford University Press, Kuala Lumpur.

9

MALAYSIAN *SOGOSHOSHAS*
Superficial cloning, failed emulation*

Chee Peng Lim and Edmund Terence Gomez

Malaysian Prime Minister Mahathir Mohamad's 'Look East' policy has entailed 'emulating the rapidly developing countries of the East in an effort to develop Malaysia' (Mahathir, 1983: 276), with specific reference to Japan. Among the major ideas which have constituted part of his 'Look East' policy has been the establishment of Malaysian *sogoshoshas*. Mahathir felt that the Japanese *sogoshoshas* merited emulation as he believed they contributed greatly to the growth of the country's economy.[1]

One reason for Mahathir's strong espousal of the *sogoshoshas* was that, by the early 1980s, the government expected not to be able to stave off the global recession much longer (see *Malaysian Business*, April 1982). The experiences of Japanese *sogoshoshas* seemed to suggest that the nature of their activities had insulated them from domestic recessions. Since *sogoshoshas* have been involved with various industries in different locations internationally, even if one industry collapsed or a business slumped, the losses could be compensated for by gains from other industries or businesses (*Intersect*, 26 October 1990). Thus, by forming large corporations, the repercussions of the impending recession on Malaysia's economy could be curtailed or minimized.

While *sogoshoshas* have generally been understood to mean large trading firms, in making the distinction between the two, Yoshihara (1982: 10) states that '[f]or a trading company to be a *sogoshosha*, it had to deal with many products (not concentrating in one product group, such as textiles or steel), engage in both export and import, have offices in various parts of the world, and wield considerable power in the spheres of marketing and finance'. Most major Japanese *sogoshoshas* – like Mitsui, Mitsubishi, C. Itoh, Marubeni and Sumitomo – have certain common traits. They have long histories; most of them were established during the Meiji era (1868–1912) when, following a long period of international isolation, the development of foreign trade and local industries became important.[2] They have huge paid-up capitals and high turnover rates,[3] and extensive world-wide branch networks which employ large numbers of personnel.[4]

Yoshihara noted two reasons why both developed and developing nations have wanted to replicate Japanese *sogoshoshas*. In the case of the former, he observed that 'there is a need to create organizations to link small and medium-sized companies to the export market', while in the case of developing companies, 'the focus is on bringing foreign trade, which has been dominated by foreign companies, under their control, and increasing exports' (Yoshihara, 1982: 1).

PROMOTION OF *SOGOSHOSHAS*

In addition to Mahathir's belief that *sogoshoshas* were integral to Japan's economic development, several other reasons have also been cited for the Malaysian government's active promotion of Malaysian *sogoshoshas* in the early 1980s. As *sogoshoshas* had played a key role in the successful promotion of Japanese products in the world market, the local incorporation of such concerns emerged as an important element of the 'Look East' policy. By bringing together major public enterprises and private companies, in line with the 'Look East' concept of Malaysia Incorporated, it was thought that Malaysian *sogoshoshas* could be created. The government also hoped that the international business of joint venture members would eventually be channelled through the *sogoshoshas*, thus increasing their trade potential and supplementing their market and distribution networks (*Malaysian Business*, 1 August 1984).

Sogoshoshas were also expected to play a vanguard role for Malaysia's export-led growth drive, acting as catalysts for the development of manufacturing, especially resource-based industries. With its relatively small Malaysian market of 16 million people in the early 1980s, industrialization was expected to require the creation of markets overseas. This, in turn, meant developing efficient marketing organizations, which the government believed the Malaysian *sogoshoshas* could become.

The government also contended that Malaysian *sogoshoshas* would assist in exporting the products of Malaysian manufacturers while acting as overseas sales and purchasing agents for them. Many Malaysian manufacturers, especially smaller ones, possessed neither the expertise nor the resources to promote effectively their products on their own in overseas markets. It was expected that while handling exports on behalf of Malaysian manufacturers, *sogoshoshas* could concurrently provide the necessary advice and information on overseas market requirements in terms of design, quality and packaging.

In addition, the government felt that *sogoshoshas* could act as consortia to cope with large orders from overseas buyers which single manufacturers could not meet. Malaysian manufacturers (like those from other countries) were often reluctant to commit themselves to large single orders, either due to limited capacity or to avoid the risks of depending on only one or a handful of overseas buyers.

By acting as trade intermediaries, *sogoshoshas* could – together with a number of manufacturers – organize the execution of large overseas orders. The *sogoshoshas* thus functioned to spread the risks. Indeed, if the orders secured by a *sogoshosha* were sufficiently large, the *sogoshosha* might well consider manufacturing the product itself, as has happened in the case of Japanese *sogoshoshas*.

Furthermore, Malaysian *sogoshoshas* could undertake export promotion and marketing activities in new, non-traditional markets such as Latin America, the South Pacific, Africa and West Asia. *Sogoshoshas* could play an effective role in helping local manufacturers to penetrate and develop new markets. Such new markets were not only important for manufactured goods, but also for Malaysia's primary commodities. In their search for new markets and products, Malaysian *sogoshoshas* could discover opportunities for participation with foreign manufacturers in joint ventures to produce such products in Malaysia. Thus, they could also serve to promote foreign investments in Malaysia.

Finally, *sogoshoshas* could also play an important role in barter or counter trade. Although not favoured by economic theory, counter trade had begun to gain significance in many countries around the world during the early 1980s. It was particularly important for those with foreign exchange constraints having problems exporting their products; some of these countries were important markets for Malaysian products, particularly palm oil. The *sogoshosha* was well placed to conduct counter trade because such trading companies could buy and sell products all over the world. The absence of *sogoshoshas* to undertake such tasks was to be one reason why Malaysia had not entered into counter trade in a big way.

Basing its promotion of *sogoshoshas* on these arguments, the government encouraged the establishment of locally incorporated international trading companies based on the Japanese *sogoshosha* model. By the mid-1980s, at least six Malaysian-style *sogoshoshas* were formed, none of which have been particularly successful. This is not entirely surprising because a close study of the nature and functions of *sogoshoshas* not only indicates their irrelevance to the Malaysian economy, but also the difficulty of emulating the Japanese *sogoshoshas*.

PROBLEMS IN DEVELOPING MALAYSIAN *SOGOSHOSHAS*

A major reason for the rapid development of Japanese *sogoshoshas* was the country's rather remote location compared with the international market in an era of maritime trade. Most Japanese manufacturers also faced language barriers when trying to promote their products. This led to a strong dependence on *sogoshoshas* for the promotion and export of their products (*Malaysian Business*, 16 July 1986). Malaysia, on the other hand, is more strategically located in terms of major sea routes. In any case, by the 1980s, geographical access had become a less serious consideration. Domination by foreign investment had limited the emergence of Malaysian manufacturers. They also faced fewer language problems than the Japanese. This meant that local manufacturers did not need to rely on organizations like *sogoshoshas* to develop their markets and to export their merchandise.

In fact, existing Malaysian trading companies could not only perform the functions to be undertaken by the *sogoshoshas*, but could also conduct them just as efficiently. For example, more than 70 per cent of Malaysia's exports were then made up of primary products, already efficiently handled by existing trading companies. As for manufacturing, the bulk of Malaysia's manufactured exports consist of electronic components, textiles and wood products. The pattern of export of these products has largely been predetermined by firm considerations and other exogenous factors. Most of the firms producing manufactured products in Malaysia have been large and foreign-owned, which means they usually have the competence and capacity to handle their own exports, with marketing usually handled by their parent companies or other subsidiaries. This leaves the products produced by small Malaysian manufacturers. Several studies have shown that small Malaysian manufacturing firms have little export potential and their products have generally not been competitive in the world market, both in terms of price and quality. In view of this, *sogoshoshas* did not have much of a role to play in Malaysia.

It was also highly improbable that the Malaysian *sogoshoshas* could quickly overcome the handicaps of small size (compared with Japanese *sogoshoshas*), acquire marketing skills and establish marketing networks which the Malaysian *sogoshoshas* needed to chalk up the large volume of sales required to sustain their operations. Consider, for example, the total sales of a Japanese *sogoshosha*. In 1980, Mitsubishi Corporation's total sales were valued at more than RM126 billion (RM: Malaysian ringgit), several times the size of Malaysia's GNP. To put it another way, in 1980, Mitsubishi Corporation alone generated sales valued at RM345 million a day, or RM43.7 million an hour. In the same year, Malaysia's total trade was valued at less than RM50 billion, or less than half the total sales of Mitsubishi.

Even if Malaysian exports grew rapidly, the nature and scale of operations of the Malaysian *sogoshoshas* would probably not be enough to enable them to compete successfully in international markets. At the same time, the volume of operations would make it impossible for Malaysian *sogoshoshas* to break even, since *sogoshoshas* are supposed to operate with very thin profit margins. The 1981 figures for the nine biggest Japanese *sogoshoshas* indicated profit margins in the range of 0.1–0.2 per cent of sales. Such profit margins were only viable if the scale of operations was large enough; this implied a total sales volume of at least RM100 million. Otherwise, Malaysian *sogoshoshas* would never be able to spread their costs over the extensive communications and transportation network they had to maintain.

In view of the small profit margins, and the large sales volumes consequently required, it is not surprising that the casualty rate of *sogoshoshas* has been high. In the past few decades, the number of Japanese *sogoshoshas* has declined from about two dozen to only nine by the mid-1980s. Besides Japan, only South Korea has so far managed to develop their version of *sogoshoshas* successfully. In all other countries where they have been established, such as Taiwan, the Philippines and Thailand, *sogoshoshas* have generally failed to achieve profitable track records. In the Philippines, *sogoshoshas* have had problems in efficiently producing exports that could compete in the world market (*New Straits Times*, 16 April 1982). Thailand's *sogoshoshas* barely achieved government targets and were not successful in opening new markets, mainly because they lacked the necessary knowledge of the relevant international businesses, and also because of the weak ties between Thai *sogoshoshas* and their associated manufacturers.[5]

In other countries, *sogoshoshas* have not been successful because most only deal with exports. Moreover, they generally do not participate in manufacturing industries through joint investments with local manufacturers, resulting in weak ties with associated manufacturers and suppliers. In addition, they have usually lacked adequate staff of qualified and experienced personnel. Many staff only have paper qualifications, but lack practical business expertise. *Sogoshoshas* can only sustain their operations if they are able to operate on a large scale. Many new *sogoshoshas* have been relatively small compared with their Japanese counterparts and have found it difficult to increase their market shares.

Even the Japanese experience suggests that *sogoshoshas* also have their disadvantages. Since *sogoshoshas* are by nature large monopolistic organizations, they tend to abuse their powers. Not surprisingly, *sogoshoshas* have a tarnished image in Japan and have been severely criticized in the past by journalists, intellectuals and the official Fair Trade Commission in Japan. They have been accused of cornering markets, causing inflation, undermining competition and corrupting the political process.

Furthermore, as competition among Japanese *sogoshoshas* has stiffened in recent decades, it has forced them to scramble farther and harder to maintain their high sales volumes. Recent changes in Japan and the world economy have also had a profound impact on the functions and operations of *sogoshoshas*. In Japan, consumer goods manufacturers sought independence by developing overseas markets on their own. Instead of continuing to operate as commission merchants, the *sogoshoshas* have turned increasingly to third country trade, counter trade, overseas investments, joint ventures, as well as more aggressive marketing of all kinds of goods.

These new areas of *sogoshosha* competition posed an even greater challenge to the Malaysian *sogoshosha*.

Another reason why Malaysian *sogoshoshas* have not been able to play a significant role in the Malaysian economy is to be seen in the fact that since they cannot rely on an adequate volume of export and import trade to finance their operations, they have had to concentrate on other income-generating activities, such as third country trade. Unfortunately, these other activities have been even more competitive; in these transactions, Malaysian *sogoshoshas* have not only had to compete with their larger and more experienced Japanese counterparts, but also with newer *sogoshoshas* from other countries, particularly South Korea, Brazil, Mexico and Taiwan. These foreign *sogoshoshas* have well-established market shares, and it was not easy for the Malaysian newcomers to provide the services which these trading companies provide. Many countries preferred to use the services of the Japanese *sogoshoshas*, which reputedly provide better marketing information, offer more competitive prices and open letters of credit.

Besides that, amendments to Malaysian banking laws made it difficult for Malaysian *sogoshoshas* to establish close tie-ups with commercial banks. This imposed a severe constraint on the trading activities of Malaysian *sogoshoshas* since trade is often related to finance. For example, in Japan, *sogoshoshas* are able to borrow at relatively low rates of interest to finance their smaller manufacturing clients at slightly higher rates of interest. It has been difficult for Malaysian *sogoshoshas* to do this since they lack close links with financial institutions. Apparently, Malaysian policy makers failed to appreciate that business in Japan, particularly foreign trade, involves tightly knit partnerships, not only between industry and the financial institutions, but also between the government and such institutions. The Japanese *sogoshoshas* are outstanding examples of such collaboration and one of the most successful manifestations of Japan Incorporated. If Malaysian *sogoshoshas* were going to emulate them, closer three way cooperation between the government, industry and financial institutions had to develop. But even then, Malaysian *sogoshoshas* have remained at a disadvantage in many other ways. For example, since Malaysian *sogoshoshas* do not have the support of the pre-war *zaibatsu* or post-war *keiretsu* system, they do not have access to 'easy', large-scale financing, nor a group of more or less captive domestic buyers and sellers.

Thus, it would appear that rather than trying to promote *sogoshoshas*, the Malaysian government should have concentrated greater attention on improving the price and quality of local export products to enhance competitiveness. It should be remembered that many other countries – West Germany, Hong Kong and Singapore – have succeeded in the export market without setting up their own *sogoshoshas*.

In short, there was no urgent need for Malaysia to set up its own *sogoshoshas*. The effort and resources expanded could have been put to better use, for example, to upgrade the technical capacities and capabilities of small firms in Malaysia. In this way, many may gradually be able to achieve international competitiveness, and thus create the need for general trading companies. The performance of Malaysian *sogoshoshas* since their incorporation has borne out these arguments.

MALAYSIAN *SOGOSHOSHAS*

Most of the Malaysian *sogoshoshas* formed involved consortia of companies, both from the private and public sectors. In all, six Malaysian-style *sogoshoshas* have been formed since the concept was first promoted.

The Malaysian International Trading Corporation (MITRA), incorporated in December 1981 as Nastra Sdn Bhd, was Malaysia's first *sogoshosha*. Among its members were publicly-listed and government-controlled Malaysian Mining Corporation Bhd, Kuok Brothers Sdn Bhd, and two other government-owned agencies, Petroliam Nasional (Petronas) and the Federal Land Development Agency (Felda). The company later changed its name to Malaysian International Trading Corporation (MITRA). Commencing with a paid-up capital of RM10 million, the company was intended to promote Malaysian products, particularly textiles, plywood and electronic products, in new markets, specifically Africa, Latin America and Eastern Europe (Gale, 1985: 181–82).

Another original shareholder, Kumpulan Perangsang, owned by the Selangor state government, pulled out of the joint venture even before MITRA commenced operations. MITRA's decline has been attributed to the different interests of the shareholders; most of MITRA's shareholders were government-owned agencies with different operating styles compared with the private Kuok Brothers, which already had reputation in commodity trading (see *Malaysian Business*, 1 August 1984).

Another *sogoshosha*, Pernas Sime Darby Trading Sdn Bhd – a joint venture between Sime Darby and government-owned Perbadanan Nasional (Pernas) – commenced trading in January 1983. Although originally capitalized at only RM5 million, by 1989, Pernas Sime Darby's paid-up capital had increased to RM13 million, still a mere pittance compared with the multi-billion dollar investments of the Japanese *sogoshosha*. Even though the company was partly owned by Sime Darby, Malaysia's largest multinational corporation, for all its resources, even Sime Darby only has a small fraction of the extensive world-wide network which the *sogoshoshas* have built up.

By 1989, however, Sime Darby Holdings had become the only shareholder of Pernas Sime Darby. A probable reason for Pernas' divestment of its equity was Pernas Sime Darby's losses. Company records indicate that by 1991, the company's accumulated losses fell to RM8.9 million from RM13.5 million in 1989. Pernas Sime Darby's turnover also indicated some improvement – rising to RM68.12 million in 1991 compared to RM56.5 million in 1989.

The Malaysian Transnational Trading Corporation Bhd (MATTRA) is a venture involving Kumpulan FIMA, then a government-owned enterprise, the Selangor state government's Kumpulan Perangsang, and two quoted companies, United Motor Works Bhd (UMW) and Palmco Holdings Bhd (Gale, 1985: 181–83). These companies were involved in a diverse range of activities: Kumpulan Fima in food processing and marketing, Kumpulan Peransang in tin mining, UMW with heavy machinery and motor vehicles, and Palmco with palm-oil products. It was hoped that by bringing together these companies involved in a wide range of activities, MATTRA would quickly become involved in a number of major industries. MATTRA also had plans to open offices in Europe, Japan, Australia and the United States (*Malaysian Business*, April 1982).

Another *sogoshosha*, Perdagangan Antarabangsa Malaysia Bhd (PAM), is a joint venture between Mitsui Co, Japan's leading *sogoshosha*, the Sarawak State Economic Development Corporation, the Sabah Marketing Corporation, the Kim Chuan Seng Group, controlled by Sarawakian tycoon Wee Boon Ping (also president of the Associated Chinese Chambers of Commerce), and the National Youth Cooperative (KOBENA), controlled by the youth wing of UMNO, the dominant party in the ruling Barisan Nasional coalition. This was the first Malaysian *sogoshosha* to have a Japanese *sogoshosha*, with vast experience in international trading, as a partner. The interests of the investing companies meant that PAM expected to inherit expertise in timber processing, engineering, trading and property development. Apart from having the backing of Mitsui's international network, PAM also entered into a partnership with UPI, a Yugoslavian company, to tap Eastern European markets (*Malaysian Business*, 16 July 1986).

Incorporated on 13 August 1974, Guthrie Malaysian Holdings Bhd (GMHB) changed its name to Multi-Purpose International Trading Corporation Bhd when it was acquired by Multi-Purpose Holdings Bhd. The company adopted the name Mulpha International Trading Corporation on 18 August 1983, and in July 1991, it was renamed Mulpha International. Among the company's subsidiaries are Mulpha (Singapore), Mulpha Trading, Mulpha Engineering and Mulpha Manufacturing. At its peak, Multi-Purpose Holdings' stake in Mulpha International amounted to around 70 per cent (Gomez, 1993: 269–71).

According to Gale (1985: 190), Mulpha was a response to Mahathir's call to establish *sogoshoshas*, with its main trade in consumer goods, foodstuffs, cosmetics and building materials; among its main principals were Canon Inc., Kanebo Ltd, Rowntree Mackintosh plc, Hume Industries (M) Bhd and Tasek Cement Bhd.

Long an unprofitable concern, by 1986, the Mulpha International group had accumulated losses totalling RM72.6 million, despite a turnover of RM230 million. The Group continued declaring losses until 1990, when it declared a profit of RM779,000 despite a much reduced turnover of RM63.22 million. Between January and June 1990, Multi-Purpose Holdings reduced its massive equity in Mulpha International, then still financially beleaguered despite the economic recovery, to a mere 6.28 per cent (*New Straits Times*, 28 June 1990).

The current majority shareholder is believed to be publicly-listed TA Securities Bhd, although there have been no major boardroom changes. In an attempt to improve the financial performance of the Group's operations, its engineering division has been closed, while its overseas operations have been expanded by opening offices in Singapore and Los Angeles. The Group also plans to diversify into garment manufacturing, and it is expected that some property development projects may be injected into the company.

Malaysian Overseas Investment Corporation (MOIC), probably Malaysia's most well known *sogoshosha*, attempted to combine ten major corporate entities, including publicly-listed Multi-Purpose Holdings, Kumpulan Guthrie Bhd, Malayan United Industries Bhd (MUI), Malaysian Mining Corporation (MMC) and Sime Darby. Three notable private limited companies were also involved – Kuok Brothers Sdn Bhd, controlled by the influential Robert Kuok, MAA Holdings Sdn Bhd, owned by Mohamad Abdullah Ang, reputedly a close friend of Prime Minister Mahathir, and Sunblest Sdn Bhd, controlled by Mohamad Hashim Shamsuddin, a former director of Bumiputera Malaysia Finance (BMF), the Hong Kong-based subsidiary of government-owned Bank Bumiputra.[6]

Incorporated in early 1983 with a paid-up capital of between RM5 and 10 million, MOIC was to spearhead Malaysia's trading and investment thrusts in the South Pacific and other Third World countries. Its first managing director was Abdullah Ang; though he resigned from the post in October 1985, he remained a minority shareholder.

By late 1984, four of MOIC's original shareholders – UMW, Pernas Sime Darby, MUI and Kuok Brothers – had sold out their interests in the company. One reason cited for their divestment was that MOIC was not fulfilling its original aim of promoting South–South cooperation and was instead concentrating on general trading, with the emphasis shifting to China (*Malaysian Business*, 16 July 1986).

By May 1986, MOIC was so immersed in debts and losses that moves were made to liquidate the company. MOIC was believed to be saddled with about RM50 million in loans that it could not repay. It was widely believed that matters might have come to a head because some of the business interests of its former managing director, Abdullah Ang, either ran parallel to or criss-crossed with those of MOIC. In July 1986, creditors agreed to the appointment of the auditing firm, Coopers & Lybrand, to liquidate the company. In late 1986, Abdullah Ang was charged and convicted in a Selangor sessions court with criminal breach of trust involving RM388,808 of MOIC funds.

CONCLUSION

Apart from Pernas Sime Darby and Mulpha International, the other Malaysian *sogoshoshas* are either defunct or keeping a low profile; none of them, however, function as major international trading companies (*Business Times*, 15 August 1990). In fact, by early July 1983, then Malaysian Deputy Foreign Minister, Kadir Sheikh Fadzir, had stated that with one exception, all Malaysian *sogoshoshas* were 'sleeping' (*New Straits Times*, 21 July 1983); in 1984, even Mahathir admitted that Malaysian *sogoshoshas* were a 'dismal failure' (*Malaysian Business*, 1 August 1984).

A number of reasons contributed to the failure of the Malaysian *sogoshoshas*. Since the owners of Malaysian *sogoshoshas* comprised large entities from both the private and public sectors, there were usually conflicts in their business operations, reflecting the shareholders' conflicting interests (*New Straits Times*, 29 February 1992). Their cooperation was thus unsuccessful as the interests of individual shareholding companies tended to take precedence over the common goals of the *sogoshoshas*. While the government had hoped that the joint venture partners would coordinate their business activities under the *sogoshoshas*, the best compromises they usually achieved among themselves were to direct some parts of new or existing businesses to the *sogoshoshas* while trying to obtain business opportunities in other trading areas (*Malaysian Business*, 1 August 1984).

Commenting on the performance of Malaysian *sogoshoshas*, Yoshihara cited two other reasons for their failure – their lack of access to finance and their limited knowledge of trading in new commodities (see *New Straits Times*, 26 August 1987). Most joint venture partners in the Malaysian *sogoshoshas* only had experience in exporting primary commodities and usually had problems securing adequate funding to finance their projects. Despite these drawbacks, a number of Malaysian *sogoshoshas* tried to expand too fast. This resulted in massive overspending which contributed to their overheads which progressively increased their losses (*New Straits Times*, 29 February 1992). In some cases, for example, MOIC, there was inadequate supervision of their operations, which contributed to the rapid collapse of the company.

Most of these *sogoshoshas* also failed to develop rapidly as their attempts to use their influence to urge the government to make it mandatory for foreign parties bidding for projects in Malaysia to source their counter purchases through Malaysian *sogoshoshas* was opposed by other Malaysian exporters and importers. These detractors argued that the government's promotion of *sogoshoshas* would lead to selective fostering of certain firms, which would in turn protect inefficiencies and force clients of these firms to pay higher prices for the services provided. There was also the danger that such measures would squeeze out small independent exporters and make local manufacturers dependent on the *sogoshoshas* for all their exports and imports.

It was also evident that these *sogoshoshas* were not supported by the government when they tried to influence changes in exchange control, and were given little support when they tried to obtain wider export credit coverage and assistance in obtaining soft loans (*Business Times*, 16 February 1985).

When considering all the problems and pressures Malaysian *sogoshoshas* have had to face, it is not surprising that none of them has earned much profit from *sogoshosha* activity. In fact, most Malaysian *sogoshoshas* have remained 'paper' companies, unlikely to do much, let alone become real *sogoshoshas*. Government leaders have been forced to acknowledge that the much-touted Malaysian *sogoshoshas* have failed to take off, and worse still, have been abused in some cases for personal gain by those entrusted with their development.

NOTES

1 However, as pointed out by Kua (1983: 279), despite the post-war occupation by the United States, most of Japan's *sogoshoshas* and *zaibatsus* (major financial cum industrial concerns) were left largely intact.

   By the early 1980s, a number of countries had begun to establish their own *sogoshoshas*. Among the countries were the United States, South Korea, Taiwan, Singapore, Brazil, Mexico, Thailand and the Philippines (*Malaysian Business*, April 1982).

2 For example, Mitsui, the oldest *sogoshosha*, was established in 1874, while Sumitomo was incorporated in 1945.

3 Marubeni, for example, had a paid-up capital of US$145 million (*Business Times*, 9 May 1983). Table 9.1 shows the gross sales of Japan's six largest *sogoshosha* in 1987.

4 Marubeni, for example, had 49 domestic offices, 80 overseas branches and offices, 210 subsidiaries and affiliates in Japan, and 156 subsidiaries and affiliates overseas. Overall, the company employed more than 10,000 workers. In the case of Mitsui, by the early 1980s, it had 181 offices overseas and more than 13,000 employees (Yoshihara, 1982: 2–3). Mitsubishi had around 200 offices worldwide, while Sumitomo has around 130 offices in 80 countries, employing 7,500 employees (*Malaysian Business*, April 1982).

5 These reasons were provided by Y. Asao, the general manager of the Asia Department of Mitsui & Co (quoted in Chee, 1985).

6 Mohamad Hashim Shamsuddin was later jailed in Hong Kong for criminal breach of trust involving funds belonging to BMF.

Table 9.1 Gross sales of Japan's six largest *sogoshoshas* in 1987 (in US$ billion)

Company	Gross sales
C. Itoh	9.9
Mitsui	9.4
Sumitomo	9.1
Marubeni	8.8
Mitsubishi	8.2
Nissho Iwai	6.7

Source: Intersect, 26 October 1990

*NOTE

This article is an edited, updated and revised version of Chee Peng Lim's 'Malaysian Sogoshoshas: No Go So Far', in Jomo K.S. (ed.), (1985) *The Sun Also Sets: Lessons in 'Looking East'*, second edition, INSAN, Petaling Jaya. *Research assistance by Shukri Rahman is gratefully acknowledged.*

REFERENCES

Chee Peng Lim (1985) 'Malaysian *Sogoshoshas*: No Go So Far', in Jomo K.S. (ed.), (1985) *The Sun Also Sets: Lessons in 'Looking East'* second edition, INSAN, Petaling Jaya.

Gale, Bruce (1985) *Politics & Business: A Study of Multi-Purpose Holdings*, Eastern Universities Press, Petaling Jaya.

Gomez, Edmund Terence (1993) 'Corporate Involvement of Political Parties in Malaysia', PhD thesis, University of Malaya, Kuala Lumpur.

Kua Kia Soong (1983) 'Why Look East', in Jomo K.S.(ed.), (1983) *The Sun Also Sets: Lessons in 'Looking East'*, INSAN, Petaling Jaya.

Mahathir Mohamad (1983) 'New Government Policies', in Jomo K.S. (1983) *The Sun Also Sets: Lessons in 'Looking East'*, INSAN, Petaling Jaya.

Yoshihara Kunio (1982) *Sogo Shosha: The Vanguard of the Japanese Economy*, Oxford University Press, Tokyo.

Newspapers and magazines

Asian Wall Street Journal
Business Times
Intersect
Malaysian Business
New Straits Times
The Star

10

HEAVY INDUSTRIALIZATION
A second round of import substitution
Chee Peng Lim

Malaysia's move into heavy industries at the beginning of the 1980s was premature. While the manufacturing sector had exhausted the limits of the initial phase, it was not yet ready to begin the steep climb towards the secondary phase. An analysis of the structure of the manufacturing sector in Malaysia towards the end of the 1970s reveals its strengths and weaknesses. Table 10.1 shows that the most important industries in Malaysia in 1978 in terms of value added were food, electrical machinery, rubber and wood products industries. Needless to say, the ranking differed when other criteria were used. Table 10.2 shows the most important industries in terms of number of establishments, total employment, value of fixed assets and revenue.

A closer examination shows that whatever the criterion used, the most important industries in Malaysia in 1978 shared certain common characteristics reflecting the shallow level of industrial development in Malaysia. First, the industries were mainly simple, light industries such as food and palm oil manufacturing. Second, the industries (such as textiles and furniture) were largely labour-intensive, making use of Malaysia's abundant labour supply. Third, the industries used simple technology and

Table 10.1 Manufacturing industries in Malaysia by value added

Industry	Value added (%)
Food	20.8
Electrical machinery	10.8
Rubber product	9.9
Wood product	9.7
Textiles	6.5
Chemicals	5.7
Others[a]	36.6
Total	100.0

Source: Department of Statistics.
[a] Each industry in this category accounts for less than 5 per cent of total value added.

244

were mainly involved in processing or assembly (example, semi-conductors and transport equipment), rather than manufacturing. Fourth, many of the industries, such as rubber and wood products made use of Malaysia's abundant natural resources. Finally, there was a relatively narrow range of industries in the Malaysian manufacturing sector. In short, manufacturing in Malaysia at the end of the 1970s was relatively 'shallow', a reflection of the immature nature and early stage of the country's industrial development.

An analysis of the manufacturing sector in terms of employment size is more revealing. Table 10.3 shows that 18,278 manufacturing establishments in Malaysia employed less than 50 workers each in 1982, indicating that the establishments were predominantly small. The proportion was unlikely to be significantly different if other measurements of size, such as value of fixed assets were used. More significantly, Table 10.3 shows that although there was a predominance of small establishments in the manufacturing sector, their contribution to output was relatively low. More specifically, although small firms accounted for nearly 75 per cent of all manufacturing firms in Malaysia in 1982, their total value added accounted for less than 10 per cent of total manufacturing value added. The relatively low contribution of the small industry sector to manufacturing output in Malaysia may be explained by the use of traditional techniques of production and inadequate access to capital and modern machinery (Chee Peng Lim, 1986). In short, at the beginning of the 1980s, the small industry sector in Malaysia had not been modernized and had yet to make a significant contribution to industrial development. Consequently, small industry would impose a constraint on the country's effort to enter the secondary stage of industrial development. The reason is that the secondary stage of industrial development involves the participation of an extensive network of modern ancillary firms able to supply high quality components or parts at competitive prices. At the end of the 1970s, the small industry sector in Malaysia was unable to play that vital role.

Another constraint on Malaysia's efforts to proceed to the secondary stage of industrial development has been the lack of research and development (R&D) facilities and a shortage of skilled manpower. Like many other developing countries, Malaysia had been spending a miniscule amount of official development expenditure estimated at less than 0.2 per cent of GNP on R&D. Moreover, a major part of its R&D expenditure is not put into critical industries such as foundry, engineering or machinery, but in agriculture instead (Chee Peng Lim, 1987a,b). Some part of this expenditure, e.g. on the Rubber Research Institute, has been cost-effective, but it has little relevance to the needs of the heavy industries Malaysia was trying to develop.

Furthermore, Malaysia was not spending enough money to train high level manpower. Table 10.4 shows that in terms of number of students enrolled in higher education as a percentage of population, the figure for

Table 10.2 Structure of manufacturing industry in Malaysia, 1981

No. of establishment	
Custom tailoring and dress making	(2,075)
Manufacture of furniture and fixtures, except primarily of metal	(1,711)
Machinery and equipment, n.e.s.	(1,139)
Total employment (no. of workers)	
Semi-conductors and other electronic components and communication equipment and apparatus	(60,791)
Sawmills	(44,326)
Printing, publishing and allied industries	(25,876)
Value of fixed assets (thousand ringgit)	
Palm oil manufacturing	(972,501)
Sawmills	(576,215)
Semi-conductors and other electrical components and communication equipment and apparatus	(534,839)
Revenue (thousand ringgit)	
Palm oil manufacturing	(4,497,187)
Petroleum refineries	(4,101,764)
Semi-conductors and other electronic components and communication equipment and apparatus	(3,425,204)

Source: Department of Statistics.

Malaysia (an upper middle income country) was not different from some low income countries such as Burma or Guinea. In 1981, Malaysia's figure was extremely low, even compared with neighbouring countries such as Thailand or the Philippines.

It would appear from the above analysis of the nature and structure of the manufacturing sector in Malaysia, and the two major constraints, at the end of the 1970s, the manufacturing sector was not yet ready to proceed with the development of heavy industries. Nevertheless, the government decided to push on with its heavy industrialization strategy.

The Government's rationale for introducing heavy industries to Malaysia was spelt out in the 1984 *Mid-Term Review of the Fourth Malaysia Plan, 1981–1985*, which stated that:

The Government has been promoting the development of heavy industries in order to strengthen the foundation of the manufacturing sector. Heavy industries are needed to create new engines of growth and to provide strong forward and backward linkages for the development of industries. Heavy industries can also have substantial effects on the growth of small-scale industries if efforts are made to establish linkages and integrate small-scale industries development with heavy industries. Projects that are planned or being implemented

Table 10.3 Number and value added of manufacturing establishments by
employment size group, 1982

Total employment size group	*No. of establishments*	*%*	*Value added (RM 000)*	*%*
Below 5	208	2.5	995	0.1
5–9	1,091	13.1	17,077	1.1
10–19	2,450	29.4	34,296	2.3
20–29	1,254	15.0	29,093	1.9
30–49	1,202	14.4	63,873	4.3
Below 50	6,205	74.4	145,334	9.7
50–99	1,063	12.7	124,681	8.3
100–199	625	7.5	201,908	13.5
200–499	301	3.6	328,726	21.9
500–999	103	1.2	301,429	20.1
1,000 and above	46	0.6	395,209	26.4
50 and above	2,138	25.6	1,351,953	90.2
Total	8,343	100.0	1,497,287	100.0

Source: Department of Statistics.

include cement plants, sponge iron plants, a cold rolling mill, a
methanol plant, an ammonia–urea plant, a pulp and paper plant, a
petrochemical complex, an automobile plant and energy-related
projects to service these industries (Malaysia, 1984: 271). (For further
details of Malaysia's heavy industry policy and programme, see INTAN,
1984).

The Government had established the Heavy Industries Corporation of
Malaysia (HICOM) in 1980 with an authorized capital of RM500 million
(RM: Malaysian ringgit). It decided to take the initiative in establishing
heavy industries for various reasons, and especially because heavy industry
projects are generally large-scale, and require huge investment outlays, have
long gestation periods and offer relatively low rates of return. Finally, in
view of their strategic importance, the Government wanted to exercise
ownership, control and management of major heavy industry projects (Lee,
1981: 3).

An initial allocation of RM125 million was provided to HICOM under
the Fourth Malaysia Plan (Malaysia, 1981). Following its inception, a
number of projects were identified for study and assessment by HICOM.
The projects covered various key industries, such as basic metal, including
iron and steel and non-ferrous metals, manufacture of machinery and
equipment, general engineering, transport equipment, building materials,

247

Table 10.4 Percentage of students enrolled in higher education in selected countries, 1960–81

Country	Number enrolled in higher education as % of population aged 20–24	
	1960	1981
Bangladesh	1	3
Nepal	1	3
Burma	1	4
India	3	8
Guinea	–	5
Sri Lanka	1	3
Bolivia	4	12
Honduras	1	8
Egypt, Arab Republic	5	15
Thailand	2	20
Philippines	13	26
Malaysia	1	5
Korea, Republic of	5	18
Hong Kong	4	10
Singapore	6	8
Japan	10	30
USA	32	58

Source: World Bank (1984).

paper and paper products, and petrochemicals (for details, see Chee Peng Lim, 1987a: 98–9).

Following its inception, HICOM invested over RM2 billion and by early 1988, it had set up nine companies employing a total of 4,350 workers (Table 10.5). Apart from HICOM Properties Sdn Bhd, which was established to develop industrial land and residential units for heavy industries, and EON, which was set up to distribute the national car product, all the other companies were involved in manufacturing of products such as cement, steel, motor vehicle and motorcycle engines. Kedah Cement was the first heavy industry project to go onstream, followed by the Perwaja Trengganu steel plant, the national motor vehicle plant, Proton and three motorcycle engine manufacturing joint ventures.

Obviously, the heavy industries projects implemented by HICOM do not constitute the entire universe of heavy industries in Malaysia. Some heavy industries had been established before HICOM was set up, e.g. Malayawata Steel Mill, founded in 1961; while others did not come under HICOM, e.g. Malaysia Shipyard and Engineering (MSE). Nevertheless, the establishment of HICOM and the implementation of its various projects marked the first major Malaysian thrust into heavy industries.

At its inception, HICOM was one of twenty selected public enterprises in which the Ministry of Finance was a major shareholder. As a major shareholder, the Ministry appointed the Board of Directors of HICOM and had a direct say in the appointment of its first Chief Executive, who turned out to be a former civil servant. The Ministry of Finance was also involved in HICOM providing subsidized loans or guaranteeing foreign loans. The loans were provided directly to HICOM and the loan rates were generally about 2–4 per cent lower than market rates.

The Implementation and Coordination Unit (ICU) in the Prime Minister's Department has been responsible for controlling HICOM. The ICU is considered a 'watchdog' for all government projects and has a unit responsible for all non-financial public enterprises, including HICOM. The ICU exercises its control through reviewing annual reports, ex-post evaluation and financing approval for new projects. However, the firms under the ICU have been powerful and relatively autonomous. Their personnel policies have been shaped more by the private sector than by government departments or statutory bodies. The ICU has not been able to develop a systematic performance evaluation system which takes into account the different objectives of the various non-financial public enterprises and to hold management responsible for results. The ICU has also been hampered in its control functions by insufficient resources and professional staff. Nevertheless, it appears that the Government was directly in charge of implementation of the heavy industries policy with little or no participation by the private sector.[1] This was probably one of the major factors contributing to problems in the implementation of the heavy industry programme in Malaysia.

Although Malaysia has not had much success in managing public enterprises, the Government was committed to the domination of public enterprises throughout the 1970s and up to the early 1980s. By 1987, there were 867 corporate public enterprises in Malaysia (more than a third of which were in manufacturing) with total sales in excess of RM26,227 million and a total government investment of RM7.8 billion at its peak in 1984. The inefficiency and mismanagement of public enterprises had not yet become public knowledge and the economy was still buoyant enough to withstand the financial losses caused by such enterprises. Thus, the Government bravely pushed on with its heavy industries policy, compounding its error by directly owning and managing the heavy industry projects.

Other factors which created problems for the heavy industry projects in Malaysia included wrong choice of industries, poor timing and lack of preparation. First, like most governments, involvement in heavy industries did not reflect an ability to 'pick winners' or successfully manage enterprises. In fact, most of the heavy industries which HICOM selected for development were 'born losers'. This applied particularly to the motor

Table 10.5 Manpower of the HICOM group of companies (as at 29 February 1988)

Companies	No. of workers	Technical/ supervisory (% of total)	Managerial
Hicom	147	7	24
Kedah Cement Sdn Bhd	383	28	6
Perwaja Trengganu Sdn Bhd	817	18	7
Hicom-Properties Sdn Bhd	9	–	–
Perusahaan Otomobil Nasional Sdn Bhd	1,353	7	8
Edaran Otomobil Nasional Sdn Bhd	1,284	3	1
Hicom-Yamaha Manufacturing (M) Sdn Bhd	63	8	6
Hicom-Honda Manufacturing (M) Sdn Bhd	59	18	–
Petro-Pipe Industries (M) Sdn Bhd	202	–	–
Hicom-Suzuki Manufacturing (M) Sdn Bhd	33	10	–
Total	4,350	–	–

vehicle plant and the steel plant complex. (For a critique of the motor vehicle plant, see Chee Peng Lim, 1983, 1984a,b.)

In addition, the timing could not have been worse. Many of the heavy industry projects were launched on the eve of a global recession which subsequently had a severe impact on the Malaysian economy. The motor vehicle project was among the most adversely affected, with projected market demand nowhere near the highly optimistic crude projections made on the assumption of an ever growing economy. A significant fall in the prices of tin and palm oil, which were among Malaysia's main exports in the mid-1980s, caused a severe recession which resulted in new vehicle sales falling by half! Lower than expected sales were compounded by chronic mismanagement of the inexperienced public officials seconded to HICOM ('Child of Nippon', *Far Eastern Economic Review*, 11 May 1991: 70).

Kedah Cement also had to cope with overcapacity. Domestic cement-producing capacity by 1986 was 6.9 million metric tons, with domestic consumption at only 2.7 million metric tons. Similarly, Sabah Gas was expected to break even if the price of methanol was US$180 per ton; however, the price prevailing then was only US$70 per ton.

Second, hardly any measures were undertaken to prepare the economy and manufacturing sector for the entry of the heavy industries. Despite much rhetoric and piecemeal effort, little was really done to implement an effective small industry policy. The weakness of small industry in precision moulding and press-die manufacturing amply illustrates the position of small industry in Malaysia. A recent study shows that small companies in these sub-sectors are still unable to deliver the quality and quantity of the products required by their customers. According to the study, those companies are undercapitalized and lack experience in modern production techniques. (For details, see 'In the same mould', *Far Eastern Economic Review*, 30 January 1992: 45.) In addition, the Government failed to commit adequate resources to human resource development for skill training, while budget allocations for research and development remained at a pathetic level. The efficient operation of heavy industries requires large numbers of highly skilled, technical, engineering, managerial and experienced shop supervisory personnel. For example, in view of its technological complexity and capital intensity, and the adverse effects of any unscheduled stoppage of production, the operation of a petrochemical plant is highly dependent on qualified and skilled personnel. Unfortunately, at the end of the 1970s, Malaysia suffered from a general shortage of skilled labour, especially skilled metal tradesmen, maintenance tradesmen, mechanical engineers and experienced managers. At the same time, because of the absence of any significant R&D activities in heavy industries, reliance was placed largely on imported technology. Expertise was not even available to assess some of the imported technology, such as the process proposed for the Perwaja Steel Mill. As a result, no serious reservations were raised over the commercially untested experimental technology imported from Nippon Steel for the RM1.1 billion Perwaja steel plant. The technology failed. Although operational losses were partly covered by compensational clauses, which did not anticipate the severe ringgit depreciation against the yen from 1985, the closing down of the direct reduction plant meant that Perwaja Steel had to operate entirely with scrap metal (instead of only 20 per cent as envisaged in the original plan). There is not much scrap on the East Coast where the plant is located and little demand for the billets produced. Therefore, transport costs alone currently come to RM60 per ton.

Similarly, Kedah Cement's problems have been exacerbated because its plant is on the island of Langkawi, off the west coast of northern Peninsular Malaysia. Though the island is endowed with a ready supply of limestone, the plant's location has raised transport supply costs for some major consumption hubs.

Sabah Forest Industries (SFI) is another example of flawed conception. Built at a cost of RM1.4 billion, it is owned entirely by the State Government of Sabah. However, the Treasury is the guarantor of the loan. Designed to produce pulp and paper from tropical hardwood, the company has been plagued by problems with the installed machinery, which was not tested due to a dispute between the management and the supplier over its appropriateness. The Treasury ended up paying the interest and principal on the loans it guaranteed.

Third, several of HICOM's projects involved high debt gearing; the debt–equity structure averaged 70:30, with the debt mostly denominated in foreign currencies. The high debt gearing, combined with the subsequent appreciation of the yen against the ringgit (by about 100 per cent) created severe financial problems for the projects concerned. For example, Kedah Cement's over-capacity problem was exacerbated by overborrowing in yen-denominated loans.

Finally, another major problem faced by heavy industries in Malaysia has been the relatively small size of the domestic market. With a population of less than 14 million in 1980 and a relatively small domestic market, it has not been easy for many heavy industries to operate at a minimum efficient scale of operation. For example, the minimum efficient scale of operation for a motor vehicle plant is said to be 250,000 units a year (Karmokolias, 1990: 6); the total demand for new motor vehicles in Malaysia in 1981 was less than half this level and was only slightly higher a decade later. Similarly, a large market is an important consideration for petrochemical production facilities. Fortunately, in this case, the constraint is more flexible. A developing country like Malaysia, where the thermo-plastics per capita consumption is less than tenth that of a developed country, can still hope to establish a viable petrochemical plant if it has surplus oil and if the facility is planned largely for export. This may be possible with the availability of cheap, wasted raw materials like flared gas and joint venture arrangements with multinational corporations responsible for marketing the products. Furthermore, in the case of petrochemicals, local production may stimulate demand not only in existing consumption sectors but also in new sectors where other natural materials are required.

In view of the above problems, it was not surprising that soon after their implementation, three of HICOM's projects ran into serious problems. Kedah Cement, the national car project and the Perwaja Trengganu steel project suffered severe cash flow problems and losses of RM103.4 million, RM42.5 million and RM42 million respectively in 1986.[2] As a result of their financial problems, the heavy industries affected had to restructure their debts. For example, Kedah Cement was forced to refinance RM315 million (or 62 per cent) of its RM507 million total debt.

The financial losses incurred by several of HICOM's projects have not only intensified the drain on the Treasury, but have also partly contributed to the significant increase in the country's external debt in the 1980s. In addition, the heavy industries strategy has created other problems for the economy. For example, the emergence of heavily financed public enterprises has tended to crowd out financially less well-endowed private enterprises. In addition to crowding out in factor markets, the spectre of heavily protected huge public corporations has generated uncertainty about factor costs as well as the potential for future sales and profits. Entrepreneurs have had to include another imponderable in their calculations of sales, margins and returns in the domestic market.

Consequently, the Government-led heavy industries strategy may have unwittingly discouraged domestic investment and dampened private enterprise in the 1980s.

Fortunately, in spite of the above problems, some of the heavy industries have managed to score a few successes after initial failures. For example, Malaysia Shipyard and Engineering (MSE), long regarded as a chronic money loser among Malaysia's heavy industry projects, finally sailed into the black after fifteen years in the red. In 1990, MSE netted RM335.3 million from its main operational activities compared with the recessionary years of 1986–87, when it was down in the dumps, with a RM21.9 million loss. Now MSE, based in Pasir Gudang, Johor, is expected to take on more challenges in furthering its commercial activities, having evolved into the premier shipyard in the country for ship repairing, construction and engineering. It may have reached a point where it can be a serious competitor to shipyards in other Southeast Asian countries.

Several factors have contributed to MSE's recent success. The recession forced the company to shed its 'excess load', which included a major staff retrenchment exercise affecting 600 of its previous 1,700 strong work force. The dedication and experience of its remaining workers have complemented the modern equipment which MSE acquired, contributing to the turnaround in its fortunes. Since 1990, the shipyard has been working at maximum capacity, catering for five ships at a time. Because of the congestion and great demand for its services, MSE has begun expanding its shipyard, which is expected to be completed soon.

Of the 1990 profit, RM145.9 million came from ship repairing, RM74.2 million from shipbuilding, RM16.5 million from related services, RM96.9 million from the engineering division and RM1.8 million from other sources such as scrap and equipment lease. Importantly, 90 per cent of the profits from the ship repair division was derived from work on foreign merchant vessels, and the rest from local ships. The shipbuilding division has also made a fair contribution to MSE's revenue, increasing from RM51.3 million in 1989 to RM74.2 million in 1990. Since it began operations in 1980, 43 vessels of various types have been built, including fast patrol craft, ferries, dredges, tugboats and sophisticated naval vessels.

Although MSE faces strong competition, especially from Singapore and South Korea, it has a comparative advantage in lower labour and material costs. It expects to see a multifold growth in its profits when it becomes involved, together with an Indonesian firm, in the construction of a cargo ship worth RM25 million. Also MSE has obtained a firm tender for the construction of two container cranes, which is to be undertaken as a joint venture with companies from Germany and Argentina. The shipyard claims a first in building Malaysia's own deep-sea fishing boat, the 500-ton K.L. Paus.

Like MSE, Perwaja Steel also suffered heavy losses at the beginning and also had to contend with a serious technology problem. However, in the year ended 31 March 1989, Perwaja posted a maiden profit of RM23.5 million. Since then, it has embarked on a RM1 billion expansion programme which will use a commercially tested Mexican direct-production process. The aim was to increase billet production from 1 million tonnes in 1991 to 1.2 million tonnes by 1992. Perwaja has also built a 400,000-tonne, RM450 million rolling mill in Trengganu to make wires for car and motorcycle parts, its first venture into downstream long products, which was due to come into operation in 1991 ('The lion's share', *Far Eastern Economic Review*, 30 May 1991: 67). In addition, Perwaja also wants to start exporting high value products, such as automotive parts, steel wire and other high quality products.

Perwaja's recovery came at a time when the steel market in Malaysia and the Southeast Asian region has been rapidly expanding. Malaysia's sustained recovery from its 1985–86 recession, and vigorous demand for steel products in the ASEAN region, have set off a surge of interest in foreign and domestic investment in Malaysian steelmaking. In the last few years, the economy has been increasingly driven by manufactured exports, which now account for more than half of all exports (compared with 22 per cent in 1980). A report by Morgan Grenfell Securities has estimated that domestic steel demand in Malaysia will double in this decade ('The millers' trail', *Far Eastern Economic Review*, 19 July 1990: 38). The forecast is based on a gross domestic product (GDP) growth rate of 6.1 per cent a year, which may be rather conservative. Other analysts say that steel consumption will grow at a rate of 8–10 per cent a year during the same period. Most probably, consumption will rise to 4–5 million tonnes from over 2 million tonnes at present (Figure 10.1). (Another way of predicting Malaysia's potential for a rapid take-off in steel consumption is to compare it with the more developed Asian economies, which have gone further down the road to industrialization. The Morgan Grenfell report found per capita steel consumption in Malaysia to be less than one-third that in the Republic of Korea and Hong Kong, and only 20 per cent of the level in Singapore and Japan.)

Apart from the growth potential of the domestic market, many Malaysian and foreign steel executives seem to have decided that Malaysia can become a base for steel exports to Southeast Asia and other parts of the Asia-Pacific region. Malaysia is favoured to command a fair share of the region's demand for steel imports now being satisfied by the world's largest steel producers. Low labour costs and cheap natural gas, which can be used to power the downstream finishing mills that make up an integrated steel complex, will help Malaysia overcome the disadvantages of not having a plentiful supply of iron ore and coking coal, the main raw materials in steel-making. In view of these bright prospects, several foreign companies have expressed interest in financing steel mills in Malaysia. These include the

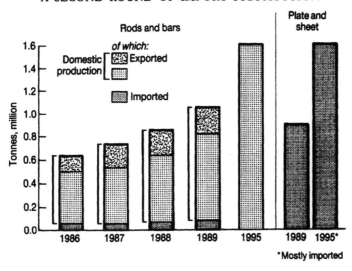

Figure 10.1 Steel consumption in Malaysia, 1986–95.
Source: MIDA, Amalgamated Steel Mills.

now aborted US$3.2 billion joint venture between Taiwan's state-owned China Steel Corp. and Malaysia's Lion Group, South Korea's Pohang Iron and Steel Co.'s proposed US$1.1 billion, 700,000 tonne-a-year cold-rolling mill in Johore and China's largest steelmaker, Anshan Steel's 200,000 tonne-a-year cold-rolling mill in a joint venture with the Trengganu State government.

Success may have been more limited for Proton, the national car manufacturer, since it is neither blessed with the prospects of a rapidly expanding market nor any particular competitive advantage. Nevertheless, after years of losses, Proton has finally started to make a profit. In March 1989, the company announced a net profit of RM32.5 million, compared with a RM58.5 million loss the previous year. There have been several reasons for Proton's improved fortunes at this juncture. The first is the heavy protection for Proton's vehicles. While Proton's rivals have to pay a 40 per cent import duty on the parts kits which they import to assemble vehicles for sale in Malaysia, Proton has been exempted from paying duty on the kits it buys from Mitsubishi and pays only half the normal excise duty on other imported components. ('Child of Nippon', *Far Eastern Economic Review*, 11 May 1991: 70). The second was a bold decision by the Prime Minister in 1988 to invite a minority partner, Mitsubishi Motor Corporation to resume control of Proton from HICOM. A third factor has been the domestic car market's gradual recovery from the recession of the mid-1980s. Total passenger car sales plunged to 38,000 in 1987, compared with 96,200 in 1983. Since then, strong economic growth and improvement in consumer buying power and attractive credit facilities have revived car sales. With official approval for a second smaller Malaysian-made car project, it is doubtful if the domestic market will ever expand enough to enable Proton to achieve the minimum efficient scale economies, though this can be achieved through greatly increased exports. Here again, Proton scored a major success when it received Generalised System of Preference (GSP) status from the UK for its seven models, all of which fulfill the UK's local content requirements. (Under British law, at least 60 per cent of a vehicle must be produced domestically before it can qualify under the GSP.) Following this, Proton has exported several thousand cars to the UK, and seems poised to increase its market share. Until then, the company had to be content with total export sales of slightly more than 1,000 cars to various countries like Malta, Bangladesh, Brunei and New Zealand ('Malaysia poised for robust growth', *Far East Business*, March 1989: 14).

Proton's success has to be qualified. Financially, the maiden profit which the company earned in 1989 was unable to cover the RM133 million in accumulated debt from its first three years of money-losing operations. More seriously, the profit was partly achieved through a book-keeping exercise by which Proton has simply charged its semi-independent domestic distributor, EON, a higher transfer price for its cars ('Saga of recovery', *Far Eastern Economic Review*, 3 August 1989: 40). Steep production costs at home (owing to low volume) and the high cost of imported components limit Proton's competitiveness in the British market. Also exports have not necessarily been beneficial to the balance sheet as the company loses money on each vehicle exported to the UK since the car sells at a slightly lower price than in Malaysia. Moreover, certain modifications in the export model's body shape and interior control panel configuration, required to satisfy British safety regulations, make it more expensive to build than models for domestic sale. Plans for breaking into the lucrative US market, originally a higher priority than the British market, have disappeared in a morass of recriminations and lawsuits between Proton and its putative US distributor, Malcolm Bricklin, who also had the US franchise for the ill-fated Yugo. While it is questionable that the Proton would have been competitive in the tough US market, it would have required additional expenses to make the necessary engineering changes required for US sales. The harsh reality is that, as noted earlier when the project was first proposed (Chee Peng Lim, 1983), Malaysia has been and will remain too small a market to achieve the economies of scale demanded by modern car manufacturing plants. According to an IFC study, 'Experience has demonstrated . . . that few countries can support an economically viable automotive industry and, fewer still, automobile manufacturing' (Karmokolias, 1990: 1; UNCTAD, 1991; Doner, 1991). Thus, Proton's future will be continuously dependent on high tariff barriers for its continued viability. While many other developing Asian countries share Malaysia's ambition to export cars, only South Korea seems to have made a recent breakthrough into manufacturing its own vehicles.

Although it may be premature to judge Malaysia's heavy industrialization strategy, some tentative assessments are possible. Whatever the success achieved by some of the heavy industry projects in Malaysia, they cannot disguise the problems and heavy costs which these projects have imposed on the economy. Undoubtedly, some employment, exports, skills and scale economies have been generated but these have been achieved at a considerable expense. For example, by 1988 HICOM had invested RM2 billion in various projects which generated less than 5,000 jobs directly, i.e. an investment–employment ratio of RM400,000 per job; exports have been almost negligible, although some technical and managerial skills have been generated. On the other side of the balance sheet, HICOM's investments have been a severe drain on the Treasury and greatly contributed to the significant increase in Malaysia's external debt in the mid-1980s. Malaysia's external debt reached a peak of RM28 billion in 1986, from less than RM5 billion in 1980 (Bank Negara Malaysia, *Quarterly Bulletin*, March–June 1990: 69).

The inefficient heavy industry projects have also burdened downstream industries, which are forced to pay higher prices for the protected products. For example, the higher costs of cement and steel have been passed on to the construction and engineering industries respectively.

Most important of all is the opportunity cost. If the RM2 billion had been spent to set up a Small Industry Corporation of Malaysia (or SICOM) instead of HICOM, Malaysia's small industry sector might have been modernized by now and the country's chances of achieving greater success with a heavy industrialization policy implemented later might have been more favourable.

Nevertheless, the heavy industries policy may still be a blessing in disguise since the severe fiscal deficit and record level of external debt, for which it was greatly responsible, forced the Government to reconsider its policy of stimulating economic growth through substantial foreign borrowings and large scale public sector investment in heavy industries. Consequently, as the economy emerged from the mid-1980s recession, the Government has committed itself to the reduction of the public sector's role in the economy through a massive privatization programme and tighter budgetary controls. This shift in government policy augurs well for the manufacturing sector in the coming decade.

CONCLUSION

Developing countries looking to Malaysia as a role model for industrial development can draw at least two useful lessons from the country's experience with heavy industries. First, adequate preparations are imperative before embarking on heavy industrialization. It is foolhardy to develop heavy industries simply because the economy has reached the limits of earlier industrial development. Adequate and intensive prepara- tions have to be made, at least with respect to technology and human resource development as well as the modernization of small industry before developing heavy industry. Heavy industries require a high degree of technical, managerial and marketing expertise. Accordingly, there is a need to strengthen these skills for the effective operation of heavy industries. At the same time, domestic technological capacity has to be enhanced in order to achieve greater self-reliance and international competitiveness. All these preparations should accompany the modernization of small industry, which have to play a significant role in the efficient operation of heavy industries. Thus, the planning and development of heavy industries should incorporate plans for ancillary firm development, which can be part of an overall promotional package for small industry development.

Secondly, where Government intervention has not proved to be efficiently and effectively pro-active, the implementation of heavy industries should rely more on market forces and private enterprise, rather than Government.

Finally, Malaysia has learned from its own experience with heavy industries and is now laying a stronger foundation for entry into technologically intensive industries. The prospects for success in this phase should be more favourable since the Government will not only be relying more on the private sector, but has also made more intensive preparations. Continued success in the emerging global environment will depend on the degree to which Malaysia can base its future industrialization strategy on long-term comparative advantage, rather than on short-term investment returns or prestige projects. The emergence of the ASEAN Free Trade Area (AFTA) can help promote the joint development of heavy and technology intensive industries, which rely greatly on economies of scale for competitive advantage.

This is the revised draft of a paper presented at the Institute of Strategic and International Studies (ISIS) Malaysia and Harvard Institute for International Development joint seminar in Kuala Lumpur on 1–3 June 1992. The views expressed by the author are solely his own and do not necessarily reflect those of the UN-ESCAP Secretariat where the author is attached.

NOTES

1 The heavy industrialization period in Malaysia coincided with the end of an era when the Government was heavily involved in economic activities. The public sector's share in Malaysia, as measured by total public sector (development and ordinary) expenditure as a percentage of gross national product (GNP), rose from about 30 per cent in the 1960s to well over 50 per cent in the early 1980s.

The recession forced the public sector to contract to its present level of around 30 per cent. The upward trend of public sector spending was a result of increasing state intervention under the New Economic Policy, while the explosion of government expenditure in the period 1980–82 was not only due to the Government's involvement in heavy industries, but also to counter-cyclical macroeconomic management. Behind the figures of public sector expansion during the last three decades is the activist role of the developmental state in economic policy-making, interest-intermediation on behalf of ethnic communities, especially in carving out strategic access for the economically backward *Bumiputera* community, and in the production and provision of social and physical infrastructure. (For details, see Mehmet, 1986.)

2 Malaysia is not the only developing country which made a precipitated rush into heavy industries. Neighbouring Indonesia also adopted a similar strategy at about the same time, and subsequently had to rephase or cancel several heavy industry projects which had caused an intolerable strain on the economy. In South Korea, the heavy industry strategy had mixed results. While boosting private investments to record levels, it introduced, in its wake, a whole range of distortions in the industrial sector of the economy, which went into a recession in 1980; following a harvest failure, the Government began to review its heavy industrialization strategy. Although technology development remains a top priority, subsequent industrial policy efforts de-emphasized the development of heavy industries, and recent interventions have been conducted along 'functional', rather than industry-specific lines. (For details, see Leipziger, 1988: 121–35.)

REFERENCES

Ariff, M. and Hill, H. (1986) 'A factor-intensity analysis of structural change in ASEAN manufacturing', *Industry and Development*, No. 19: 77–102.

Bank Negara Malaysia (1992) *Annual Report 1991*, Kuala Lumpur.

Chee Peng Lim (1979) 'Small Industry: Its Role in Malaysian Industrial Development', in Cheong Kee Cheok (ed.), *Malaysia: Some Contemporary Issues in Socio-Economic Development*, Malaysian Economic Association, Kuala Lumpur.

Chee Peng Lim (1982) 'From Import Substitution to Export Promotion: A Study of Changes in Malaysia's Industrial Policy', in K. Yoneda (ed.), *Trade and Industrial Policies of Asian Countries*, Institute of Developing Economies, Tokyo: 41–98.

Chee Peng Lim (1983) 'The Malaysian Car Dream: a Need for Reconsideration', in Jomo K.S. (ed.), *The Sun Also Sets*, INSAN, Kuala Lumpur.

Chee Peng Lim (1984a) 'The Malaysian Motor Vehicle Industry at the Crossroads: Time to Change Gear?' in Lim Lin Lean and Chee Peng Lim (eds.), *The Malaysian Economy at the Crossroads*, Malaysian Economic Association, Kuala Lumpur: 437–54.

Chee Peng Lim (1984b) 'The Malaysian Car Project: Problems and Prospects', Paper presented at the Institute of Strategic and International Studies (ISIS) workshop on the Malaysian Car, 10 October, Kuala Lumpur.

Chee Peng Lim (1984c) 'Changes in the Malaysian Economy and Trade Trends and Prospects', Paper presented at international conference on the 'Global Implications of the Trade Patterns of East and Southeast Asia', organized by National Bureau of Economic Research, Kuala Lumpur.

Chee Peng Lim (1984d) 'Industrialization in Malaysia – Perception and Policy: Preparing Malaysia for Heavy Industry', Paper presented at seminar on

'Population and Demographic Issues in Malaysian Industrialization', Port Dickson, Malaysia, 6–8 December.

Chee Peng Lim (1986) *Small Industry in Malaysia: Profile, Problems and Policies*, Berita Publishing, Kuala Lumpur.

Chee Peng Lim (1987a) *The Malaysian Industrial Master Plan*, Pelanduk Publications, Kuala Lumpur.

Chee Peng Lim (1987b) 'Science, Technology and Development: ASEAN Regional Cooperation', *Development & South–South Cooperation*, Vol. III, No. 5 (December): 147–78.

Chee Peng Lim (1988) 'Foreign Investments in Malaysia: Changes in Policy and Pattern', *East Asian International Review of Economic, Political and Social Development*, vol. 3: 109–35.

Chee Peng Lim and Fong Chan Onn (1983) 'Ancillary Firm Development in the Malaysian Motor Vehicle Industry', in K. Odaka (ed.), *The Motor Vehicle Industry in Asia: A Study of Ancillary Firm Development*, University of Singapore Press, Singapore: 85–109.

Chee Peng Lim *et al.* (1979), *A Study of Small Entrepreneurs and Entrepreneurial Development Programmes in Malaysia*, University of Malaya Press, Kuala Lumpur.

Chen, E.K.Y. (1977) 'Domestic Saving and Capital Inflow in Some Asian Countries: A Time-Series Study', *Asian Survey*, July.

Chen, E.K.Y. (1980) 'Export Expansion and Economic Growth in Some Asian Countries: A Simultaneous-equation Model', in R.C.O. Mathews (ed.), *Measurement, History and Factors of Economic Growth*, Macmillan, London.

Department of Statistics, Malaysia (1984), *Industrial Survey 1982*, Kuala Lumpur.

Doner, Richard F. (1991) *Driving a Bargain: Automobile Industrialization and Japanese Firms in Southeast Asia*, University of California Press, Berkeley.

Edwards, C.B. (1975) 'Protection, Profits and Policy – An Analysis of Industrialization in Malaysia', PhD dissertation, University of East Anglia, Norwich, UK.

Garnaut R. and K. Anderson (1980) 'ASEAN Export Specialization and the Evolution of Comparative Advantage in the Western Pacific Region', in R. Garnaut (ed.), *ASEAN in a Changing Pacific and World Economy*, Australian National University Press, Canberra: 374–413.

Hoffman, L. and J.E. Tan (1980) *Industrial Growth, Employment and Foreign Investment in Peninsular Malaysia*, Oxford University Press, Kuala Lumpur.

INTAN (1984) 'Prospects for Heavy Industry in Malaysia', Kuala Lumpur (mimeo).

Ismail Md. Salleh (1991) 'Privatisation: the Malaysian Experience', in H. Yokoyama and M. Tamin (eds), *Malaysian Economy in Transition*, Institute of Developing Economies, Tokyo.

Jones, R.W. (1971) 'A Three-factor Model in Theory, Trade and History', in J. Bhagwati and others (eds), *Trade, Balance of Payments and Growth*, North Holland Publishing, Amsterdam.

Jomo K.S. (1990) *Growth and Structural Change in the Malaysian Economy*, Macmillan, London.

Karmokolias, Y. (1990) 'Automobile Industry: Trends and Prospects for Investment in Developing Countries', IFC Discussion paper, No. 7, International Finance Corporation, Washington DC.

Khor Kok Peng (1984) 'Industrial Policy in Malaysia – Problems and Prospects', Paper presented at the Malaysian Economic Association – FEA Symposium on 'Issues and Prospects Towards An Industrialized Nation', Kuala Lumpur, 31 July.

Krueger, A.O. (1977) *Growth, Distortions and Patterns of Trade among Many Countries*, Princeton Studies in International Finance, No. 40, Princeton University Press, Princeton, New Jersey.

Krueger, A.O. (1981), 'Export-Led Industrial Growth Reconsidered', in W. Hong and L.B. Krause, (eds), *Trade and Growth of the Advanced Developing Countries in the Pacific Basin*, Korea Development Institute, Seoul.

Lee Cheng Tiong (1981) 'Role of Government in the Heavy Industries', Paper presented at AIESEC Seminar on 'Heavy Industries: Vision of the 1980s', Kuala Lumpur, 17 October.

Lee Kiong Hock (1984) 'Malaysian Manufacturing Sector Protection: Ideas, Structure, Causes and Effects', Faculty of Economics & Administration, University of Malaya (mimeo).

Leipziger, D.M. (1988) 'Industrial restructuring in Korea', *World Development*, Vol. 16, No. 1, January: 121–135.

Lew Sip Hon (1980) 'Industrialization Policies for the Eighties', Paper presented at the Sixth Malaysian Economic Convention, Penang, May.

Lim D. (1973) *Economic Growth and Development in West Malaysia*, Oxford University Press, Kuala Lumpur.

Lim Lin Lean and Chee Peng Lim (eds) (1984) *The Malaysian Economy at the Crossroads*, Malaysian Economic Association, Kuala Lumpur.

Malaysia (1971), *Second Malaysia Plan, 1971–1975*, Government Printers, Kuala Lumpur.

Malaysia (1979) *Mid-term Review of the Third Malaysia Plan*, Government Printers, Kuala Lumpur.

Malaysia (1981) *Fourth Malaysia Plan, 1981–1985*, Government Printers, Kuala Lumpur.

Malaysia (1984) *Mid-term Review of the Fourth Malaysia Plan, 1981–1985*, Government Printers, Kuala Lumpur.

Malaysia (1986) *Fifth Malaysia Plan, 1986–1990*, Government Printers, Kuala Lumpur.

Malaysia (1989) *Mid-term Review of the Fifth Malaysia Plan, 1986–1990*, Government Printers, Kuala Lumpur.

Malaysia (1991) *Sixth Malaysia Plan, 1991–1995*, Government Printers, Kuala Lumpur.

McTaggart, William Donald (1972) *Industrial Development in West Malaysia, 1968*, Center for Asian Studies, Arizona State University.

Mehmet, Ozay (1986) *Development in Malaysia: Poverty, Wealth and Trusteeship*, Croom Helm, London.

O'Brien, L.N. (1989) 'The Relative Significance of Foreign Investment in the Manufacturing Sector in Malaysia', Institute of Australian Geographers 23rd Conference, The University of Adelaide, 13–16 February.

O'Brien, L.N. (1990) 'Indices of industrialization: capital goods production in Malaysia', *Journal of Contemporary Asia*, Vol. 20, No. 4: 509–19.

Odaka, K. (1983) *The Motor Vehicle Industry in Asia: A Study of Ancillary Firm Development*, University of Singapore Press, Singapore.

Teh Kok Peng (1977) *Protection, Fiscal Incentives and Industrialization in West Malaysia since 1957*, Monograph Series on Malaysian Economic Affairs No. 4, Faculty of Economics and Administration, University of Malaya, Kuala Lumpur.

UNCTAD (1991) 'Structural changes in the automobile and components industry during the 1980s with particular reference to developing countries', UNCTAD/ITP/46, Geneva, 1 November.

UNIDO (1981) 'ASEAN Cooperation in the Field of Industry – A Background Study on Past and Present Activities', Vienna, 6 February (mimeo).

UNIDO (1982) 'Regional Industrial Cooperation - The Approaches Pursued by ASEAN', Vienna, 27 April (mimeo).

UNIDO (1985a) *Malaysia*, Vienna, July.

UNIDO (1985b) *Medium and Long Term Industrial Master Plan Malaysia, 1986–1995*, Vienna.

UNIDO (1991) *Malaysia*, Industrial Development Series, Vienna.

Wheelwright, E.L. (1965) *Industrialization in Malaysia*, Melbourne University Press, Melbourne.

Wheelwright, E.L. (1972) 'UNIDO Industrial Development Mission to Malaysia', final report, Sydney (mimeo).

World Bank (1978) *Employment and Development of Small Enterprises*, IBRD, Washington DC.

11

THE PROTON SAGA
Malaysian car, Mitsubishi gain*
Jomo K.S.

In Malaysia, the saga of the Malaysian car – Proton – is generally portrayed and seen as a success story. Since Malaysia's recovery from its mid-1980s economic slump, sales of Proton cars have soared. Protons now dominate Malaysia's roads and have also acquired a reputation for quality – or rather 'value for money' – within its price range in Britain. After losses in its early years in the mid-1980s, Proton has been in the black since 1989. Riding on the economic boom since 1987, its huge 'protected' market share and growing exports have made it a source of national pride for many.

The Proton Saga has captured over 70 per cent of the Malaysian passenger car market in its engine capacity range (i.e. under 1600cc), and is likely to retain its market lead, if only because it is exempt from the 40 per cent import duties imposed on its locally assembled competitors and the far higher duties on imported completely built-up (CBU) units. Proton now has significant exports to Britain: in the first year, sales totalled 10,000 units, setting a record for new market entrants in the UK. In 1989, Proton announced its first profits ever of RM32.5 million, after four years of consecutive losses, while still bearing some RM136 million in accumulated losses on its books. In the following year, profits wiped out these losses, and subsequent profits have ensured Proton's listing on the Kuala Lumpur Stock Exchange in 1992.

Is Proton's 'success' illusory, or have there been real tangible benefits for Malaysia? In evaluating its success, or otherwise, it would be helpful to measure Proton against its objectives, which include profits, boosting Malaysian manufacturing, especially heavy industry, technology transfer, labour training, job creation, enhancing consumer welfare and advancing Malay ownership as well as involvement in industry. Balanced analysis of Proton's achievements must consider issues such as the state of the auto industry before and after Proton's inception, the terms and conditions of Proton's establishment, technology transfer, local content and export sales.

BEFORE PROTON

The motor industry in the region began in 1926, when the Ford Motor Company of Malaya was incorporated in Singapore. That was, however, a rudimentary operation, and it was only after independence in 1957 that the Malaysian government developed a policy in 1963 to promote an integrated auto industry, ostensibly to strengthen the country's industrial base. Then came separation from Singapore in 1965, which upset these plans as the expected Malaysian common market was thus substantially reduced. Nevertheless, the government began processing applications for auto assembly and component manufacture. In 1967, the first plant (Swedish Motor Assemblers) went into operation. The government's main objectives in trying to create a viable motor industry were to promote import substitution, save foreign exchange, create employment and nurture the evolution of a supporting auto components manufacturing industry that would enhance overall industrial development through its multiplier effects.

Despite much exhortation and numerous guidelines from the government, the Malaysian auto industry never progressed beyond minimal assembly operations and local content requirements, reflecting a low level of import-substituting industrialization. Progress was stymied by the large number of makes and models in a small market, weak local linkages and poor prospects for export. From the lone Volvo plant in 1967, the industry mushroomed to include 11 assemblers by 1980, who produced 25 makes of commercial and passenger vehicles, 122 models and 212 variants. This proliferation of makes and models made it very difficult for parts makers to achieve economies of scale. Consequently, local parts were expensive and local content in Malaysian-assembled cars dismal; by 1979, local content only averaged 8 per cent and was largely limited to tyres, batteries, paint and filters.

Conflicting government objectives did not help. The Motor Vehicle Assemblers Committee (MVAC) – an inter-departmental agency set up under the Ministry of Trade and Industry to oversee the auto sector – had a sweeping brief. Its regulatory powers included prices, local content, import regulations and control of the number of assemblers, makes and models. But the committee's efforts ran up against other government policies: 'jobs had to be created, investment was necessary and Malays had to be promoted economically' (Doner, 1988). Thus, the original MVAC decision to license only six assemblers proved meaningless. Disqualified plants exerted political influence to engage in subcontracting assembly work, and in 1977, the MVAC licensed another five assemblers for whom criteria for entry were modified to favour *Bumiputera* (indigenous) assemblers.

Attempts to achieve greater local content also met with failure, at least initially. Again, this was not for lack of trying, for the government successively issued directives that included protection for parts producers, mandatory local content increases (rising from 10 per cent in 1972 to 35 per cent in 1982) and other indirect measures to increase local content; those failing to meet local content requirements were penalized. However, such measures were later abandoned for a number of reasons. First, the government felt they might conflict with an ASEAN regional complementation scheme. There were also fears that they would raise car prices, which could cause a political backlash against the government. Finally, and this was especially significant, during the 1960s and early 1970s, foreign assemblers and their local partners effectively resisted localization. The number of parts producers was small and few had much influence on policy making.

The situation began changing in the late 1970s. A group of six large parts producers – led by Malaysian Sheet Glass – moved to rationalize their industries, and in 1978, the Malaysian Automotive Component Parts Manufacturers Association (MACPMA) was formed. By the end of the year, MACPMA consisted of the 50 or so largest producers, of whom there were 200 at the time. MACPMA's strenuous lobbying efforts proved successful. In 1979, the government announced its decision to move towards an all-Malaysian car through what it called mandatory deletion of CKD (completely knocked down) vehicles. Basically, this involved the prohibition of certain components in imported CKD kits, thereby creating market opportunities for local parts manufacturers. These deletions were backed by ample protection – incentives, tariff protection for parts makers, duty exemptions and penalties for assemblers, etc. Thus, local content levels increased more rapidly from 8 per cent in 1979 to 18 per cent in 1982 and 30 per cent in 1986.

INDUSTRY WEAKNESSES

Despite some increase in local content level during the 1970s and early 1980s, the automobile industry contributed little to Malaysian industrialization in spite of the tremendous increase in automobile sales. Automobile sales surged from RM160 million in 1978 to RM418 million in 1983. By 1984, Malaysia had a person-to-car ratio of 1 to 20.8, second only to Singapore in the ASEAN region, and much higher than either South Korea (1 to 146) or Taiwan (1 to 51). However, the automobile industry contributed little to the national economy. Its share of gross domestic product (GDP) dropped from 1.2 per cent in 1978 to 0.6 per cent in 1983 while the industry's contribution to total manufacturing output actually declined, in relative terms, from 2.0 per cent in 1978 to 0.79 per cent in 1983. Meanwhile, the surge in automobile sales during this period saw Malaysia's import bill for transport equipment rise from RM484 million to RM1,200 million (RM: Malaysian ringgit).

The prices of locally assembled vehicles remained high – one estimate put their costs at 50 per cent over their imported CBU equivalents due to extensive market fragmentation, the high price of locally made components, the 'deletion allowance' problem and the failure, or refusal, of Japanese assemblers to reduce the prices of their imported CKD packs by the same amount as the price charged by local producers for parts deleted from their packs (*Malaysian Business*, 1 December 1984). In the early 1980s, locally assembled vehicles actually cost at least 20 per cent more than equivalent imported cars, before taking into consideration the price effects of protective tariffs. Meanwhile, local assemblers complained that the government continued to overregulate while maintaining contradictory policy objectives (Doner, 1988). For example, as noted earlier, the government wanted to rationalize the industry, but the desire to increase *Bumiputera* participation seemed more urgent, and it therefore allowed more car assembly plants to open. It wanted to raise local content while also attempting to raise tax revenues by levying high duties on imported materials essential to the manufacture of locally made parts.

After 1970, the government also sought to raise *Bumiputera* participation in the auto sector. According to figures from the Automotive Federation of Malaysia, *Bumiputera* equity in the auto assembly sector in 1984 came to 30.3 per cent, less than the Chinese holdings of 42.9 per cent. Meanwhile, foreigners, especially the Japanese, wielded disproportionately greater influence in the sector – than suggested by ownership data – owing to their control of technology. *Bumiputera* capital was considered even weaker in the auto parts sector, which was largely Chinese-dominated. And the one area where *Bumiputera* equity seemed significant – i.e. the distribution of imported, luxury CBUs – has been widely believed to be riddled with abuses, e.g. the hawking by *Bumiputeras* of their approved permits (APs) – necessary for the import of cars – to the highest (often Chinese) bidders (Chan, 1988).

The Malaysian car assembly industry had been disadvantageous to Malaysian consumers in terms of both price and quality, while reducing potential revenue from import taxes which would otherwise accrue to the government. The main beneficiaries from past government promotion of the assembly industry have been foreign car companies and their local subsidiaries or partners in a position to derive oligopolistic profits from the protected market. Arguably, their employees also enjoyed some of this 'rent' in the form of wages and remuneration. It has been argued that if completely built-up cars were imported and sold at protected prices, there would still be a considerable excess after paying the government foregone tax revenue and the employees wages for doing nothing (Edwards, 1975).

MITSUBISHI'S REGIONAL STRATEGY

In the 1970s, the Japanese car industry became increasingly export-oriented. By the early 1980s, more than half the passenger cars produced in

Japan were exported. The main overseas markets for Japanese cars have been North America and Southeast Asia. However, the debilitating global competition to sell cars also resulted in cooperation between American and Japanese car makers from the 1970s. While the Japanese Big Three – Toyota, Nissan and Honda – have their own market shares, which are relatively large percentages of the total world market, second-line companies, such as Mazda and Mitsubishi Motor Corporation, have had to cooperate with American auto companies to successfully compete in the world market. The American companies, for their part, have thus gained access to Japanese technology (and capital) to make up for their own lack of technology and experience in producing small, energy-saving cars, for which American consumer demand dramatically rose from the 1970s, following the two oil crises and greater environment as well as resource consciousness.

In 1985, Mitsubishi Motor Corporation (MMC) was the fifth largest Japanese car maker after Toyota, Nissan, Honda and Mazda. MMC produced 1,153,00 units in 1985, of which 55 per cent were exported. The major shareholder in MMC is Mitsubishi Heavy Industries, while the Chrysler group, the third largest American car maker, owned 24 per cent of MMC's shares. This capital tie up between MMC and Chrysler began in 1971, when Chrysler purchased 15 per cent of MMC's shares.

The spread of MMC into East Asia, Southeast Asia and the Pacific area has been unusual among Japanese car makers; MMC, often together with Mitsubishi Corporation, has majority or part-ownership in several production units in East and Southeast Asia as well as Australia. In addition to providing technology and staff training for the factories in which it has shares, MMC has also provided such services, on contractual terms, to other factories in these regions. Eventually MMC developed a long-term strategy called the 'Pacific Production Area Plan' to enable MMC and related companies to use cheaper parts from anywhere in the Pacific area, especially East and Southeast Asia.

The basic premise of the plan involved an international division of labour, in which any assembly plant in MMC's network can purchase the cheapest parts and components from any factory managed by or associated with Mitsubishi. According to this plan, Japan's role in the distant future would mainly be in developing new technology, long-term planning, designing, coordinating, marketing and financial control. However, for years to come, the main parts and components – including engines – for production points in the Asia–Pacific area would still be provided by factories in Japan. Proton can therefore be seen as part of MMC's Pacific area plan.

From Mitsubishi's perspective, the Proton project represented an opportunity to increase greatly its share in one of ASEAN's fastest growing auto markets, from 8 per cent in 1982 to over two-thirds by the second half of the 1980s. Mitsubishi thus also consolidated its regional production scheme, in which the firm located various facilities for vehicle production in the ASEAN region to achieve economies of scale, and thus dominate the much talked about ASEAN car industrial complementation scheme (see Chapter 12 by Machado, in this volume). Hence, the

> Proton Saga was seen as a golden opportunity to secure a strong foothold in the increasingly prosperous Asian region (in the face of aggressive competition) where Toyota dominates the Indonesian archipelago of 170 million inhabitants, Mazda has the upper hand in the 75 million strong market of the Philipines, while Nissan is the number one car manufacturer in Thailand, a market of 65 million.
>
> (Bartu, 1992: 71).

PROTON'S BEGINNINGS

Malaysia's heavy industrialization strategy from the early 1980s has been closely identified with Mahathir's early years as prime minister. The Heavy Industries Corporation of Malaysia (HICOM), set up to spearhead the drive, was established in 1980, during the tenure of Mahathir's predecessor as premier, Hussein Onn, when Mahathir was Deputy Prime Minister and also Minister of Trade and Industry. Mahathir first placed HICOM within the Ministry of Trade and Industry, and then took it with him when he became Premier in mid-1981 to the Prime Minister's Department, where it was really activated. The Proton, or national car project was promoted as the answer to the problems of the auto sector, by bringing about the rationalization so badly needed. Politically, there was an additional spin-off as opportunities for *Bumiputeras* to pick up managerial positions and technical expertise would be created, in line with the expectation that state enterprises serve the government's ethnic redistributive targets.

If there was one person responsible for the Proton Saga, it would have to be Mahathir. The idea of a made-in-Malaysia car was apparently first mooted in 1980 when Mahathir ordered the Malaysian Industrial Development Authority (MIDA) to carry out a feasibility study for the project. Aware that Malaysia could not possibly do it alone, MIDA began talks with Daihatsu Motors, which dragged on for nearly two years before breaking down; apparently, Daihatsu was only willing to put up a body stamping plant and offer technical assistance. This was not the 'Malaysian car' that Mahathir envisaged then, although production of the the second, smaller Malaysian car – the Perodua Kancil – from 1994 involves Daihatsu as the principal technology supplier.

In October 1981, Mahathir – by then already Prime Minister and on an official visit to Japan – had talks with Mimura, Mitsubishi Corporation's president, and 'a verbal agreement was reached that Mitsubishi would come in' (*Malaysian Business*, 1 December 1984). In February 1982, Dr Kubo,

Mitsubishi Motor Corporation's chairman, visited Malaysia and reached an understanding with Mahathir on the type of car desired (Paul Chan, cited by Doner, 1988). In October 1982, Mahathir was able to announce Southeast Asia's most ambitious automotive project to date, the manufacture of a made-in-Malaysia automobile. By all accounts, work started even before Cabinet approval had been obtained in December 1982. By then, the project team – then working under HICOM – had prepared a market feasibility study and Mitsubishi had flown a clay model of the Proton prototype, prepared in its Japanese factories, to Kuala Lumpur for Mahathir's inspection and approval (Doner, 1988).

Officially, the project began with the incorporation of Perusahaan Otomobil Nasional Sendirian Bhd, or simply Proton, in May 1983. The Proton project was conceived of as the lynchpin of a broader state-led effort to accelerate and balance the country's industrialization. 'Automobile manufacture promised technological advancement, development of engineering skills, and generation of supply industries with export potential' (Machado, 1989: 510). State sponsorship for heavy industry was also seen as a way to strengthen the economic position of the indigenous *Bumiputera* to better achieve the ethnic redistribution targets set by the New Economic Policy (NEP).

However, the government made no attempt to improve its bargaining position *vis-à-vis* Mitsubishi by contacting other foreign or local auto firms, thus privileging Mitsubishi without any semblance of competitive bidding (*Asian Wall Street Journal*, 8 July 1985). By all accounts, Mahathir seemed to believe that Mitsubishi was the best of the Japanese automakers when it came to understanding Malaysian national ambitions or at least, his desires. Indeed, MMC seemed not only the most understanding of Japanese firms as far as local sourcing was concerned, but also in complying with the South Korean national auto development programme by working with Hyundai (Doner, 1988). Unlike the other Japanese automakers, who apparently believed the Proton project to be neither necessary nor desirable, Mitsubishi had come up with a specific proposal; 'according to Proton Saga's first general manager, there was hardly any choice' (Bartu, 1992: 70). To secure MMC participation and financial viability for the project, the government assured market dominance for the new 'national car' by granting Proton substantial protection, most important, by exempting it from a newly imposed 40 per cent import duty on CKD kits (Machado, 1989: 509, 510, 514). Simultaneously, it raised the CKD import duties for other brands by threefold so that the incidence of taxes to the landed price of CKD packs for non-Sagas became almost 100 per cent (*FEER*, 14 February 1985). As a result, it has been estimated that the Treasury lost about RM120 million in foregone import duties in 1987 alone. Thus, Proton can import parts at prices 33 per cent cheaper than those paid by other assemblers. As a result, the price of the Proton Saga has been 20 to

30 per cent cheaper than those for similar cars manufactured by other assemblers. In 1987, the 1300cc Proton Saga price was RM21,000, while that of other 1300cc cars ranged from RM28,000 to RM29,000. Proton's market share increased steadily from 47 per cent in 1986 to 65 per cent in 1987 and 73 per cent in 1988.

Thus, Proton was set up as a joint venture between HICOM and Mitsubishi. HICOM contributed 70 per cent of the total paid up capital of RM150 million, with Mitsubishi Corporation (MC), and its subsidiary, Mitsubishi Motor Corporation (MMC) each taking up 15 per cent stakes. Paid-up capital was RM150 million (about US$60 million) in mid-1987, while the proposed total capital was RM400 million. However, most of the funds required for plant construction and operating equipment came from Japanese sources – Proton raised a total of some 33 billion yen from Mitsubishi-related banks (*Malaysian Business*, 1 January 1986). The 900-hectare Hicom industrial estate in Shah Alam, some 15km from Kuala Lumpur, was purchased for a high RM88 million from a Sime Darby plantation holdings subsidiary in 1983 and the factory built at a cost of US$245 million. By mid-1985, a year ahead of schedule, the first Sagas were rolling off the assembly line. At the time, the plant was only running at 25 per cent of installed capacity, producing 105 cars a day. It was initially designed for 21.3 units per hour, with an output of 40,000 units per year on a single shift, or 120,000 cars a year over three shifts.

Unfortunately, however, the Proton Saga was not really a Malaysian car. In the words of Mitsubishi consultant, Hiroshi Satoh, 'Proton took a short cut. Instead of trying to start from scratch, we opted to use existing components and make modifications to the bodyline'. The Proton Saga is essentially a four-door Mitsubishi Lancer Fiore, in 1300cc and 1500cc engine size. Most of the car is shipped to Malaysia in knocked-down kit form and assembled there (*Asian Wall Street Journal*, 19 December 1985, in Bartu, 1992: 74). In any case, Mitsubishi was not spending very much. While HICOM's profits were uncertain, Mitsubishi's profits were guaranteed by the turn-key project terms, at least from technical assistance, plant construction and the supply of equipment and parts. It was envisaged, for example, that Mitsubishi would provide key components such as engines and transmissions. Initial increases in local content were achieved with the newly established body stamping plant built, equipped and run by MMC. 'Mitsubishi was assured not only of important upfront earnings for the installation of the factory, but also of continued royalty payments for its technology transfer' (Bartu, 1992: 72). Details of the contract are not public, but what is known is that Mitsubishi promised the following: construction of the plant, starting dates, equity shares, training of Malaysian personnel, and new design changes every two years, with model changes once every five years. Quite a few things were left vague, however, including future local content levels, CKD payments, royalties, the use of non-Japanese technology, technology transfer and exports – which 'seemed to provide Mitsubishi with significant advantages', and adversely affected Malaysia's subsequent bargaining position and capacity.

Given the near total secrecy in which the negotiations were carried out, there has been a dearth of information about the project. This has not stopped discussion, however. Indeed, outside the Malaysian press, the project was widely criticized as not viable; an economist was quoted as saying 'I have yet to talk to a single economist who thinks the project is viable'. More damaging, however, was a secret report from the government sponsored Institute of Strategic and International Studies (ISIS) that concluded the project was 'not viable, from an economic point of view' (*Asian Wall Street Journal*, 19 December 1985). 'A secret report commissioned by the government also concluded that the final cost of such a venture could be hundreds of millions of US dollars and that there was no guarantee the national car project would be able to survive fierce international competition' (Bartu, 1992: 70). A 1985 United Nations Industrial Development Organisation (UNIDO) report put it starkly. The possibilities for gain, it said, 'appeared far more secure for Japan and Mitsubishi than for Malaysia. . . for the former, the sun may continue to rise, but for the latter, first light could still turn to darkness'.

The government, however, had based its optimistic projections on growing auto sales of 6 per cent a year and a feasibility report by the HICOM project group, done in collaboration with local market researchers, SGV-Kassim Chan, that concluded that the project was feasible. According to their scenario, Proton would produce 40,000 units in 1986, 80,000 units in 1988 and 120,000 units by 1994. Later, however, the projections were revised to begin with 20,000 cars in 1985, increasing to a maximum of 100,000 cars yearly by 1991. The production levels expected were lower than the production capacity envisaged for the complex, i.e. 80,000 cars per year in 1985 rising to 120,000 by 1988. Two basic body models were envisaged, namely the four-door saloon produced from 1985 and the three-door hatchback from 1987. Both would be front wheel drive models, and each would accommodate two engine sizes of 1,300cc and 1,500cc respectively. Operations were originally scheduled to start in 1986, but subsequently, as noted earlier, plans were brought forward and the first car came off the line in 1985.

Many informed observers in Malaysia questioned the Proton car plans, although few did so openly, usually citing the Prime Minister's strong personal commitment to the project. However, Mahathir's own strong personal commitment does, of course, raise questions about the commitment of subsequent Malaysian government regimes to the Proton project despite other politicians' current avowals to the contrary. The main problem often mentioned has been the limited size of the local market, which limits economies of scale and thus prevents Proton from ever becoming truly internationally competitive, i.e. without subsidization. International estimates of optimum annual production capacity are in the region of 200,000 to 400,000 units per annum, while an output level of 100,000 to 200,000 cars per year is generally considered the economic minimum.

Malaysia's national car project was initially only oriented towards supplying the Malaysian domestic market. Hence, the size of the Malaysian passenger car market was to define and limit the size of Proton's operations. Before the launching of Proton, the Malaysian Government had employed consultants to estimate both the domestic demand for passenger cars and the likely market share of the Proton Saga. As noted earlier, Proton was established in 1983, when the sale of passenger cars in Malaysia reached a record high. Proton's economists estimated that the annual growth rate of passenger car sales would stay around 6.69 per cent between 1986 and 1990. This rather optimistic forecast was probably based on the relatively robust performance of the Malaysian economy up to 1984. However, the shortfall between actual sales and these projections grew embarrassingly large over the mid-1980s, with dire consequences for Proton.

In 1981, Malaysian car sales totalled only 108,000 for the whole of Malaysia, including Sabah and Sarawak. These sales figures were achieved before the full effects of the mid-1980s recession and yen appreciation were felt in Malaysia, and also before taxes on cars were raised (e.g. a 15 per cent import duty on knocked-down kits was introduced in 1982) to increase government revenue and to protect further the local market for Proton. Also, though the sale of new cars actually declined in 1982, HICOM's plans were apparently predicated on forecasts that demand would increase steadily by 8 per cent per year from 1981.

Table 11.1 Forecasted demand for passenger cars in Malaysia, 1985–95

Year	(Most likely) (units)	Proton Saga (units)	(%)	Others assembled locally (units)	(%)	Imported CBU units (units)	(%)
1985	118,010	7,500	6.4	99,510	84.3	11,000	9.3
1986	125,900	40,250	32.0	75,030	59.6	10,620	8.4
1987	134,330	67,600	50.3	56,660	42.2	10,070	7.5
1988	143,310	84,400	58.9	49,510	34.5	9,400	6.6
1989	152,900	95,200	62.3	49,100	32.1	8,600	5.6
1990	163,150	100,200	61.4	55,300	33.9	7,650	4.7
1991	173,150	105,100	60.7	61,520	35.5	6,530	3.8
1992	183,770	108,200	58.9	70,380	38.3	5,190	2.8
1993	195,030	114,000	58.5	77,350	39.6	3,680	1.9
1994	206,980	120,000	58.0	85,030	41.1	1,950	0.9
1995	219,670	120,000	54.6	99,670	45.4	0.0	

Source: Malaysian Industrial Development Authority (MIDA), *Industrial Master Plan, 1986–1995.* These figures assume 100% of the Proton Sagas are sold.

Just as Proton was ready to begin production, auto sales slumped badly. In 1985 and 1986, the country went into its worst economic recession since Independence. The number of passenger cars sold in Malaysia in 1985 was 67,888 units, or only about 58 per cent of forecasted sales. In 1986 and 1987, the disparities were even worse, with the percentage of real against forecasted sales dropping to 41 per cent and 28 per cent respectively. Total passenger car sales plunged to 38,200 in 1987 from a peak of over 100,000 in 1983. As a result, total Proton production for the years 1986 and 1987 hovered around 25,000 units per annum. Total domestic sales of the Proton Saga were 7,492 in 1985, 24,148 in 1986 and 24,858 in 1987. 'With such an insignificant output the company was losing 35,000 ringgit (US$15,000) on each vehicle sold. Unofficial estimates put these losses still higher' (Bartu, 1992: 74).

The weakened economy and the resulting balance of payments deficit also caused a depreciation of the Malaysian ringgit against the currencies of its major trading partners. The *endaka* (i.e. the steep appreciation of the Japanese yen after September 1985) caused Proton's start-up loan of ¥33 billion to increase alarmingly in ringgit terms. 'Loans of 34 billion yen were taken by Proton in the first half of the 1980s during a time when RM1 was worth about 100 yen. By mid-1986, it took about RM1.7 and by mid-1988 about RM2 to buy 100 yen. HICOM renegotiated lower interest rates on part of Proton's loans. By late 1988, Proton's loans still stood at 34 billion yen, but by then, represented a debt of about RM680 million' (Machado, 1989: 518–9).

The ringgit costs of CKD imports rose sharply with the yen appreciation. Thus, for the year ending 31 March 1985, even before the plant had actually begun production, Proton had accumulated losses of RM11.6 million.

> The venture was also badly hit by the rapid appreciation of the yen, which increased the production cost of the Proton Saga by more than 70 per cent and inflated Proton's outstanding yen debts of some 34 million yen (US$ 250 million). A concerned Mahathir appealed to Tokyo for a debt relief, but failed to get any concessions since such a move would have set a dangerous precedent. Tokyo only agreed to a token reduction in the interest rate. But in order to be seen to be responsive to Kuala Lumpur's request, the Japanese government extended a multi-million dollar cash contribution to the construction of Malaysia's first planetarium.
>
> (Bartu, 1992: 74)

EXPORT SALES

Malaysia's GDP grew at 7.8 per cent in 1980, 5.6 per cent in 1981, 5.9 per cent in 1982, 6.3 per cent in 1983, and 7.8 per cent in 1984. But in 1985, the growth rate fell to minus one per cent, while in 1986, GDP increased by a mere 1.2 per cent. Growth of GDP picked up a little to 4.7 per cent in 1987. The sale of passenger cars, however, fell to its lowest level in 1987. Sales climbed upwards again from 1988. The original Proton project did not plan to export cars during the first stage of development, but the plan called for exports to begin after 1990. However, the unexpected drop in domestic demand for passenger cars accelerated the export of Proton Sagas ahead of schedule as it was seen as the only way to utilize excess capacity.

Mahathir himself had originally downplayed any possibility of export, but he switched tack abruptly after sales began falling. He demanded exports – first within five years, and then within two years of commencing vehicle production. Mitsubishi appeared reluctant at first; they did not have to be enthusiastic as the contract had left the export question vague – 'exports of Proton Saga cars were not provided for in the agreement with Mitsubishi. In fact they were excluded, at least during the first phase of the project' (Bartu, 1992: 75).

> Officially the Japanese promised to "consider" the proposal. In reality, they resisted it from the very beginning, and when the pressure from the Malaysians grew stronger, they tried to stall the idea by suggesting that extensive market research was necessary which would take up to two years, that the technical modifications to make the Proton exportable would last as many years, and that this export plan would require massive new investments. The Japanese knew, of course, that the Proton Saga was not made for export and were deliberately misleading their Malaysian partners. Mitsubishi had installed an obsolete plant in Shah Alam which produced second-class vehicles made of thin and inferior steel, composed of many light plastic parts and equipped with overall technology that was not sufficient to enable the car to pass the strict regulations prevailing in overseas markets, especially in the United States. Even the engine was of inferior quality in terms of noise and pollution emissions.
>
> (Bartu, 1992: 76–7)

> The vehicles are designed to Malaysian requirements only. . . . Their windshield glass isn't up to European standards, dashboards are made from plastic materials that could shatter in an accident, bumpers aren't adequate, and starters aren't suitable for temperate climates.
>
> (*Asian Wall Street Journal*, 19 December 1985, in Bartu, 1992: 76–7).

In other words, the Proton Saga was a deliberately downgraded Lancer Fiore, good enough for Malaysia, but certainly not good enough for export. Suddenly, the Malaysians discovered the truth about their national car.

> (Bartu, 1992: 77)

While Bartu exaggerates Malaysian public awareness about the nature of the Proton, he is essentially correct about the character of the vehicle.

Mitsubishi's reluctance stemmed mainly from three factors. First, they did not want the Saga to compete with their other products. A Mitsubishi plant in Australia already manufactured the Lonsdale, which the company had hoped would sell well in Britain. The Proton would qualify for duty-free import into the UK under the Generalised Scheme of Preferences (GSP), which would make it difficult for the Lonsdale to compete with it (*Business Times*, 2 December 1989). The Sagas could also eat into the US market share of other Mitsubishi cars, marketed by Chrysler Corporation. Secondly, the Japanese also felt that the Proton would rapidly become outdated; staying ahead in the international auto market presupposes constant changes in model design, and the Japanese were unconvinced that Proton could keep up. Mitsubishi was also unconvinced that Edaran Otomobil Nasional (National Automobile Distributorship or EON) had the marketing ability to sell the car overseas. Nor did they believe that Proton could consistently adapt technology for the different markets. EON had no experience with international marketing, and Malaysia had few, if any, international marketing channels for auto sales. Third, the Saga's low quality – especially its seats, dashboard and floor mats, among other items – would damage Mitsubishi's image. A second-class Mitsubishi Lancer Fiore was bad publicity it could ill-afford.

Initial efforts by Proton seemed to confirm Mitsubishi's worst fears. When the Prime Minister took ten Sagas with him to China on a trade mission, the cars went equipped with air-conditioners, instead of heaters to combat the frigid Beijing winter. The cars themselves could not be used; their engines were equipped to use high-grade Malaysian petrol, instead of the much lower grade fuels used in China.

> While an impatient Mahathir and his desperate Malay managers pushed the Japanese to upgrade the car and to make it exportable, a totally uninterested Mitsubishi Corporation dragged its feet. [Then] an apparent white knight in the person of the American entrepreneur Malcolm Bricklin entered the scene. . . . When Bricklin was introduced to the Malaysian Prime Minister, he brought along a letter of recommendation from none other than Henry Kissinger, the former United States Secretary of State. Bricklin impressed Mahathir with bullish Proton Saga sales projections for the United States market. The idea of breaking into the rich North American market was an irresistable temptation for Proton, as it is for all East Asian industrialists. In December 1986, Proton signed a letter of intent with Bricklin Industries Inc. of New York, tentatively naming the company its sole distributor in the US. Bricklin Industries had successfully imported a Yugoslavian car, the "Yugo" to the US in 1985.

Bricklin announced his intention to sell 100,000 Sagas in the car's first year in the US, four times the total 1986 output. Bricklin Industries also planned to spend US$10 million to modify the Proton Saga for US certification and to build a distribution network. It established a subsidiary called Proton America Inc. to sell the Saga in the US. It was announced that the price would be between US$5,000 and US$8,000, later raised to US$9,000.

Bricklin planned to start importing Sagas to the US in February 1988. In June 1987, Proton America announced a US$4.4 million engineering and administration programme with Britain's Canewdom Consultants Group for the Proton Saga. Canewdom would convert the Saga into a right-hand drive vehicle. The development programme was also aimed at reducing the use of parts imported from Japan and priced in Japanese yen. The cost savings would be more than US$500 per vehicle, whereas by using Japanese parts, the Saga could not meet the target price in the US.

Proton's agreement with Bricklin sent shock waves through Mitsubishi's executive offices. At once, the Japanese abandoned their stalling tactics. Instead, they became extremely cooperative and took great interest in Kuala Lumpur's links with Bricklin. But in the event, their fears were proven unjustified because Bricklin did not keep his promises. Not only did he fail to obtain the technical approval from the United States authorities for Proton Saga imports, but even worse, he suddenly sold off his company in the midst of negotiations with the Malaysians. Bricklin's dishonourable exit cost Kuala Lumpur millions of ringgit and put a sudden end to Mahathir's dream of exporting the Proton Saga to the United States.

(Bartu, 1992: 77–8)

Plans for penetrating the lucrative US market – originally considered more important than the UK – eventually resulted in recrimination between Proton and its intended US distributor. Under the terms of the agreement, Bricklin had until November 1988 to get the approvals. Proton threatened to sue for breach of contract, but the key factor in the project's demise was Proton's own internal changes. The replacement of the Malaysian management with a team from MMC in mid-1988 allowed the Japanese partners to show their own disapproval of the project by letting it die from neglect.

Planning for US distribution had been hasty. The Malaysians put high hopes on the US market and apparently did not carefully consider the intense competition in that market nor the high costs of modifications to meet US standards. Even if the plan to export to the US had not failed, it has been estimated that car export price subsidies to the US would have been at least RM5,000 per vehicle, or over 40 per cent of the original expected retail price of US$5,000. This would have been higher than the RM4,500 per vehicle capital cost subsidy then believed to exist for cars produced for the local market.

By April 1990, more than 12,900 units had been exported to various countries including Bangladesh, Eire, Sri Lanka, Brunei, Singapore, Jamaica, New Zealand, Malta, Nauru and the UK. The UK showed the most promise, with a total of 10,170 units sold there in its first year – exceeding Proton's expectations by some 4,000 units. Quality has not turned out to be a problem; British newspaper and auto review magazines gave the Saga favourable ratings. The main problem has, in fact, been meeting demand. The first 500 Sagas sent to Singapore sold out within a week, surprising both Proton and its Singapore distributor, Cycle and Carriage. Indeed, from late 1989, even Malaysian buyers have had to contend with waiting periods of between two to four months before delivery.

Proton has also begun to export pressed parts to Thailand. These exports are expected to increase following the free trade accord between ASEAN countries signed in early 1992. Whether Proton will make money on its overseas sales is unclear. In Parliament, Mahathir denied that the Proton was being subsidized for export; the overseas prices do not seem significantly lower than domestic prices. When the car made the tenth spot in a London *Sunday Times* rating of economy cars costing up to 7,000 pounds sterling (RM30,800), it was also the most expensive except for one other model; costing only a little less than its retail price in Malaysia (RM32,000). According to a MIDA official, Proton's then managing director, Kanji Iwabuchi, maintained that 'export sales contribute to the company's results'. Indeed, Iwabuchi maintained that 'we will still make profits on Britain-bound exports even without tariff advantages under the GSP' (*Malaysian Business*, 1 September 1989). Industry analysts, however, generally feel that Proton loses on overseas sales, at least in Britain, pointing to high unit production costs as a result of low volume and the high cost of imported Japanese components. There are also over four hundred costly modifications made to the British-bound Sagas, required to fulfill various British standards.

MANAGEMENT CONTROL

As pointed out earlier, one of the apparent motives for the national car project was to redress ethnic economic imbalances. As Chinese entrepreneurs had dominated Malaysian auto assembly, it became an obvious target for restructuring. Hence, despite their obvious lack of relevant experience, Proton's management was largely Malay from the outset. The three top-ranking Malaysian executives in Proton – president (Tan Sri) Jamil Jan, vice president Mohammed Saufi Abdullah, and managing director Wan Nik Ismail – were all ex-civil servants whose first experience of heavy industry came through HICOM established in 1980. 'One of Mahathir's top priorities has been to entrust the car project to Malay hands and for this reason he installed an almost exclusively Malay management team. More experienced experts were excluded from the decision-making level purely on racial grounds' (Bartu, 1992). None of Proton Saga's managers had ever been confronted with the difficult task of building up a car industry. Although some were well trained and highly motivated, they had limited experience, mainly in protected and publicly-funded corporations. The task of building and selling cars in a competitive world was quite alien to them.

Proton's management apparently also suffered from internal conflicts and misunderstandings. Part of the reason for the company's mismanagement has been its recruitment and promotion of inexperienced managers. If HICOM or the Malaysian Government had employed experienced Malaysian managers of existing heavy industries – instead of civil servants – as Proton managers, the management of Proton would probably have been more successful. The government thus tied its own hands at the outset, and as a result, the 'national car' project was firmly under Mitsubishi control for a long time.

From this weak basis, the situation deteriorated as larger forces beyond the control of the management team worked against Proton. As noted earlier, the escalating yen, coupled with low domestic demand, led to four successive years of losses, culminating in losses of RM52 million and RM58 million in 1987 and 1988. In late 1987, Proton's management even had to ask the government for a soft loan to help ease its yen burden; the government agreed, but nothing else seemed to be working well.

Then, the Bricklin fiasco erupted and this both outraged and humiliated the Prime Minister. For weeks, the local press had played up the issue and presented it as yet another great national achievement, but once Mahathir had to admit that exports to the United States had to be abandoned (he used the expression 'postponed'), Proton's all-Malay management team was blamed. In June 1988, Finance Minister Daim Zainuddin complained that the government was fed up with hearing excuses from managers for their poor performances: 'A good management team is able to adapt the company to changes, to look for alternatives and not to make excuses one after another. If you fail, you must have the courage to resign. If you don't, you may be sacked' (*Far Eastern Economic Review*, 1 September 1989). A day after Daim's outburst, Proton's deputy chairman, Mohammed Saufi Abdullah resigned. On 1 August 1989, Proton's executive director, Wan Nik Ismail was replaced by Kenji Iwabuchi, the former managing director of MMC. The MMC management control of Proton was consolidated when another MMC manager, Kyo Fujioko, was appointed head of the new corporate planning division.

Some of these criticisms were not very fair, however, because Proton's management had not really committed the major blunders on the export issue. Proton's losses stemmed mainly from the collapse of the car market due to the economic recession, yen appreciation and higher taxation – incorrectly blamed on the management team. It was not they – but the government – who had chosen Bricklin as Proton's US car importer and distributor. When they learnt that the government was going to sell the Proton cars to Bricklin Industries at a price below direct (marginal or variable) production cost, they apparently opposed the exports, arguing that 'poor Malaysian tax-payers would be subsidising rich American consumers'. After scapegoating the Proton management, the Prime Minister appointed an MMC manager to head the management team (Bartu, 1992: 78–9).

'Though Proton Saga remains, on paper at least, Malaysia's national car project, many important decisions are now no longer taken by the Malaysians. Increasingly, control has been moved from Shah Alam to the Mitsubishi Motor Company's head office in Japan' (Bartu, 1992: 79). It was a blow to Malay and Malaysian pride, and suggested that the government thought that only Japanese management could save the project. However, some implications of what may fairly be described as a Mitsubishi takeover only became clear later.

A German high technology car-brake producer's proposal to the Malaysian government to set up a joint venture to produce high quality ABS brakes in Malaysia for use in the next generation of Proton Saga cars was shot down by Mitsubishi despite great enthusiasm from the authorities in Kuala Lumpur. The Japanese head of the Proton factory refused to receive the German representatives from Europe. This incident reinforced Malaysian desire to break the tight Japanese control. The order for cosmetic changes to the Proton Saga that followed went to a British company, and not to Mitsubishi, who reportedly always charged very high fees. The freight charges for shipping engines from Japan to Shah Alam were exorbitant, with domestic transport costs inside Japan (from the Mitsubishi factory to the port) much higher than the costs of shipping the engines from Japan to Malaysia. Similarly high costs were incurred in assembling Proton Saga engines, all of which were initially assembled by Mitsubishi in Japan. However, in order to increase local content, they were partly dismantled before shipping and then later reassembled in Malaysia. And when the Malaysians insisted, for instance, on the use of locally made spark-plugs, Mitsubishi Japan sent the engines fitted with cheap dummy plastic plugs for which the Malaysians had to pay dearly. The 'deletion credit' issue has also been a major ongoing problem between the two parties (Bartu, 1992: 80). 'The company often uses massively inflated internal transfer prices which are well above going world market prices. [It] also resists every attempt made by the Malaysians to diversify Proton's part suppliers away from Japanese firms' (Bartu, 1992: 82).

'The general manager supervises the production with army-like discipline and members of the Malaysian staff admit that many fear the Japanese boss. "In the past, we had a say in the project. Now we only take orders from the Japanese", one Malaysian manager complained' (Bartu, 1992: 80). Numerous Japanese technicians, most of them unable to communicate in either English or Malay, control the production process. According to one, the Japanese technicians are so important that the company could not function for a single day without them. This statement does not only reflect badly on the government's recruitment policy, but also on Mitsubishi's training programme (Bartu, 1992: 82).

MMC's position in the joint venture was strengthened by Proton's recovery and profitability after the management change in 1988. This turnaround was, however, largely due to the improved economic situation and increased domestic demand. The yen appreciation also helped speed up the localization process, and by 1991, almost 60 per cent of Saga components were supplied locally (Bartu, 1992: 80–1).

LOCAL CONTENT

Although the Proton Saga has been touted as a made-in-Malaysia car, ironically, at least at the outset, local content was actually lower than that for some other locally assembled cars. For example, one Malaysian-assembled Nissan car had 38–40 per cent local content (in price terms) in 1988, but failed to secure pioneer status like Proton. Thus, the local content argument was a dubious rationale for giving Proton special status as a pioneer industry. In fact, the Proton is essentially still a Mitsubishi car, with an exclusive body design involving largely cosmetic changes, and locally assembled with a higher and growing proportion of locally produced components, initially largely accounted for by the Mitsubishi-supplied and serviced body-stamping plant. Selling parts to Proton is one way for Mitsubishi to increase its profits.

The first Proton had local content (by value) of 'less than 20 per cent' (Bartu, 1992: 72), rising soon to about 36 per cent. After that, increases came slowly, mainly because of Mitsubishi's reluctance to commit itself to supposedly 'inferior quality' local components. Instead, a great deal of components have been imported, at great cost, from Mitsubishi plants in Japan. Nevertheless, efforts to further raise local content have since become more feasible due to greater scale economies and lower relative production costs as well as relocation of small and medium Japanese ancillary firms in Malaysia after the appreciation of the yen. Since 1985, some Japanese car parts makers, who had been supplying MMC with car components made in Japan, began setting up factories in Malaysia. Now, they make parts in Malaysia for the Proton Saga, and often for other assemblers as well. This relocation has also been encouraged by the massive yen appreciation against the ringgit, Japanese government (MITI) support and new processes (e.g. just-in-time) involving reduced inventories and requiring suppliers located close by.

Some Malaysian manufacturers have complained about Proton's bias against local parts suppliers. The Malaysian Plastic Manufacturers Association (MPMA) alleged that Proton preferred to import plastic components from Japan though they were more expensive than Malaysian-manufactured parts. Also, MPMA claimed that Malaysian plastic manufacturers have both the ability and technology to produce components for Proton. In fact, Japanese electronics and electrical factories in Malaysia have been using more plastic parts manufactured in Malaysia, especially since the second half of the 1980s.

In some areas, Malaysia actually has considerable experience. For example, many electrical components for the car industry are produced in Malaysia. Electro-magnetic relays manufactured by Fujitsu Component (Malaysia) Sdn Bhd (FCM) are being used by car manufacturers in Japan, Europe and the United States. The electro-magnetic relays are also used in electronic equipment, digital switching systems, audio-visual equipment and automatic control devices in vending machines. Yet, car assemblers in Malaysia, including Proton, are not buying local electrical components. Instead, assemblers still source parts from associated companies in Japan, which have a close relationship with the Japanese parent company. Also, Malaysian component companies often lack the design technology necessary to adjust to changing assembler needs in Malaysia.

Automobile parts usually supplied locally in Malaysia include batteries, radiators and radiator hoses, seatcovers, windscreens and other glass, absorbers, paint, alternators, starter motors, fuel tanks, wiper motors, mud flaps, tyres, carpets, body side moulding, and wire harnesses. However, most movement components have not been supplied from Malaysia. Engines and other movement parts, like transmissions, are difficult to manufacture and relatively expensive since they require more sophisticated technologies.

However, things have changed since. Strong pressure from MACPMA and the government, coupled with the high costs of importing from Japan because of the stronger yen, have catalysed this change. The yen appreciation led to Proton sourcing from other countries, including Taiwan, Thailand, South Korea, India, Australia and the USA.

The emergence of Proton has also catalysed the emergence of Malaysian parts exporters. Three companies – UMW, Tan Chong and Oriental Motors – have gone into parts production in a big way, with the first two reporting turnovers of between RM75 and RM100 million in parts manufacture; interestingly, 15 to 20 per cent of their production in 1988 was for export to places like Australia, Japan and the Middle East (Doner, 1988). Proton too has joined the parts exporting business. As planned by Mitsubishi Motor Corporation, Proton is exporting doors to Sittopol, a Thai car maker which, like Proton, is partly owned by MMC. The designs of the Proton Saga and the Sittipol car are very similar, both being based on the same Mitsubishi car.

The strong yen has also induced the relocation of Japanese parts maufacturers from Japan to Malaysia, where they mainly produce parts for export; Proton and other local assemblers also buy some of their production. But the supply of local parts is still limited.

> In reality. . . many Proton Saga components are still imported from Japan. In building up its network of suppliers Mitsubishi gave priority to Japanese firms and the few Malaysian component-makers that the Mitsubishi Motor Company considered suitable for the Proton venture were coerced into expensive technological assistance arrangements with Japanese firms.
>
> (Bartu, 1992: 81)

On the one hand, the localization of parts would be expected to reduce the cost of the Saga, but on the other hand, Mitsubishi's control – coupled with the high yen costs of imported parts – has raised the price of the Proton Saga considerably.

In cost terms, 55.2 per cent of the parts of Proton Sagas produced in July 1988 were imported from Japan. This means that 44.8 per cent of the parts were purchased, though not necessarily made in Malaysia. In many cases, Proton buys parts from Japanese subsidiary companies in Malaysia. These companies import parts or assemble products from Japan or other countries, so the real ratio of local parts is smaller than this. This ratio also changes as exchange rates – and relative production costs – fluctuate. By mid-1990, according to Proton officials, the car's local content was to reach 65 per cent. By the late 1980s, Proton manufactures 453 components, while 356 other parts were sourced from 56 local vendors. Another 133 parts were to be developed by local manufacturers, and when the company completely localizes engine manufacture, local content will exceed 72 per cent. In August 1988, the Proton plant began engine assembly.

DISTRIBUTION

Edaran Otomobil Nasional was appointed the sole distributor for the Saga. Unlike Proton, however, EON was an ethnic compromise; while HICOM retained the largest shareholding (45 per cent), extensive Chinese participation was encouraged to tap their auto marketing experience and to avoid alienating Chinese car buyers. Thus, a UMW subsidiary held 35 per cent, while Tan Chong became involved through directorship holdings. Later, to placate *Bumiputera* indignation at these 'compromises', 15 per cent of equity was offered to UAS, a diversified *Bumiputera* company, and 5 per cent was alloted to Pekema, representing the Malay Motor Traders

Association. In this way, the government reasoned, it could spread the gains from the Proton project.

On an independent footing from Proton, EON quickly began setting up dealerships throughout the country. It also began racking up profits from the outset, with the relatively low 'tranfer prices' paid for Proton's cars by EON. Besides these 'friendly' transfer prices, EON also enjoyed high profit margins from selling cars loaded with virtually mandatory, expensive 'accessories' or 'options' – a strategy that the distributor remorselessly used, much to the chagrin of many consumers. A customer who did not want any of EON's 'options' had to wait a very long time for car delivery. Beside accessories, EON also derived commissions from finance companies; all Proton buyers have to go through EON's panel of 30 finance companies which charged an interest rate including an EON commission from each transaction of 0.9 per cent. It is estimated that a further 20 per cent of EON's profits comes from servicing.

However, when the US export plan was shelved in the late 1980s Proton began selling their cars to EON at higher prices. Relations between Proton's and EON's managements had never really been very good. The Japanese began clamouring for participation in EON, to streamline and better coordinate production and distribution functions. Early in 1989, the government agreed. HICOM retained its 45 per cent share, but 25 per cent finally got assigned to a private company controlled by the Ministry of Finance, with the remaining 30 per cent going to Kuala Pura, an MMC subsidiary (*Business Times*, 2 December 1989). The effect was to bring EON more firmly under Proton's control, apparently cutting into the profitable margin EON previously enjoyed. According to the then new chief executive of EON and now Proton chief executive officer, Mohd. Nazmi Mohd. Salleh

> if we sell the car bare from Proton, we will lose money as the cost of the car from Proton compared to the price we sell to customers does not leave enough for us to be profitable. We recover our costs from accessories and hire purchase commissions (*Far Eastern Economic Review*, 3 August 1989).

OTHER ASSEMBLERS

According to MIDA's forecast, Proton's market share would be 62 per cent in 1989, while the share of other Malaysian assemblers would be 32 per cent. This meant that other Malaysian assemblers would be able to produce less than 50,000 units per year by the late 1980s, just half their peak production in 1983. Proton's appearance in the market was therefore clearly critical for private local assemblers. As Proton increased its market share, the 'rationalization' of the Malaysian auto industry proceeded.

Sales of other cars fell sharply, not only because of declines in their market shares, but also because total car sales had shrunk. Nissan's sales fell from 24,548 units in 1984 to 3,800 in 1987, while Toyota's sales declined from 21,692 in 1984 to only 1,620 in 1987. Their assembly plants laid off many workers. Two other assembly factories were closed down; Mitsubishi, which sold 8,302 units in 1983, was closed in 1986, while Mazda shut down its plant in 1988. Others simply reduced output or switched to the production of vehicles that would not compete with Proton.

Importing completely finished passenger cars into Malaysia has not been attractive since the 1960s as the government imposes very high import duties on cars imported from abroad. Such protection has been common among developing countries pursuing import-substituting industrialization. As a result of this policy, many major car makers established assembly operations in Malaysia to protect or capture market shares, especially if they deemed it potentially profitable. Many leading car makers – including Nissan, Toyota, Honda, Ford, Daihatsu, Mazda and Mitsubishi (MMC) – had established factories by the 1980s. Between 1977 and 1983, the average growth rate of the car assembly industry in Malaysia was a little more than 9 per cent. In 1983 – the peak year for car assembly in Malaysia before Proton – they assembled about 100,000 passenger car units, mostly for the domestic market.

Assemblers, owned by Malaysian and foreign companies, imported knockdown sets (KD sets) and paid about 50 per cent in import duties, 45 per cent in tariffs and 5 per cent in other duties in 1988. They also purchased local car parts, as required by the government to reduce tax and penalty payments. But as the quality of locally made parts was generally not as good as that of imported parts, and foreign suppliers allowed only minimal deductions for deleting locally available components from CKD packs, such imports continued. Hence, assemblers usually mainly purchased products made locally from Malaysian raw materials. Importing components into Malaysia allowed the parent companies abroad to profit from exporting parts.

By 1987, the Malaysian car industry was in a terrible condition. One Malaysian newspaper reported, 'Apart from Proton, the producer of the national car, the rest are saying that the industry is in critical condition and requires treatment from the "doctor"', presumably implying that Dr Mahathir should approve government intervention in its favour. The car producers asked for help in the form of reduced import and excise duties. They claimed that if no help was forthcoming in 1988, there would be more jobless people, not only from among assembly plant executives and workers, but also from sales and service staff. More than 5,000 workers in the Malaysian car industry lost their jobs in 1985 and 1986, while wages of the remaining workers were cut as well. The Transport Equipment and Allied Industries Employees Union, the relatively militant national industry union, had about 7,000 members in 1984, but only 2,500 in 1988. The government does not allow Proton workers to join this union; only an in-house union is allowed.

The car project was expected to eventually create only 3,000 job opportunities – a total much lower than the number of workers already involved in the local assembly of cars. Hence, except for the few absorbed into Proton (which generally employed inexperienced, rather than retrenched workers), many car assembly workers and even sales and distribution personnel were displaced as the Proton cornered the market. Fortunately, however, the economic boom and employment expansion since 1987 has minimized such adjustment costs.

Ethnic preferences were clearly reflected in Proton's recruitment. In 1988, the plant employed 1,300 people, 94 per cent of whom were ethnic Malays. Most Proton personnel were inexperienced, while very few experienced workers laid off by the other assembly firms – mainly non-Malays – were hired. The chief executive of Proton at the time, Wan Nik Ismail was quoted as saying 'if we'd wanted to employ such "veterans", we would have to get permission from the PM's Department' (*Business Times*, 19 July 1986). This meant that workers laid off by other plants were left unemployed. The government only responded by saying that the car industry had to undergo a rationalization process. According to the Industrial Master Plan (IMP), this meant closing down inefficient producers so that eventually, only Proton and two other car manufacturers would be left, but ignoring the issue of retaining relatively skilled and experienced workers from the other car assembly plants in the industry.

There was little public opposition to the government's forced rationalization of the car industry. Many industry appeals, however, were sent to the government, all of which were ignored. Most of the larger Chinese-owned firms jumped on the bandwagon instead. United Motor Works (Toyota), Tan Chong Motors (Nissan) and Oriental Motors (Honda) all got into components manufacturing; and when the first two – the largest assemblers after Proton – were offered stakes in EON, the sole distributor of the Saga, they happily accepted, much to the chagrin of some *Bumiputera* businessmen.

TRAINING

Of Proton's 1,300 workers in 1988, a total of 323 persons, including 250 workers, 55 staff members and 18 managers, were trained in Japan by Mitsubishi Motor Corporation between 1983 and 1986. Of the 323, 90 per cent were Malays, 6 per cent were Chinese and 4 per cent were Indians. In 1988, 16 Japanese engineers and management staff were employed at Proton. In 1987, there were about 30 Japanese staff. Initially, in 1985, the number of Japanese staff was about 100. The Japanese engineering staff are not supposed to control and advise their Malay colleagues too much, but rather allow them to solve problems by themselves. However, a Japanese staffperson claimed in 1987 that, after three years of commercial operation, Proton's production line could not be operated, even for one day, without the Japanese staff team. Even in early 1994, scores of MMC employees from Japan were still working on the Proton shopfloor, rotating every few months and hence not considered Japanese expatriate staff on Proton's payroll.

Of the 323 trainees, 138 trainee workers received financial support from the Malaysian government as part of the 'Look East' policy. These 138 Proton workers learnt the Japanese language for one year in Malaysia before they went to Japan for 4 to 8 months of technical training. Another 185 trainees were Proton trainees paid wages by Proton. The first group (5 staff and 7 workers) went to Japan in mid-1983. They did not learn the Japanese language beforehand, so the first 4 weeks in Japan were devoted to language training. During the fifth week, they studied courses on Japanese history and society. After that, they went to Mitsubishi Motor Corporation's Mizushima Factory for practical operations and engineering training. They stayed in Japan for 12 months. The second group (13 workers) went to Japan in November 1983 and participated in a similar programme for 11 months. By 1986, eleven groups in all had been sent to Japan for 6 to 12 months training. These workers and staff trained in Japan were later employed as foremen or supervisors in Proton's factory. Proton managers also went to Japan for training. In 1984, they were trained there for periods ranging from 34 to 88 days. Proton did not recruit managers from car assembling or allied industries in Malaysia, so they were not experienced in the industry, causing many difficulties.

The training programme for workers and staff has been large and ambitious. First, the number of trainees is great and the training period in Japan rather long. Few Japanese companies overseas have conducted such a huge training programme for such inexperienced new foreign workers in Japan. Secondly, the curriculum contains non-technical subjects, such as language training and background education about Japan and its society, in line with Mahathir's "Look East" policy from the early 1980s, as well as details of other Mitsubishi companies, though such information is not really useful for Malaysian operators and engineers.

The training was oriented towards gaining proper knowledge of operations and ordinary maintenance. But since this knowledge was limited to certain machines, the training was only good for the operation of some special sections of car assembly. In terms of its implications for technology transfer, the training was also strictly limited to car assembly itself. It did not include design, research and development – prerogatives MMC reserves for itself. The curriculum for managers was even more dubious. The training programme lasted up to 88 days in Japan. Since the newly employed Proton managers were not experienced in car assembly plants, 88 days was hardly enough for management trainees to gain adequate knowledge of the industry.

PROTON'S CHEQUERED SUCCESS?

As noted earlier, after four years of losses, Proton finally came into the black in 1989, posting a pre-tax profit of RM32.6 million on a turnover of RM820 million. The reasons for this turnaround include increased domestic demand and higher prices paid by EON. In 1990, Proton registered sales of over RM1 billion for the first time, and its pre-tax profit of over RM159 million effectively wiped out its accumulated losses. The company kept improving its finances. In 1991, turnover jumped to RM1.79 billion and pre-tax profits were in the region of RM261 million, enabling Proton to be listed on the Kuala Lumpur Stock Exchange in February 1992, with 150 million shares, out of a possible 500 million shares, offered to the public at RM5 a share. However, HICOM and the Ministry of Finance remain the largest shareholders, with 29 and 18 per cent respectively. The Japanese stake was trimmed down to 17.4 per cent, while the rest is held by two Malaysian institutions and members of the public.

For the year ended 31 March 1992, Proton registered a turnover of over RM2.1 billion, with pre-tax profits of RM408 million. The boom, however, may not last though auto sales hit an all time high of 136,000 units in 1991. Indeed, the national car maker expects profits to remain flat, especially with the availability of Perodua Kancil from mid-1994. Nevertheless, it is undeniable that in recent years, the national car project has been a financial success for Proton, made possible mainly by the heavy and generous protection accorded to Proton. With exemption from high import duties, Proton can offer their cars at prices that undercut equivalent imported vehicles by almost 30 per cent (Bartu, 1992: 73).

Proton's launch shook up an industry that was in sore need of rationalization. The costs, however, have been high. The economic burden of the Proton project in the first decade of its existence was estimated to be at least 1.6 billion ringgit (Chee, 1985). The Treasury, for instance, lost about RM120 million in foregone import duties in 1987 alone. The authorities have continued to assist Proton. In early 1991, for instance, the central bank passed tough guidelines restricting loan financing for new cars to four years from five previously. The directive was ostensibly aimed at limiting runaway consumption and related inflation, but only affected cars priced above RM40,000. Thus, Proton was exempted from the new regulation while all its competitors were adversely affected. The directive may now affect Proton. Already, its new 1993 upper end model costs more than RM40,000, but many observers think that the authorities will simply revise the limit upwards if the price of the most popular Proton models exceeds RM40,000.

However, protection also decreased a little in 1991, when Proton, for the first time, had a 5 per cent import duty imposed on its CKD packs – still much lower, however, than the 40 per cent borne by all other manufacturers. Most analysts do not expect more increases for Proton. If anything, increases could be imposed on the other manufacturers. In 1991, when vans – which were price comparable with Proton – were found to be increasingly popular with consumers, hefty import and excise taxes were introduced for them. Thus, despite calls for Proton's protection to be 'gradually reduced' – in response to the relatively high auto prices in Malaysia compared with the pre-Proton era – this is unlikely to happen.

While the Malaysian car project has achieved some economies of scale from the standardisation of locally produced components, previously produced inefficiently, expensively and often poorly by about 75 local ancillary manufacturing firms, the car industry needs much greater economies of scale to become truly internationally competitive. The domestic Malaysian market is simply too small to support such an industry. Most competitive car factories manufacture more than 200,000 units per year, whereas, in spite of the economic boom, Proton sold only 136,000 units in 1993 – a level which, by Proton's own estimates, cannot be sustained for the next two years. Thus, the only way for Proton to eventually become viable, without protection, is to export in a big way. However, whether it can ever become a major exporter will depend on various factors, including Mitsubishi's willingness to cooperate. For the time being, however, the fate of the Malaysian car project depends primarily on the protection and other help it enjoys to keep competitors at bay assuming, of course, that domestic demand continues to ensure sufficient sales to maintain profitability.

Protection of the Proton has increased the prices of all cars. Many consumers also claim that the protection forces them to accept poorer quality Protons, while some complain of less choice as a consequence of the 'rationalization' of the industry. The more heavily protected market has also meant a reduction in the range of available models in the local market. Government revenue from taxes on imported cars has also declined as consumers have virtually been forced – by the price differential – to buy the Proton.

Thus, Mitsubishi's strong interest in the Malaysian car project has proved to be very profitable. The protection of the local market for Proton has ensured handsome profits for Mitsubishi. Besides profits from the sale of cars, Mitsubishi has made substantial gains from the supply of car parts, production equipment, technical and managerial support, etc. on turnkey project terms. Hence, Mitsubishi has certainly profited, even while the Proton car project was incurring losses for HICOM. With an investment of only RM54 million, Mitsubishi has captured a huge share of the Malaysian car market. This is indeed impressive since Mitsubishi's previous market position was not particularly impressive. In the early 1980s, Mitsubishi held fifth place in the market, accounting for only 8 per cent of the car market in 1982. In contrast, Proton commanded over 70 per cent of the car market by the early 1990s.

It is still not clear what Malaysia or the government will gain in the long term for giving MMC a dominant position in the domestic market. National pride may have been strengthened by the propaganda accompanying the project. Big new machines and modern management techniques have been brought in, but Malaysia's own real car manufacturing technological capacity remains very limited. Proton's operations and viability remain very much subordinated to Mitsubishi's interests. Fortunately, the Malaysian parties have slowly enhanced their bargaining capacities in some important ways, though not without great cost.

While it is increasingly acknowledged that the Proton car project has been economically burdensome, especially for consumers, it has been argued by some that the car project is essential for the pursuit of a new stage of industrialization involving the development of heavy industries. It certainly cannot be denied that the car industry has played a major role in the industrial growth of both the United States and Japan. But for various reasons, Malaysia cannot realistically expect to follow suit by trying to replicate the experiences of these economies in fundamentally different domestic and international economic and technological circumstances.

Proton's dependence on Mitsubishi continues, although new strains have been showing. In 1991, Prime Minister Mahathir announced plans for a second national car, a smaller one with an engine capacity of less than 1,000 cc and costing much less than the Proton. Much to the chagrin of Mitsubishi, which makes small cars as well, the Japanese partner picked was Daihatsu, associated with Toyota. Mainly involving private *Bumiputera* business interests, the new car project is expected to begin production in 1994 with much the same privileges enjoyed by Proton. Although touted to create a new 'lower middle class' car market segment, it is likely to encroach on the 'lower end' of Proton's market share, and may thus enhance the Malaysian government's leverage and bargaining position *vis-à-vis* Mitsubishi.

In March 1994, it became clear that Mahathir had become increasingly irritated with Mitsubishi for several reasons, including slow technology transfer, steep management and technology fees and a persistently high dependence on Mitsubishi in Japan. That could be one reason why the Proton Saga facelift, the Iswara, was designed by British engineers, and not by Mitsubishi. In July 1994, it was announced that Proton would collaborate with Citroen and Diversified Resources Bhd, a *Bumiputera* company favoured by Mahathir, to produce two new models in Malaysia. However, the need to ensure the continued viability of Proton may ensure that Malaysia's relationship with Mitsubishi will endure. Indeed, the Japanese have become even more important to the project as management dependence actually increased in the late 1980s, a development at odds with fulfilment of the goal of building a truly 'Malaysian' car.

*NOTE

The author would like to acknowledge the research of Shiode Hirokazu on the Proton in the late 1980s.

REFERENCES

Friedemann Bartu (1992) *The Ugly Japanese: Nippon's Economic Empire in Asia*, Longman, Singapore.

Business Times (BT) 25 March 1985. 'Saga dealership issue: Common sense prevails'.

Business Times (BT) 19 July 1986.

Business Times (BT) 2 December 1989, supplement on the Proton project.

Paul Chan, 'Economics of Regulation In Malaysia with Reference to the Motor Vehicle and Components Industry', cited in Doner (1988).

Chee Peng Lim (1985) 'The Malaysian Car Industry At A Crossroad', paper presented to the 7th Malaysian Economic Convention, Kuala Lumpur.

Richard F. Doner (1988) 'The Dilemmas and Limits of State Autonomy in Malaysia: The Case of the National Car Project', paper presented at the Asian Studies Association annual meeting, San Francisco.

C.B. Edwards (1975) 'Protection, Profits and Policy: An Analysis of Industrialization in Malaysia', PhD thesis, University of East Anglia, Norwich, UK.

Far Eastern Economic Review (FEER) 24 December 1982.

Far Eastern Economic Review (FEER) 3 August 1989.

Far Eastern Economic Review (FEER) 1 September 1989.

S. Jayasankaran (1993) 'Made-in-Malaysia: The Proton Project', in Jomo K.S. (ed.) *Industrializing Malaysia: Policy, Performance, Prospects*, Routledge, London.

Jomo K.S. (1983) 'Project Proton: Malaysian Car, Mitsubishi Profits' in Jomo K.S. (ed.) *The Sun Also Sets*, INSAN, Kuala Lumpur.

Kit Machado (1989) 'Japanese Transnational Corporations in Malaysia's State Sponsored Heavy Industrialization Drive: The HICOM Automobile and Steel Projects,' *Pacific Affairs*, 62: 504–31.

Malaysian Business (MB) 1 December 1984.

Malaysian Business (MB) 1 January 1986: cover story on the Proton project.

Malaysian Business (MB) 1 September 1989, 'Auto makers opt for parts'.

Malaysian Business (MB) 16 April 1990: cover story on Proton/EON.

Shiode Hirokazu (1989) *Japanese Investment In Southeast Asia – Three Malaysian Case Studies*, Centre for the Progress of Peoples, Hong Kong.

The Asian Wall Street Journal (AWSJ) 8 July 1985, 'Malaysia gambles for growth with car'.

The Asian Wall Street Journal (AWSJ) 19 December 1985.

UNCTC (1983) *Transnational Corporations in the International Auto Industry*, United Nations Centre for Transnational Corporations, New York.

United Nations Industrial Development Organisation (UNIDO) report, 'Japan and Malaysia's Car: Rising Sun or False Dawn of Economic Cooperation', Vienna, cited in *Far Eastern Economic Review*, 14 February 1985.

12

PROTON AND MALAYSIA'S MOTOR VEHICLE INDUSTRY

National industrial policies and Japanese regional production strategies

Kit G. Machado

Structural changes underway in the world political economy have affected and promise further to affect the power and wealth of states, corporations, financial institutions, classes, groups and individuals. Which states, organizations and people move ahead or fall behind in these terms depends largely on the extent to which they are able to advance or maintain their relative position in a very fast changing international division of labour (Frobel *et al.*, 1980: 45; Caporaso, 1987). Worldwide relocation of whole or partial manufacturing facilities proceeds apace in many industries. No states have been more involved in this on-going process than those of the Pacific Basin. Firms from the world's advanced capitalist states have made substantial new investment in and relocated numerous manufacturing plants to most of the less developed states of the region. This process has altered the latter's role in the world economy, and it has contributed to the economic advance made by some of them. Wide dispersal of production sites does not, however, assure commensurately wide dispersal of the economic benefits of production. These are determined primarily by where value is added and how it is shared. These questions are continuously at issue between those at different levels in the global division of labour as those below the top seek to move up and those on top seek to stay there.

Today, the ASEAN (Association of Southeast Asian Nations) states seek to accelerate and deepen industrial development. At the same time, Japanese firms expand and, in some sectors, seek to organize and integrate industrial production throughout the Pacific Basin as part of larger strategies for maintaining or enhancing their position in the international division of labour. The ASEAN states' industrial policies derive from various combinations of international and domestic considerations. Japanese strategies along with other international factors form an important matrix of opportunities and constraints which shapes the outcomes of these policies. This can be seen in various sectors (e.g., electronics, machinery), but it is particularly notable in the motor vehicle industry. The recent development of that industry in Malaysia provides a good example of the intersection between the ASEAN states' industrial policies and Japanese industrial strategies. As part of a larger heavy industrialization drive, the Malaysian government in 1983 formed a national auto firm in joint venture with Mitsubishi, and in 1993, a second such venture was formed with Daihatsu. These projects were, among other things, intended to promote rationalization (i.e., concentration into fewer but larger companies) and localization (i.e., increased use of locally produced parts) in a sector where most other participants were also associated with Japanese auto firms. At the same time, Japanese firms have, for both strategic and narrower economic reasons, sought to promote regional production of motor vehicles and to control the character and pace of localization. The primary purpose of this chapter is to describe and explain the outcomes of such Malaysian and Japanese efforts to date.

What follows is informed by debates in political economy concerning the prospects for Third World industrialization. Some hold that the capitalist world system imposes such severe constraints on states seeking to improve their position in the international division of labour that they may at best achieve dependent and distorted industrial development (Cardoso and Faletto, 1979; Evans, 1979). Others give greater weight to domestic factors and assert that 'hard', purposeful, high capacity Third World states that enjoy substantial autonomy from society (Deyo, 1987; Haggard, 1990) or that build effective public–private sector coalitions (Doner, 1991) can exploit opportunities in the world system to build a solid industrial base. Still others, encouraging synthesis, stress that national political economic developments are shaped by both global and domestic factors and that the important matter is to assess their relative weight in particular cases (Frieden and Lake, 1991; Ellison and Gereffi, 1990). The following analysis of the effects of global and domestic political economic trends on the development of the Malaysian motor vehicle industry certainly finds both to have been important.

Malaysia is a particularly suitable subject for this analysis. The country has long exhibited classic characteristics of economic dependence (Khor, 1983), but it has been systematically attempting to reduce the limitations imposed by this circumstance. It more closely matches the model of the 'hard', autonomous state than most Third World countries. Malaysia's national leaders and private businessmen have sometimes worked in concert to advance national goals. At the same time, Malaysia's highly complex ethnic situation has an impact on most state undertakings (Milne and Mauzy, 1986). The government's commitment to advancing the economic position of the *Bumiputera* (i.e., indigenous Malays) in relation to the large Chinese and Indian communities has been considered at every turn in pursuing other policy objectives, including industrialization and managing relations with transnational capital (Bowie, 1991; Jesudason,

1989). Examination of the Malaysian case should thus bring the importance of external constraints and opportunities and of domestic characteristics and initiatives into sharp relief.

The focus of this chapter is on the interaction and bargaining between the national and transnational participants in the Malaysian motor vehicle industry as they pursue their respective strategies within the context of world and national political economic trends (for excellent studies of such bargaining in the automobile industry, see Bennett and Sharpe, 1985; Doner, 1991). It first briefly analyses Malaysia's heavy industrial and motor vehicle policies. It next assesses Japan's regional and global economic strategies and its motor vehicle firms' specific strategies. It then examines the intersection of Malaysian policy and Japanese strategies in the transformation of the Malaysian motor vehicle industry through early 1994, considering (1) the formation and early development of the 1983 auto project and the formation of the 1993 project, (2) transfer of management control of the first project from Malaysian to Japanese hands during a critical five-year period (1988–93), and (3) the localization process. Finally, it looks at the intersection of Japanese strategies and both Malaysian and ASEAN policies in the early stages of regional auto production schemes advanced by Mitsubishi and other Japanese auto manufacturers. I conclude that while Malaysia has effectively exerted influence on Japanese transnational auto firms and thereby derived some real economic benefits and advanced some of its national industrial goals, these gains have been realized at the cost of accepting new forms of dependence for the foreseeable future.

MALAYSIAN HEAVY INDUSTRIAL AND MOTOR VEHICLE POLICIES

Policy development and management

A large-scale, state sponsored heavy industrialization drive, centred initially on motor vehicle and steel manufacture, was launched in Malaysia in 1981 (Bowie, 1991: Ch. 5; Machado, 1989–90). This was largely the work of Datuk Seri Dr Mahathir bin Mohamad, who became the prime minister that year. He simultaneously defined 'learning from Japan' as crucial to national development and vigorously promoted this orientation under his 'Look East' policy. Heavy industrialization would rely extensively on Japanese capital, technology, and finance, but the priorities would be set by Mahathir. Joint ventures would be established between Japanese corporations and the Heavy Industries Corporation of Malaysia (HICOM). Mahathir had created the latter as a former Trade and Industry Minister and had recruited its top managers mainly from the public sector. In 1981, he took jurisdiction over HICOM with him to the prime minister's department, where it has effectively answered to him. It was not formed as a government agency but a 100 per cent government-owned holding company established, like a private firm, under the Companies Act. This fact reduced the governmental control and scrutiny normally exercised over public undertakings (Puthucheary, 1984). The role of HICOM is exemplary of a long-term shift in policy making power in Malaysia from career bureaucrats to the top political leaders – a shift which was accelerated greatly by Mahathir. Inter-agency bodies work out the details of narrow industrial policy issues, but the coordinating body for general industrial policy making is the cabinet. HICOM projects are closely identified with the prime minister, and he has made many key decisions in their development. Political insiders say that dealing with Japanese participants in these projects is the exclusive domain of the prime minister.

External and domestic factors in heavy industrial policy

Malaysia's leaders had long attempted to promote manufacturing, but Mahathir's strategy was a new departure in industrial policy. He aimed to push Malaysia into the ranks of the Newly Industrializing Countries (NICs) by the end of this century. His goals were, in part, to reduce Malaysia's economic dependence on world primary commodity markets and on Western capitalist states and to increase the benefits to the country of relations with transnational corporations. Malaysia has long been highly vulnerable to fluctuations in primary commodity prices. Long-term trends in the prices of its exports and imports have resulted in substantial decline in its terms of trade over the past 30 years (Khor, 1987: 76–80). During the first post-independence decade, industrial development was based on import substitution. In the late 1960s, the promotion of export-oriented manufacturing began. This was based mainly on primary product processing and labour-intensive assembly, packaging, and final processing operations. Many of these industries were foreign-owned and operating in Free Trade Zones (FTZ) where they had few links to the rest of the economy. An Industrial Master Plan (IMP) prepared under the auspices of the UN Industrial Development Organization (UNIDO) in the early 1980s was intended to form a coherent framework for further industrial development (MIDA/UNIDO, 1985). Its main goals were rationalization of protected import-substituting industries and both diversification and deepening of export-oriented industries. The IMP aimed to push modern manufacturing activity beyond FTZ enclaves and to stimulate spin-offs. The intention was to reduce the dependence of Malaysian industries on imported raw materials and intermediate inputs and to foster an expanding network of linkages between these industries. The decision to promote heavy industries antedated the formulation of the IMP, however, and had to be taken as a given by its authors.

Mahathir's economic policies were partly responses to such external constraints, but his critique of these problems and his reactions to them followed from more than his reading of the economic situation. These derived from his sense of nationalism, from his efforts to mobilize nationalist sentiment to bolster his administration and, most importantly, from his ideas concerning national development and its requisites and his long-standing concern with what he regards as serious defects in Malay values and behaviour. His views on these matters were originally set forth in his controversial book, *The Malay Dilemma* (Mahathir, 1970). He asserted that rural Malays lacked sufficient individual enterprise, independence, initiative, pride in work, or competitive ability, and he stressed that effecting changes in *Bumiputera* values and behaviour was essential to national development. These assumptions also underlay his 1980s 'Look East' policy, which emphasized the need for Malays to learn from Japanese work ethics and attitudes. Mahathir stressed the rural roots of alleged Malay deficiencies. He argued that the solution was 'to urbanize the Malays', and he emphasized that they 'must acquire skills through working . . . not be subjected to theoretical lessons' (1970: 105–106). He said that *Bumiputera* economic problems could not be solved politically without supporting changes in their values and behaviour (1970: 31), which must ultimately come through their own efforts (1981: 33). For Mahathir, promoting industrialization to stimulate changes among *Bumiputera* was as important as promoting it to hasten economic development. It is these views that are most important to understanding his industrial policies.

Heavy industrialization was also part of Mahathir's effort to further structural change in Malaysia's political economy (Milne, 1986). He was disappointed by the slow progress made in meeting New Economic Policy (NEP) goals. The NEP required restructuring 'society to eliminate the identification of race with economic functions' (Government of Malaysia, 1981: 1), meaning primarily increasing *Bumiputera* participation in the modern sector of the economy. A 1990 target of 30 per cent *Bumiputera* ownership and control in the corporate sector was clearly not going to be met. Creation of state industries went well beyond an Industrial Coordination Act-mandated equity restructuring exercise that had given state trust agencies a stake in many private companies after the mid-1970s. Establishing state firms in sectors that had been wholly or partly dominated by Chinese, often in combination with foreign capital, represented an advance in economic restructuring and in efforts to expand the *Bumiputera* managerial and entrepreneurial classes. Reliance on state firms also followed from the factors that deter private investment in such projects – large initial investments, big risks, long gestation periods before profits can be expected, and low rates of return (HICOM, 1984: 14–15). Moreover, such initiatives created new opportunities for dispensing patronage, which was of growing importance to top leaders of the United

Malays National Organization (UMNO), who were seeking to expand and to cement their political dominance (Gomez, 1990).

Although Mahathir remains committed to advancing Malaysia to NIC status as part of his Vision 2020 and to promoting changes in *Bumiputera* values and behavior, he has fostered important shifts in the thrust of national economic policy in general and industrial policy in particular in the early 1990s. Under the National Development Plan (NDP) that succeeded the NEP in June 1991, economic equity for *Bumiputera* is no longer defined in terms of specific shares and target dates, and there has been greater emphasis on market forces. Privatization has extended to the heavy industrial sector. The national auto firm was partially privatized in 1992 as was HICOM (renamed HICOM Holdings) in early 1994. Simultaneously, emphasis on heavy industry has been reduced and emphasis on small and medium industries (SMIs) has been greatly increased. Mahathir's approach to fostering the latter industries is called the 'umbrella concept'. SMIs are encouraged to develop subcontracting ties or, if they lack the necessary capital and technology for this, to form joint ventures with transnational corporations. This meshes perfectly with Japanese regional production strategies, and specific Malaysian government policies to improve the performance of such industries appear to derive from advice proffered under Japanese technical assistance programmes (*Business International Country Report*, 1992; *Far Eastern Economic Review*, 1992: 44).

Objectives of the national auto projects

It was Mahathir's decision to promote the manufacture of a national car in 1983. He saw this as a central pillar of industrialization and defined it as a key to national 'coming of age'. He described it as 'another step toward enhancing the nation in the eyes of the world [and] a symbol of Malaysians as a dignified people' (*New Straits Times*, 1985). Auto manufacture promised technological advance, the development of engineering skills, and the generation of supply industries with export potential. The auto project was partly an effort to reduce import dependence by forcing rationalization of the industry. After more than a decade of local assembly of imported Completely Knocked Down (CKD) automobile kits, finished vehicles still contained no more than 18 per cent local content by value. Automobile assemblers and their primarily Japanese partners had not only consistently resisted government localization policies, but, with government forbearance and protection, they had created an industrial structure that was itself an obstacle to localization. The large number of makes and models of cars being assembled for a very small market made it difficult economically to produce component parts locally (Ariff, 1982; Chee, 1984). Moreover, as local Chinese entrepreneurs dominated auto assembly, it was an obvious target for restructuring. The second national car project was instituted in

1993 to extend heavy industrialization, to deepen the local parts and components manufacturing sector, and to gain increased access to the technology necessary to achieving the latter goal.

JAPANESE REGIONAL AND GLOBAL STRATEGIES

National and corporate strategies

Forced from Southeast Asia in defeat in 1945, the Greater East Asian Co-prosperity Sphere apparently in ruins, the Japanese soon returned and rapidly became the predominant economic force in the region. In the 1970s, Japan became the largest or the next to largest trading partner of and investor in all of the ASEAN states (Akrasanee, 1983; Sekiguchi, 1983). During the next decade, Japanese firms accelerated cumulative investment in ASEAN from US$6 billion in 1980 to US$23 billion in 1990 (Dobashi, 1988; JETRO, 1991), though owing to economic difficulties at home their investment has slowed since 1990. Today, the Japanese seek to maintain and extend their predominant economic position in Southeast Asia under the best possible terms. They aim to reduce the economic uncertainties inherent in the current period and to maximize their global competitiveness. In pursuit of these goals, they seek to promote greater regional economic integration under their leadership. Top Japanese political leaders made proposals to these ends in the 1960s and 1970s. These proposals were met with little enthusiasm by their neighbours, who perceived them as promising advantages mainly to the Japanese. Tokyo's top leaders have consistently denied that they seek regional economic domination and have for some time concentrated on supporting ASEAN as well as broader regional arrangements proposed by others (Sudo, 1988a,b). Japanese academics and technocrats simultaneously project colourful images of Asia developing under Japanese leadership. Japan has been variously portrayed as the leader of geese flying in 'V' formation and as the 'Asian brain'.

More practically, the Japanese work to build the structural underpinnings for the position they seek in the region one piece at a time. Both government and private sector interests favour and attempt to promote complementation or 'agreed specialization' between Japan and its economic partners to optimize complementarity in the division of labour between countries and within specific transnational industries (Kojima, 1970; Aoki, 1986; Dobashi, 1988; RIM Studies Group, 1988; Ohata, 1989). The 1987 Japanese Ministry of International Trade and Industry (MITI) New Asian Industries Development Plan sets a framework for investment in and relocation of export-oriented industries to the region (Unger, 1990). Follow-up Japanese studies done with specific ASEAN governments recommend products in which their countries should specialize (*Wall Street Journal*, 1990; *Far Eastern Economic Review*, 1991a: 54). Japanese transnationals design and promote integrated regional production schemes based on an intra-industry international division of labour. Institutions set up to recycle some of Japan's trade surplus in Southeast Asia, such as the Japan–ASEAN Investment Corporation and the ASEAN–Japan Development Fund, finance projects that conform to such goals. Japanese banks are acquiring stakes in local banks in the region to provide better for the needs of Japanese investors there. Many investment, financing, and aid decisions are thus made within the framework of the broader Japanese strategy.

Recent Japanese direct foreign investment, much of it in export industries, is supported by Japanese government agencies, private financial institutions, and trading companies, and it is driving increased integration of the Asia–Pacific region. New investments by Japanese transnationals as well as recent relocations of small and medium Japanese firms in other regional states follow from both domestic problems and global strategies. The impact of a severe labour shortage on wages, inflated land prices, and yen appreciation since 1985 have all contributed to increasing production costs in Japan. These mounting costs have had an adverse impact on the price competitiveness of some Japanese manufactured exports in world markets. This has been a particularly important consideration in the decisions of many small and medium Japanese industries to locate elsewhere in Asia where labour is cheaper (Phongpaichit, 1988). It has even been argued that Japan 'agreed to yen revaluation in accordance with its own industrial policy for phasing out sunset industries at home and for the purpose of accelerating its direct foreign investment' (Hollerman, 1988: 17). In any case, Japan's wish to hold down its trade surplus with, and to circumvent quotas in, the United States and the European Community (EC) is a further spur to regional investment by its transnationals, as it means that products made by companies under Japanese control can enter these markets from other Asian countries. This consideration has become particularly important as Japanese global strategies have led to the increasing presence of their manufacturing plants in other advanced capitalist states. To enhance price competitiveness in these markets, these plants will be supplied in part by Japanese-controlled companies elsewhere in Asia (Dobashi, 1988).

Hollerman (1988: 8–11) offers a convincing explanation of such trends, arguing that Japan's 'domestic industrial policy . . . has evolved into geopolitical strategy' which 'coordinate[s] Japan's external relations with the transformation of its indigenous industrial structure, . . . [including] calculated disaggregation . . . of the production process, with some stages being assigned abroad and some retained at home'. In this process, 'Japan retains for itself the higher value-added operations that yield the best rates of return'. At the same time, 'export of plants and equipment [establishes a] dependency relationship (in terms of financing, maintenance, management, and distribution of output) . . . between Japan and its clients'.

Hollerman (1988: xi) thus contends that Japan aims to become a 'headquarters country' able to 'impose central management on a world network of joint ventures, subsidiaries, and affiliates' and to 'coordinate the relations of its foreign clients with each other as well as . . . with itself'. This project is far from realization. The total portion of Japanese industrial production by value located offshore is still only 6.6 per cent. It is expected to increase through the early years of the next century, and in some industries, it is expected to grow rapidly. (For comparison, the current United States figure is almost 26 per cent.) Internationalization of some Japanese industries proceeds apace, and Japanese strategies form an important matrix within which both governments and business people throughout Asia must operate.

Auto industry strategies

Japan's auto makers, like its other manufacturers, have been reluctant transnationals, historically preferring to produce at home and export. Current and feared import restrictions in North American and EC markets have been the primary spur to change. The major Japanese auto firms now have global strategies looking mainly to replace some exports with cars produced on both continents, where they have invested US$10.5 billion since the mid-1980s (*Far Eastern Economic Review*, 1991c: 59). Nissan, having started the earliest, has gone the furthest with this process. In 1989, it announced that it planned during the next decade to reverse its domestic to overseas production ratio from what it was then (2:1), to make it 1:2 by the turn of the century. About the same time, the firm was reorganized to create what its president called a 'tripolar corporate management structure, with integrated operations headquarters in Japan, North America, and Europe, . . . [making] it easier to coordinate our overall activities from a global perspective' (*Asian Wall Street Journal*, 1989). Nissan set out to strengthen the global planning capacity of each of its departments as a step toward establishing its corporate functions on a worldwide basis in order 'to reinforce Nissan's ability to coordinate business plans for its overseas operations in harmony with domestic operations' (*Japan Times*, 1990). It also began building a global research and development (R&D) network. Mitsubishi, Honda and Toyota have to varying degrees been moving in the same direction. They are now conducting R&D and producing vehicles alone and/or in tie ups with local manufacturers in North America and/or Europe.

Japanese auto firms' Asian regional strategies are similarly inspired, as they also face import restrictions in what they regard as an increasingly promising market. At the same time, however, production of both cars and parts in lower labour cost states of the region are ultimately intended for export to North America and the EC countries. Parts are also intended for import and use in Japan. In 1988–89, for example, Nissan was instructing some 100 of its affiliated parts makers to locate in ASEAN and China to set up a 'global buying network' (Steven, 1990: 102). Japanese motor vehicle firms are apparently attempting to reproduce their subcontracting-based domestic industrial structure on a regional basis. As noted, this meshes very well with current Malaysian policy. It does not necessarily auger well for Malaysian or ASEAN companies that join with Japanese parts firms to supply Japanese auto makers. The latter are basically assemblers and rely heavily on networks of 200 to 300 external suppliers to provide them with components and subassemblies that make up about 70 per cent of their total manufacturing costs. Many subcontractors do exceedingly well, but their employees are often among the first to feel economic downturns. Moreover, successful principal–subcontractor relationships centre on large measures of trust (Smitka ,1991). It is difficult at this point to imagine Japanese companies entering easily into such relationships with non-Japanese suppliers. Japanese organizations appear to offer two classes of citizenship, one for Japanese and one for foreigners; and it has been argued that the auto firms make this distinction with respect to their off shore suppliers (Womack et al., 1990). In any case, the extent to which the Japanese auto firms' global strategies shape their Asian regional strategies should be borne in mind as we turn to a more detailed consideration of their intersection with Malaysian policies.

MALAYSIAN POLICIES AND JAPANESE STRATEGIES IN THE TRANSFORMATION OF MALAYSIA'S MOTOR VEHICLE INDUSTRY

Formation and development of PROTON

Having opted to promote auto manufacture, Mahathir instigated efforts to find a Japanese transnational corporate partner. HICOM ultimately formed a joint auto venture, Perusahaan Otomobil Nasional (PROTON), with Mitsubishi Motor Corporation (MMC) and Mitsubishi Corporation (MC) (Doner, 1991: Ch. 5; Machado, 1989–90). The establishment and development of PROTON has involved ongoing bargaining between the Malaysian and Japanese partners. At the outset there appeared to be substantial convergence between MMC/MC's corporate interests and Mahathir's definition of Malaysian interests. The terms of the final joint venture agreement favoured the Japanese side, but Malaysia got more or less what it initially wanted. PROTON was set up as a HICOM subsidiary under the Companies Act. HICOM required foreign partners to take minority shares in its projects on the assumption that this would commit

300

them to their success. MMC/MC put up 30 per cent and HICOM 70 per cent of the RM150 million equity in this RM490 million project. MMC was to design and build a plant with an annual capacity of 80,000 (expandable to 120,000) units to manufacture Malaysia's national car, the Saga, a slightly modified Mitsubishi Lancer. The Saga was initially to be built exclusively for the local market. The PROTON plant was to do body stamping, assembly, painting and trim and final assembly of the car. Bodies were to be added to imported, locally assembled CKD kits. MMC reluctantly agreed under heavy pressure to use in the Saga most locally produced parts used in other makes under the existing local content programme. Local production of bodies assured that the Saga would have higher local content than other cars, but they required imported steel, which was to come primarily through MC from Japan. Managerial, technical, clerical, and production jobs would be created, primarily for Malays, and many PROTON managers and workers would be trained by Japanese counterparts in Malaysia or by MMC in Japan.

Production and sales of the Saga were to be carried out by separate companies, but – in an arrangement unusual in both the Japanese and Malaysian auto industry – they were not under common control. HICOM entered a partnership with a private firm, UMW Holdings, in the Saga marketing company, Edaran Otomobil Nasional (EON). HICOM had only a minority share, while UMW had effective control of EON. The head of UMW was a prominent Chinese entrepreneur who was on the boards of HICOM and some other state-controlled concerns and was considered to be very close to Mahathir. He had acquired the Toyota franchise in 1982 with the intention of taking the dominant place in the local auto market, and PROTON was a major blow to these plans. Some auto industry insiders believe that Mahathir permitted him to take the lead in EON partly to remedy the damage done to his interests. Others believe that Mahathir, and possibly MMC/MC as well, recognizing the lack of marketing experience among PROTON's management, simply wanted to bring in an experienced party to assure the effective sale of the Saga. MMC/MC was not keen on the structure of this arrangement, but accepted it as a local matter. In any case, it was to become the source of a costly schism in the car project.

MMC/MC derived great leverage in negotiating the PROTON agreement from their control of capital and technology. As all RM340 million in finance for this highly leveraged venture came from associates of the Mitsubishi group, MMC/MC enjoyed greater influence in the project than their minority equity position would suggest. This influence was acquired at very low risk, for all loans were guaranteed by the Malaysian Treasury, as required by the Japanese lenders. MMC/MC used this leverage at the very outset to ensure that construction arrangements were advantageous to themselves. They were in charge of contracting for the turn-key plant construction project. The majority of contract payments went to Japanese firms, particularly MMC and MC, who were key suppliers of equipment and machinery. Their equity share in PROTON was equal to about 13 per cent of the RM354 million turn-key project. It is likely that their profits were about the same as their equity shares, meaning that the Malaysian side in effect paid most of the costs of the project. MMC and MC could also look forward to continuing profits as suppliers of CKD kits and steel for cars bodies, even if not as minority shareholders in PROTON.

Malaysia enjoyed only limited leverage in negotiating the auto agreement, primarily because MMC was the only Japanese auto firm willing to meet its desire to develop a manufacturing facility. Hence, there was no competitive selection process. There were also divisions between a lukewarm production side and a more interested commercial side of Mitsubishi concerning the advisability of the project. HICOM thus negotiated the final agreement with a somewhat hesitant MMC after the latter's selection was in effect certain. The weakness of HICOM's position was reflected most notably in provisions on key issues such as local content, pricing, and technology, which were all left very vague in accordance with Japanese preferences. The question of export was left as a subject for possible future discussion. The details of such matters have from the outset been the subject of continuous difference between HICOM and MMC and have had to be negotiated on a case-by-case basis – a circumstance that is seen as disadvantageous by the Malaysian side.

Most of the leverage Malaysia did have with Mitsubishi was expended simply to secure MMC's participation in the PROTON project. This leverage derived primarily from the government's power to set terms and conditions of participation in the national economy in ways both more and less advantageous to Japanese firms. The Economist Intelligence Unit (1985: 24) reported that in promoting heavy industrialization, Malaysia was seeking to 'obtain technological benefits . . . in return for . . . favorable consideration of Japanese interests in [its] trade and investment policies and . . . the award of contracts . . . (especially for construction . . .) [and] to use its enormous natural resources to bargain for industrial assets'. Mitsubishi Bank, Chemical, Electric and Gas all operate in Malaysia. Mitsubishi Corporation also has a variety of interests there, including minority participation with PETRONAS (the national oil company) in the Malaysia Liquefied Natural Gas project in Sarawak. Mitsubishi officials must certainly have understood the potential long-term group benefits of participating in a project so important to Mahathir, and the Malaysian side may have capitalized on this. According to one Japanese industry analyst highly knowledgeable about Mitsubishi affairs, terms being negotiated in the gas project were linked by Malaysia to MMC participation in PROTON and from the group's point of view the profits from the gas project would cover its exposure in the car project. How bluntly such leverage may have been used is known to only a few. In any event, it appears that Mitsubishi Corporation's multiple interests in the country, contrary to expectation, may have enhanced rather than weakened Malaysia's leverage in this case.

The government's capacity to grant protection was of particular importance to MMC. To secure MMC participation and, it was presumed, the financial viability of the auto project, a 40 per cent import duty was imposed on CKD kits, and PROTON was granted exemption from that duty as well as the excise tax imposed on other assemblers. Thus, MMC was assured instant domination of the Malaysian passenger car market at the expense of its Japanese competitors. A Mitsubishi manager said that the company entered the venture expecting to take between 55 and 60 per cent of the market. With this assurance, MMC could see Malaysian goals meshing with its larger regional and international strategies. The company had a relatively weak place in the Japanese and Malaysian markets in the early 1980s, and it was seeking to develop external markets as part of its strategy for gaining on the firms ahead of it at home and abroad. At that time, the ASEAN countries comprised Japan's largest Third World market and Malaysia was its largest ASEAN passenger car market (Economist Intelligence Unit, 1985: 13–14). In the longer run, MMC aimed to promote regionally based production of an auto for export to Western markets, and it was determined that Malaysian body parts might eventually be used in this scheme.

The formation of PROTON was only the first step in a process of ongoing bargaining between the Malaysian and Japanese sides. Differences between them soon emerged and widened as conditions prevailing at the time of their initial agreement changed rapidly and substantially. Just as PROTON became operational in 1985, it was hit with multiple problems. Deepening recession resulted in a sharp decline in the demand for Malaysia's traditional exports. This event was soon translated into rapidly shrinking domestic demand for motor vehicles. With rapid yen appreciation, PROTON's all yen debt soon doubled in Malaysian ringgit. The cost of servicing it mounted accordingly, and it became a severe burden on the company. A multi-million-ringgit difference quickly developed between a losing PROTON and what proved to be a very profitable EON over what had been agreed concerning the transfer price of the Saga. As the companies were not under common control, this conflict proved quite intractable. By 1988, PROTON's accumulated losses were close to RM150 million (HICOM, 1985–88). As PROTON foundered financially, it pushed for reduced interest on its debt, accelerated localization, export of the Saga to third countries, and other measures to improve its earnings. MMC cooperated with some initiatives but resisted others. In the context of negotiations over these matters, MMC placed its own people in top management positions in PROTON and pressed for its regional complementation scheme. UMW's majority shares in EON were transferred to the Ministry of Finance, Inc. (25 per cent) and to a joint venture between MMC/MC and a *Bumiputera* company (15 per cent each), thus giving Mitsubishi a voice in marketing operations and improving the coordination of PROTON and EON policies.

The recession finally abated for Malaysia in 1988. Demand for automobiles, has increased more or less steadily since that time, though there was a dip in 1992 occasioned partly by government efforts to dampen demand generally. PROTON has a 67 per cent share of the market. With stronger demand and a more favourable pricing arrangement with EON, PROTON has recorded modest profits since fiscal year 1988–89. Projected demand by late 1992 was such that PROTON began gearing up to expand plant production capacity to 120,000 units by the end of 1993 and 150,000 units by 1995 (*Financial Times*, 1992). It appeared that PROTON would eventually attain a measure of economic viability as long as it continued to enjoy special protection and as long as the Malaysian economy continued to generate demand for what would, with that protection, remain a very expensive Saga. For example, in mid-1993 the cost of a new Saga ranged from about RM30,000 to RM50,000 (*Business International Country Report*, 1993), whereas GNP per capita was RM7,556 (Asian Development Bank, 1993: 171). Some of the other main objectives of the auto project are also being met. As Table 12.1 shows, a large measure of rationalization has taken place in the auto industry. The Saga now accounts for 70 per cent and the top three makes, 86 per cent of all production. The number of parts makers has also increased, largely on the basis of supply to PROTON. The Saga is with modest success being exported to several markets and to the UK. Between 1987 and mid-1993, about 65,000 units had been exported (Xinhua News Service, 1993). About two-thirds have gone to the UK, where the General System of Preferences (GSP) limit for duty exemption is 14,000 units a year. Saga exports to the United Kingdom are already close to this ceiling. In any case, these advances are being accompanied by increasing rather than declining dependence. Malaysia lost national management of PROTON to MMC during a critical five-year period, and its motor vehicle industry as a whole seems on its way to be being incorporated into Japanese-organized and controlled regional production schemes. This process is in an early stage, it moves in fits and starts, and its outcome is still uncertain, but the die appears to have been cast.

MMC takes management of PROTON

By mid-1988, both the Mahathir administration and the MMC had become quite concerned about PROTON's problems. Malaysia's finance minister attributed these to management inadequacies and, given the state of the economy, made what seemed exaggerated and unusually harsh public criticisms of the project's managers. He told the press that '[t]he recession

Table 12.1 Rationalization of the Malaysian passenger car industry

	1975	1980	1981	1982	1983	1984	1985	1986	1987	1988	1989
Total PC production	38.6	80.4	87.8	85.3	100.2	96.4	69.8	41.9	33.5	61.3	93.8
% Production PROTON Saga	–	–	–	–	–	–	12.3	59.5	71.6	72.9	70.1
Total no. of makes[a]	19	15	15	16	13	13	12	12	10	11	11
% Production/ top three makes	44.2	67.2	61.2	63.1	63.5	64.6	64.9	81.8	87.0	87.9	86.2

Sources: Ariff (1982: 127); HICOM (1985–89); and Malaysian Motor Vehicle Assemblers Association (1980–89).
[a] With production of at least 100 PC units

is only part of the problem, . . . [and if management cannot show results], they should do what people in Japan do – commit *harikiri* [sic]' (*New Straits Times*, 1988). By this time, most of the original Japanese counterpart managers had returned to Japan, and PROTON was largely in the hands of Malay managers. MMC began pushing for management changes. The prime minister ordered the formation of a task force comprised of HICOM, PROTON, and MMC/MC to look into the company's affairs. This task force was primarily an MMC undertaking, however, and MMC assumption of the company's management was clearly to be the end result of its work. HICOM and PROTON managers were opposed to this but were unsuccessful in their effort to fend it off. The Malaysian managing director was relieved of his responsibilities and replaced by a former MMC managing director in August 1988. Two additional MMC managers were made heads of the newly formed business and corporate planning divisions. This change was engineered in a face-saving way for the company but not for its top management. It was described as a Malaysian initiative. It was emphasized that the MMC managers were responsible to PROTON's Board not to MMC, and that this arrangement was to be for only two years while a 'turn around' exercise was to be carried out. In light of the nationalistic thrust of Mahathir's heavy industrialization drive and its important part in the effort to promote the development of Malay entrepreneurs, the irony of this episode was lost on few politically attentive Malaysians.

The primary reason for the change was said by both sides simply to be to streamline PROTON's management and to bring it to profitability, but this was not a complete explanation. With local market contraction, PROTON began to push hard to export the Saga. MMC reluctantly went along with exports only to small markets (e.g., Jamaica, Bangladesh, Sri Lanka) and was most displeased when Mahathir took independent initiatives to begin exports to the United Kingdom and the United States. With steep yen appreciation, PROTON also began to press for acceleration of localization and a search for suppliers outside of Japan. Locally produced parts had always been more expensive than Japanese ones because they were produced in such small numbers, but this situation changed rapidly as the value of the yen went up. With the rising costs of Japanese-made auto parts in world markets, MMC also became increasingly interested in promoting a complementation scheme in which there would be a measure of 'agreed specialization' among regional states in making parts and subassemblies. These components would then be traded among MMC regional operations for use in vehicle assembly. The aim of producing components in one country for regional use was to take advantage of economies of scale. The MMC apparently found PROTON's management too keen on exporting the Saga and on hastening localization and not keen enough on regional complementation. Therefore, it wanted to be in charge while the details of all three were being worked out. According to one Japanese auto industry analyst, MMC officials had concluded that their company's degree of control over PROTON was not commensurate with what was going to be its increasing involvement in the project.

In pushing for the PROTON management change, MMC's leverage was increased because its cooperation was essential to improving PROTON's economic performance. MMC controlled the loan renegotiation process, the price of the CKD kit, the technology needed to make changes required if the Saga was to be exportable to markets with standards higher than Malaysia's, and the pace of localization. How bluntly MMC used this leverage is uncertain. PROTON efforts on the foregoing fronts were not progressing well. Mutual recognition of the strength of MMC's position could not but have helped shape the outcome of discussions between the two sides. The intractability of the PROTON-EON conflict also strengthened MMC's hand, as it could be cited as evidence of a serious management problem. Malaysian acquiescence to the management change also appears to have stemmed partly from the belief that this conflict could be better resolved with persons not directly party to the dispute being in charge. In any case, soon after the change, the pricing dispute between PROTON and EON was settled. Impasses on other matters at issue were also soon broken. HICOM was able to renegotiate lower interest rates on part of PROTON's loans. A long-standing PROTON request for a small discount on the CKD kit was granted. An engine assembly line long under negotiation was started at the PROTON plant. This step would help boost the local content of the Saga over the 60 per cent necessary to permit it to enter the United Kingdom under the GSP (for GSP purposes, local content includes labour costs). PROTON's new MMC manager stressed that one of his main priorities would be to make the Saga internationally competitive. Such facts are consistent with the observation of one Japanese auto industry insider that by putting a high-level person in the top slot at PROTON, MMC had given the Malaysians a hostage guaranteeing that the auto project would not be allowed to fail.

By early 1990, MMC personnel had assumed the five top positions in PROTON, and neither HICOM officials nor Japanese auto industry experts believed that their terms would, in fact, be limited to the originally specified two years. They were proven correct. In June 1990, MMC announced in Tokyo that Mahathir had asked them to stay on and that they would remain 'for the next several years' (*Ward's Automotive International*, 1990: 4). The Japanese managers in fact remained in place until after the first model change was effected, and management was turned back to Malaysians in July 1993. The timing and details of the bargaining over the duration of MMC management are known only to a narrow circle of participants. The extent of MMC's involvement in the PROTON project by August 1990 was such that it is hard to imagine it having been willing even to consider withdrawing its managers at that point. PROTON's technological dependence on MMC could have made it very costly for Mahathir to press for these managers' departure if he had been so inclined. The early export effort was enjoying modest success, but expanding on that would require MMC's cooperation. Introduction of a left-hand drive model would, for example, be necessary to increase the potential overseas market for the Saga. A further increase in local content, perhaps to 80 per cent, may be necessary to qualify for GSP in the European Community after 1992. These factors gave MMC leverage that would have been very difficult to counter in bargaining over the tenure of MMC management or other policy questions. In any case, the Japanese managers of PROTON were able to make decisions during this critical period on such matters as localization and complementation which assured that MMC would set the direction and pace of these processes for some time. A privatization exercise in March 1992 – in which the MMC/MC stake in PROTON was somewhat reduced, the HICOM stake was both reduced and partly dispersed to other public agencies, and 30 per cent of company shares were floated – did not materially change this.

Localization

Increased localization of the Malaysian auto industry was a central goal of the national car project. The combination of Malaysian pressure and new departures in Japanese strategies following from yen appreciation have favored this development. Parts makers have grown in both number and strength, largely on the basis of supply to PROTON. At the end of 1988, PROTON was producing 337 parts in-house and procuring 46 parts from about 30 locally based companies. By 1993, it was producing almost 400 parts in-house and about 2,500 parts were being supplied by 125 locally based vendors. PROTON was assisting an additional 30 vendors to begin production of more than another 100 parts. In early 1993, local content of the Saga was reckoned to be 69 per cent, and it is expected to reach 80 per cent by GSP definition in 1994 (Kyodo News Service, 1993). Mahathir is said to have been under pressure in the Cabinet and from the parts makers to push MMC as well as HICOM and PROTON to hasten this process. In March 1994, he publicly criticized MMC for being too slow in transferring technology to PROTON and said that Malaysia might source 'knowledge from manufacturers other than the Japanese partners' (*New Straits Times*, 1994).

The Toyota and Nissan affiliates have also expanded their capacity for in-house production and worked to develop suppliers. Both have become suppliers to PROTON. They are expected to achieve 60 per cent local content within a few years. This is a sharp departure from the pre-1985 situation, but it is also somewhat deceptive. Such figures mask continuing conflicts over the nature and pace of localization. These are rooted in the very fundamental issues of where value is added and of how it is shared that help to determine the livelihoods and well-being of a great many people. Many Japanese worry that a rush of small and medium businesses or the transfer of higher value added component production overseas will result in 'hollowing' of the nation's industrial structure (i.e., deindustrialization). Firms fear that loss of control over technology will harm their profits. Hence the Japanese have strong motivations to limit the pace of localization.

Many auto components counted as 'local content' under current regulations in Malaysia rely heavily on imported intermediate goods. This fact shows up clearly in the country's trade statistics. Malaysia enjoyed a modest trade surplus with Japan in the early and mid-1980s, but it became a small deficit in 1988, which was, it should be noted, after the peak of yen appreciation. This deficit increased six times to RM3.8 billion in 1989 and to RM11.4 billion in 1991 (*The Straits Times*, 1992)). The major items in the import bill (67 per cent) were capital goods, mainly machinery and transport equipment, and a fair portion of these were bound for assembly and finishing plants (*Asian Wall Street Journal*, 1991). Much of this, of course, translates into exports, though their value is often only slightly in excess of the cost of the imported intermediate goods. The import of capital goods should eventually decrease with deepening industrial development. The basic point is, however, that many foreign participants in the Malaysian economy, including the Japanese parts suppliers that license technology to or are in joint ventures with Malaysian parts makers, have little reason to hasten change in these regards. The hostility of Japanese interests to autonomous Third World industrial progress was made clear in their government's 1989 submission to the Trade Related Investment Measures negotiating group under the General Agreement on Tariffs and Trade (GATT). It proposed worldwide abolition of requirements concerning local content, export percentages, and technology transfer, calling them restrictions on investment which distort trade. While this frontal assault on localization is likely to fail, Japanese firms are in a good position to set the pace at which it occurs in the Malaysian motor vehicle industry. In negotiations on this issue, they have the upper hand primarily because they control the technology that must be transferred if localization is to take place.

Such localization centres on supply to PROTON, and progress can be sustained only by continuing government pressure on MMC to accelerate local sourcing of parts for the Saga. This is not an easy task. Without a clear agreement with MMC on the specifics of localization, advances have to be negotiated on a case-by-case basis. PROTON echoes two standard complaints of assemblers of Japanese cars concerning the process of replacing CKD kit parts with local ones. The first is that MMC delays the testing of local parts proposed as replacements in order to slow the localization process. The other is that in itemizing the prices of parts in the CKD kit, MMC underprices the most easily replaced ones and overprices the others in order to keep its profits up when the former are deleted and replaced. To hasten localization, PROTON pressed MMC to begin engine assembly at the Saga plant. The latter argued that this was premature but reluctantly agreed. By early 1990, all engine requirements were met with local assembly. Local content of engines was initially only two to three per cent, but it increased with the opening of a HICOM Engineering Complex for casting and machining in 1991. Replacements for engine CKD kit parts still have to be negotiated on a part-by-part basis, and this has not been much easier than has been the deletion and replacement of auto CKD kit parts.

As MMC has come under added pressure on local content, it has taken new tacks to retain its control over the development of the Saga. While MMC managers were at PROTON's helm this was comparatively easy. MMC attempted to fragment control over technology. PROTON, for example, wanted to make the whole Saga brake assembly in-house with the HICOM Engineering Complex taking the lead. PROTON's MMC managers opted instead to go to two outside companies to supply parts of the assembly. This decision was hard to criticize because it advanced *Bumiputera* companies and because it represented localization. At the same time, it kept PROTON from controlling the technology for the whole assembly. This situation means that PROTON remains in the stage of making things up from subassemblies, and this is contrary to its larger goals. HICOM wanted to establish a joint venture with a local firm that had been supplying PROTON with some plastic parts, but a Japanese plastic company that is an MMC supplier in Japan made a better offer to the latter than HICOM could. This event was not purely an economic matter in HICOM's view, as it assured MMC continuing control over product technology.

As MMC's vendors in Japan have expanded operations in Malaysia to supply PROTON, concern is increasing that this is being done at the expense of established parts makers or national goals. A recent change in the sourcing of safety glass for the Saga provides a good example of the lengths to which Japanese firms may go to favour their own suppliers. A well established and very successful company, itself in partnership with a Japanese firm, had been supplying PROTON with safety glass. MMC management apparently wished to shift some of this business to another company with ties to a Japanese glass company that is part of the Mitsubishi Group. MMC set a new standard for safety glass, which was that completed windows could have no handling equipment marks on the edges. The original supplier spent RM7 million for new equipment to meet this standard, but the other company did not match this investment and did not reach the standard. The standard was then relaxed, and the other company got 40 per cent of the business anyway. It appears to private sector parts makers that PROTON's MMC managers give preference to Japanese companies even when MMC affiliates are not available as suppliers. One firm with very small Japanese participation claimed that it received a letter of acceptance to supply a specific part for the Saga and that it was then told that this was a mistake. The part was procured instead from a 90 per cent Toyota-affiliated firm which had not made a bid to supply it. Such practices are bound to be more common if MMC succeeds in organizing and controlling a comprehensive regional auto production scheme.

Formation of M2

The formation of the second national car project, popularly called M2, as a joint venture with Daihatsu Motor Company in February 1993 appeared to be wholly a Mahathir initiative. Daihatsu is a mini-car maker and an affiliate of Toyota Motor Corp. Mahathir raised the issue of a second project during a 1991 trip to Japan, and negotiations for creation of a joint venture were announced late that year. The concept of M2 was to build a relatively inexpensive mini-car that would dominate the lower end of the market in the way that the increasingly expensive Saga dominated its larger middle sector. The immediate aims of the project were to extend heavy industrialization and to deepen the parts and components manufacturing sector. As noted, there was considerable dissatisfaction with the pace at which MMC was transferring technology, so M2 was also no doubt intended to accelerate the transfer of motor vehicle related technologies to

Malaysia. The result was a joint venture between Daihatsu Motor Co. (20 per cent); Daihatsu Malaysia Bhd., the latter's local distributor (5 per cent); Mitsui Co., the trading company associated with the Mitsui group with which Daihatsu is associated in Japan (7 per cent); Permodalan Nasional Bhd. (PNB), a public investment house intended to advance *Bumiputera* share holdings (10 per cent); UMW Holdings Bhd., the local Toyota assembler and distributor in which PNB holds a controlling interest (38 per cent); and Med-Bumikar MARA Bhd, a subsidiary of MARA, a public agency for advancing *Bumiputera* participation in the economy (20 per cent). This is a RM400 million venture with initial paid-up capital of RM140 million. It is slated to begin assembly of a car based on Daihatsu's MIRA mini-car in July of 1994. The plant will have a capacity to produce 45,000 units per year, but will begin by producing only 20,000.

Although M2 is not yet in operation at the time of writing, it is perhaps worthwhile to make some preliminary observations about its formation in light of PROTON experience. As with the earlier project, Mahathir was personally the prime mover of the joint venture with Daihatsu. As with Mitsubishi, Daihatsu's control of necessary technology was a source of its attraction and its bargaining strength. Like Mitsubishi, Daihatsu had initial reservations about entering into a car venture in Malaysia but ultimately concluded that its larger strategy and perhaps broader group interests could make this worthwhile if the venture was formed largely on its terms. With continuing economic stagnation in the United States, the EC and Japan, the smaller Japanese car makers particularly have been aggressively trying to enter new, smaller markets. Daihatsu withdrew from the American market in early 1992 and began pursuing an Asia centred strategy, which has included efforts to promote production ventures in China and Indonesia and to expand sales in South Korea. It no doubt came to view the Malaysian project in this context. As in the case of PROTON, the Malaysian side negotiated the M2 agreement with the only significant candidate for participation (a small role for Peugeot in the project was for a time considered). As in the negotiations with Mitsubishi, the Malaysian side was in a relatively weak bargaining position. Negotiations with Daihatsu remained at an impasse through most of 1992. Differences over pricing, equity structure, and management control were mentioned in press accounts as the major sticking points during this period.

According to industry observers, the final agreement was very much like Daihatsu's initial proposal (*Far Eastern Economic Review*, 1993: 60). Mahathir personally intervened in the negotiations in October, 1992, when he criticized the Malaysian side (primarily MARA subsidiary Med–Bumikar representatives) for insisting on management control. He warned that 'excluding Japanese management may bring losses, as experienced during the early years by PROTON' (Kyodo News Service, 1992). It appears that Daihatsu managers will at the outset play the predominant role in managing the second car project. Like PROTON, M2 will enjoy the tax holidays and duty exemptions that are necessary to secure its intended niche in the auto sector. It is said that the second car will initially have 35 per cent local content and that it will reach 70 per cent in 1997. PROTON's experience shows, however, that the value of this undertaking to Malaysia will in part hinge on whether any agreements concerning local content and technology transfer have been made explicit and contain targets rather than being left hopelessly vague and, thus, subject to constant haggling. MMC was opposed to and very critical of the second car project, taking the view that a lower end car should be based on the Saga. Whether there are ways in which the second project can be used by the Malaysian side to gain leverage with Mitsubishi to hasten localization and technology transfer remains to be seen. What, if any, prospects there may be for export of the second car to regional markets also remains to be seen. If, as expected, Daihatsu managers are predominant in the venture, they will certainly have a decisive voice in decisions concerning technology transfer and exports.

JAPANESE STRATEGIES, MALAYSIAN AND ASEAN POLICIES, AND REGIONAL COMPLEMENTATION IN THE MOTOR VEHICLE INDUSTRY

National governments and private businesses as well as transnational corporations (TNCs) operating in the ASEAN states have long asserted interest in promoting regional economic cooperation. Governments and local businesses have, however, feared transnational corporate domination of arrangements created to facilitate regional industrial cooperation. One of the earliest (1971) regional production initiatives – from Ford for an 'Asian car' – came to naught for this reason (Young, 1986: 691). Among the mechanisms for regional industrial cooperation that have subsequently been established, the 1981 ASEAN Industrial Complementation (AIC) scheme (ASEAN-CCI, 1987; Chee and Suh, 1988) is of concern here. AIC projects normally require the participation of industries in at least four member countries. To gain the benefits of producing in larger volume, industries in participating countries specialize in making selected components for the same end product and then trade these among themselves. The countries agree to tariff reductions on traded components and temporary exclusive production rights for the country making each of them. AIC proposals originate with national and regional industries but are advanced by the ASEAN Chambers of Commerce and Industry (CCI). Proposals are then evaluated and recommendations are made by the ASEAN Committee on Industry Minerals, and Energy (COIME); and final decisions on them are made by the ASEAN economic ministers. The CCIs of some countries, Malaysia for one, include transnational firms, whereas others do not. The role of firms with foreign participation in these schemes has consistently been a source of conflict among various interests in the member states and among the states themselves. The only AIC proposal approved through 1987 was made by the ASEAN Automotive Federation, and five of the six items it included were produced by foreign-controlled or -dominated firms (Young, 1986: 695). This effort ultimately foundered as a result of competing national concerns.

Japanese motor vehicle companies tended generally to be unenthusiastic about complementation schemes initiated by ASEAN. As complementation promised to make local production of auto parts economically viable by expanding the size of the market and thus production volumes, it could clearly cut into the profits the Japanese firms derived from the export of CKD kits. However, several factors combined to increase the interest of Japanese firms in this idea in the second half of the 1980s. Rapid yen appreciation upped the costs of Japanese-made auto parts and components in world markets. Parts could now for the first time be made more cheaply in ASEAN countries if they could be produced in sufficient volumes. They could then be used in vehicles assembled not only in ASEAN countries but also in Japanese firms' worldwide operations, and this step would help to keep increasing prices in Japan from hurting sales. ASEAN states were at the same time becoming increasingly assertive in demanding accelerated localization. Complementation offered Japanese firms the prospect of complying in a way that left much of the process under their control. Japanese firms might now also export ASEAN-made vehicles to North America and the EC under GSP quotas for Third World made vehicles with sufficient local content. With heightened interest in complementation, Japanese firms would attempt to organize and control it themselves.

MMC was the first to act. It had long been more receptive to the idea of complementation than any of its Japanese competitors, and it had already gone further than any of them in integrating regional production. It had operations in Indonesia, Thailand, and the Philippines – in addition to its PROTON involvement in Malaysia – and plants in the latter three countries were already exchanging parts among themselves on a limited basis without AIC benefits. In early 1987, MMC proposed a Brand-to-Brand Complementation (BBC) scheme to COIME under AIC provisions. This was simply to provide a general framework for specific agreements that would have be worked out between interested companies. Complementation was to be on a brand-to-brand basis, meaning that only parts for one make of vehicle could be exchanged under any specific agreement. Diverging from the AIC formula, BBC agreements could be concluded between firms in as few as two countries. BBC's key features were to be a margin of tariff preference for ASEAN-produced auto parts traded among participating companies and, much more importantly for export potential, local content accreditation by each participating country for each traded part. MMC's immediate aims in taking the lead on BBC included boosting

313

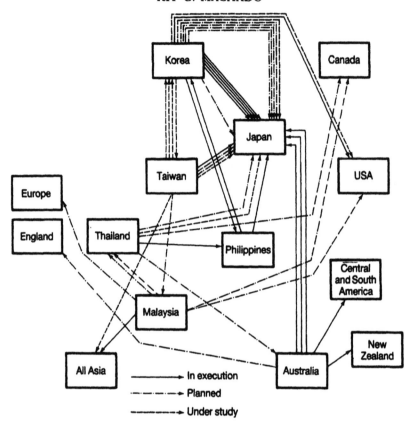

Figure 12.1 Mitsubishi Motor Corporation Asian regional division of labour in global context.

Source: This figure is adapted from Kikai Shinko Kyokai Keizai Kenkyujo (1988): 204–5. The original is derived from various newspaper accounts and shows reports of current, planned and possible exchanges of motor vehicle parts and components among MMC regional affiliates and some such connections outside the region in mid-1987.

slumping sales in ASEAN markets. It hoped to secure an edge in price competition by eliminating duplication of investments in making the same parts at each ASEAN facility and gaining the cost advantages of higher volume production. More basically, however, according to the general manager of the Kuala Lumpur MMC office, BBC was meant to advance the firm's plan to use ASEAN as a production and export base (*Investors Digest,* 1988: 7). This was, however, to be developed within a much more extensive regional and international MMC network (See Figure 12.1). An idea that had, despite several efforts, been unimplemented for nearly twenty years was again revived.

The ASEAN states and MMC carried on negotiations on the BBC proposal during 1987. Changed circumstances gave MMC some notable sources of leverage in this process. By 1987, new economic realities had made some in ASEAN more receptive to regional complementation under Japanese auspices than they would have been earlier. Yen appreciation had substantially increased the costs of imported CKD kits and thus changed the economics of motor vehicle assembly in the ASEAN states. In Malaysia, for example, 1.3 litre CKD kits that cost 550,000–600,000 yen in early 1985 had by 1988 dropped to 350,000–450,000 yen, owing to deletion of parts by then being produced locally as well as discounting by the manufacturers. Nonetheless, with yen appreciation, this translated into an increase in the import price from RM5,500–6,000 to RM7,000–8,000 over the same period, and the parts deleted from the CKD kit during these years had to be purchased elsewhere at additional cost. The ASEAN states and motor vehicle assemblers were being pinched by this situation, and BBC appeared to offer some possibility of relief. Moreover, as the high yen and domestic economic considerations made Japanese auto firms more interested in production of parts and components in the ASEAN countries for use in local assembly as well as in Japan and other countries, some in ASEAN began to see this development as containing promise for increased localization of the auto industry and increased exports. These facts clearly enhanced MMC's position as it pushed for BBC, and it was additionally in a position to offer inducements that were or at least appeared to be supportive of ASEAN states' interests in these regards to gain their assent to BBC.

The ASEAN states also had some leverage in these negotiations. Such ASEAN undertakings require full agreement, so any one of the ASEAN governments could have killed BBC simply by refusing its assent. Furthermore, as already noted, each state has the power to set the terms and conditions under which foreign firms operate within its borders. How directly, if at all, the ASEAN states asserted such leverage to secure inducements is unknown, but their capacity to withhold assent was obvious to all participants in the negotiations. The ASEAN states had never been shy in making their interest in increased localization and exports known to the Japanese auto firms, and it seems only reasonable to assume that these interests were reaffirmed to MMC in connection with deliberations on its BBC plan. The MMC agreement to produce gasoline engines in Thailand was reported to be in part to gain the Thai government's assent to BBC (*Tokyo Business Today*, 1988: 25). MMC announced several other decisions that appeared to further localization and/or exports around the time that its BBC plan and follow-up proposal for a specific complementation agreement were under consideration or soon after they were approved. It cannot be stated with certainty that any such decisions were explicit tradeoffs demanded by the ASEAN states or proffered to them by MMC for signing

315

off on its BBC plan. It can only be noted that MMC offered some things that the ASEAN states wanted and that the latter did agree to BBC.

MMC shepherded a Memorandum of Understanding (MOU) on BBC through COIME and on to approval by the ASEAN economic ministers in October 1988 (ASEAN, 1988; *Investors Digest*, 1988: 5–9), but it fell short of what MMC had hoped for. The ASEAN states clearly exerted their leverage in setting some critical features of the MOU. MMC wanted participation of the four ASEAN states where it had assembly operations, but Indonesia – the country with the largest potential market in the region – was unwilling to participate. The Indonesian government was concerned that it would have to buy far more from its much smaller neighbours than it could sell to them, and it believed that the scheme would limit its ability to develop its own parts industry. It ultimately signed the MOU, which required agreement of all ASEAN governments, making it possible for other members to participate. MMC wanted a 90 per cent margin of tariff preference on traded parts but had to settle for 50 per cent. According to participants in the COIME deliberations, MMC's initial proposal gave the lead firm a very large measure of control over participating companies. It could specify which parts and components each participating company should produce and which it should buy. MMC clearly envisioned a single source per included component. This was unacceptable to ASEAN representatives, and they made it clear that they would not agree to it. They were concerned about the costs of supplier monopolies and about the prospect of Japanese auto firms giving such monopolies to local subsidiaries of their Japanese suppliers or local ventures tied to them. Hence, the final MOU leaves companies in a complementation agreement free to purchase included parts from any maker in a participating country, and it states emphatically that there will be 'no mandatory single-sourcing of parts/components' (ASEAN, 1988: Sec. 11). A firm proposing a complementation agreement is required to list the parts to be traded for specified vehicle models and the source and purchasing countries for each part. This proposal must be approved and formally certified by COIME and the ASEAN economic ministers. In subsequent deliberations on MMC's specific BBC proposal, it was further agreed informally that as a rule there should be no exchange of parts already being produced in an importing country.

Malaysian support for BBC came primarily from the Mahathir administration and local parts makers. HICOM and PROTON managers objected to MMC-led complementation because they believed it incompatible with the national car concept and feared that it would impede effective localization. Hence they played virtually no role in the COIME deliberations. Their lack of support for BBC was no doubt one reason that MMC wanted management control over PROTON. In any case, Malaysia's initial positions were formulated by concerned officials, primarily in the Trade and Industry Ministry and MIDA. As negotiations progressed, however, they received important input from the Malaysian Automotive Components and Parts Manufacturers' Association (MACPMA), the body representing private sector parts makers. Both government and many local makers shared the general ASEAN concern about the prospects of supplier monopolies and favoured free choice in sourcing. The Malaysian parts makers' views on this and other matters were important in shaping the version of the MOU that was finally approved.

In negotiating the MOU on complementation, MMC advanced the interests of Japanese and some European motor vehicle manufacturers as well as its own. This was not its objective, however, and it was clearly not consulting with its competitors. Its intention was simply to gain an edge on them. MMC had a specific BBC plan ready for submission as soon as the MOU was signed, and it was quickly approved in March 1989. Although not initially as keen on complementation as MMC, both Toyota and Nissan had become increasingly interested in the idea. They submitted their plans for consideration in mid-1989, and these were approved in November 1989 and May 1990 respectively. Like MMC, both were eager to have Indonesian participation in their schemes, but they ultimately had to proceed without it. Volvo and Mercedes Benz, both of which have assembly operations in several ASEAN states, also quickly launched BBC plans that include Malaysian affiliates. Whether Daihatsu will seek approval of such a scheme remains to be seen.

Both Toyota and Nissan consulted with their regional affiliates on their BBC plans, but like MMC's scheme, their plans are widely perceived in Malaysian industry circles to have been wholly designed in Japan. Toyota has a significant stake and thus a management say in its local affiliate, UMW Toyota, whereas Nissan is far less involved in the affairs of its affiliate, Tan Chong Motors. In any case, both UMW Toyota and Tan Chong Motors were more favourably disposed to BBC than PROTON. First, as private firms, their chief purpose is profit making and not advancing national development. Unlike PROTON, they are not concerned with having an autonomous identity, and they are not defined as the vanguard of the national heavy industrialization drive. At the same time, they find BBC advantageous as they are obliged to adapt to the new national policy regime. Following the Industrial Master Plan-mandated push for rationalization of the motor vehicle industry, UMW and particularly Tan Chong expanded investment in parts making both in-house and in joint ventures. This was to insure their economic survival, and it meshes very well with the thrust of BBC. They must also comply with increasing local content requirements. Both also expect parts production to help keep their cars more affordable and thus to reduce the adverse impact on their sales of government protection for PROTON and yen appreciation.

MMC's regional complementation plan centres on Thailand (*Tokyo*

Business Today, 1988: 24–25). In its initial stage, it has primarily involved incorporation of transmissions made by its Philippine affiliate and doors produced by PROTON into a Mitsubishi Lancer assembled in Thailand by MMC Sittipol (48 per cent Mitsubishi owned) along with exchange of a few smaller parts. The immediate trade consequences of the plan for Malaysia have so far been limited. Malaysian industry insiders believe that MMC is not so keen on the plan that was finally approved and that the changes forced in the MOU slowed it down. While that is no doubt true, MMC appears to hope for expansion of trade in parts both within ASEAN and beyond. Its initial proposal to COIME for the BBC plan for the Lancer listed more parts for exchange than were initially traded. For example, Malaysian companies were certified to sell 20 items to MMC Sittipol, and Thai companies to sell 40 to PROTON. MMC also requested COIME certification for additional parts in May 1990. In any case, the general manager of MMC in Kuala Lumpur indicated that the company does not 'expect (BBC) to be realized quickly' (*Investors Digest*, 1988: 7). Whatever the eventual extent of the parts trade, by producing in these three countries, MMC is assured protection in all of them. At the same time, in conformity with its global strategy, the Thai-assembled Lancer acquires enough local content to qualify for export to North America and the EC under GSP provisions. In 1988, MMC Sittipol began fulfilling a six-year contract to sell 100,000 Lancers to Chrysler Canada, which markets them as Plymouth and Dodge Colts. Canada was intended primarily to be a way-station en route to the US market following ratification (January 1989) of the US–Canada Free Trade Agreement. It was no doubt with this possibility in mind that MMC Sittipol undertook to double its production capacity and began engine assembly during the following two years. Thinking well ahead, Mitsubishi also submitted a plan for the development of an auto industry in Vietnam to that country's government in 1993 (National Trade Data Bank Market Report, 1993). As part of that plan, PROTON is slated to enter a joint venture with Mitsubishi and the Vietnamese government to produce vehicles in Vietnam.

Of the other two schemes, Toyota's is the most ambitious. It centres on exchange of engines produced in Thailand, electrical equipment and steering systems from Malaysia, and transmissions built in the Philippines for a range of Toyota four-wheel vehicles. In 1990, a 100 per cent Toyota-owned management services company was established in Singapore to coordinate ASEAN operations and the BBC plan. Nissan's scheme involves exchange of engines and stamping dies made in Thailand, clutch and electrical components from Malaysia, and wiring harnesses from the Philippines for its small cars and light trucks. It also includes various subcomponents from Taiwan, which will not receive AIC benefits. Governments and local affiliates pressed successfully to make COIME approval of the Toyota plan conditional on Toyota investment in completely new plants for making the named components in Malaysia and the Philippines. These investments were consistent with Toyota's aims, so the leverage gained by imposing these conditions appears primarily to have been used to influence their details. In any case, combined with its establishment of a new engine assembly plant in Thailand and establishment of a new car assembly operation in the Philippines after a five-year absence, Toyota planned a total investment of US$215 million over three years beginning in 1989 to advance its BBC scheme. While Nissan's plan places greater reliance on existing firms, it has also invested in increasing the capacity of its regional affiliates and promoted a number of joint ventures between its parts suppliers and local companies.

Components produced by plants participating in both schemes are expected to be exported to Japan and to worldwide production sites. Nissan planned to do about 5 per cent of its Japanese sourcing from ASEAN by 1992 and eventually to increase this to 10 per cent. In 1989, Toyota Motor Thailand, the leading assembler in that country, was designated one of Toyota's few 'global vehicle suppliers' and is projected to be an exporter of complete vehicles. Its 1989 output of 50,000 units was expected to triple by the mid-1990s. Plans for construction of a major new plant outside Bangkok were finalized in 1993. Toyota expects its plan to be well under way by 1993, while Nissan's is developing more slowly. Nissan has not designated a lead exporting country as its two competitors have (i.e., Thailand), but its Malaysian affiliate has since 1989 exported vehicles to Singapore and Brunei with Nissan's approval. It is planned that BBC exchanges will boost the local content of both makers' ASEAN-produced vehicles from around 30 to 40 per cent to the magic GSP number of 60 per cent within a few years.

CONCLUSION: GLOBAL AND DOMESTIC FACTORS IN THE DEVELOPMENT OF MALAYSIA'S MOTOR VEHICLE INDUSTRY

Both global and domestic factors have clearly shaped the recent development of the Malaysian motor vehicle industry. What remains is more systematically to analyse the mix of such factors in this case. It should first be stressed that while Mahathir's economic policies stemmed partly from Malaysia's long-standing problems in the world economy, these problems did not determine the specific strategy that he selected from among a variety of possibilities. His emphasis on heavy industry was based largely on his reading of domestic political economic imperatives, particularly his understanding of the requirements for *Bumiputera* advancement and his desire to further specific NEP goals. It was also partly for such domestic reasons that Mahathir opted to rely primarily on Japan in pursuing his industrial strategy. In doing so, he tied Malaysia to the country whose government and transnational firms have the most elaborate and integrative global and regional strategies among the advanced capitalist states. In promoting the auto projects, it was Mahathir, not the Japanese firms, who took the initiative. He was, however, able to secure MMC's participation in PROTON only because it served MMC's larger strategic purposes and because Malaysia was willing to underwrite most of the costs. This situation was still not without opportunities, but they existed within very circumscribed limits, and Malaysia had to push very hard and with great persistence to gain any advantages. This was particularly so both because PROTON's localization and export goals made it a potential challenge to industrial interests in Japan and because it was so heavily dependent on Japanese capital and technology. In any case, Mahathir had the will and the power to engage in some necessary pushing.

In the mid-1980s, trends in the world economy imposed severe constraints that heavily affected the auto project's prospects. Indeed, one of the most apparent facts about Malaysia shown here is its continuing and extreme vulnerability to forces in the world economy over which it has no control. The vagaries of the business cycle in the advanced capitalist states, world commodity prices, and international currency fluctuations form a shifting matrix in which the country's industrial policy is pursued – sometimes for better, often for worse. The auto project was partly an effort to overcome the vulnerability inherent in its over-dependence on world commodity markets, but this long-standing problem along with new ones occasioned by yen appreciation set this effort back and put it on a somewhat different track. The auto project's problems in the mid-1980s went beyond shrinking domestic markets and rapidly escalating debts. PROTON's economic troubles contributed greatly to the situation in which MMC was able to press the advantage it had thereby gained to assume management control, and thus a larger role in setting the auto project's future direction. Economic troubles for all ASEAN states squeezed by yen appreciation, including Malaysia, created the context in which these states accepted a complementation scheme of which most had long been suspicious. Now, however, it will be organized and controlled by Japanese auto firms. Some of MMC's primary motivations for taking management control of PROTON and promoting BBC were its own problems with the rising yen and North American and EC market restrictions along with pressure for localization and exports from its regional affiliates, including PROTON.

External constraints weigh most heavily in the explanation of the outcomes to date of Malaysia's motor vehicle polices, but it is far from complete without reference to constraints of internal origin and to domestic capacity to make the most of some opportunities found in partnerships with Japanese transnationals. PROTON's ill-conceived arrangement with EON was based entirely on domestic considerations, and this greatly aggravated its economic problems. The intractability of the resultant domestic conflict also helped to justify, but did not determine, the decision for MMC's assumption of PROTON's top management. The PROTON–EON conflict affected the course of the auto project, but the effects were more of timing and detail than ultimate outcome. More positively, Malaysia undertook active efforts to shape the adjustments of the auto project to adverse trends in the world economy and to its own internal problems. It was very assertive in trying to extract concessions from MMC in order to gain more advantages for PROTON. The overriding fact is that MMC increased its influence over the direction of PROTON during the period of adjustment, but it is also the case that it was obliged to accommodate certain Malaysian demands. Had the Malaysian side been less assertive in pursuing its interests, it is unlikely that the Saga would have reached the 60 per cent local content required to enter Western markets under GSP provisions, or that exports, particularly to the United Kingdom, would have gone ahead. Moreover, the aggressive national auto policy regime, which centres on the car project, is the primary factor driving desired changes in the private sector. It has, for example, pushed Toyota and Nissan assemblers to become substantial parts makers.

Malaysian reliance on Japanese transnational corporations for further development of its motor vehicle industry increased rather than decreased Malaysian dependence, at least for the foreseeable future. This survey of Japanese strategies and practices suggests that Japanese transnationals are unlikely to agree willingly to the changes in economic relationships that would be necessary to elevate Malaysia's place in the international division of labour significantly unless this development occurs within a framework largely of Japanese making. For PROTON, this reality was revealed earlier than it might otherwise have been as a result of the economic crisis, which induced Malaysian efforts to force the issue of Saga exports and accelerated localization. These issues would eventually have been joined, and it is difficult to imagine MMC assenting except on terms that made PROTON more dependent. MMC's promotion of regional auto complementation is exemplary of the larger Japanese regional integration strategy. Conditions were such that neither Malaysia nor other ASEAN states, save Indonesia, were inclined to reject this scheme, but at the same time, MMC could not simply force its terms on them. The ASEAN states were scarcely powerless in this situation, but they are now more tightly woven into an emerging Japan-centred regional production network. From now on they will have to negotiate such issues as localization and exports within this framework. Malaysia could derive significant economic benefits from this arrangement, but these benefits are likely to be concessions granted on MMC terms rather than gains securely anchored in national industrial strength. Malaysia has demonstrated considerable skill in winning such concessions, but whether the cumulative effects of these efforts can in the long-term alter the asymmetrical structure of its relationships with Japanese auto firms is at best problematic.

This chapter is an abbreviated and updated version of a chapter that originally appeared under the title 'ASEAN State Industrial Policies and Japanese Regional Production Strategies: The Case of Malaysia's Motor Vehicle Industry' Ch. 9 in Cal Clark and Steve Chan, eds, *The Evolving Pacific Basin in the Global Political Economy: Domestic and International Linkages*, Lynne Rienner Publishers, Boulder CO. (1992). Reprinted with permission of the publisher. I thank the Fulbright Faculty Research Abroad Program, the California State University, Northridge Foundation, and Waseda University for financial support and the Institute of Strategic and International Studies (ISIS), Malaysia, for institutional support of the research for this chapter. I am particularly grateful to the numerous persons in Malaysia and Japan who granted the interviews between 1988 and mid-1990 on which much of this research is based. Most were government or private-sector employees and were assured that their responses were not for attribution. I have thus not cited interviews but, where appropriate, have identified the general position of sources in the text. I am alone responsible for the text.

REFERENCES

Akrasanee, Narongchai (ed.) (1983) *ASEAN–Japan Relations: Trade and Development*. Institute of Southeast Asian Studies, Singapore.

Aoki Takeshi (1986) 'Development of High Technology, Industrial and Trade Networks in the Pacific Region'. *Asia–Pacific Economic Symposium Papers* 42–89.

Ariff, Mohamed (1982) 'The Motor Vehicle Industry in Malaysia', in *The Scope for Southeast Asian Subregional Cooperation in the Automotive Sector*, eds. United Nations, Economic Commission for Asia and the Pacific. UN/ESCAP, Bangkok.

ASEAN (1988) 'Memorandum of Understanding: Brand-to-Brand Complementation in the Automotive Industry under the Basic Agreement on ASEAN Industrial Complementation', mimeo.

ASEAN–CCI (ASEAN Chambers of Commerce and Industry) (1987) *ASEAN: The Way Forward*. ISIS for the Group of Fourteen on ASEAN Economic Cooperation and Integration, Kuala Lumpur.

Asian Development Bank (1993) *Key Indicators of Developing Asian and Pacific Countries*. Oxford University Press for the Asian Development Bank, Manila.

Asian Wall Street Journal 20 December 1989.

Asian Wall Street Journal 8 July 1991.

Bennett, Douglas C. and Kenneth E. Sharpe (1985) *Transnational Corporations versus The State: The Political Economy of the Mexican Auto Industry*. Princeton University Press, Princeton.

Bowie, Alasdair (1991) *Crossing the Industrial Divide; State, Society, and the Politics of Economic Transformation in Malaysia*. Columbia University Press, New York.

Business International Country Report (Malaysia) 25 February 1992.

Business International Country Report (Malaysia) 26 March 1993.

Business Times 23 November 1990a.

Business Times 6 March 1990b.

Caporaso, James A. (ed.) (1987) *A Changing International Division of Labor*. Lynne Rienner Publishers, Boulder.

Cardoso, Fernando Henrique and Enzo Faletto (1979) *Dependency and Development in Latin America*. University of California Press, Berkeley.

Chee Peng Lim (1984) 'The Malaysian Car Industry at the Crossroads: Time to

Change Gear?' in *The Malaysian Economy at the Crossroads: Policy Adjustment or Structural Transformation*, eds. Lim Lin Lean and Chee Peng Lim. Malaysian Economic Association, Kuala Lumpur.

Chee Peng Lim and Jang-Won Suh (eds) (1988) *ASEAN Industrial Co-operation*. Asian and Pacific Development Centre, Kuala Lumpur.

Deyo, Frederic C. (ed.) (1987) *The Political Economy of the New Asian industrialism*. Cornell University Press, Ithaca.

Dobashi Kenji (1988) 'Restructuring of Japanese Industries and the Impact on Asian Economic Development.' *Asian Perspectives* (Nomura Research International, Hong Kong) 5: 2–28.

Doner, Richard F. (1991) *Driving a Bargain: Automobile Industrialization and Japanese Firms in Southeast Asia*. University of California Press, Berkeley.

Economist Intelligence Unit (1985) *The ASEAS Motor Industry: Problems and Prospects*. EIU, Special Report No. 205, London.

Ellison, Christopher and Gary Gereffi (1990) 'Explaining Strategies and Patterns of Industrial Development'. in *Manufacturing Miracles: Paths of Industrialization in Latin America and East Asia*, eds. Gary Gereffi and Donald L. Wyman. Princeton University Press, Princeton.

Evans, Peter (1979) *Dependent Development; The Alliance of Multinational State, and Local Capital in Brazil*. Princeton University Press, Princeton.

Far Eastern Economic Review 2 May 1991a.

Far Eastern Economic Review 28 March 1991b.

Far Eastern Economic Review 28 February 1991c.

Far Eastern Economic Review 30 January 1992.

Far Eastern Economic Review 18 February 1993.

Frieden, Jeffry A. and David A. Lake (eds) (1991) *International Political Economy: Perspectives on Global Power and Wealth*, 2nd edition. St. Martin's Press, New York.

Frobel, Folker, Jurgen Heinrichs and Otto Kreye (1980) *The New International division of Labour: Structural Unemployment in Industrialized Countries and Industrialization in Developing Countries*. Cambridge University Press, Cambridge.

Gomez, Edmund Terence (1990) *Politics in Business UMNO'S Corporate Investments*. Forum, Kuala Lumpur.

Government of Malaysia (1981) *Fourth Malaysia Plan, 1981–1985*. National Printing Department, Kuala Lumpur.

Haggard, Stephen (1986) 'The Newly Industrializing Countries in the International System'. *World Politics 38*: 343–70.

Haggard, Stephen (1990) *Pathways From the Periphery: The Politics of Growth in the Newly Industrializing Countries*. Cornell University Press, Ithaca.

HICOM (Heavy Industries Corporation of Malaysia) (1983–89) *HICOM Annual Reports, 1983–1989*. HICOM, Kuala Lumpur.

Hoffman, Kurt and Raphael Kaplinsky (1988) *Driving Force: the Global Restructuring of Technology, Labor, and Investment in the Automobile and Components Industries*. Westview Press and the UN Centre on Transnational Corporations, Boulder.

Hollerman, Leon (1988) *Japan's Economy Strategy in Brazil: Challenge for the United States*. Lexington Books, Lexington, MA.

Investor's Digest November 1988. Kuala Lumpur Stock Exchange, Kuala Lumpur.

Japan Times 18 January 1990.

Jesudason, James V. (1989) *Ethnicity and the Economy: The State, Chinese Business, and Multinationals in Malaysia*. Oxford University Press, Singapore.

JETRO (Japan External Trade Organization) (1991) *Business Facts and Figures: Nippon*. JETRO, Tokyo.

Khor Kok Peng (1983) *The Malaysian Economy: Structures and Dependence.* Marican & Sons for Institut Masyarakat, Kuala Lumpur.

Khor Kok Peng (1987) *Malaysia's Economy in Decline.* Consumers' Association of Penang, Penang.

Kikai Shinko Kyokai Keizai Kenkyujo (Machine Industry Promotion Association Economic Research Institute) (1988) *Kikai sangyo no kozo henka to ajia to no sogoison no genjo – 21 seiki e mukete no waga kuni kikai sangyo no doko* [*Current Changes in the Structure of the Machine Industry and Interdependence with Asia – Trends in our Country's Machine Industry As We Face The 21st Century*]. Kikai Shinko Kyokai Keizai Kenkyujo, Kikai Kogyo Keizai Kenkyu Hokokusho 62–3 (Machine Industry Promotion Association Economic Research Institute, Machine Industry Economic Research Report 62–3), Tokyo.

Kitazawa Yoko (1987) 'Setting Up Shop, Shutting Up Shop'. *AMPO: Japan–Asia Quarterly Review* 19: 10–29.

Kojima Kiyoshi (1970) 'An Approach to Integration: The Gains from Agreed Specialization'. in *Essays in Honor of Roy Harrod*, eds. W.A. Eltis, M.F.G. Scott, and J.N. Wolfe. Clarendon Press, Oxford.

Kyodo News Service 20 October 1992.

Kyodo News Service 23 February 1993.

Machado, Kit (1987) 'Malaysian Cultural Relations with Japan and South Korea in the 1980s: Looking East'. *Asian Survey* 27: 638–60.

Machado, Kit (1989–90) 'Japanese Transnational Corporations in Malaysia's State Sponsored Heavy Industrialization Drive: The HICOM Automobile and Steel Projects'. *Pacific Affairs* 62: 504–531.

Mahathir bin Mohamad (1970) *The Malay Dilemma.* Asia Pacific Press, Singapore.

Mahathir bin Mohamad (1981) Interview with *Far Eastern Economic Review* 30 October 33; 38–39.

MMVAA (Malaysian Motor Vehicle Assemblers Association) (1980–89) *Annual Report.* MMVAA, Kuala Lumpur.

MIDA/UNIDO (Malaysian Industrial Development Authority/United National Industrial Development Organization) (1985) *Medium and Long Term Industrial Master Plan – Malaysia, 1986–1995.* MIDA/UNIDO, Kuala Lumpur.

Milne, R.S. (1986) 'Malaysia – Beyond the New Economic Policy'. *Asian Survey* 26:1364–82.

Milne, R.S. and Diane K. Mauzy (1986) *Malaysia: Tradition, Modernity, and Islam.* Westview Press, Boulder.

National Trade Data Bank Market Report 15 January 1993.

New Straits Times 2 September 1985.

New Straits Times 28 June 1988.

New Straits Times 22 March 1994.

Ohata Yashichi (1989) 'The Developing Countries of the Pan–Pacific Region: The Interdependence of Economic Relations with Japan.' *Waseda Journal of Asian Studies* 11: 1–18.

Ozawa Terutomo (1979) *Multinationalism Japanese Style: The Political Economy of Outward Dependence.* Princeton University Press, Princeton.

Phongpaichit, Pasuk (1988) 'Decision-Making on Overseas Direct Investment by Japanese Small and Medium Industries in ASEAN and the Asian NICs'. *ASEAN Economic Bulletin* 4: 302–15.

Puthucheary, Mavis (1984) 'The Political Economy of Public Enterprises in Malaysia'. in *The Malaysian Economy at the Crossroads: Policy Adjustment or Structural Transformation*, eds. Lim Lin Lean and Chee Peng Lim. Malaysian Economic Association and Organizational Resources Sdn. Bhd., Kuala Lumpur.

RIM Studies Group (1988) 'International Division of Labor in the Pacific Rim Area'. *RIM – PACIFIC Business and Industries*, 5–19 August.

Saravanamuttu, Johan (1988) 'Japanese Economic Penetration in ASEAN in the Contest of the International Division of Labour'. *Journal of Contemporary Asia* 18: 139–64.

Sekiguchi Sueo (ed.) (1983) *ASEAN–Japan Relations: Investment*. Institute of Southeast Asian Relations, Singapore.

Shiode Hirokazu (1989) *Japanese Investment in Southeast Asia*. Centre for the Progress of Peoples, Hong Kong.

Smitka, Michael J. (1991) *Competitive Ties, Subcontracting in the Japanese Automotive Industry*. Columbia University Press, New York.

Steven, Rob (1990) *Japan's New Imperialism*. M.E. Sharpe, Inc., Armonk, New York.

Sudo Sueo (1988a) 'Japan–ASEAN Relations: New Dimensions in Japanese Foreign Policy'. *Asian Survey* XXVIII: 509–25.

Sudo Sueo (1988b) 'From Fukuda to Takeshita: A Decade of Japan–ASEAN Relations'. *Contemporary Southeast Asia* 10: 119–43.

The Straits Times 18 October 1992.

Tokyo Business Today April, 1988.

Unger, Danny (1990) 'Japanese Manufacturing Investment and Export Processing Industrialization in Thailand' (mimeo).

Wall Street Journal 20 August 1990.

Ward's Automotive International June, 1990.

Womack, James P., Daniel T. Jones and Daniel Roos (1990) *The Machine That Changed the World*. Rawson, New York.

Young, Evans (1986) 'The Foreign Capital Issue in the ASEAN Chambers of Commerce and Industry'. *Asian Survey* XXVI: 688–705.

Xinhua News Service 19 May 1993.

13

EAST ASIAN ECONOMIC REGIONALISM

Moving to the next level

Ghazali Atan

GENESIS

The call for an East Asian Economic Group (EAEG) was first made by the Prime Minister of Malaysia in December 1990 to work out a collective regional response to the failure of the Uruguay Round of negotiations earlier that month and to strengthen trade and economic links between countries in East Asia, regardless of the success or failure of the Uruguay Round negotiations. The idea was 'sounded' to ASEAN (Association of Southeast Asian Nations) member governments by the Malaysian Minister of International Trade and Industry in early 1991, and after some explanations, received their tentative support.

The idea was formally tabled for consideration at a special meeting of the ASEAN senior economic officials meeting (SEOM) in Bandung, Indonesia on 15–16 March 1991. No decisions were made during this early stage. There were also some uncertainties expressed about how the concept would fit in with the other regional initiatives that were already on the table such as the Asia Pacific Economic Community (APEC) and the ASEAN Free Trade Area (AFTA).

The ASEAN senior officials meeting (SOM) held in Kuala Lumpur in May 1991 decided to form a working group to study the EAEG idea in more detail and to report to the ASEAN Foreign Ministers meeting in July 1991 and to the ASEAN Economic Ministers meeting in October 1991. The working group agreed that EAEG should be viewed as an initiative to be taken by ASEAN as a group, to strengthen ASEAN's economic cooperation with other economies in the region. The working group noted that expanded intra-regional cooperation in East Asia would help enhance trade and development within East Asia. Furthermore, the group could be used as a vehicle for promoting free trade, using East Asia's large market size and economic strength for leverage in such efforts. It was also agreed that ASEAN should form the 'core' of the proposed East Asian grouping.

Recognizing the role of APEC in enhancing cooperation in the wider Pacific area, the working group agreed that EAEG must not duplicate

APEC. In addition, it was agreed that the EAEG must not be confrontational vis-a-vis third parties. It was also agreed that the EAEG must not develop into a trade bloc. Furthermore, noting Japan's ambivalence to the idea and that its membership was essential for the proposed grouping, it was agreed that the proposal must take into account Japan's position so as to ensure its support and effective membership. The underlying principles of the EAEG proposal, as set out by the working group, were as follows:

1 open and outward looking;
2 involving mutual respect among participants;
3 mutually beneficial;
4 'GATT consistent';
5 should build on ASEAN's strength and enhance ASEAN identity, interests and influence;
6 should foster better economic interdependence among countries in East Asia;
7 should enhance trade and investment; and
8 be compatible with APEC.

Suggested membership of the group included the ASEAN six, Japan, the Republic of Korea, the People's Republic of China, Hong Kong, Taiwan and Vietnam. The approach towards cooperation was to be carried out in a step-by-step, evolutionary and consensus-building manner. Once the group was formed, the proposed areas of cooperation were to include:

1 consultation on the Uruguay Round and subsequently on post-Uruguay Round issues relating to implementation;
2 cooperation in the form of:
   a exchanging views on the North American Free Trade Agreement (NAFTA) and the European Economic Community (EEC);
   b exchanging information on economic and trade policies and regulations;
   c undertaking regional economic forecasting and research;
   d exploring trade liberalization measures;
   e cooperating on export promotion programmes;
   f undertaking joint initiatives to enhance direct foreign investment (DFI);
   g consultations on the services sector; and
   h consultations on economic reconstruction of regional economies such as Vietnam and helping their integration into the regional and global economy.

After considering the working group's report, the 23rd ASEAN Economic Ministers Meeting on 7–8 October 1991 in Kuala Lumpur agreed to the convening of an East Asian Economic Caucus (EAEC) to discuss issues of common concern to East Asia and to meet as and when the need arises. The name 'Caucus' was agreed upon at this meeting in response to Indonesia's reservations on the use of the word 'Group'. Malaysia and the others agreed on the understanding that whatever name was given, the intentions would remain essentially the same.

The ministers agreed that the EAEC would work towards expanding intra-regional cooperation. There is, however, no agreement to initiate an institutionalized body for this purpose. The ministers also agreed that the EAEC would not be a trading bloc. These findings were reiterated by the ASEAN Foreign Ministers meeting on 23 January 1992 in Singapore.

The Fourth ASEAN Summit held in January 1992 in Singapore subsequently issued the Singapore Declaration of 1992. On the EAEC idea, the Declaration stated the following:

> ASEAN recognizes the importance of strengthening and/or establishing cooperation with other countries, regional/multilateral economic organizations, as well as Asia-Pacific Economic Cooperation (APEC) and an East Asian Economic Caucus (EAEC). With regard to APEC, ASEAN attaches importance to APEC's fundamental objective of sustaining the growth and dynamism of the Asia-Pacific region. With respect to an EAEC, ASEAN recognizes that consultations on issues of common concern among East Asian economies, as and when the need arises, could contribute to expanding cooperation among the region's economies, and the promotion of an open and free global trading system.

Further to this declaration, a Joint Consultative Meeting (JCM) was ordered to elaborate on the EAEC concept and to recommend a plan of action. The JCM met in July 1992 in Manila. The ASEAN Ministerial Meeting on 21–22 July 1992 endorsed the JCM's request that the Secretary-General of the ASEAN Secretariat (as chairman of JCM) would study an appropriate modality for the EAEC. To date, the study has still not been officially presented to ASEAN.

Meanwhile, the idea of the EAEC has been discussed at many forums, seminars and conventions involving participants from East Asian countries. The aims of these activities are to increase awareness, encourage open discussions and help arrive at certain acceptable modalities for the EAEC.

THE AGREED PARAMETERS

The viable and generally agreed upon parameters for the EAEC, gleaned from the various discussions held by ASEAN and in the other forums surveyed above, can be summarized in the following ten principles:

1 The EAEC must work on the basis of an open and outward looking regionalism;
2 It must be GATT consistent;
3 It must be investment and trade generating, and must not create unnecessary barriers to third country imports;
4 It should ensure better management of East Asia's increasing interdependencies and be an example of North–South relations;
5 It must not be too narrowly focussed (e.g. be restricted to trade issues only);
6 It must contribute towards creating a sense of psychological well-being and a sense of economic security in East Asia without being threatening to others;
7 It must be compatible with APEC;
8 It must enhance the prosperity of ASEAN and must complement the ASEAN process;
9 It must not be inward-looking;
10 In its proceedings, the EAEC must establish a democratic egalitarian process based on mutual respect and mutual benefit.

THE EAEC VISION

The following points help summarize some of the currently available views on what the EAEC can or should be:

1 The East Asian economies, being trading nations strongly dependent on free trade, need to champion free trade and safeguard their position against protectionist actions that may be taken by the strong groupings that are emerging in Europe and North America. To achieve this, East Asia too must be organized and must consolidate its strength into a 'viable political-economic force'. Only in this way can it act as a significant counterweight to other regional groupings. Such a counterweight will provide much needed negotiating leverage in the Uruguay Round and other international forums where East Asia can 'speak with one voice'.
2 Should the world trading environment deteriorate, the EAEC can also play the role of a mutual protection society to safeguard against Japan-bashing, NIE-bashing, East Asian-bashing or against collusion by regions which see themselves as being hurt by East Asia's economic dynamism and export competitiveness.
3 An integrated and organized East Asia will also create a large market base to attract both investors and traders from abroad, whether North America, Europe, Oceania or elsewhere. In addition, the EAEC can also be a mechanism to 'psychologically' anchor Japan in its natural

constituency (East Asia) and prevent it from overly concentrating its industrial and investment activities in Europe or North America.

4 The above objectives, namely the defence of free trade and the active encouragement of intra-regional trade and investment flows, require that the region remain open. The EAEC proposal, in calling for an 'organized relationship', should thus not be a call for the formation of a trading bloc. This will be contrary to its role as an organization for prising open any attempted trading blocs.

5 In addition to the above objectives, the EAEC will also function as a consultative forum to resolve internal frictions and problems, discuss trade, investment and economic policies as well as harmonize rules and regulations, standards, rates and procedures.

6 EAEC will also be a mechanism for enhancing mutual help and cooperation. Such cooperation can be in the form of flows of investments, exchanges and discussions on development strategies, training, planning, administration, etc.

7 The closer linkings and interactions that result from these activities will, in addition to bringing prosperity and development to the whole region, also create a certain degree of Asian consciousness and a degree of pride in being Asian. Such pride and sense of oneness will help to foster peace, good relations and political stability in the region.

NAGGING DOUBTS

While the ASEAN countries are generally agreeable to the idea of an EAEC, each, however, has certain queries which require clarification and attention if the EAEC is to make the difficult transition from concept to reality.

Singapore is the most supportive of the idea, particularly with regards to its commitment to the formation on an open grouping which is GATT consistent and which seeks to complement APEC and enhance ASEAN solidarity. Singapore sees the EAEC as a viable consultative group with some leverage in discussions with the USA, and which can be complementary to efforts made in ASEAN and APEC. Singapore, however, feels that there are many sensitive issues that need to be resolved and clarified using a step-by-step consensual approach.

The Philippines holds similar views to Singapore, but also wants to know whether EAEC will remain a consultative forum or will evolve into having its own structures and institutions. The Philippines is also unsure how ASEAN can be the 'core group' in both APEC and the EAEC at the same time. In addition, there are questions as to how the EAEC can seek a 'common voice' when internal interests are so diverse. Thus, in the Uruguay Round negotiations, they note that Japan's (and even Korea's) position was often contrary to views generally held by developing countries.

The Thais, while supporting the idea, also want some clarification on how and in what ways EAEC will be different from ASEAN and APEC. Their query, however, is not meant as a criticism, but to secure a working modality which they can support. They also seek clarification on how the conflicting needs of the diverse parties involved in the grouping may be reconciled.

The questions posed by the Indonesians are even more fundamental. They ask what the present schemes of consultations, namely ASEAN and APEC, do not provide that the proposed EAEC can deliver. The relevance of EAEC is thus questioned, particularly if the aim is not to create a trade bloc or group, but simply to consult, because consultative forums already exist via APEC and ASEAN. They also question the wisdom of anchoring EAEC on one economic power, i.e. Japan, when in fact ASEAN is in agreement with Japan on certain issues, but in conflict on others. The Indonesians therefore call for the proposal to be 'x-rayed', i.e. examined in detail for feasibility and modalities. In addition, the Indonesians feel that the EAEC needs to address Japanese attitudes and US disquiet very carefully so as not to cause negative reactions.

Japanese views have also been mixed. Basically, the key consideration for Japan has been how to improve its relationship with East Asia, and perhaps play a critical role in the region, without hurting its relations with other parties, particularly the USA. To enable it to clarify its position, Japan has wanted ASEAN to clarify, in detail, the modality for the EAEC.

The Koreans hold a similarly ambivalent and guarded viewpoint as the Japanese. China, Hong Kong, Taiwan and Vietnam, however, are favourably disposed to the idea. All, however, welcome detailed clarifications on the modalities.

The Bush administration's views were more categorical. It opposed any East Asian grouping, even one operationalized in the form of a caucus, if the USA is left out.

HOW IT WILL ALL FIT IN

The world economy has now developed a tripolar pattern, with important economic regions centred in Europe, North America and East Asia. While the two older growth poles of Europe and North America are larger, with aggregate gross domestic product (GDP) around US$6 billion and US$6.2 billion respectively, East Asia, whose GDP is US$3.9 billion, is the most dynamic. By 2020, the three economic regions are expected to be of approximately equal size in economic terms.

All three have a degree of intra-regional economic integration and cohesion. Thus, while intra-regional exports account for around 65 per cent of European export trade and 41 per cent of North American trade, such intra-regional trade already accounts for 39 per cent of East Asian trade.

Institutionally, however, Europe is the most integrated. North America, on the other hand is coming close to formal integration via a free trade area agreement among the USA, Canada and Mexico. *Only East Asia remains an identifiable economic region which does not have any formal institutional arrangement.* Such formalization is necessary if East Asia is to be able to negotiate and deal effectively with the other two regions.

In addition to being the youngest and most dynamic, East Asia also has the most up-to-date and undistorted production structure. Thanks to the policy of divestment and outward investment of older and no longer viable industries, the Japanese industrial structure does not carry a deadweight of old, no-longer-viable industries requiring high levels of protection to survive. Similar adjustments have been made in the East Asian newly industrializing economies (NIEs) and more recently in ASEAN. Despite desires to the contrary, both USA and Europe are finding it politically difficult to adjust because of the strength of opposition from unions and industrial interests representing their older industries. Europe's inability to accept the Uruguay Round agricultural package and Clinton's problems with labour interests that fear relocation of US industries into Mexico with the proposed NAFTA are but a few examples of such inward-looking tendencies. *East Asia, being the youngest and least dependent on protectionism, is thus the world's best chance for free trade.*

Politically, the end of the Cold War and the disintegration of the USSR have left the world with only one superpower, namely the USA. Despite their economic wealth and economic superpower status, Japan and Germany have no ambitions to become military superpowers. Russia and China are busy undertaking economic liberalization and have disavowed taking military ventures. Even US military power is somewhat lame, reflecting its economic weakness. This political scenario, combined with the globalization of production and closer trade and investment relations between nations, have resulted in the dominance of economic over political relations.

In East Asia, the world is seeing a US 'withdrawal' from its key bases in the Philippines following the USSR's demise as a military threat in the Pacific. These factors, combined with Japan's continued disavowal of militarism, China's preoccupation with economic reform and developmental issues, the economic liberalization of Vietnam, closer economic relations among China, Korea, Taiwan and Hong Kong, and tentative efforts towards economic liberalization in North Korea have given rise to what has been termed 'the outbreak of peace'. As a result, *East Asia today is in a period of its greatest peace and political stability in decades.* There is no obvious hegemony in sight and the whole region is split into relatively non-antagonistic, pluralistic sub-regions and entities such as ASEAN, Japan, China, Asian NIEs, Vietnam and Indochina. Furthermore, the identities of these regions are defined on economic, rather than political or strategic grounds.

The time is thus both ripe and opportune for organizing the East Asia economies on a formalized basis in order to:

1 enhance regional economic integration and facilitate continued economic growth and advancement;
2 integrate the former socialist economies of China and Indochina into liberal market economies;
3 discourage and counteract any movements towards protectionism in the other two regions;
4 'freeze' the existing pluralistic political structure and ensure the continuation of regional peace and stability over the long term.

To achieve this, a formal East Asian entity, called by the name of EAEC or whatever, and based on the principles already enumerated, needs to be established. This entity can help ensure the success of APEC as a consultative mechanism because the APEC process will be sidetracked or will fail if any single party, such as the USA within NAFTA, has the ability to exercise dominance or hegemony, over other parties in the group. *Other members will clearly not cooperate to make the relationship meaningful if they see APEC merely as a vehicle for exercising US hegemony.* With the presence of an East Asian grouping under the APEC umbrella, the three regional groupings (NAFTA, EAEC and Australia New Zealand Closer Economic Relations and Trade Agreement (ANZCERTA)) will be represented in a more or less balanced manner. In this way, APEC will become an important vehicle for ensuring pluralistic, open, fair and non-hegemonic relations between the three regions within the Pacific.

It is obvious that to function within APEC *vis-à-vis* NAFTA and ANZCERTA, EAEC has to be formalized beyond the level of a merely *ad hoc* consultative process. In other words, it cannot be set up with the same degree of looseness as APEC as it would then degenerate into a consultative framework within a bigger consultative framework. A formal organization, without involving a free trade agreement, remains the most appropriate way for organizing EAEC. For example, the EAEC may be organized in a manner similar to ASEAN prior to the development of AFTA.

THE NEXT STEP

To start off the EAEC, a formal agreement is needed, perhaps in the form of a *region-wide treaty of amity and cooperation*. Thereafter, the EAEC can function as follows:

Set up a *pluralistic series of frameworks*, at both official and private sector levels, with the following broad agendas:

a enhancing regional cooperation, friendship and relations;
b conflict resolution;
c mutual help and matching of needs and capabilities of the various parties; and
d cultural and other exchanges to enhance East Asian consciousness.

In addition, the EAEC should meet and *function as a caucus in negotiations affecting all parties*, e.g.

a Caucus in Uruguay Round and post-Uruguay Round talks;
b Caucus prior to APEC; or
c Caucus prior to G7 meetings, in which Japan will also speak on behalf of the group.

Finally, the EAEC can also work as a group which meets regularly with the EC and NAFTA with regard to trade, investment and other issues with the aim of smoothing such relationships as well as further enhancing cooperation with these regions.

SUMMARY

The EAEC will thus be an open group, which can act as a counterweight to NAFTA and the EC, and which can function as a strong voice for Asia. It will, as such, be Asia's insurance policy against the degeneration of world trade into closed trade bloc arrangements.

The EAEC will also be an insurance policy against any deterioration in the current reign of peace enjoyed by Asia and against the continuation of hegemonic tendencies by the USA, or the development of such tendencies by China, Russia or Japan. Just like ASEAN in the 1970s and 1980s, the EAEC can play the critical role of 'freezing the peace' and enhancing cooperation among member countries. It can be a mechanism by which East Asians can learn to know one another as friends. The existence of EAEC will thus help ensure that East Asia's political stability and plurality is similar to Europe's while its economy continues on its current dynamic growth path.

14

JAPANESE CULTURAL IMAGES IN MALAYSIA

Implications of the 'Look East' policy

Wendy A. Smith

This chapter will discuss the nature of Japanese cultural images in Malaysia, as they are used by the Malaysian state in the 'Look East' policy, and as they are created by the Japanese presence in Malaysia at both the general social level and at the factory level in ideologies of Japanese management.

The 'Look East' policy, a personal project of Dr Mahathir Mohamad, implemented in 1981 soon after he became Prime Minister, emerged right in the middle of Malaysia's twenty-year project of economic and social restructuring, the New Economic Policy (NEP). Politically speaking, it was designed to have a catalytic effect, to mobilize Malaysians to achieve Mahathir's goals.[1] It is thus a highly significant phenomenon representing the crystalization of culture-based ideological resources which are always present within economic processes.

At the time of the formulation of the 'Look East' policy, Japan was the major source of investment capital in Malaysia, with 329 ventures in 1980, investing a total of RM1.6 billion (Saravanamuttu 1985: 318–22). By 1990, the figure had risen to RM4.2 billion.[2] Japan is also Malaysia's major trading partner.[3]

Japanese capital entered Malaysia in the import substitution stage in the 1960s, and rapidly increased in the 1970s, when the government placed heavy emphasis on export-oriented industrialization by foreign investment to create employment. Malaysia's need for foreign investment corresponded with the period of Japan's rapid economic expansion overseas to utilize cheap labour and to capture markets for consumer products. The NEP also encouraged the growth of the middle class in Malaysian society[4] and a materialist, 'conspicuous consumption' ethos, not only among the new middle class, but also among the first generation of wage earners from rural peasant social backgrounds. In 1991, at the end of the NEP era, consumer spending expanded 11.6 per cent over the previous year, and this rate of growth was only moderated to 8–9 per cent in 1992 by government policies restricting credit (*Economist*, 17 October 1992: 26).

The conjunction of Japanese overseas expansion and Malaysian economic growth under the NEP has resulted in the overwhelming majority of electrical appliances and cars in Malaysian middle class homes now being Japanese brands, with the working class owning Japanese motor bikes, reconditioned Japanese cars or aspiring to own the new Malaysian mini car based on the Daihatsu, planned to capture this new market (*FEER* 13 February 1992: 44; Chee, 1985: 397).

Thus, the Japanese economic presence in Malaysia, especially after the 'Look East' policy, has had ramifications far beyond the economic sphere: along with Japanese technology and capital came the Japanese expatriate community of managers, families, teachers, service workers, as well as Japanese consumer products, lifestyles and cultural practices. Although many of these non-economic activities originated in the West, in many cases, it is the 'Japanized' versions which have come to Malaysia and have been embraced enthusiastically by the Malaysian public.

In this paper, I will first outline the nature of the 'Look East' policy and comment on the Japanese reaction to the policy. Second, I will analyse the ideological potential of 'Japanese Management', a key element in the 'Look East' policy as it relates to work organization. Third, I will examine some of the more significant socio-cultural ramifications of the increased Japanese presence in Malaysia since the advent of the 'Look East' policy.

THE 'LOOK EAST' POLICY

What then does the 'Look East' policy consist of? Briefly stated, the key elements in the initial 'Look East' policy statement of December 1981 were: to introduce Japanese work ethics and management systems to Malaysia in order to improve productivity and overall economic performance and hence enhance Malaysia's industrialization with Japanese technology and capital (Lim, 1984: 231). In support of these were concrete proposals in two areas: first, in human resource development, to train large numbers of Malaysian students in Japanese undergraduate courses, to set up a Japanese language training centre at the University of Malaya to prepare students for this, and to send more workers to Japan for on-the-job training through the AOTS (Association for Overseas Technical Scholarship) scheme already established;[5] second, to set up economic institutions new to Malaysia, but already existing in Japan, for example, general trading companies (*sogoshosha*) (Milne and Mauzy, 1986: 148), and 'Malaysia Inc.', a concept similar to 'Japan Incorporated' (Jomo, 1990: 211), and to expand the incidence of in-house unions. These can be seen as directly inspired by the Japanese model.

The public Japanese reaction to the 'Look East' policy was restrained but positive. Embarrassed by the unilateral declaration of solidarity inherent in the policy, Japan was nevertheless put in a position where it had to make some concrete response. This took the form of soft loans and other financial aid even at a time, in the 1980s, when Japan herself was claiming financial difficulties (Lim, 1984: 235). Although the Japanese may regard the 'Look East' policy as a nuisance (*meiwaku*), nevertheless its formulation must have reassured them. The Japanese foreign investment pattern is overwhelmingly one of joint ventures, in which they hold minority equity but nevertheless retain managerial and financial control (Chee and Lee, 1985: 275; Imaoka, 1985: 17). Because of the fear of national takeovers, as happened in Iran, a major factor in any Japanese company's decision to invest overseas is the stability of a country's political regime. Both Japanese businessmen and diplomats have always been most concerned that Mahathir's regime should continue.[6]

A policy such as the 'Look East' policy, while placing the Japanese under obligation, nevertheless proves to be to their advantage in the long-term because the Japanese will not only make direct economic gains from the 'Look East' policy, but also indirect gains through heightening the Japanese socio-cultural profile in Malaysia. Built into the whole Japanese economic advancement is a cultural agenda, the Japanization of the world through a consumer culture and lifestyle based on Japanese products. It is therefore of significance to observe the socio-cultural ramifications of the 'Look East' policy in Malaysia.

WORK ETHICS AND MANAGEMENT

Officially, the main thrust of the 'Look East' policy has been to introduce and spread the ethics of hard work, efficiency and productivity among Malaysian workers since these are perceived to be the key reasons behind Japan's economic success. In formulating this policy, simplistic stereotyped views of Japanese society and management have been adopted without a critical understanding of their historical underpinnings, or even their interrelationship with various other aspects of Japanese society: for instance, the relative job security of regular employees in a large Japanese firm is supported by a large cohort of part-time and temporary workers who work side by side with them and by very flexible arrangements with subcontracting firms whose employees have very little security of tenure. Consequently the 'Japanese management system' has been embraced in a utopian way and the emphasis given to work ethics within the 'Look East' policy clearly demonstrates its ideological intent (Muzaffar, 1985: 337).

In examining the ideological potential of utopian views of Japanese society, one must dissect the stereotype which has come to be accepted internationally as *the* explanation: that is, the vertical theory of Japanese society expressed by Professor Chie Nakane in her book *Japanese Society*, originally published in English in 1970.[7] It is significant that her view of the society as a whole is closely linked to theories of Japanese management; indeed, Nakane's model is largely based on her analysis of business organization, which is then extrapolated to the whole society.[8]

The basic elements of Nakane's view of Japanese society may be summarized as follows: 1) its social structure is unchanging over time; 2) all groups are structured according to the same vertical principle, hence the society is homogenous; 3) the society is conflict-free and harmonious because of the obedience of its members to those higher up in the hierarchy; 4) the society is basically egalitarian; all people despite their different levels of ability, find equally useful places in the vertical structure; 5) the vertical nature of social groups contributes to great efficiency in mobilizing members of the group, hence Japan achieved rapid modernization.

These attributes constitute a classic example of a 'utopia' as expounded by Dahrendorf (1958). According to Nakane, Japanese society is unique because of the above characteristics. Nakane uses the analogy of Japanese companies to illustrate the principle of the absence of conflict in the following manner. *Within* companies, there can be no conflict because of the intrinsic nature of their vertical organization. Furthermore there will only be 'competition', not conflict, *between* rival companies A and B.[9] However, under the vertical principle, their cooperation can be secured by a higher agent, such as the government.

The prevailing Japanese management paradigm can be seen to be closely linked with Nakane's utopian conceptualization. The supposed uniqueness of the three pillars of the Japanese management – guaranteed lifetime employment (*shushin koyo*), the seniority system in wages and promotions (*nenko joretsu*), and enterprise or in-house unionism (*kigyobetsu kumiai*) – has taken a tenacious hold on the popular imagination although it has been refuted many times on the basis of international statistical comparison (Koike, 1983), Japanese economic history (Crawcour, 1978) and theoretical analysis of internal labour markets (Smith, 1983). A journal special issue on 'Japanese Management in Southeast Asia' by Japanese economists faithfully listed the three pillars in the Introduction (see *Southeast Asian Studies (Kyoto)*, 1985: 336). The stereotype relies heavily on culturalist, ideological factors – such as feudal loyalty and paternalism – for its validity (Shimada, 1983; Smith, 1983).

Control is a central focus of discussion in our understanding of the labour process in general. Management systems must secure willing, productive, accurate work from employees without a perception of the exploitative nature of the class relations involved which might lead to dissent or even resistance. To a great extent, this is exactly what the 'work ethic' component of the 'Look East' policy hopes to achieve.

Large Japanese firms, while sharing characteristics with Western firms such as a hierarchical job structure in which workers are promoted through a process of individual rivalry, and the internal labour market which is the outcome of this – may nevertheless be evaluated as extremely successful in securing productive labour from their workers. This can be explained in terms of the historical development of employment systems in Japan, where, due to the scarcity of skilled labour and consequent high labour mobility in the early days of industrialization, employers in concert created paternalist systems with seniority-based renumeration schemes to discourage workers from leaving their firms after they had been trained in modern production techniques (Crawcour, 1978: 234).

In the modern era, the system of work organization on the shopfloor which is found in Japanese firms strongly emphasizes job rotation. This creates a great range and adaptiveness in skilling workers (Koike, 1984) and promotes a *de facto* egalitarianism, as veteran workers can perform tasks which would normally be left to supervisors, due to their wideranging experience in the production process. The Japanese case is a prime example of what Friedman has called the 'responsible autonomy' type of control strategy 'which allows workers a wide measure of discretion over the direction of their work tasks and enhances their identity with the competitive aims of the enterprise so that they act "responsibly" with the minimum of supervision' (Friedman, 1977: 48).

Enterprise, as opposed to craft, unionism enhances this system. Job rotation in a firm where workers are members of several craft unions creates job demarcation disputes, but under enterprise unionism, the workers' material interests are identified with the profitability of the firm and the demarcation of duties is of low priority in the issues bargained for by the union.[10]

Second, a highly sophisticated system of wage determination exists in large Japanese firms; typically, the Japanese wage stucture has three components, length of service, age and ability. The relative weight of the first two components is decided by collective bargaining, but the third depends on the individual's annual merit assessment. As the base wage thus determined is used to calculate the annual bonus (which may be up to six months' wages paid in two lump sums annually), this merit assessment is crucial. Because of this component, a wage table cannot be drawn for workers in Japanese firms as it can be for workers in Malaysia, where all workers' wages can be located on a wage table decided by collective bargaining (Smith, 1988: 454).

Hence, the Japanese worker is under pressure to actively participate and cooperate in quality control circles (QCCs) and other managerial campaigns, and to show initiative and innovation in his or her work as these are all key items in the annual merit assessment. In contrast, the Malaysian worker has little to gain in salary terms by performing with more 'responsible autonomy'. At best, he or she stands to gain a double increment, perhaps awarded to two workers out of a section of 50. He or she can make more money by leaving work at the end of the shift, for instance, to help a relative run a small street stall, instead of participating in unpaid QCC activities after hours.

339

Similarly, Malaysian workers will guard their job categories jealously to ensure their own employment security. The specifications of a job are very likely to be written into the firm's collective agreement. So, to impose the Japanese system, a central feature of which is job rotation, on existing Malaysian firms is organizationally impossible; it is similarly unrealistic to expect Malaysian workers to adopt Japanese-style work ethics under the present system of renumeration.

PRE-1945 CULTURAL IMAGES OF THE JAPANESE

In the pre-war era, the Japanese community in Malaysia was made up of migrant petty traders[11] (barbers, photographers, bicycle shop owners), prostitutes (*karayuki-san*),[12] and businessmen in the extraction sector (rubber and iron ore) (Shaharil, 1984: 96). The post-war stereotype among Malaysians of the pre-war Japanese community is that they were a fifth column, consisting of active spies, or reluctant collaborators co-opted into the war effort for the information and other services they could provide.

Even more negative stereotypes emerge from the years of Japanese Occupation: the massacre of masses of innocent people, especially members of the ethnic Chinese communities, often associated with public displays of extreme brutality (Cheah, 1980: 78–80) – these have left an indelible imprint in the post-war Malaysian world view. The atrocities committed by the Japanese army remain in people's memories in the form of superstitious perceptions of geographical areas, misfortune and illness.[13] The scientific validity of these explanations is not so important as the fact that these stereotypes still persist in people's minds fifty years after the events took place, and they remain even after the peasant or small trader generations of the wartime years have been transformed into a middle class using predominantly Japanese products as part of their middle class lifestyles.

The Japanese Occupation is also associated with the disruption of the economy and of the pre-existing social order. Food supplies were requisitioned by the occupying forces and normal patterns of subsistence agriculture were disrupted. (Cheah, 1980: 87–8). Families lived in fear of their daughters being raped or sexually exploited by Japanese soldiers, as has been borne out in the recent revelations of the 'comfort women'.[14] Men were rounded up to work on the Death Railway and the majority never returned. But most significantly, the Japanese Occupation exacerbated the ethnic divide between the Malays and the ethnic Chinese, as Malays were seen as collaborators with the Japanese,[15] whereas the Chinese population received the full brunt of Japanese aggression, which spilled over from the atrocities committed in China itself, because of their support for the predominantly Chinese resistance force, the Malayan People's Anti-Japanese Army of the Malayan Communist Party (Cheah, 1980: 89–92).

SOCIO-CULTURAL RAMIFICATIONS OF THE JAPANESE PRESENCE IN MALAYSIA

The contemporary Japanese community in Malaysia is still subjected to the Japanese military stereotype of the Occupation years. Most Malaysian Chinese families can recall at least one relative killed by the Japanese during this time.[16] But since the 1970s, this has been pushed into the background by economic factors. Likewise, from the 1970s onward, Japanese cars and consumer products were not avoided because they were considered to be very good value for money before the rising yen, or *endaka*, phenomenon which took place after the Plaza Accord of 1985. However, in addition to the pervasiveness and prestige associated with Japanese consumer products, the 'Look East' policy with its implied emphasis on the superiority of Japanese society due to its high economic growth rate, has given great 'face' to the Japanese in Malaysia[17] and has led to a growing mood of cultural imperialism.

The Japanese community in Malaysia, presently more than 5,000 in number (*FEER*, 1991: 120), consists mainly of expatriate businessmen and their families whose stay is temporary. As the community grows in strength and importance, a sub-community of supporting Japanese workers has grown up; the teachers, chefs and waitresses in restaurants, tour guides and other service workers, who are also transients.

In this section, I will deal with some effects of the 'Look East' policy for Malaysian society and culture. The increased Japanese economic presence in Malaysia and the closer Japan–Malaysia relations in the wake of the 'Look East' policy have been accompanied by the predictable lip service paid to 'cultural exchange',[18] not unlike discussion of the 'benefits' of foreign investment, such as technology transfer. The contents of this supposed cultural exchange, which is actually a one-way flow of material culture and values from Japan, will now be examined. Unfortunately, such cultural activities also ideologically obscure the unbalanced underlying economic relations. No amount of supposedly neutral cultural contact between Japan and Malaysia could alter the fact that Japan benefits more than Malaysia from the relationship.

The following discussion of Japanese cultural influences upon Malaysian society will be grouped into three sections: 1) institutional forms, such as education structures and resources, aid programmes; 2) leisure activities, such as golf, restaurants, clubs, tourism and popular culture; 3) consumer related issues, such as supermarkets and department stores, consumer goods and so on. Although some of these categories overlap and are difficult to separate from their essentially economic origin, they are articulated in the cultural sphere because of their overtly Japanese characteristics, with all the positive value that this implies under the 'Look East' policy.

Institutional forms

Information networks

In the post-war era, the flexible specialization of Japanese professionals and the openness of organizational structures creates the possibility of information gathering for the national interest in a more open way than was possible in the pre-war years. Japan is famous for the secondment (*shukko*) system (Hamada, 1992), whereby employees of the parent company are seconded to the joint venture in Malaysia, even though it is a separate company, legally constituted in Malaysia. *Shukko* is not limited to the business world. Japanese academics have been seconded as diplomats overseas, including to Southeast Asia. Some prominent academics also serve on a contract basis or as permanent advisors to major Japanese multinationals. Newly employed graduates in government departments and major Japanese companies have been sent to enrol in undergraduate courses in the University of Malaya to study Bahasa Malaysia for several years before rejoining their employing institutions and being posted back to Malaysia as representatives.[19]

The links between business, academia and government are very strong and the boundaries of duty are blurred. Similarly, the information-collecting activities of the Japanese trading companies and the Overseas Operations Divisions of Japanese multinationals are highly developed, complementing and often surpassing those of academic and governmental institutions.[20]

There are also many dedicated young Japanese working in Malaysia under the *Nihon Kaigai Kyoryoku Taiin* (Japan Overseas Cooperation Volunteers), who bring their special skills – mechanical, horticultural, child and health care – to the impoverished rural areas and urban squatter settlements. However, similar to the US Peace Corps, their presence has two facets. The regular monthly reports which they submit to their parent organization in Japan are analysed by academics and government officials and become a primary source of base-line intelligence on economic and social conditions in Malaysia. Since the 'Look East' policy was announced, more of these volunteers are being used to fulfil language teaching roles, thus reducing the aid once given to poor communities.

Books

In Japan's own modernization, books played a crucial role. As with Malaysia, the national language was non-European and an ambitious translation programme was needed to create access to Western learning. Translation activities developed on a very large and comprehensive scale. Almost all Western literary classics were made available in Japanese in cheap paperback editions. Famous academic texts in English and other European languages were translated and one publishing house survived on its specialty of translating Marxist texts. Even today, academic works of outstanding merit and best-sellers on Japan are translated immediately.[21] Bodies such as the Japan and Toyota Foundations allocate funds to seek out worthy texts on Southeast Asia for translation into Japanese. In the present era of Japanese economic dominance, this enthusiasm and capacity for translation has also been applied to Japanese texts, and the foundations allocate funds for the translation of Japanese books into English and the Southeast Asian languages. For instance, the *Institut Penataran Ilmu* translates English works into Malay, under the Toyota Foundation's 'Know Thy Neighbour' project.

Books which present a conservative, ideologically acceptable view of Japanese society are earmarked for translation. Since the 'Look East' policy, demand for books about Japan has grown, as they supposedly supply the key to Japanese-style affluence. In Malaysia, a tendency has been observed for Malaysian scholars, who want to earn money by translating books about Japan into Bahasa Malaysia under these programmes, to nominate books of their own choice, for instance the famous text *The Anatomy of Dependence* by Takeo Doi, Professor of Mental Health, on *amae*, an emotion supposedly central to the Japanese personality. Often, the Malaysian scholars are relatively uninformed about the wide range of sociological perspectives in Japanese studies, and they nominate books already translated into English, which convey simplistic and stereotypical views. Hence, the overall quality of books about Japan translated into Bahasa Malaysia is unbalanced.

The Japan Foundation, which has maintained a permanent representative in Kuala Lumpur since 1988, also distributes free books on Japan to institutions with Japanese language programmes. Those in English are usually translations of the supposed classics of Japanese scholarship and rarely express an alternative view of Japanese society.

Academic training and exchange

For many years, the Japanese Ministry of Education (*Mombusho*), through the Japan Information Service in the Japanese Embassy, has sponsored academic training and exchange programmes between Japan and Malaysia. It offers a number of undergraduate and postgraduate *Mombusho* scholarships as part of its worldwide student programme. This continues to be open to all Malaysians. However, since the 'Look East' policy, one of whose objectives is to have more Malaysians graduate from Japanese universities, large groups of Malaysian students sponsored by the Public Services Department (PSD) of the Malaysian Government have been sent to do undergraduate studies after first receiving Japanese language training in the Japanese Language Centre at the University of Malaya.[22] This scheme has mainly benefited Malays, as most PSD overseas tertiary scholarships are awarded to them.

There are several ironies here. First, degrees from Japanese universities were not officially recognized in Malaysia before the 'Look East' policy and Malaysians who had studied privately in Japan often found themselves employed by Japanese companies in Malaysia and working with expatriate Japanese staff who graduated from the same universities, but at lower rank and with reduced authority, for much lower renumeration and with poorer promotional prospects. Second, the first batch of 'Look East' policy graduates returned to Malaysia in 1987 with almost all of them being recruited immediately to work in Japanese companies operating in Malaysia.[23] Some were recruited through the parent companies in Japan before they had even finished their courses. Fresh from several years of living in Japan, they will have been well exposed to the values of loyalty and submission to group interests which are considered to be highly desired characteristics of new recruits in Japanese companies.

Since the 1970s, there has been a Japanese visiting professor in the History Department of the University of Malaya. Sometimes, the person is not a historian by training. For some time too, under the 'Look East' policy, there was a Visiting Professor post in the Faculty of Economics and Administration of the University of Malaya for a Japanese expert in Japanese management. A detailed examination of their academic records shows that several of these academics had done little research, if any, in Japanese firms and had held overlapping government and academic duties in the past. As such, they could be expected to espouse the official Japanese line on 'Japanese management'. Besides imparting an ideological view of Japan to Malaysian students, these year-long postings for Japanese scholars serve as valuable fact-finding missions on the Malaysian economy.

Architecture

The self-confidence of the Japanese in their cultural presence in Malaysia is reflected in the architecture of the new Japanese Embassy planned and built in the 1980s in the prime location along Jalan Tun Razak near the US Embassy.[24] The building is a box-like structure with functional windows, and a high fence with slits, reminiscent of apertures for military defence. Given the graceful nature of traditional Japanese architecture and the fact that most other newly constructed embassies in the locality reflect their national architectural styles, the Japanese Embassy is a disappointment. It is said to be reminiscent of the former US embassy in Saigon; functional, military, representing the country's dominance in the region at the time. Ironically, the new US Embassy nearby is a graceful building, dominated by a sloping roof and large windows, reflecting a more classic American architectual style.

Leisure activities

Restaurants and clubs

The Japanese business community members, who are largely transient, staying usually from three to six years, are supported by permanent insitutions such as the Japanese Chamber of Commerce, JETRO (Japanese External Trade Organisation), the Japan Club and the Kuala Lumpur Japanese school (*Kuara Runpuuru Nihonjin Gakkoo*).[25] These institutions are closed to non-Japanese although the women's group of the Japan Club runs a very popular bazaar each year at the YWCA.

As a support structure to the growing Japanese community and as part of the structural change in patterns of Japanese direct foreign investment and the increased volume of Japanese tourists since the *endaka*, the 1980s has seen the proliferation of Japanese investment in the service sector, in hotels, restaurants, clubs and bars, department stores, travel and advertising agencies.[26] Japanese restaurants and *karaoke* bars have sprung up all over the business district of Kuala Lumpur. These are not only for the Japanese community, but attract middle class Malaysians in varying degrees of popularity. Most large hotels now have a first class Japanese restaurant which caters to Japanese expense account diners and their clients. Even though the chefs are Japanese and the standard of food served is very high, the prices are a fraction of what would be paid for the same dish in Japan.[27] There are a growing number of cheaper establishments for business lunches, but generally, Japanese restaurant food does not appeal to Malaysians, being too bland and too little in quantity.

To the casual observer, there is a 'neo-colonial' feeling about the Japanese presence in Kuala Lumpur nowadays. Since the 'Look East' policy, several Japanese-style exclusive clubs have opened.[28] Usually located in several stories of prestigious office blocks in the centre of Kuala Lumpur, the clubs offer membership (with suitable sponsorship) to those who can pay the joining fee of several thousand ringgit plus a monthly service fee of usually not more than RM50 plus any chits signed for meals or drinks. They offer sports and gym facilities, as well as dining and drinking areas with Japanese-style hostess service. The system is modelled on the operational style of the old colonial clubs of the British days. While these historic clubs, such as the Selangor Club and the Lake Club, still survive with considerable prestige attached to membership, in the last decade, there has been a wave of modern clubs established, on similar operational principles, to cater for the leisure needs of the growing middle class. It is a measure of their self-confidence in the region that the Japanese also are establishing clubs based on the colonial pattern.

Karaoke

Karaoke bars are perhaps Japan's most significant cultural export world-wide in the past decade and their popularity in Malaysia is no exception. Karaoke bars arose from the custom of groups of salarymen from large companies drinking together regularly after work, one of the main leisure activities of males in Japan. These gatherings are not only composed of those of the same status in the firm, but have a hierarchical component. The group consists of those who work together in one workplace or office, from the lowest ranking member to the section head.[29] The well-known activity of singing in these group occasions, no matter whether one has talent or not, is a tension releasing, social equalizing mechanism.

Usually, the group sits around a low table on the *tatami* mats, the table piled high with bottles of beer, ceramic *sake* containers with the little *sake* cups, and *otsumami* (snacks of grilled fish, salty pickled vegetables, dried squid, and other things designed to make one thirsty). Everyone is usually quite drunk, or if not biologically inebriated, then falling into that drunken carefree mode of behaviour, which soon becomes less than artificial.

The singing, traditionally a solo performance without any backing except clapping, proceeds in order around the table. It is mandatory to make one's contribution; no value judgments are placed on those who can sing in tune or not, the act of singing, sharing one's soul, is important. As most people are genuinely drunk and thus without inhibitions, they generally sing rather well. Even the one who is patently out of tune is patiently listened to, enthusiastically applauded and thus enjoys the experience of performing in public, without having to worry if he has caused the listeners discomfort, since excellence is not the issue here.

The advent of *karaoke* has helped the amateur performer because now he has musical support. A *karaoke* machine is a special type of tape recorder which plays tapes of popular songs in which one layer of the recording, the vocal, is left empty (*kara*), leaving the orchestral (*oke*) backing. This allows for the patrons of the *karaoke* bar to take it in turns to sing their favourite songs with authentic musical backing.[30]

A whole subculture of *karaoke* bars has sprung from this custom of the after work drinking/singing party. With the mushrooming popularity of *karaoke* bars in Japan in the last decade, the electrical appliance companies have found a way to commoditize this traditional tension-releasing mechanism for males in Japanese society. Much more expensive than ordinary tape recorders or compact disc decks, *karaoke* machines are being bought by families and are even used by lone individuals performing to the public in parks. *Karaoke* bars originally opened in the world's major cities for the Japanese businessmen stationed overseas but are becoming popular with the indigenous inhabitants. This is certainly the case in Kuala Lumpur where there are *karaoke* clubs with Chinese songs for mainly Malaysian

Chinese patrons. Indeed, most of the local pubs of British origin are now renamed '*Karaoke* Pub' or '*Karaoke* Bar', but in Malaysia, they are associated more with the individual pursuit of leisure than with work group activities, increasing the participation of pub patrons from a passive one of merely drinking while watching others make music. Malaysian middle class families also buy *karaoke* sets costing RM15,000 as a status item in the home. The *karaoke* concept has thus been readily transferred to another cultural context.

Golf and Japanese business culture

Golf is also a very important activity in Japanese corporate culture. Similar to *karaoke*, it combines leisure and business in a harmonious fashion. In Japan, executives spend Sundays travelling to golf courses several hours away and playing, not primarily for pleasure, but in the context of their work responsibilities.[31] Second only to social drinking, so important is the ability to play golf to advance one's career that practice ranges, high netted but compact enclosures, have been built since the 1970s even in the inner areas of crowded Tokyo and substantial areas of agricultural land around the perimeter of the metropolis have been sold to golf club developers. Hence, playing golf well serves as a source of prestige and success in one's career.

The golf course functions as a place where business negotiations or political discussions can be conducted without fear of eavesdropping. But club membership is very expensive, ranging from ¥100–400 million, several year's salary for the individual, and is often purchased as an investment. One Japanese expatriate was able to buy an apartment in Japan after his retirement by selling his membership in a prestigious Japanese golf club.

In Malaysia and other Southeast Asian countries, the Japanese preoccupation with golf as a corporate sport and the building of golf clubs as one type of overseas investment has been a notable feature of their presence. In order to understand this phenomenon, we must examine the golf industry in Japan itself. The building of golf clubs and associated resorts has become big business in Japan after two Prime Ministers, Tanaka in 1972, and Nakasone in 1987, instituted large-scale domestic construction programmes to offset crises in Japan's international economic position. These policies resulted in indiscriminate national development projects as land use regulations were relaxed. The proliferation of golf courses in Japan is associated with 'three evils' also relevant to Malaysia: 1) environmental destruction and pollution, as water catchment forests are destroyed, mountains levelled and downstream water supplies polluted by herbicides and pesticides used on the greens; 2) the takeover of land that could be used for agriculture, each course occupying on average 100 hectares; 3) the encouragement of corrupt social practices, as there have been cases of local administrators taking bribes from golf course developers.

In its developed form, the golf course industry has been transferred directly to Asia.[32] In Malaysia, golf course development is mainly in the hands of the Japanese, sometimes in partnership with local capital. It has entered the Malaysian economy at the full blown level of big business; golf clubs are associated with resort development, accompanied by a hotel, condominiums, international golf star course designers, and huge membership fees which are seen as investments. They are also associated with the three evils: the proposal to build an international resort on Penang Hill including golf courses, hotels, condominiums, a retirement village for Japanese, restaurants, *karaoke* lounges, shopping malls and theme parks would lead to massive destruction of the environment. The Templar Park Country Club, developed by a subsidiary of the Kyowa Company is located on government land covering a third of the protected Templar Park. Its membership is 25 per cent Japanese, with a joining fee of US$22,200 (*Aliran Monthly* 1991, 11, 9: 7). As in Japan, in Malaysia now, golf memberships are regarded as investments which can later be resold at a profit. A major scandal arose regarding the overpriced purchase by Mara Holdings of 450 memberships worth US$11.3 million in the prestigious Rahman Putra Golf Club, in which over a quarter of the members are Japanese (*FEER*, 12 November 1992: 30).

Compared with the time spent reaching golf clubs in Japan and the expensive membership and green fees, golf clubs in Malaysia are accessible and cheap. In fact, some Japanese find it cheaper to fly regularly to Malaysia just to play golf. Existing clubs have been overburdened with Japanese corporate memberships and players at weekends taking advantage of the excellent, but inexpensive facilities.[33] Some local members of the club have been heard to complain that the course is swamped with Japanese businessmen at weekends, using the facilities as guest members which they, the regular members, have paid for with their membership subscriptions. As in many other contexts, it is the Japanese 'over-presence' which creates anti-Japanese feeling.[34]

Tourism

The high yen phenomenon has led to an influx of Japanese tourists, including college students and young unmarried working people who can afford to stay in the top hotels in Kuala Lumpur, such as the Pan–Pacific, the Regent and the Shangri La. However, Japanese tourism does not bring much revenue to Malaysia as several hotels, and most of the tour buses, gift shops, restaurants and tourist facilities which they patronize are Japanese-owned.[35]

A different type of Japanese tourism must also be mentioned. As part of the strong emphasis in Japanese Buddhism placed on proper burial ceremonies and honouring the dead through attendance at their graves at regular intervals, since the war, there have been many visits by Japanese groups to find the bones or honour the graves of Japanese war dead. However, in the 1980s in Japan, in the wake of such controversial issues as the representation of Japanese wartime roles in Asia in school textbooks and the fingerprinting of 'alien residents' in Japan, including ethnic Koreans born in Japan, there has been a growing awareness of Japan's political identity and responsibility in Asia. In this context, a party of Japanese school teachers came in 1984 to visit a mass grave of Malaysian war victims newly discovered in Sungei Lui, a little town near the border of Negri Sembilan and Pahang.[36] Japanese environmentalist groups and a study tour in 1991 of the Asian, Latin American and African Association – made up of Japanese publishers, academics and students – have also visited Malaysia to see, among other things, the Asian Rare Earth site, polluted by radioactive waste, near Ipoh, and another wartime massacre site near Lenggeng, Negeri Sembilan. In such cases, we see evidence that the Japanese approach to Malaysia is multi-dimensional, reflecting the many facets of Japanese society itself, and does not merely consist of a cultural imperialism resulting from economic hegemony, although this is the dominant mood.

Popular culture

In the field of popular culture, growing Japanese influence can be observed in television programmes, where there have been a number of long-running Japanese daily serials shown on the Malaysian national television channels, dubbed into Bahasa Malaysia, besides several other weekly series for different target audiences. The popular Japanese cartoon series *Doremon* is shown in the prime 7.30pm viewing time after the Maghreb (sunset) prayer.

Japanese popular songs are often broadcast or requested on the FM stations. Some Japanese singers record Malay songs and manage to enter the Top 10 Chart, for example Miss Suzuki singing *Ikan Kekek*. Video clips of Japanese pop stars singing in Malay or Japanese are also featured on Malaysian television.

In the spirit of cultural exchange, it must be added that Lat's *The Kampong Boy*, a collection of cartoons on Malaysian rural life, has been translated into Japanese by a Japanese journalist, and has become a bestseller in Japan.[37] But Lat has also been co-opted into the service of culturally familiarizing Malaysians with Japan: national dailies have often carried his cartoons representing scenes from Japanese life, based on his trips to Japan (for instance, *New Straits Times*, 22 and 24 April 1989). However, in his inimitable style, he remains a major source of wry comment on the 'Look East' policy: one memorable cartoon in which a cleaner greets the Prime Minister on equal terms, parodies the 'egalitarian' nature of Japanese work relationships.

The Japan Information Service regularly sponsors free film shows and performances by Japanese artistes. These concerts, which are of very high quality, are attended by Cabinet Ministers and sometimes even by the Prime Minister himself. One recent dance performance captured the spirit of cultural exchange in its literal meaning. It included Japanese folk dances in front of a Japanese backdrop of kite motifs, alternating with Malay traditional dances by the national dance troupe, to a backdrop of a tropical beach scene. The highlight came when Japanese members donned *batik* and participated in the Malay item, but a bigger surprise was when Malay dancers were revealed to have participated in an intricate Japanese number, having been disguised beneath facecovering straw hats. But the cultural exchange inherent in the 'Look East' policy is very much between Japanese and Malay culture. Such activities have intensified so much that a Japan Cultural Centre, with only Malay and Japanese staff, has been set up with official Japanese Government support in the early 1990s.[38]

Consumer culture

Consumerism is perhaps the major area in which we observe the Japanese influence expanding since the early 1980s. Malaysia is fast becoming a consumer society: not just the middle classes but low wage factory workers buy expensive brand sports shoes and video games (*FEER*, 9 July 1992: 58). Because of the recent proximity of their own transformation into a 'middle class' consumerist society, the Japanese manufacturing companies were better able to anticipate what Malaysians would like to buy as their first status acquisitions in the home. In comparison, the marketing strategies of Western appliance makers, whose market consisted of the small historically entrenched middle class of pre-NEP professionals, were rigidly defined and they were caught unawares by the rapid social change generated by the NEP.

As mentioned previously, Japanese trading companies are famous for their exhaustive information-gathering approach. This, coupled with a long-term strategy and a willingness to invest time and manpower in investigating and maintaining a presence in small, backward or politically unpopular countries, means that they have a very sensitive awareness to the advent of huge new consumer markets in countries embarking on large-scale industrialization which generates a new working class of first-generation cash wage earners in factories and the public sector, plus a middle class of the managerial supervisors of production and civil servants to whose lifestyle the workers aspire. These forecasts are passed on to the manufacturers in the trading companies' *keiretsu* (industrial groupings). Thus, the Japanese consumer goods manufacturers were able to predict and make available the items of mass consumption for both the new working class and new middle class generated in Malaysian society after the NEP.

Those poor village folks who listed their occupation as *kerja kampong* (village work) previously survived with very little cash expenditure in daily life. Items purchased with cash from small-scale rubber tapping, the sale of goats for ritual slaughter, and so on, would include a new set of clothes for *Hari Raya*, cooking oil, soy sauce, *Ajinomoto* seasoning, batteries for a radio, etc. Some families in the *ulu* (remote) regions would not have enough ready cash to regularly purchase a sixty sen bar of soap or a RM10.50 *kain pelekat* (cotton sarong). When the children of these families migrated to urban areas to work in factories, they sent back consumer durables or cash remittances to their ageing parents and younger brothers and sisters. They also sent back grandchildren to be looked after by the grandparents. Village agriculture declined, as only the very old and the very young were left. But village households came to have Japanese gas ring stoves to replace the charcoal fires, fans to ward off the heat radiated from corrugated iron roofs, televisions and 'compo' stereo sets.

At the same time, it must be imagined what the middle generation of such rural families, who have become the urban working class, or lower middle class, often aspire to buy for themselves usually through hire purchase: as well as a stereo and television (and now in the 1990s, a CD player and VCR),[39] a fridge, rice cooker, toaster, blender for processing chillies, a set of Pyrex or Corelle plates, a zip-up collapsible wardrobe, an electric fan – a pattern and level of consumption associated with Japanese families in the 1950s and 1960s. Moreover, rapid economic growth and the relatively high standard of living in Malaysia by Third World standards have meant that the middle class market is also expanding rapidly. Here, the diversity of Japanese consumer brands manaufactured or sold in Malaysia, from high technology/high price range brands like Sony to durable image/low price range brands like Sanyo, plus the fact that the company managers, rather than seeing themselves as rivals, meet regularly once per month to devise a concerted market strategy, has created an indelible hold on the Malaysian market by Japanese manufacturers.

The leading brand of home appliances in Malaysia is National, and their market strategy in the 1980s was to tidy up the dusty rural town electrical shop into a sparkling *Kedai National* (National Shop),[40] where the shelving and window displays are like the modern shop style in Kuala Lumpur. In these *Kedai National*, one can purchase almost every type of home appliance one might aspire to own. However, the models on sale are about a decade behind those currently marketed in Tokyo. For instance, the one-colour rice cooker with lift-off stainless steel lid is still the common type in Malaysia, while the hinged, heavy streamlined lid type with pastel flower motifs, the common model in Japan for over a decade, is prohibitively expensive, even in Kuala Lumpur, and unavailable in rural shops.

The marketing of Japanese automobiles in Malaysia presents a similar story of long-range strategy and competent analysis of the Malaysian consumer's mind. Prestige cars for the old rural middle class in the 1960s and early 1970s were European makes such as Fiat, Alfa Romeo, Peugeot, BMW or Volvo (before the latter two became much more expensive, prestigious and symbols of the urban elite). These cars were seen as robust and having very good roadholding abilities for the village roads, with economical fuel consumption despite their high performance. Fiat also had a range of models from very large to very small, which suited them to all income groups within the middle class. Other popular small cars were the Mini and the VW.

When the Japanese began to dominate the world car market in the 1970s, on the basis of their small economical cars, these small European models were already well established in Malaysia. The Japanese car companies' strategy then was to take over the European car dealerships in Malaysia, and to close them down in rural areas so that sales came to a standstill and spare parts were very difficult to obtain. Thus, people turned to Japanese cars and and felt they were getting a good deal in terms of low purchase price and fuel economy, although the Japanese brands did not measure up to the European ones in terms of road holding or performance. Until the yen exchange rate rose, most middle class families were choosing to buy either a Toyota or a Nissan. But by the late 1980s, these dealerships had to be trimmed all over the country due to the rising price of these brands, and to the enormous popularity of the lower priced, heavily protected Malaysian car, the Proton Saga, which is essentially a modified Mitsubishi Lancer Fiore (Jomo, 1985).

Supermarkets and department stores

Although some supermarkets collapsed in the mid-1980s recession, a noteworthy phenomenon since the early 1980s has been the establishment (after the success of Yaohan in Singapore) of Japanese supermarket/ department store chains: Kimisawa, Jayajusco, Chujitsu, Yaohan (*FEER*, 28 March 1991: 50). These consist of several storeys and usually combine a supermarket on the bottom floor with two floors above of department store items (including many Japanese and other imported brands).

While these are mostly representative of the cheaper provincial or suburban chains in Japan, in Kuala Lumpur, they represent the pinnacle of luxury shopping for the new middle class, in terms of the variety of fresh and imported food offered in the supermarket section (including Japanese foodstuffs largely bought by Japanese expatriates) and brands of household goods which may be considered to be 'high quality' for money. These products (cosmetics, tapes, and so on) are often sold much more cheaply in Malaysia than in Japan, simply because they would be impossible for Malaysians to afford if sold according to the normal conversion rate (which doubled after the 1985 *endaka*). Many Japanese tourists also travel to

Southeast Asia with the intention of buying leading Japanese consumer goods such as cosmetics, VCRs and video cameras, made in Japan itself, but sold overseas at a cheaper price.

Japanese department stores are also responsible for bringing in quality ready-to-wear clothing, where up till the 1980s, even urban-dwelling Malaysians would previously have had everything more formal than a T-shirt individually tailored. This sets the pattern of the middle-class style of purchasing clothes found in the West. Second, Japanese department stores consolidated the practice of 'no bargaining' for goods. While there had been several British fixed price department stores from the late colonial period, these catered mainly to the Anglophile elite. However, for the general population, haggling for food items in the wet markets or for items of daily use in the stalls or shops run by individual proprietors has been the norm in Malaysia and not to do so is to be taken for a fool and sometimes overcharged. However, since the 1980s, with the advent of a middle class consumer culture, with spending patterns revolving around prestige brand names, highly capitalized chain stores and fast food outlets, such as Kentucky Fried Chicken and Seven Eleven, haggling has become a class indicator and has been losing its pervasiveness. A tradition of fixed prices already existed in the indigenous Chinese emporiums, but they sell household items at 'value for money' prices. Formerly luxury items or investment items such as gold jewellry would be haggled over precisely because they were expensive. However, the Japanese department stores of the 1980s popularized the phenomenon of selling luxury items at high prices for which there is no bargaining – not unlike the English-style department stores from the late colonial period which catered for the Anglophile elite.

Even for lower income earners, so strongly is the consumer influence felt in relation to Japanese household items such as kitchenware, plastic containers, and so on, that local companies are making imitation items with Japanese writing (cute nonsense slogans) printed on the side. So, the image of 'quality' goes with supposedly being made in Japan. Whereas it was once embarrassing to observe the nonsense English slogans on clothing and other items in Japan,[41] now nonsensical Japanese writing can be seen on T-shirts and children's clothes in Malaysia.

The Japanese supermarket/department stores can be seen as trend-setters in the development of Malaysian middle-class consumer taste. Although only middle-class salary earners could afford to shop there regularly, the stores are thronged with factory workers and rural folk looking at the items on display. This is true not only of the 'department store' area but of the supermarket area also, reinforcing the phenomenon of the prestige of being able to purchase a modern packaged item with a foreign brand name.[42] Thus, working class window shoppers will wander around the Japanese supermarket as a leisure activity and perhaps purchase a small item at the checkout before leaving. In this way the affluent shopping malls become a major focus in the development of consumer lifestyles and generate a 'material consumption', 'brand conscious' set of values among the working class long before their incomes allow them to fully engage in these levels of consumption.[43]

CONCLUSION

While insisting that the 'Look East' policy does not mean that Malaysia will become a client state of Japan, Mahathir's 'Look East' policy has nevertheless given virtual 'Open Sesame' to Japan in matters of investment type and managerial style in its Malaysian ventures, reinforcing Malaysia's economic dependence upon Japan and cementing the relationship with a cultural hegemony which extends from the media and the information sector to the consumerist material culture of the daily life of all Malaysians.

Despite the persistence of negative wartime stereotypes of the Japanese, the Malaysian public has generally been positively disposed to Japanese investment, products and culture, because of the demonstrated economic success of post-war Japan, outstripping even that of other Western economies, because of the success of the government's 'Look East' policy as an ideological campaign and because the consumerist environment accompanying Japanese investment in Malaysia corresponded with new levels of purchasing power among two social classes whose numbers expanded dramatically under the New Economic Policy: the newly waged industrial workers and the emerging middle class.

Ironically, the impact of the 'Look East' policy has been stronger in unintended areas, such as lifestyles, than in the concrete areas delineated under the original policy statements. In the case of management practices, it has been quite difficult to transfer Japanese elements such as job rotation systems, consensus decision making, egalitarian work roles and sophisticated merit-based reward systems, which are the key elements in the functioning of successful large Japanese enterprises. This is because of differences between Malaysia and Japan in workplace culture, labour legislation and the greater degree of social stratification in Malaysian society. Thus, elements of so-called Japanese management practices have been transplanted in a piecemeal fashion, such as uniforms, morning exercises, slogan campaigns and QCCs. These have often failed as there is no merit-based system of renumeration and promotion to provide incentives to employees such as those in Japan itself. Similarly, a call for workers to develop Japanese work ethics would need to be backed up with the sophisticated pay schemes found in large Japanese enterprises, plus the unwritten but largely maintained guarantee that the company will try all other measures first before retrenching its workers in the event of an economic downturn.

A second objective of the 'Look East' policy, manpower training, has been successful on a modest scale, but the graduates from Japanese universities have been mainly employed by Japanese companies, so the ultimate benefits to Malaysia remain uncertain. As Machado (1987: 653) points out, the number of Malaysian students in Japan is only a fraction of those studying in the West.

Conversely, the socio-cultural effects of the Japanese presence in Malaysia in the 'Look East' policy era have been substantial and in sometimes unanticipated directions. Still, these could have been predicted from an examination of Japanese military practices and cultural policies under the Occupation, which strove to impose the Japanese language, spiritual values and other cultural forms on the local population through the establishment of new educational policies and training institutions.

In the institutional arena, information-gathering networks of the Japanese in contemporary Malaysian society have been the most striking theme. The secondment system, and other mechanisms like informal but institutionalized regular meetings, multiple role playing, etc, create strong information-exchange networks between government, business and academia. These have been transferred to Malaysia within the roles played by members of the Japanese expatriate community. This phenomenon replicates the 'flexible specialization' or 'job generalism' concepts of Japanese management within a wider social context.

Japanese cultural influence has made unexpected gains in the area of leisure pursuits of Malaysians, for instance in the form of the extreme popularity of *karaoke*. Ironically, it could be said that the effect of the 'Look East' policy has been the spread of *karaoke* rather than Japanese work ethics, reflecting the intense alienation of Malaysians in the era of rapid social and economic change, especially concerning the restructuring within and between the ethnic communities, as people drown their sorrows with entertainment (Shamsul, 1991: 5). Here too is the theme of flexible specialization, job generalism and egalitarianism, as the *karaoke* experience gives everyone a chance to be a star and mitigates against the norm of only those with a special talent having the right to sing in public.

Third, consumer culture is the area which shows the most striking impact of Japan on post-'Look East' policy Malaysian society. Where values pertaining to traditional material expressions of status in peasant societies are translated within one generation into a modern urban consumer culture, this produces a form of consumerism more extreme than that found in the developed societies where the consumer items originate. In Malaysia, the transition of a large proportion of the population from rural peasant to urban wage earner was effected in a dramatically artificial way, in comparison with the parallel process in the West, as it took place in the span of one generation and within the highly politicized context of the social restructuring of an ethnically divided society under the NEP.

355

Japanese investment and technology transfer have been key elements in the logic of economic development under the NEP and the 'Look East' policy can be seen as a logical outcome of this. Hence, the Japanese were well-placed to fill the material needs and cultural gaps in a society 'inventing itself' into the consumerist world too rapidly.

NOTES

1 Mahathir has continued to use culturally based value systems as a stimulus to economic growth. His latest initiative has been to promote an Islamic work ethic through the establishment of a new think-tank, the Malaysian Institute for Islamic Understanding (IKIM) which aims to overcome resistance to goals of economic advancement among Malay Muslims by arguing that 'Islam is not incompatible with industrialization and modern standards of productivity'. Moreover 'Hard work could be defined as *jihad* or holy war'. *Far Eastern Economic Review* (*FEER*), 20 May 1993: 32

2 Japan was briefly overtaken by Taiwan as the most significant foreign investor in 1990, but the Taiwanese interest in Malaysia has subsequently declined in view of the attractiveness to Taiwanese investors of economic reforms in China, and wage and other investment incentives in Vietnam and Indonesia. (*FEER*, 18 March 93: 46).

3 In 1989, Japan took 16.1 per cent of Malaysia's total exports, ranking third as an importer from Malaysia, and supplied 24.2 per cent of total imports to Malaysia, ranking first as an exporter to Malaysia. In contrast, Malaysia ranked 12th as an exporter to Japan and 14th as an importer to Japan. Malaysia's trade deficit is increasing and stood at RM4,359 million in 1990 (MIER, 1991: 48). This reflects the flow of Japanese intermediate goods used in Japanese assembly plants in Malaysia and the reluctance of Japan to buy manufactured goods from Malaysia over and above the traditional purchases of oil and commodities (*FEER*, 1991: 129). This state of affairs, while heavily balanced in Japan's favour, is a product of the conjunction of mutually compatible stages in the economic development of the two countries in the post-war era.

4 In recent research by Savaranamuttu (1989) on the Malaysian middle class, the overall expansion of the middle class since the beginning of the NEP era is demonstrated through an examination of the 1980 Census data on income and occupational distribution. He calculates that the largest rate of change is shown among the Malays, whose membership of the middle class has increased by 35 per cent, with Chinese membership increasing by 20 per cent for the same period. See also Crouch (1993: 141–4).

5 For a description of the AOTS training scheme, see Koike and Inoki (1990: 63–6). Despite the many positive results achieved with this scheme, Malaysian participants mention difficulty in communicating in Japanese as a major problem.

6 Milton-Smith (1986: 401) notes that in the calculation of risk in decisions on foreign investment in Singapore, the Japanese primarily emphasized the factor of political climate, whereas the Germans emphasized tax incentives and the British and Americans, freedom of equity participation.

7 Sections of Nakane's work were translated into English by the Japanese Ministry of Foreign Affairs and distributed freely by Japanese embassies all over the world under the title, *Human Relations in Japan*. Thus, her vertical theory of Japanese society became the view authorized by the Japanese government.

8 For a detailed examination of Nakane's work, see Hata and Smith (1983).

9 For an example of the extreme consequences which this 'competition' between the two major Japanese car manufacturers, Toyota and Nissan, had for the lives of workers on the production line, see Kamata (1983).

10 Although the establishment of enterprise, or 'in-house' unions has been a key element in government labour policies since the 'Look East' policy era, and there have been cases, even in the 1970s, where the government intervened to replace troublesome unions with in-house unions, for example, the MAS case of 1979, according to Jomo (1990: 220) 'so far very few new in-house unions have been registered where no unions existed before'.

11 For a situation similar to that of pre-war Malaya, see the account of *toko jepang*, Japanese retail shops, in pre-war Indonesia, in Shimizu (1991: 41).

12 See the account in Yamazaki (1972) and also Shimizu (1991) on *karayuki-san* in Indonesia.

13 For instance, some large houses and public buildings throughout Malaysia are said to be haunted, unlucky, uninhabitable or to cause sickness and misfortune for their occupants because they were used as Japanese army headquarters during the Occupation and were the scene of torture and violent death. Similarly, if children or other sensitive people living in a particular area constantly fall ill or are subject to disturbing dreams or unpeaceful sleep, this is attributed by the Malays to the place being formerly the site of a Japanese massacre. Labu, near Seremban, the state capital of Negeri Sembilan, is an area with such a reputation. Accident-prone spots on country roads may also be linked to buildings or sites nearby where incidents took place during the Japanese Occupation.

14 'Although military prostitution has been common throughout history, the brothels run by the Japanese military during the war were unusual because of the degree of coercion involved. The women were described as "war supplies". . . . These facilities were rapidly extended to wherever the Japanese military were found, from the border with Siberia to equatorial New Guinea. . . . Officers, NCO's and men were charged different rates for visits to the women. The rates also differed by nationality. Japanese women were the most expensive, followed by Okinawans, Koreans, Chinese and Southeast Asians' (*FEER*, 18 February 1993: 33).

15 For instance, Malay school teachers were trained to become Japanese language teachers under the cultural propaganda policies of the occupation forces. The substitution of *Nippongo* for English was a key element in the cultural policy of the Japanese. See Akashi (1991: 117–172).

16 See, for instance, a documentation of the Japanese war atrocities in one state in Malaysia in a book privately published by the Negeri Sembilan Chinese Assembly Hall, *Senmeilan Zhonghua Dahuitang Chuban: Rizhishiqi Senzhou Huazu Mengnan Shiliao*, 1988 (A Historical Record of the Suffering of the Negeri Sembilan Chinese People under the Japanese Occupation). See also the account of wartime images of the Japanese in 'Kinder Co-prosperity', (*FEER*, 30 October 1991: 32–38).

17 For example, reports compiled for the Kuala Lumpur office of JETRO in 1990 and 1991 on the state of plastic parts and press die manufacture in Malaysia by Japanese executives in the industry, made recommendations for 'Just-in-Time' (JIT) style production improvements that would tie the small Malaysian companies more closely to the Japanese electronics companies they supply in Malaysia. The report on this in *FEER* (30 January 1992: 45) concluded: 'the tone of the documents supports criticism that Japanese technical assistance in

Malaysia . . . is tailored to Japan's own industrial agenda. In Malaysia's case, this has been made easier by Prime Minister Datuk Seri Mahathir Mohamad's "Look East" policy, which espouses Japan as a role model'.

18 This is clearly illustrated in a recent policy statement by the Japanese *Keidanren* (Federation of Economic Organizations) in which its special committee for international exchanges advocated increased cultural exchange especially in the form of foreign student contact with Japanese companies, with attention to be given to Southeast Asian exchanges. They stated that it was 'vital for companies to promote cultural exchange and mutual understanding to ensure smooth international economic activities'. Towards this aim, they proposed the donation of books on Japan to Southeast Asian universities and institutions, the support of Japanese studies programmes (*Japan Times*, 26 April 1989), and the organization of special orientation programmes for newly arriving Southeast Asian students, such as offered by the Toyota company (*Japan Times*, 11 June 1989).

19 The career of one such Japanese graduate of the University of Malaya in the early 1970s included postings as a member of the Jakarta JETRO office, head of the Kuala Lumpur JETRO office, head of the Jakarta JETRO office, then Professor of Malay Language at a university in Tokyo. An earlier Japanese graduate of the University of Malaya returned to Kuala Lumpur in the 1980s as a senior diplomat in the Japanese Embassy. From the 1980s there have been an increasing number of post-graduate students from Japan coming to do research, especially on rural society in Peninsular Malaysia, or in Sabah and Sarawak. They either enrol directly in a Malaysian university, or seek local supervision while being enrolled in their home university in Japan. Senior Japanese academics visiting Malaysia briefly call these younger researchers together for formal meetings. Thus, the information exchange potential of a widespread network of researchers is maximized.

20 According to Shinohara, the trading conglomerates 'have telecommunications equipment and intelligence-gathering networks that rival anything the CIA or the Pentagon can come up with' (cited in Milton-Smith, 1986: 410).

21 In the Japanese case, it may have been easier to implement the translation programme, as, unlike Malay, Japanese existed in a literary as well as vernacular form due to the borrowing of abstract and scientific vocabulary from Chinese. For an excellent discussion on literacy and orality in the Malay world, see Sweeney (1987).

22 For details of the training schemes implemented under the 'Look East' policy, see Machado (1987: 649–56).

23 Personal communication from a representative of the AOTS Malaysian Alumni.

24 See Kahn (1992) for a post-modern discussion of architectural metaphors in a political context.

25 The Kuala Lumpur Japanese School is run by the Japanese government and staffed by Japanese teachers seconded from Japan, Japanese living locally and Malaysian teachers. It is open to children of expatriate Japanese couples only; children of mixed Malaysian–Japanese parentage are not admitted. As such, it is an institution devoted to helping Japanese children who are temporarily absent from Japan due to their fathers' overseas postings to keep up with the rigorous demands of the Japanese curriculum upon their return. But the posting of Japanese overseas has become so pervasive (over two million businessmen and their families (Hamada, 1992: 136) that the difficulties faced by returning Japanese children (*kikokushijo*) in adapting successfully to the school system in

Japan, both in a scholastic and cultural sense, has become the subject of much study and concern (see White, 1988).

26 The same phenomenon has been described in Thailand. See Lehmann (1987: 193).

27 For example, *kaiseki ryori*, traditional Japanese cuisine, which would cost at least ¥10,000 (RM200) per person in Japan, cost RM40 at the Nadaman restaurant in the Shangri La hotel.

28 See *Malaysian Business*, 16–31 January 1989: 5–8, 'Japanese Lounges – Yen for Nite-Life'.

29 It is openly acknowledged that the informal drinking activities are a time when superiors have the chance to get to know their subordinates on a personal level, learn about their personality quirks, family problems, psychological disposi-tions, attitudes to politics, the company, and so on. Given that the annual assessment of workers' performance – on which a sizeable part of the monthly wage and hence the considerable annual bonus depends – places great emphasis on personality attributes, and attitudes to life in general, not just the job or the company, these so-called informal drinking occasions conducted after working hours are in fact a near compulsory part of the Japanese employees' working life. To refuse to attend, or to intimate that one had better things to do with one's time, is to set oneself apart from one's work group (Atsumi, 1979: 63), to avoid evaluation of one's personality and motives, and hence invite a negative annual assessment, with all the consequences which that might imply for future income. The informal drinking sessions have become stereotyped as times when Japanese workers and middle class salarymen get drunk, and let their hair down, after the tension of maintaining strict decorum and bottling up feelings of rivalry and frustration which have to be sublimated for the good of the company in the daily workplace. The phenomenon of drinking in Japan is well described by Smith (1992: 147) 'the Japanese have a positive attitude toward drinking and a great tolerance for drunken behaviour; they hold the belief that, at least theoretically, any thing said or done when drunk should be forgiven and forgotten because the alcohol, not the drinker, caused the mischief. Thus in Japan, the exchange of drinks affirms the bond between individuals – even people of different rank – while the alchohol defines a context in which relaxed standards of decorum are not only tolerated but expected, permitting a freer flow of information and expression of affect than is acceptable in normal social intercourse'.

30 The machines have been developed to high degrees of technological sophistication. The singer can have his performance recorded to take home. The machines can assess the performance according to accuracy of key and other qualities and award each singer a point score (thus introducing a new emphasis on performance, which did not exist before). With the advent of compact disc technology and video disc, the words of the song can now be displayed on a screen for the singer to follow, and so on.

31 As a consequence, wives and children who do not see them on week nights, due to the custom of social drinking with work colleagues after hours, also do not see them on weekends. Time spent by the salaryman with his family is actually called 'family service' in Japan.

32 Already, there is evidence of environmental destruction and the take over of agricultural and forest land by Taiwanese golf course developers in Vietnam (*FEER*, 20 August 1992) and Hong Kong developers in China (*FEER*, 29 October 1992).

33 Compared with the journey they would need to make, it is of no consequence

for a Japanese businessman based in Kuala Lumpur to drive one hour from Kuala Lumpur to play golf at the Seremban International Golf Club. Even clubs which are primarily golf clubs have excellent swimming, gym, tennis, sauna, squash and dining facilities, as well as libraries, TV rooms and gambling rooms. Hence, Japanese businessmen are able to bring their families and park them by the pool all day while they play golf. Japanese wives also take up golf in Malaysia, but during the week, while their children are at school.

34 Yet golf clubs which have a waiting list for Malaysian prospective members actively invite short-term individual expatriate or corporate membership by foreign companies as a source of revenue. For instance the Seremban International Golf Club, whose membership at RM7,500 is temporarily closed to Malaysians, offers expatriate short-term membership of 5 years at RM10,000 for individuals or corporate membership for five employees at RM28,000 annually. Needless to say, the majority of these expatriate members are Japanese.

35 It is difficult to show Malaysian-style hospitality to Japanese friends visiting Malaysia, that is, invite them to stay in one's home and show them around the countryside at a leisurely pace. In the author's experience, friends from Tokyo could only spare three days for their holiday in Malaysia, and when they booked their airline tickets in Japan, they also booked accommodation at the Hilton Hotel and a Japanese tour guide to take them around Kuala Lumpur and Malacca. There was very little left for the Malaysian friend to do. See Takagi (1988). 'The overseas trips that Japanese take are generally quite short: usually four days to a neighboring Asian country . . . most Japanese won't risk taking all their vacation time if no one else in the company does. After the short vacation is over, they give fellow workers presents bought overseas or whiskey purchased at the duty-free shop. The presentation of these gifts is often accompanied by deep apologies for the long absence. According to Naito Kunio, a senior journalist in the Mainichi newspaper, 'in local (Southeast Asian) eyes, the Japanese are really something fearsome. All they do is work, work, work. And the tourists spend all their time shopping. They are so single-minded, with no time for anything else', quoted from 'Hatashite Nihon-jin wa Minikui ka?' [Are the Japanese Really Ugly?], *Bungei Shunju*, September 1977.

36 See the volume cited in note 16.

37 Ratto [Lat], *Kanpon no Gakidaisho* [The Kampong King of the Kids], 1984, Tokyo: Shobunsha. Translated by Sanae Ogishima and Mieko Sueyoshi.

38 Personal communication, Jomo K.S.

39 A comparative analysis of media contact between Malaysia, Thailand and Indonesia in 1984 showed that the ownership of video cassette recorders was highest in Malaysia, 56.4 per cent, as opposed to an average of 36 per cent in the other countries (Ito, 1987: 32). Despite the fact that ownership of these high cost items was concentrated in the Malaysian middle (47.3 per cent) and upper classes (35.7 per cent), still, 16.9 per cent of those classified as lower class in the sample of 600 respondents, of which 35.9 per cent were designated as lower class (Tsujimura, 1987: 9–10), owned VCRs. The same survey showed that Malaysia had 1.3 million television sets in 1983, one per 11 people, or a dissemination rate of one unit for every two households. (Tsujimura, 1987: 6–7). For a survey sample living in and around Kuala Lumpur, 99 per cent possessed television sets (Khor Yoke Lim, 1987: 125).

40 This marketing system is modelled on the network of 25,000 'National Shops' in Japan itself, from which 80 per cent of the sales are of National products.

For a description of this system of quasi-vertical integration of sales channels by large Japanese corporations, see Kono (1984).

41 An example of a decorative English text on a child's dress sold in Japan: 'Feel Wind and Love Always. Time is my Sweat Friend'. In another case, English is used to give an international flavour in the marketing of a set of bedsheets in Japan: 'refreshing space of residence on the produce. Make be overflow with interior feeling to your room'. Here, we have the use of foreign texts as elements of design or as immediately visible symbols of life-style, rather than as a conveyor of useful information which would persuade the potential buyer.

42 Factory workers also aspire to eat at fast-food outlets such as Kentucky Fried Chicken and Long John Silver, because of the prestige attached to these middle-class lifestyle activities. Even though delicious pieces of fried chicken have always been available at the traditional eating stalls, and the workers acknowledge that the food in the commercial outlets is more expensive and not as nice, they are still willing to invest occasionally a substantial amount of their income to take the family to eat in such places for the status value. So far the Japanese have failed to capitalize on this market, although the food fair basement of Yaohan Department store has some popular stalls selling Japanese-style snacks.

43 Working class shoppers would wander around the expensive Japanese shopping malls for entertainment, but purchase goods at the cheaper indigenous department store/supermarkets which have Chinese names and the flavour of Chinese material culture as the dominant theme of their wares. Nevertheless, these are stores which have items which are locally produced, but with Japanese language logos, or imitation Japanese brand names on them to give a feeling of Japanese 'quality' or fashionable appeal. These stores sell good quality items at prices within the range of working class incomes. Those located near the large bus stations, where the routes from rural areas come together, do extremely good business.

REFERENCES

Akashi, Yoji (1991) 'Japanese Cultural Policy in Malaya and Singapore, 1942–1945', in G. Goodman (ed.), *Japanese Cultural Policies in Southeast Asia during World War 2*, St Martin's Press, New York.

Atsumi, Reiko (1979) 'Tsukiai – Obligatory Personal Relationships of Japanese White-Collar Company Employees', *Human Organization*, 38, 3: 63–70.

Cheah Boon Kheng (1980) 'The Social Impact of the Japanese Occupation of Malaya (1942–1945)', in A.W. McCoy (ed.), *Southeast Asia Under Japanese Occupation*, Yale University Southeast Asia Studies Monograph Series Number 22: 75–103.

Chee Peng Lim (1985) 'Proton Saga: No Reverse Gear! The Economic Burden of Malaysia's Car Project', in Jomo (ed.), *The Sun Also Sets*, pp. 387–401.

Chee Peng Lim and Lee Poh Ping (1985) 'Japanese Joint Ventures in Malaysia', in Jomo (ed.), *The Sun Also Sets*, pp. 270–77.

Crawcour, E.S. (1978) 'The Japanese Employment System', *Journal of Japanese Studies*, 4, 2: 225–45.

Crouch, H. (1993) 'Malaysia: Neither Authoritarian nor Democratic', in K. Hewison, R. Robison and G. Rodan (eds) *Southeast Asia in the 1990s*, Allen and Unwin, Sydney.

Dahrendorf, R. (1958) 'Out of Utopia: Toward a Reorientation of Sociological Analysis', *American Journal of Sociology*, 64, 2: 116–27.

Far Eastern Economic Review (1991) 'Malaysia: Look East – and Up', *Japan in Asia*, Review Publishing Company, Hong Kong.

Friedman, A. (1977) 'Responsible Autonomy vs Direct Control over the Labour Process', *Capital and Class*, 1: 43–57.

Hamada, T. (1992) 'Under the Silk Banner: The Japanese Company and its Overseas Managers', in Lebra, T.S. (ed.), *Japanese Social Organization*, University of Hawaii Press, Honolulu.

Hata H. and W.A. Smith (1983) 'Nakane's Japanese Society as Utopian Thought', *Journal of Contemporary Asia*, 13, 3: 361–88.

Imaoka, H. (1985) 'Japanese Management in Malaysia', *Southeast Asian Studies*, 22, 4: 9–26.

Ito Shinichi (1987) 'Cassette and Video Tape Recorders', *East Asian Cultural Studies*, 26, 1–4: 31–42.

Jomo K.S. (ed.) (1985) *The Sun Also Sets – Lessons in 'Looking East'*, 2nd edition, INSAN, Petaling Jaya.

Jomo K.S. (1990) *Growth and Structural Change in the Malaysian Economy*, Macmillan, London.

Kahn, J. (1992) 'Class, Ethnicity and Diversity: Some Remarks on Malay Culture in Malaysia', Kahn, J.S. and Loh K.W. (eds) *Fragmented Vision – Culture and Politics in Contemporary Malaysia*, Allen and Unwin, Sydney, pp. 158–78.

Kamata, S. (1983) *Japan in the Passing Lane – An Insider's Account of Life in a Japanese Auto Firm*, George Allen & Unwin, London.

Khor Yoke Lim (1987) 'Television and Family Life in Malaysia', *East Asian Cultural Studies*, 26, 1–4: 125–32.

Koike, K. (1983) 'Internal Labour Markets: Workers in Large Firms', in T. Shirai (ed.), *Contemporary Labour Relations in Japan*, University of Wisconsin Press, Madison, pp. 29–61.

Koike, K. (1984) 'Skill Formation Systems in the U.S. and Japan: A Comparative Study', in M. Aoki, (ed.), *The Economic Analysis of the Japanese Firm*, Elsevier Science Publishers, North Holland, pp. 47–75.

Koike, K. and T. Inoki (eds) (1990) *Skill Formation in Japan and Southeast Asia*, University of Tokyo Press, Tokyo.

Kono, T. (1984) *Strategy and Structure of Japanese Enterprises*, Macmillan, London.

Lehmann Jean-Pierre (1987) 'Variations on a Pan–Asianist Theme: the "Special" Relationship between Japan and Thailand', in R. Dore and Radha Sinha (eds), *Japan and World Depression*, Macmillan, London.

Lim Hua Sing (1984) 'Japanese Perspectives on Malaysia's "Look East" Policy', in *Southeast Asian Affairs 1984*, Institute of Southeast Asian Studies, Singapore, pp. 231–45.

Machado, Kit G. (1987) 'Malaysian Cultural Relations with Japan and South Korea in the 1980s – Looking East', *Asian Survey*, 27, 6: 638–60.

MIER (1991) *Proceedings of the MIER Dialogue on Japanese Investment in Malaysia*, Malaysian Institute of Economic Research, Kuala Lumpur.

Milne, R.S. and D.K. Mauzy (1986) *Malaysia: Tradition, Modernity and Islam*, Westview Press, Boulder.

Milton-Smith, John (1986) 'Japanese Management Overseas: International Business Strategy and the Case of Singapore' in S.R. Clegg, D.C. Dunphy and S.G. Redding (eds), *The Enterprise and Management in East Asia*, Centre of Asian Studies University of Hong Kong, Hong Kong pp. 395–411.

Muzaffar, Chandra (1985) 'Hard Work – The Cure All', in Jomo (ed.), *The Sun Also Sets*, pp. 337–45.

Nakane, Chie (1970) *Japanese Society*, Weidenfeld and Nicolson, London.

Saravanamuttu, J. (1985) 'The Look East Policy and Japanese Economic Penetration in Malaysia', in Jomo (ed.), *The Sun Also Sets*, pp. 312–36.

Saravanamuttu, J. (1989) 'Middle Class in Malaysia: A Problem of Identification', a paper for the Conference on 'Wither Malaysian Politics: Continuity or Change?', 2–5 February 1989, Universiti Sains Malaysia, Penang.

Shaharil Talib (1984) *After Its Own Image: The Trengganu Experience, 1881–1941*, Oxford University Press, Singapore.

Shamsul A.B. (1991) 'Dasar Pandang Timur dan Etika *Karaoke*' [Look East policy and *karaoke* ethics], *Dewan Masyarakat*, November, p. 5.

Shimada Haruo (1983) 'Japanese Industrial Relations – A New General Model', in Shirai T. (ed.) *Contemporary Industrial Relations in Japan*, University of Wisconsin Press, Madison, Wisconsin.

Shimizu Hiroshi (1991) 'Evolution of the Japanese Commercial Community in the Netherlands Indies in the Pre-war Period (From Karayuki-san to Sogo Shosha)', *Japan Forum*, 3, 1: 37–56.

Smith, S.R. (1992) 'Drinking Etiquette in a Changing Beverage Market' in J.J. Tobin (ed.) *Re-Made in Japan: Everyday Life and Consumer Taste in a Changing Society*, Yale University Press, New Haven, pp. 143–58.

Smith, W.A. (1983) 'The Relevance of the Japanese Model of Industrial Relations for The Analysis of Management Labour Relations: A Case Study of a Japanese-Malaysian Venture', *Proceedings of the International Industrial Relations Association, Sixth World Congress*, Kyoto, Japan, Vol. 5, pp. 144–81.

Smith, W.A. (1988) 'Skill Formation in Comparative Perspective: Malaysia and Japan', *Labour and Industry*, 1, 3, pp. 431–62.

Southeast Asian Studies, (Kyoto) (1985) 22, 4, Special Issue 'Japanese Management in Southeast Asia'.

Sweeney, A. (1987) *A Full Hearing*, University of California Press, Berkeley.

Takagi Nobuo (1988) 'Japanese Abroad: Armed with Slippers and Soy Sauce', *Japan Quarterly*, 35, 4: 432-6.

Tsujimura Akira (1987) 'The Spread of Mass Communication', *East Asian Cultural Studies*, 26, 1–4: 6–10.

White, Merry (1988) *The Japanese: Can They Go Home Again*, Free Press, New York.

Yamazaki Tomoko (1972) *Sandakan Hachiban Shokan* [Sandakan Brothel No. 8], Chikuma Shobo, Tokyo.

INDEX

For Product Safety Concerns and Information please contact our EU
representative GPSR@taylorandfrancis.com
Taylor & Francis Verlag GmbH, Kaufingerstraße 24, 80331 München, Germany

www.ingramcontent.com/pod-product-compliance
Ingram Content Group UK Ltd.
Pitfield, Milton Keynes, MK11 3LW, UK
UKHW021835240425
457818UK00006B/202